Letitia Baldrige's Complete Guide to Executive Manners

Other books by Letitia Baldrige:

Roman Candle
Tiffany Table Settings
Of Diamonds and Diplomats
Home
Juggling
Amy Vanderbilt's Everyday Etiquette
The Entertainers
The 1978 revision of *The Amy Vanderbilt Complete Book of Etiquette*

Letitia Baldrige's Complete Guide to Executive Manners

Edited by Sandi Gelles-Cole

RAWSON ASSOCIATES : *New York*

Rawson Associates
Macmillan Publishing Company
866 Third Avenue, New York, NY 10022
Collier Macmillan Canada, Inc.

Library of Congress Cataloging in Publication Data

Baldrige, Letitia.
Letitia Baldrige's Complete guide to executive
manners.

Includes index.
1. Business etiquette. I. Gelles-Cole, Sandi.
II. Title. III. Title: Complete guide to executive
manners.
BJ2193.B33   1985   395'.52   84-43161
ISBN 0-89256-290-0

Macmillan books are available at special discounts for bulk purchases
for sales promotions, premiums, fund-raising, or educational use.
For details, contact:

Special Sales Director
Macmillan Publishing Company
866 Third Avenue
New York, N.Y. 10022

15   14   13   12   11

Printed in the United States of America

Designed by Jacques Chazaud
Illustrations by Remo Bramanti

To three wonderful people whose lives I made miserable
during the five years it took to write this book:
my husband, Bob, and our children, Clare and Malcolm.
They constantly admonish me to practice
what I preach in these pages, but no one is perfect.

Contents

Managers, Etiquette, and the Opposite Sex · How the Polished Female
Executive Can Help Herself and Other Women · Helping Her Community ·
Sex and Romance in the Office · Talking About Your Sex Life · Flirtation and
Affectionate Body Language · Coping with Unwelcome Sexual Advances ·
Colleagues and Their Spouses · When a Colleague (or Client) Marries ·
Competition Between Spouses · Be Nice to a Commuting Couple · Executives
and Their Children · Pregnancy in the Office · Congratulations for an
Executive Mother · Etiquette for the Executive New Mother · Diplomatically
Handling the News of a Miscarriage or Abortion · Divorce Etiquette in the
Office · When an Office Colleague Is Widowed

THE ART OF CONVERSATION: How You Sound to the Outside World · The
Quality of Your Voice · The Relationship Between Voice and Vocabulary ·
Good Body Language Is Part of Good Conversation · Finding Help for Voice
and Speech · Being a Good Conversationalist · Small Talk · The Art of
Listening · Important Conversational Aptitudes · Subjects to Avoid ·
Conversation When the Young Executive Is Alone with a Senior Executive ·
Business and Small Talk · The Immorality of Eavesdropping · Party Talk and
Table Talk · The Host's Responsibilities for Meal Conversation · The Tradition
of Switching Conversation Partners at Large Dinners or Lunches
EXECUTIVE TELEPHONE MANNERS: Deciding How Your Telephone Will Be
Answered · The Heroes of the Business World Answer Their Own Telephones ·
How You Train Your Secretary Is Crucial · Screening Calls · How Good Are
Your Own Telephone Manners? · The Hold Button: A Necessary Evil ·
Cutting a Telephone Call Short · The Art of Taking Good Messages · The
Answering Machine: An Aggravating Necessity · Dealing with an Answering
Service
THE PERSONAL SIDE OF BUSINESS LETTER WRITING: Proper Form of the
Business Letter · The Etiquette of Who Signs the Letters · The Office
Letterhead Is Meant for Business Matters · Handling an Executive's Mail in
His or Her Absence · Proper Content of the Informal Business Letter ·
Letters Pertaining to Favors · Letter Informing a Person Why He Didn't Get
the Job or an Agency Why It Didn't Get the Account · Letters of Reference
and Recommendation · Letters of Resignation · Letters of Acceptance and
Regret in Answer to an Invitation to Join the Board of a Nonprofit Institution ·
Letter Declining to Endorse or Praise Anything for Commercial Purposes ·
Complaint Letters · Acknowledging a Compliment · The Interoffice Memo ·
The Form of a Memo · Letters of Friendship in Business · Letters to
Congratulate or Mark Special Occasions · Letters to Consolidate a Contact ·
Letters of Encouragement · Letters for Difficult Circumstances · Letters
Marking a Time of Transition · Letters of Acknowledgment and Thanks ·
Retirement Letters

Art · A Small Company Can Also Support the World of Art · Communicating
a Corporation's Generosity · Institutional Advertising to Support the
Nonprofit Sector · Corporate Support and the Employees · Service on the
Board of a Nonprofit Institution · Corporate Good Manners Toward Nonprofit
Institutions · An Institution's Good Manners Toward a Sponsoring
Corporation

Gift · Liquors and Wines as Gifts · Bar Accessories · For Special People and
Special Occasions · Occasions on Which Fine Gifts Should Be Given · Gifts
for the Retiree · Gifts Relating to Art · An Exchange of Gifts at Merger and
Acquisition Time · Giving and Returning the Inappropriate Gift · Company
Policy Prohibiting the Acceptance of Gifts · Accepting and Acknowledging a
Gift

List of Illustrations

Acknowledgments

The faith demonstrated by my friend and fellow Women's Forum member Eleanor Rawson in undertaking to publish this gargantuan project is monumental in itself. An experienced woman executive, Eleanor has developed her own excellent overview of social behavior in the workplace, which made our task much easier. I also want to thank her associate, Toni Sciarra, coordinating editor of Rawson Associates, for the invaluable aid she gave us in keeping things moving.

I must salute the Herculean labors of my editor, Sandi Gelles-Cole, who physically is one-half my size but mentally probably my superior. We were the Mutt and Jeff of the publishing world during this past year. With grace and supportiveness she daily browbeat me into rewriting an ungainly manuscript of 1700 typed pages into one that is a shadow of its former size. Much of my writing ended up on the cutting room floor, but as she kept reminding me, my mission was not to rewrite the Bible, but to provide a book of helpful information and guidance.

I thank Remo Bramanti for interpreting my hopelessly inept drawings into his own charming illustrations; his is a gift for making order out of chaos!

I must also thank my great good friend Nancy Tuckerman, who worked long, hard, and lovingly on this project in its beginning years, and also Nancy Dunnan, who did brilliant research.

My Letitia Baldrige Enterprises assistant, Nana Katsiff, not only helped in many ways to whip this manuscript into shape but also survived my frequent outbursts of frustration and complaining over working twenty-four hours a day—running my company, writing this book and a column, and fulfilling my roles as wife, mother, cook, and dog walker. My husband is also grateful to Nana, because she absorbs my complaining all day five days a week, which means he only has to do so in the evenings and on weekends.

Lily Lodge, of course, was my staunch support structure in writing this book, just as she is my staunch vice-president of the "Corporate Manners" division of my company. Wise, intuitive, and full of insight, Lily has been my partner "of the politest sort" in our executive management training activities.

There are names scattered through the text of people who have helped me, but many names of people who have also helped me are missing. To all of them I say, thank you, thank you, and thank you. (I hope three thank-yous are polite enough.)

Author's Note

It seems fitting that I begin this book on a crucial point of etiquette. The advent of women into the work force and, in particular, the executive suite, made it necessary for me to search, throughout the writing of the book, for a pronoun that would cover both genders without sounding clumsy. In the five years it has taken me to write this book, I was unable to find such a pronoun, nor was I able to find a way to overcome the clumsy phraseology of including *he* and *she* for every point I made. Therefore, I have chosen, in most cases, to go with the classic *he* when I mean both sexes.

It makes me proud to think that women have come so far that I must begin this work on executive manners with an apologia to explain why women must read themselves into the male pronoun.

Letitia Baldrige's Complete Guide to Executive Manners

Why We Need a
Book on Business Manners

Th_his is a book about manners but also
about the *quality of excellence.* It is a book about the importance of detail and
about how details linked together can create the strong, effective executive
presence that propels an individual upward in his or her career. This is, therefore, a book about success.

This is a book of information, parts of it relevant to some executives,
parts of it relevant to other executives, parts of it relevant to *all* executives.
The computer genius, for example, who communicates all day—not with a
person but with a terminal—may need a reminder to smile and say hello when
he meets a colleague in the hall. The chief executive officer may need a
reminder that certain VIPs on his mailing list are properly addressed with
"The Honorable" in front of their names. A young lawyer may be sorely in
need of tips on the handling of senior clients; a banker making a foreign trip
may need information on a country's social climate in order to avoid a major
gaffe. Salesmen may need assistance with manners in a prospective customer's office; a company host may need some ideas on how to survive an evening
in a restaurant with important clients.

This book is based on the theory that good manners are cost-effective,
because they not only increase the quality of life in the workplace, contribute
to optimum employee morale, and embellish the company image, but they
also play a major role in generating profit. An atmosphere in which people
treat each other with consideration is obviously one in which a customer
enjoys doing business. Also very important, a company with a well-mannered,
high-class reputation attracts—and keeps—good people.

On the other hand, sloppy manners, a lack of awareness, and an absence
of caring are highly visible on any job and make everyone present extremely
uncomfortable. "Negative behavior," whether based on selfishness, careless-

ness, or ignorance, can cost a person a promotion, even a job. It can also cost him a good social life, which most of us strive for.

Good manners are part of working smart.

Good manners are not incompatible with being tough in business. Strength can exist without meanness. If you have to make a tough decision, you make it and take action quickly, but there usually are several options available for how you carry out that decision.

When I revised *The Amy Vanderbilt Complete Book of Etiquette* a few years ago, I included a short chapter on business manners. This chapter was read by people who had never before thought to consult an etiquette book. Parts of the chapter were reprinted in company house organs and in-flight magazines. I began to receive telephone calls from all over the country, requesting information on everything from how to word a tricky business invitation to what kind of treatment should be given a visiting Saudi prince. I fielded questions on the design of executive stationery, the etiquette of giving out business cards, and the dilemmas of seating a high level dinner. ("What are we supposed to do when France's ambassador to Washington and France's ambassador to the United Nations are both coming?") Young managers cornered me at cocktail parties with such questions as, "When is it okay to invite the boss home to dinner without looking like you're apple polishing?" and, "What are you supposed to do when you're entertaining your Number One client and he is completely, abusively drunk?"

By 1980, it was very clear that there was a big market for information of this nature. There was no detailed manual in existence that gave information on the social side, the *human* side of business. There were a lot of self-help books telling you how to get rich; there was nothing to tell you how to behave on your way there. The managers and professionals now "moving up" in business had survived a turbulent time in their youth, beginning in the mid-sixties and lasting through the seventies. During this period, there was tremendous upward social and economic mobility. We became one great middle class; the youth rebelled, and women left home and went to work, changing the workplace forever.

It is this complicated, multifaceted revolution that is the real reason this book had to be written. During that time of change and adjustment, education effectively advanced in most fields, but it regressed in the field of manners. While today's senior managers have rules in their heads, there are very few concrete rules on paper for the benefit of those who have not shared the experiences of seasoned senior executives. There is a lot of trial-and-error behavior, most of it with inefficient and expensive results. There is no concerted effort in management training to teach appropriate social behavior. There *is* a need—to teach young managers what they should have learned at home but too often didn't.

Never before have so many executives of such diverse business backgrounds shared the same workplace. Not only do we have an ever-increasing influx of other nationalities entering the executive workplace, Americans themselves, depending on the age group into which they fall, were raised under very different cultural and sociological influences. If one were to attempt to summarize differences in their training in social behavior, one would separate them into three age categories: senior, mid to senior, and young.

Senior managers in their late fifties and early sixties were products of a totally different era. Theirs was a society of strong families, in which women stayed home and the family gathered around the dinner table every night and on Sunday noon. There was either a conscious schooling in manners, or the children learned them by osmosis. Even if the children fought discipline and social comportment, they were exposed to it. They therefore grew up knowing how to behave in all kinds of social situations and often don't understand people who don't. For them, this kind of knowledge is automatic and academic. Today, however, these managers often face social situations for which protocol itself has changed.

Mid-to-senior managers now in their late thirties and forties were products of several simultaneous social revolutions, the most serious of which was the youth rebellion. Individualism and protest flowered in their youth, while communication between parents and teenaged children withered. The young people denigrated the establishment, and the subject of manners was considered archaic by anyone over the age of fourteen.

Today, these managers face many business situations requiring social skills that leave them ill at ease. They work hard on attaining the right kind of "manners awareness" so they know whether they are doing something appropriate or not.

Young managers now in their twenties and early thirties were products of the new technology and innovation in education. Theirs was a growing-up period in which family life was segmented. Multi-marriages proliferated, and so did activities that took them out of the home or kept them in their rooms with their earphones on. Basically very conservative, they received very little education in manners and comportment after eighth grade.

There are many situations in which these young managers do not feel at ease, but their "manners awareness level" also tends to be low. They often don't understand "the proper thing to do," so do not necessarily agonize over slip-ups and omissions in social behavior. However, if shown the difference between good and bad social behavior, they eagerly adopt the former.

Manners are the very keystone of good human relationships. They govern how people treat each other, whether in the coal mines or in a mahogany-paneled boardroom. When people who work together in either place adhere to the rules of social behavior, their workplace becomes efficient. There is an absence of confusion and wasted time. When people treat each other with consideration, they do not run into each other; there is a minimum of stumbling about, feeling awkward, groping for words, or wondering what to do next.

An awareness of good manners automatically propels human beings in the same affirmative direction. Up to now, management has given this subject little thought, particularly in how it relates to profit. It is time not only to think about it but to give it priority attention in management training. Today's young manager is well-educated, well-motivated, and highly intelligent. Yet often he feels awkward when confronted by a situation presenting several options of behavior. He often doesn't know how to extricate himself from an embarrassing situation, not realizing that manners consist two-thirds of logic or common sense and one-third of kindness. Once he becomes aware of manners, he usually realizes the wisdom of living by the Golden Rule—when you're nice to others, they're nice to you in return.

Someone who is well-mannered eight or nine hours a day at work does not lapse into egocentricity and lack of consideration of others when he's at home. You can't turn good manners on and off like a faucet. They're bonded into your character and behavior.

For this book, I made the decision to approach executive social behavior from two perspectives: as an interpersonal human relationship and as protocol-governed ritual. A good attitude and a show of kindness and consideration are basic to good personal relationships at work just as in social life. Knowing the rules for what to do, when to do it, and how to proceed properly are basic to the protocol of executive manners. There are signposts along the way on both sides. In this book, the reader will find that being aware, thinking ahead, and using common sense are integral factors in both an executive's success and his or her social development.

Even though this is the most comprehensive book yet written on social behavior in American business, it is impossible to cover in every detail many situations that crop up only sporadically for the majority of those in the business community. For example, a comprehensive treatment of the subject of social practices in international business alone would require many books. However, you will find the most important points of etiquette covered here. Moreover, if a business person accepts the basic theory that consideration of others is the key to good social behavior, then uses the information offered in this book as a further guide, he or she will be able to handle him- or herself with ease in any business-related situation, whether in Sioux City, Iowa; Paris, France; or Tokyo, Japan.

There is no snobbism inherent in real manners; they are not an affectation. Often they translate simply into assisting someone in need of assistance. In its most minor form, this might entail helping someone with his coat in a crowded airplane aisle; in its most extreme form, the assistance might consist of going to the aid of someone in trouble, without giving a second thought to one's own safety.

For those who maintain that manners are a question only of character and not of training, I quote a senior executive who once remarked during his address to a business audience, "You certainly can't teach an S.O.B. to be well-mannered, but if you catch him early enough and teach him a thing or two, you feel you might have kept him from turning into one!"

His words reinforce better than anyone's my conviction that manners should be part of the curriculum of management training. It is why I have gone into the business of teaching manners via seminars and lecture programs. It is a new and most important element of human management training.

I have been asked more than once, "And just why do you set yourself up as such an expert on this subject?" The question deserves to be answered, and my reply here is a classic example of justifiably throwing aside the charming asset of modesty.

I have worked in an executive capacity for thirty-seven years in four countries. I have run my own public relations and marketing consulting company since 1964. I was Tiffany's first Director of Public Relations and Burlington Industries' first Director of Consumer Affairs. I served as an aide to the United States' ambassador at the American embassies in Paris and Rome and as Chief of Staff for Mrs. Kennedy in the White House during the John F. Kennedy administration. I have been a corporate director for ten years and a consultant to large corporations and small businesses. Business experience aside, I have been writing books, articles, and a syndicated newspaper column on manners since my postgraduate days when I went to Europe. I was a social observer long before I took over the writing of the late Amy Vanderbilt's etiquette books. I have watched heads of state in action in their palaces and company managers in action in their conference rooms. I have sat in on approximately 8000 meetings during that time, watched companies start up, watched others go belly up. In all that time spent working and listening, making my own mistakes and paying for them, I have come to the important but unremarkable conclusion that people are the same everywhere, character-wise. There are the good and the bad, the rude and the courteous, the sensitive and the completely insensitive. There are regional differences in social customs and, of course, differences in social behavior from one business to another, but there is a unifying factor in any profession or business: the desire to please and do what is right.

It's distressing to see a man (or woman) succeed when he is thoughtless and boorish, with unattractive personal habits. Do the executives in his organization regard him as a role model—someone to emulate, someone whose attitudes should be slavishly copied as the keys to success? I think not. I think people admire true leadership in the executive workplace—someone who cares about others, who has a sense of fairness and practices ethics in his business.

I have queried executives at all levels of management for this book. I have asked their opinions, heard them voice their problems, and sought their advice on which option of behavior they consider the best in given situations. I have talked to chairmen of the board, students in business schools, bankers, engineers, lawyers, salespeople, and more. I have talked with managers on a fast track and managers struggling to get on one, with administrative assistants and executive secretaries, with entrepreneurs who are successful and those who are just starting.

I have tried to write their opinions on what constitutes good behavior—and my opinions as well—with a light personal touch, so that no one will consider this subject intimidating. It's not. It's warm, human, and cost-efficient. Having made many mistakes myself in high places, I know how it feels to be embarrassed, even mortified by one's own faux pas. I've committed the worst gaffes one can commit—and in the glare of the limelight, including several in foreign capitals and the White House. And I know what survival is. I have survived all of those gaffes, picked myself up off the figurative floor and carried on, convinced that "this time wasn't so bad after all; the next time will probably be much worse!"

Some of the information that follows, on large-scale entertaining, for example, may appear to apply only to large corporations with big budgets. But in reading through the material, one can learn a great deal about the organization of much lower-budgeted projects as well. There are times in a bad economy when even a corporation used to going first-class all the way must drastically cut corners and "trade down," so to speak, in its corporate lifestyle. That need not affect its class image, for class goes far deeper than outward appearances. The people who work for the company are what provide its class.

I hope this book will help people find a comfortable way through all kinds of situations. If at times I write about the rich and the powerful, it is meant to show the young, entrepreneurial and non-powerful what to look forward to in the future and how to get one's act together right now. That's what it's all about—learning, copying, and adapting to the situation at hand.

In using this book, I hope you will learn to rely on the index. Certain aspects of organizing business events are in the Entertaining section, for example, and others are in the Meetings section. By using the index, you will both find answers to problems at hand and see problems anticipated that you had not thought of before but can look up now—*before* a difficulty arises. I hope that senior and junior management alike will read this book, because often the former knows far less than he thinks he does, while the latter will often learn enough to teach the former a thing or two. I also hope that whoever reads the book from cover to cover will conclude that, yes, good manners mean good business and, yes, they mean good character, too. Is there a better combination?

PART I

HUMAN RELATIONS AT WORK

A generation and a half ago a business book would never have contained a chapter on men's and women's relations in the executive office. There would not have been anything to report. With rare exceptions, there simply weren't many women whose jobs could be categorized as "executive." Perhaps it was the arrival of women on the management side of business that caused the emphasis in the business world today on human relations, on interpersonal relationships. Sensitivity did not use to be an issue in management's thinking. But the arrival of women in the executive suite has caused male executives to be more mindful of their business manners. That, plus the burgeoning interest in the human potential movement, has raised everyone's sensitivity quotient. As a consequence, productivity and profits have been proven to be directly related to good working and personal relationships within the organization. As we approach the third millennium, one person's sensitivity to another has become a surprising keystone of companies' preoccupation with future growth and success. Nothing is more important than men and women getting along with each other, equally and gracefully, in the work force. A chauvinistic attitude denotes a loser.

1

The Personal Qualities That Make Life at Work More Livable

Moses never passed out any business commandments, but he must have had the business world in mind when he came down from the mountain with his tablets. It is impossible to divorce good business behavior or even business protocol from good character and kindness.

An executive who understands and lives by the unwritten rules of social sensitivity moves with absolute ease through both the business and the social world. Like everything in the field of manners, these rules are based on kindness and efficiency. We are not talking about phony, affected behavior or elitism but about someone simply knowing how to put his best foot forward. It makes good business sense.

The Prototype of a Good Manager

As proof that business dexterity and good character traits combine in the makeup of an excellent manager, you have only to consider what personal qualities in a good manager make life at work more liveable for everyone.

A good manager

- Never expects others to follow rules he himself does not.
- Makes time *to listen to his subordinates* as well as give them orders.
- Keeps his promises, both large and small.
- Insists on good internal communications—candid, accurate, and two-way—so that management is responsive to employee needs and he is aware of any discontentment.
- Respects the ideas of others.
- Contributes meaningfully to meetings, rather than wastes time with interruptions and trivia.
- Sends copies of letters and memos to anyone concerned with a project, so that egos are not bruised.
- Does not thoughtlessly encroach on another's territory.
- Vigorously defends any staff member who has been unjustly accused.
- Accepts the blame for his group, even if he was not personally at fault.
- Gives full credit to whoever merits it.
- Criticizes those he must in a constructive rather than destructive manner, and always in private.
- Is sensitive to whether his office is better run in an informal or more formal manner.
- Returns telephone calls within twenty-four hours, or has someone else return them for him.
- Answers important mail within four days and unimportant mail within two weeks.
- Grants quality time to young interns, trainees, and new staff members and helps in their adjustment to the company.
- Doesn't boast, but shows off his considerable knowledge only to make an effective contribution to the discussion.
- Does not pretend to be an expert on what he is not.
- Is thoughtful about forwarding clippings and items of interest to colleagues who would enjoy seeing them and who would profit by reading them.
- Draws attention at meetings to people who have worked hard behind the scenes to make a presentation a success.
- Makes sure the office environment is the best it can be in terms of lighting, comfortable seating, and good work conditions.
- Fights for benefits for his employees.
- Goes out of his way to help a colleague who has had a tragedy in his life or who has been working out a serious problem.
- Writes personal letters as an instant reaction to news, whether to congratulate, commiserate, help, praise, or thank.
- Always returns borrowed property promptly and in good condition.

- Never repeats a rumor that would hurt someone's reputation.
- Allows others to draw attention to his accomplishments, remembering that "self-praise is worthless, while from the lips of others, it is gold."
- Shows compassion when there is bad news in an employee's personal life.
- Corrects someone who has just made an incorrect statement in front of a group either in a quick, casual, good-natured way on the spot or else later in private.
- Goes out of his way to be considerate to newcomers or loners in the group.
- Knows how to dress on and off the job, and understands appropriate attire for business.
- Answers all invitations promptly, either by writing or calling.
- If unable to attend an event to which he has accepted an invitation, calls immediately and apologizes.
- Doesn't talk about invitations around those who haven't been invited.
- Never brings a guest to an event without first calling to receive permission to do so.
- Is a considerate host, always mindful of his guests' comfort.
- Is a considerate guest, always ready to help out his host and to contribute to the success of the affair.
- Is deferential in office situations when it is proper to be so.
- Knows how to introduce people properly and in a manner that makes them feel good.
- Knows how to compliment someone and how to graciously accept a compliment himself.
- Is punctual or, if delayed, always informs his host in advance that he will be late.
- Acknowledges in writing any item or gift sent to him.
- Picks up the check in a bar or restaurant when it's his turn.
- Realizes that the quickest road to social failure is to be pushy and aggressive in getting himself invited to business social affairs or in getting close to the important people at a function.

When You're the New Kid on the Block

When you join a company, either in your first executive position or as a transfer from another company, you might as well accept the fact that you will be an object of curiosity and probably of some suspicion as well. You might also be a hate object for someone who thought he was going to obtain the position you have been retained to fill.

Remember, time is the great healer and dealer. It doesn't matter how cool the atmosphere may be when you arrive in your job. What matters is that you take your time to establish good personal relations and proceed slowly and carefully—the opposite of a shotgun approach. Here are some tips on how to handle yourself:

- *Listen and learn, rather than do all the talking.* Don't think you have to justify yourself to everyone. Spend your energies observing and asking smart questions rather than trying to let everyone know how much you know and how important you are.
- *Be equally nice to everyone.* The messenger may some day turn out to be your best friend in court. The receptionist may one day be able to give you the most important information of your life. The junior executive you don't think is very important in the office next to yours may one day be your boss.
- *Don't make snap judgments* about who's nice, who's important, who's going to be your friend. You may change your mind about most of the people in the office, so it's smart not to form an opinion of anyone until you know them well and have seen them interact. Don't listen to negative stories about who's out to get whom, who's about to get fired, who's cheating, etc. Resolve to keep an open mind and to make your own judgments later—much later.
- *Ask your peers to lunch, one by one* (once a week, for example). Get to know them on an easy informal basis. It will be money well invested. Assume an "I honestly need your help to learn how this company works" attitude. If you make your peers understand that you need their assistance, that you know less than they do but need to know more in order to become a good *team member,* you will find they will help you. They won't mind your asking for information. What does *not* work is arrogance; what *does* work is modesty.
- *Don't ask prying personal questions about others in the office.* If you try to collect gossip, you'll instantly acquire the kind of reputation you don't want. You'll become known as a gossip yourself, someone not to be trusted.
- *Get on the good side of the secretarial and clerical staff right away.* If you treat them with consideration and friendliness, they will always be eager to help you. Never make unrealistic demands on them; don't harp on clerical errors; don't demand impossible deadlines. Always thank them for any job they do for you; always give them a generous helping of praise when they do a good job. Make friends.

If You Supervise People
Who Are Much Older Than You Are
(See also A Young Woman Boss and Her New Employees,
Chapter 2)

The situation of a young manager in charge of one or more executives who are older than he or she requires tact and sensitivity. I have seen it work wonderfully well many times. The newly appointed younger person should have a private talk individually with each older manager in the group and make the following kind of statement to the older person:

- "I know the fact that I am so much younger is not easy for you."
- "I know that you are a very good, effective worker. I have looked into your record and am impressed with your experience and your achievements. I will be glad to count upon that experience. My own will complement yours."
- "I am fully qualified to run this division (section, group), and if I obtain the cooperation of everyone in it, we will outperform every other division in this company and it will benefit us all. I know what I'm doing."
- "I don't think it necessary to refer ever again to the difference between my age and that of some of the older members of this team. I hope you agree?"

To Squeal or Not to Squeal
on Anti-Company Behavior

If you have the inside track on someone in your division who is stealing company funds, misreporting, or committing any kind of crime against the company or its people (and this includes sexual harrassment), it is your duty *not* to ignore it.

Step One: Talk to this person in private. Tell him or her you are aware of the offending activity, that you are not going to report it but serving a warning so that it will cease.

Step Two: If the illegal behavior continues, invite three or four of your peers to discuss it and to decide what action might be taken. The best procedure may be to call in that person, to confront him with the fact you know he is continuing his illegal activities, and to serve him with a final warning.

Step Three: If he does not desist, take him to court, so to speak. Report him to senior management as a committee. One person reporting him is not as effective as a group reporting him. (If the perpetrator is the head of the company, the committee should quietly contact the outside senior director on the board of directors and give him or her the information.)

One of the reasons that ethics have declined so rapidly in the business world is that we seem to be afraid of getting anyone into trouble—or we may be lazy about it and not want to bother with the inevitable fuss that will occur. To allow an individual's known anti-company behavior to continue is a crime in itself. The right thing to do is to give the perpetrator fair warning, and if he continues, to report him to the top.

Someone who is stealing from the company or hurting it in other ways is hurting the job future of everyone in the company, as well as the money invested by each and every stockholder. It is a solemn responsibility to protect everyone's rights and investments.

Put-Downs, Unjust Criticisms, and Outright Attacks

If you're an effective manager, you'll accept criticism for errors made or failures in your work, shoulder the blame, promise to do better—and then *do better*. However, if you are *unjustly* criticized in front of a group or attacked by someone in the presence of your boss, you must react, not just slough it off as something not worth responding to. At times there is a fine line between rising above negative criticism and simple cowardice. Self-defense in the workplace is an art, because it implies understanding appropriateness and the nuances of timing.

When you are unfairly attacked, the first thing you must do is command yourself to keep cool. Bite your tongue, if you have to, as a reminder not to blurt out heated words that may make you sound out of control. Give yourself time to think about what you are going to say. Deliberately drop your voice and speak in a low, calm tone. All eyes will be upon you. Your self-control will command your peers' respect. You'll have their attention, because they will all be waiting for you to blow your stack.

You may want to react like this:	*Instead, react like this:*
"That's not true! You're a bloody idiot to say something like that. You're a damn fool. You don't know anything about the subject, and yet you have the gall to criticize me about something that I know everything about and you know *nothing* about!"	"You talk about my project like someone who's had the same experience with it as I have, who's been studying it for as long as I have, and who's had the same access to the research data I've had. Since that isn't the case, I'd like to explain to the others who have just heard you why my actions were right ones. If you take the time to listen, then I'll recognize your right to criticize, but not before.

If you are unfairly criticized in front of your boss, do not try to defend yourself in front of your accuser and perhaps others, for it puts you at a sputtering disadvantage. Just say to your boss, "Jack, obviously I'm not going to leave that accusation unanswered. It deserves a strong response, and I have one. I'll see you in your office right after this meeting, if you don't mind." (Your accuser will now be the one placed at a distinct disadvantage.)

Put-Downs at Social Gatherings

It is very important, too, to remain in strict control of your emotions and actions when you are unfairly attacked at a business-related social gathering or in a group that includes people from outside the company. Again, maintaining control of your temper is the key to successful defusion of an unpleasant situation. React to the verbal attack with something like,

"That wasn't a very helpful remark to make," or

"That remark does not add to this conversation," or

"I don't think this is the place for an unfair remark like that."

Use an "in-charge" tone of voice. And never try to force an apology out of anyone, for that will instantly exacerbate your opponent's hostility. (Be grateful if you *ever* receive an apology, even years later!)

If your adversary continues to harangue against you, interrupt him. "Look, we're supposed to be enjoying ourselves. I think that for the benefit of our host—and everyone else—you and I should continue this discussion tomorrow, *at the office.*" Then begin talking on a new subject with the others around you, an important step to help make them feel more comfortable. Innocent bystanders often become as intimidated as the protagonists in a verbal battle such as this.

If the person who made the negative remarks about you is inebriated, you might say something like "I'm obviously going to ignore what you said." That reply may infuriate the other person, but it gives you license to ignore any further abuse from him. If the antagonist continues his tirade, obviously to everyone's discomfort, it's up to the host to arrange to have the hostile guest removed from the situation. If the host isn't nearby, then it's up to a sensitive guest who's present to go find the host, explain what's happened, and suggest that action be taken. (In a situation like this, it is the host's role, not the guests', to do something to remove the person who is out of control.)

Often when people are relaxed in a social situation under the influence of alcohol or other drugs, they exaggerate their feelings of hostility against their peers, and their remarks should be judged with consideration of their condition at that time. However, if someone continues to attack you—either to your face or behind your back—in or out of the workplace, you should cease being a victim. In the office it's a question of reporting the situation to your superior. At a party it's a question of hoping your host steps in to quiet him or remove him. If that does not happen, leave the party. Direct confrontation only serves to place you in a no-win situation.

When Someone Else Is Unjustly Put Down in Your Presence

If you hear a colleague being criticized unfairly—even in cocktail party chitchat—speak up. Defend the victim calmly, not aggressively: "I don't think that's fair. I know him well and work with him every day. That's not the way I see him." Or, "I really don't think you're giving the whole picture." Or, "Why don't you make those accusations to his face, instead of behind his back?"

When someone makes a malicious, funny remark about a colleague, don't join in the laughter. Others who know you are his friend will be watching you to judge your reaction; if you laugh, you are sanctioning the remarks made. If the negative remarks continue after you have made your defense, leave the group without making a drama out of it. Just leave. "Good-bye, I'll see you later." By quietly leaving, you have sent a strong message to that group that you consider their behavior unreasonable, petty, and unfair.

Should you tell your colleague about what happened at that cocktail party? Not necessarily. It could worry that person far beyond the importance of the occasion. It may have been a one-time episode, prompted by sheer jealousy of his obvious success or good fortune. (Often these episodes occur after a manager has made a sudden jump in his career or has had good fortune.)

When Someone Has an Irritating Habit

If a colleague has an irritating habit that continually grates on his peers' nerves, or if he has done something wrong without being aware of it, kindness and friendship should prompt you to inform him. It should be done in a spirit of helping him out, not as an act of criticism.

These are some habits that patently irritate others:

- Always interrupting another's conversation
- Exaggerating his own abilities
- Bragging about his excellent social contacts
- Talking about how personally close he is to the big brass
- Taking credit for something undeserved
- Refusing to be serious about something that requires seriousness

When It's Your Job to Criticize and Evaluate

Every manager who works up from the bottom slot has to give those under him helpful criticism and advice at times in the performing of their functions. Often this takes the form of the annual "review." The executive chosen to handle the review of his or her people, must perform this unpleasant task efficiently and with sensitivity. That means:

- Everyone is judged on the same basis; no favoritism is shown.
- A person's good points and main contributions are mentioned at the beginning and at the end of the discussion.
- The person being subjected to the review is told the negatives very slowly and clearly so there is no doubt he understands the conversation perfectly.
- The reviewer gives the reviewee all the time he needs to protest or to explain, excuse, or rationalize his behavior.
- The reviewer makes the reviewee understand what steps he must take to improve his performance. In other words, you don't criticize someone without suggesting ways of helping to correct the situation.
- The discussion is held at a time and place conducive to quiet conversation. Nothing should be pressured or hurried.
- If you're lucky enough to have a staff member who has a *completely* positive review, take your time and enjoy giving the review. It happens all too infrequently.

When You're the One Being Reviewed

- *Be prepared* when you go to the lunch or meeting where you are being reviewed. Bring written notes of your accomplishments, things of which you are proud. Bring notes of areas in which you may not have done your best, so that you will be receptive to possible criticism.
- *Be enthusiastic about your ability to correct anything that was not A-plus* in your performance during the preceding review period.
- *Hear the other person out.* If he says something you disagree with or consider unfair, don't interrupt to protest. Let him finish. Jot yourself a note—just a word—while he's talking, to remind you how to answer his statement when it's time for *you* to talk.
- *Don't sound paranoid.* Many executives make the mistake of blaming their mistakes on everyone but themselves. It takes guts to say, "Yes, I did do that badly," but then you also sound sincere when you add, "but that won't happen again" or "I'll remedy that at once."
- *Don't give an excuse for something that went wrong* unless it is legitimate.
- *End the conversation on a very positive, "up" note.* Make it clear to the other person that
  You accept the criticism.
  You clearly understand it.

You will correct a failing in the future.

You appreciate the courteous way in which the reviewer handled you.

When You Have to Let Someone Go

(*See also* Letters of Reference and Recommendation, in the
Personal Side of Business Letter Writing section of Chapter 3.)

Having to tell someone that he or she is fired or "let go" is one of the worst tasks in the whole business world. Don't make someone in Personnel do your dirty work, whether it's a secretary or a division vice-president. Do it yourself for your own people. True, if the person is a good friend or has grave financial problems, it will be very hard for you. Even if the person is incompetent, firing someone is a difficult, wrenching task—you somehow feel you have taken the responsibility for ruining his or her life.

When someone has committed an act such as robbery, of course, you don't have to waste time being nice. But in the case of someone who couldn't do his job properly, even after fair warning, you should talk to him in a kind, constructive, and reassuring manner. "You didn't make it here, but you'll learn a lot from this experience and do a much better job the next time. Just remember the reasons why I have to let you go (and enumerate them again). In your next job you'll have an opportunity to correct all that. I'm sure you can do it. You need to direct your energy in a constructive manner, etc."

For a person who has to be let go for reasons other than incompetency, the key to doing it well, as far as the "victim" is concerned, is for you to be *compassionate and concerned, but also prepared.* If you are letting him go for economic reasons, give him some figures that show that it is economics and not his shortcomings that are behind the termination. Research every possible avenue of assistance that may be open to this person when he or she receives the news. Give the person the bad news in complete privacy, right at the beginning of your conversation—don't stall and make chitchat. Have at your fingertips a list of what the company will do for him and, if he is a good friend, what you personally will do for him, so that he leaves your office knowing there are avenues of help already functioning for him.

The company, for example, might arrange the following for the executive:

- Satisfactory severance pay
- The services of an outplacement firm to help him find another position
- The use of an office for a period of anywhere from a month to four months (depending, of course, upon the rank of the executive and his length of service with the company)
- A letter from the CEO for his files stating the economic reasons for having to terminate his employment and commending his work

Your own assistance might consist of the following:

- The promise to make telephone calls to colleagues in other organizations to see if there might be a place available within their executive ranks
- If the executive in question will relocate, letters to close friends in other cities, asking for their help in leads to pursue

If the person is someone you wish you did not have to let go, keep reminding him that "this is not the end of the world." Help him to see this will mean opening new doors, following new pathways, experiencing new challenges—he may even be much happier once he has found another position. If his termination occurs during an economic slump, reassure him: "If anyone can find a good position, *you can.* Don't get discouraged. You have so many resources. You have energy and fight. You'll find something good." Build up his confidence, remind him of his qualifications and experience. Tell him, "We'll help you," and make good on your word.

If the person you let go is on in years, double your efforts in calling around to see if there are positions available for him. Try to arrange a consulting relationship with the company so that he will have some income while he is looking; make good use of his talents during that period. Inspire him to do some research, writing, and lecturing while he is looking, so that he won't be as easily depressed.

Keep in touch with a friend. Keep checking on his progress while he continues his job search. Give him all of your trade publications to read so that he won't get out of touch with your trade, industry, or profession.

When You Have Been the One Let Go

The way to have *everyone* on your side when you have been let go is to show your colleagues you are turning your energies toward finding a new job, not lamenting or complaining about what has happened to you. In other words, don't bend everyone's ear about what a "rotten deal" the company gave you. If you discuss the steps you are taking to find another position and ask your colleagues for tips, they will consider you the noble one and the company the ignoble one. Don't make yourself the object of office gossip by being sulky or negative every time they see you in the halls during the interim period when you have the use of a free office. Take the positive view that you are looking hard, that you will find something even better than what you had at this company, and that you'd appreciate "any tips" anyone has.

The smart executive does not line up loyal forces on his behalf to talk and talk about the injustice he has suffered. The smart executive, whether he or she has been let go for financial or other reasons, does not allow the company to lose valuable executive and employee time spent in commiserating with him or gossiping about him.

The smart executive does not try to give "tips" to his replacement or to criticize the direction his replacement is going in projects or policy. The executive who has been let go should be respectful, particularly if the company gives him a free office and perhaps relocation consulting advice.

He should conduct himself with dignity and leave the premises for a new life as quickly as he can. His presence is a reminder of a failure—either his or the company's—and the sooner he leaves, the better. He should, in other words, *get on with his life.*

SENSITIVITY AND SOCIAL SAVVY

The first pages of this chapter have dealt mostly with being motivated to interact in the office environment with kindness and consideration and with understanding for people's feelings and emotions. What follows has to do with the same subject, but it is also geared to social situations: everything from introducing a stranger to the group to knowing when and when not to talk to the boss when you are traveling together. In other words, the next few pages deal with knowing how to act both in what may seem familiar circumstances and in uncharted territory. Every executive should want to have the reputation of being "socially savvy." It's the same as being socially sensitive.

When You Keep Someone Waiting

Often an executive must keep someone waiting who has an appointment, either because the executive is badly organized or has a series of emergencies with which he must cope. However, it is understandable that a person resents being kept waiting by the person with whom he has an appointment.

Visitors

When you must keep a visiting executive waiting in your office, go out to the reception area to greet him or her, apologize, and explain the delay. Offer coffee, a glass of water, or a soda; make interesting material available to read, and the use of a telephone if he needs it. If you can't go out to talk to him, have your secretary or receptionist bring a note into your office, so the visitor at least knows that you are aware of his arrival. What really aggravates a visitor is to feel no contact has been made with the person he has come to see. He will feel he is arbitrarily being manipulated by the staff.

If you and your staff are really gracious and apologetic about keeping him waiting, the visitor's irritation will be greatly decreased. Your secretary should be trained to check on your progress every so often, even if it is just a matter of sticking her head into the doorway of your office or keeping watch on the telephone button and apologizing for your still being on a long distance call.

If you are going to keep someone waiting longer than thirty minutes, explain your predicament yourself (this is *not* the secretary's job), apologize, and give your visitor the option of waiting or rescheduling the appointment at his convenience.

Make certain that your waiting area is equipped with comfortable chairs, good reading lights, and interesting reading material, including, of course, your company's annual report.

Colleagues

Although colleagues often keep each other waiting during a usual office day, a colleague deserves the same courtesies you show to visitors from the outside. If someone comes to your desk, for example, and you are on the telephone or engrossed in your work, trying to meet a deadline, you should make a quick nod of acknowledgment and say something like "Glad to see you; be with you in a minute." Wave the visitor into a seat by your desk or on the sofa or wherever you want him to sit. When you've finished, apologize and give him your full attention, without letting other interruptions occur during your conversation. (Of course, the colleague should be there on pressing business, not just to pass the time of day.)

Showing Deference

Deference is defined as high regard and respect owed an elder or superior. In the business world we should also pay deference to visitors from the outside. We should learn how to do it at an early point in our careers, and continue practicing it until we have reached a point where we merit it ourselves!

Standing and Rising

When someone of either sex comes into the office from the outside, the executive and any staff person present should rise and properly greet that person. (I am not speaking here of the arrival of a messenger with a package or of a colleague who drops in from down the hall.) When a visitor arrives, the company people present should rise simply as an act of courtesy, so the outsider feels welcome and honored. When an older, more senior member of management walks into the office of a junior executive, the latter should rise at once as a form of greeting that also shows deference.

Naturally, if a senior executive walks in and out of a junior executive's office constantly during the day and the junior executive is deeply involved in work at his desk or computer terminal, the younger person does not have to jump to his feet each time. However, he should always stop whatever he is doing, look up, and acknowledge the presence of the senior person, as if to await instructions.

Seatsmanship

Knowing when and where to sit is something every young executive should learn. A junior person who comes barging into a room and then takes any seat of his choice, catches the disapproving eye of senior management. There is an unwritten protocol about where and when people sit. Young people are not supposed to take their seats until their seniors have either signaled to them where they should sit or until their seniors have taken their own seats.

The young manager should wait until signaled to sit down, whether he or she is in an executive's office, at a meeting in the conference room, at a table in a restaurant, or approaching a waiting limousine.

Once a senior person waves or points a young executive toward a seat, the young person should move quickly into place and say, "Thank you." It is very awkward to have people standing around in a room (whether it's the conference room or an executive's living room), wondering where to sit down. The meeting chairman should indicate the proper places for people to sit around the conference table; the host should indicate the proper places for people to sit in his living room.

When guests assemble for cocktails or dinner in a space where the seating is low and consequently difficult to get in and out of, the host executive should make sure there are some straight, comfortable chairs available. (That's not deference; that's kindness!)

Elevator Etiquette

Everyone at the very front of a crowded elevator car should automatically get off when the doors open, even if they are not at their destination floor. The people behind cannot possibly emerge with ease if the people in front do not exit to give them enough room to move. If everyone on the car is going to get off at the same floor, then the people in front should step off smartly and to the side, again to make it easier for those following behind.

Traditionally, it was customary for "gentlemen" to perform every kind of contortion necessary to allow the ladies behind them to leave the elevator car first. After the ladies, the man most senior in rank and importance was supposed to leave the car. In a few places today (e.g., in the homes of heads of state), these protocol customs are still rigorously followed.

The late playwright and friend of many famous people Marc Connelly used to tell the story of his visit to Stockholm for the performance of his play *The Green Pastures.* He was the guest of honor at a U.S. embassy reception following the performance and found himself with Sweden's Prince William in an elevator going to the reception floor of the American minister's home. (In those days we were represented by a minister instead of an ambassador in Stockholm.) When the elevator stopped, the prince deferred to Mr. Connelly, insisting the latter exit first. Connelly refused. "After you, Your Royal Highness." "No, no," replied Prince William. "Since you are my country's guest, you must let me be hospitable."

Connelly could not bring himself to do it; it was a denial of the code of manners with which he was raised. "Sir," he finally said, "do you realize that at this moment, we are on American territory and that, according to international law, you are now a guest of the United States?"

The prince was ready. "You have made an error, my dear friend. One foot ahead of us may technically be United States territory, but right now we are in a Swedish lift and right above Swedish ground."

So they emerged from the elevator shoulder to shoulder. No one was first, and no one was last, a compromise in the same sense that a round table, with no head or bottom place, is used for international conferences, so that no representative of a state will feel he and his country have been downgraded.

Fortunately, in today's workplace, he or she who is at the front of the elevator exits first, and no one should have to stand back or crunch against the side to allow another person to pass.

If you accidentally push against someone in an elevator, your saying "I'm sorry" or "Please excuse me"—quickly and with conviction—will calm the other person's hostility. As far as elevator etiquette goes, my own pet peeve, second to someone's smoking on an elevator (a federal offense), is a person on the car staring relentlessly at me. I begin to wonder if I have mascara dripping on my cheek or a bit of today's chicken salad on my chin. An elevator is much too close quarters for staring activities.

Going Through Doors

Our grandparents were taught that ladies should always walk through the door first. Not so in today's workplace. Common sense and efficiency dictate that whoever arrives at the door first, male or female, should hold it open for the others directly behind and keep it open until all have passed through. However, younger executives should still defer to very senior ones—by managing to get to the door fast, ahead of the others, to hold it open. And the executive the outside people have come to see should act as their host, including opening doors for them and motioning them to walk ahead.

As for *swinging doors,* the executive who is host to the others should push through the swinging door first, so that he can be there when the others emerge, ready to direct where they should go next. If an executive knows that a particular swinging door is very heavy and difficult to move, he should go ahead and push hard to help those coming behind. (A woman host would do the same.) If the visitor is elderly or handicapped in any way, the host executive should precede him and maintain a very slow pace, to allow the handicapped person to come through at a safe, slow speed.

"Door protocol" is simply a matter of thinking ahead and using common sense.

When Junior and Senior Executives Travel Together

When a young executive travels with a member of senior management, he should be helpful in handling details, but without being obsequious. He should offer to see to all transportation, the checking in and out of the hotel, tipping, the limo, etc., managing all logistical aspects of the trip. The older executive may have a lot of important work to do and not wish to be disturbed. If he has time to talk, it is, of course, the perfect opportunity for the younger person to get to know him, to learn some important management lessons, perhaps even to make a few brownie points of his own with the boss. The younger person should be very careful before engaging in long conversations to make sure the senior executive wants them as much as he does. In other words, the junior executive should follow the senior executive's lead. (*See also* Conversation When the Young Executive Is Alone with a Senior Executive, in Chapter 3.)

In the Limo

A younger executive should take it for granted that when a group goes in the limo, he or she occupies one of the uncomfortable jump seats. (The next most uncomfortable spot in the limo is in the middle of the back seat.)

The seat next to the limo driver is very comfortable; the only difficulty is that one is usually cut off from the conversation taking place in back. This negative is often a plus, because most limo drivers are fountains of information, and often a young executive can learn more about the company, the town, and future trends from the driver than he can from the manager of the local plant they are going to visit.

Someone exceedingly long-legged should be put in the front seat if the jump seats are in use, for the latter cut into the legs even of short people sitting behind them.

In an Executive's Own Car

A junior executive driving with his boss and others on a long trip should ask, "Where do you want me to sit?" instead of taking a choice seat himself. I once watched an aggressive young manager take the comfortable front seat next to the company president, who was driving his own car, while the chairman and two other executives were wedged into the small back seat. When I saw the CEO the next day at a North Carolina furniture plant and asked him how the three-hour drive had been, he said, "Fine, but I learned something about young _____ that I had never known before." Before I could ask what, he continued, "Anyone who is insensitive enough to hog the best seat in the car during a very hot, long ride either has to be the chairman of the company or someone on his way out of the company. I'll let you guess which one *he* is!"

Corporate Jet Etiquette

Often a corporate jet brings directors and VIPs to headquarters for meetings. If you are someone's guest on a corporate jet, the most important thing to remember is not just to be on time, but to *be early*. If you hold up the departure of a jet by as much as ten minutes, you can cause the plane to wait in line for another hour or two before obtaining a new clearance.

As a guest you should wait to board until after your host has boarded; you should take the seat to which you are shown, and not try to choose your own.

There is usually only a limited amount of refreshment on board. The pilot, copilot, or steward (if there is one) will offer you what there is. Don't embarrass your corporate host by asking for something special; just take what is offered.

Treat the crew with great respect and carry your own baggage whenever you can—they are not your porters.

Don't use the jet to transport your Christmas packages and large personal items. Space is at a premium. If you are not the boss of the corporation, as a passenger you should "travel light."

Be careful when eating and drinking on the plane. Organize your litter neatly. I heard a pilot complain one day that every time a certain person traveled with the flight group, it was necessary to vacuum the entire interior of the plane. Said the pilot, "Even the cages in the zoo look better than our plane when he's been aboard."

When you land, always thank the crew and compliment them on a "beautiful flight." If the flight was a rough one because of weather, mention what "skillful pilots" the crew are.

If you have received a ride on a corporate jet, write a thank-you note to the executive who was responsible for your getting a seat on the flight. Don't forget to praise the crew in that letter.

Outside directors who are flown in to board meetings at company headquarters on the corporate jet always with the same crew should remember each member of the crew at Christmas with something like a book, candy, or fruit.

The Art of Introducing People

The most important thing to remember about introducing people is *to do it,* even if you forget names, get confused, or blank out on the proper procedure. Introducing people is one of the most important acts in business life, and yet very few people know how to do it.

Making proper introductions is actually sheer logic:

- Introduce a younger person *to* an older person.
- Introduce a peer in your own company *to* a peer in another company.
- Introduce a nonofficial person *to* an official person.
- Introduce a junior executive *to* a senior executive.
- Introduce a fellow executive *to* a customer or client.

Explain who people are when you introduce them. For example:

"Mr. Cogswell, I'd like to present my daughter Cynthia. Cynthia, this is Mr. Gregory Cogswell, the president of our company."

"Mr. and Mrs. Johnson, I'd like to introduce to you a fellow executive from Standard Oil, Timothy Greet. Tim, this is Mr. and Mrs. Oleg Johnson, good friends of my parents."

Introducing a Stranger to Your Group

When someone you know comes up to your group, and you are obviously the only one who knows the newcomer, it would be very rude of you to go on talking without introducing him to the others. It is very hard on the newcomer to be left standing there, feeling alien and unwelcome, wondering how he can extricate himself from this situation. You should interrupt the group's conversation in order to welcome the newcomer.

"Frank, it's good to see you! I'd like to introduce my colleagues from East-West—John Morton, Joan Corleone, and Ed Schmidt. And this is Frank Brissell, a neighbor of ours in Winnetka who's with Putnam, Schroeder and Baker."

It's helpful to provide the group with a little information about the person you're introducing. It helps make the conversation continue to flow. Someone will mention a friend of his in the same law firm, someone else will make a remark about Winnetka, and the newcomer will feel instantly welcomed.

Using Titles in Introductions

When introducing people of equal standing, you do not have to use a title unless you are introducing an older person, a professional, or someone with official rank. For example: "Harry, I'd like to introduce a young vice-president of our company, June Jordan . . . June, this is Dr. Henry Pratt."

It is considerate when introducing a widow to give both her given and her late husband's names: "Mrs. Treadwell, may I present my brother, Douglas Stewart. Doug, this is Ann Treadwell. Her late husband, Anthony, was a great friend of my father's, and she's one of the bastions of this community."

Use a person's official title when talking to or introducing him, even if he no longer holds that position. For example, a man who used to be mayor would be introduced as "former Mayor Cantwell or just "Mayor Cantwell." A man who used to be an ambassador would be introduced as "Ambassador Smith." A woman who is a retired colonel in the air force would be introduced as "Colonel Schmidt."

What Is in a Name?

Concentrating on and Practicing Names

The ability to remember names is an outstanding asset. Concentration is the key to remembering a large number of them—at least for a short space of time, such as during a party or a weekend meeting.

When you meet a person, concentrate on his name as it is given to you. Repeat it mentally while you say it aloud. "Glad to meet you, Mr. McChesney," you might say as your mind repeats the name silently two or three times and you also search for an identifying word association. He may have one wisp of hair standing up straight on his head" ("McChesney—wisp on top of head"). He may have unusual colored eyes ("McChesney, green cat's eyes"), very broad shoulders ("McChesney, wrestler's shoulders"), or an unusual pattern in his suit ("McChesney, tic-tac-toe suit"). If the name can be used in a word association with the person himself, concentrate on that. For example: "Mr. Burns, red hair," "Mr. Long, very tall," "Mrs. McIntosh, wearing a raincoat," etc. Remember one salient detail and it will fasten to that person's name like Velcro, at least for a while.

If you don't understand a name when it's given to you (and many introducers are hopelessly inept at articulating names when making introductions), don't be shy about asking for the name again: "I'm sorry. I didn't understand your name, and I want to know it." The other person should be flattered that you care enough to want to know it.

If the other person repeats it but you still do not understand, ask for a repetition, even more apologetically this time: "I'm sorry, I just can't seem to catch the name."

This time the person should pronounce his name slowly so that you are able to understand it. If you repeat it aloud, his name will now stick in your mind. If his name is very complicated (like Dobyczescowitz, for example), ask him for his business card; if he doesn't have one, ask him to write his name on your notepad. By now he will either be very irritated or immensely pleased by your interest.

If you see someone you've met before but can't remember the name, say something like, "I remember meeting you at that American Express lunch at the Hilton last spring. I'm Agnes Catwell." The other person will be flattered to have been remembered, even if you didn't recall his or her name.

If you are entrusted with the responsibility of introducing people to each other at a corporate function, you will have to go through a lot of hard work in order to remember people's names and in order to pronounce them properly. When you do a good job of it, you cast a fine reflection on your company and on your own talents. People like to have their names and titles remembered and stated correctly. It's one of the emoluments in life to which one feels entitled.

How to Finesse Names and Titles

We all forget names. It's a very human error, and some of us—me, for example—are more human than others. I have forgotten my college room-mate's name when introducing her. I have forgotten my boss's wife's name at my own party. In my zest for introducing people, I have introduced husbands to wives. I also introduced a man and woman to a roomful of guests as man and wife when both were married to others. One of my more memorable gaffes was introducing the man a friend was with as "her dear father." The man was her husband.

During the seven years I spent introducing officials at the American embassies in Paris and Rome, as well as during the three years I spent in the White House, I made every mistake there was to make, but I survived. People forgave me; they knew my heart was in the right place and *that at least I tried.*

What irritates people most, I believe, is to be ignored. If they are expected to fend for themselves—whether at a business gathering or social party—they are not going to feel comfortable. Every corporate host, whether in his or her office or at home, should endeavor to have everyone feel comfortable.

If you suffer a memory lapse on a name when trying to introduce people, don't think it an unsolvable crisis. Admit your memory lapse. It happens to everyone. It is not as terrible as you may think at the time. Look incredulous and say, "How could I *do* such a thing! I know your last name *so well!*"

While the easiest solution is to admit you have temporarily forgotten a name, there is another alternative. It's called the "talk fast and maybe they won't guess the truth" solution. If you have forgotten the name of the person who has joined your group, begin talking quickly in a pleasant, even funny exaggerated way. Build up the ego of the person whose name you can't recall:

"Listen, everyone, this is someone I haven't seen for a long, long time, but he was such a fantastic salesman that the rumor is he almost sold the office building to his company president!"

If the only thing you can remember about a person is where he lives, you can almost always drag out a little story that will cause everyone to smile. Soon they are shaking hands and everyone is introducing himself all around. Probably the newcomer and the others in the group don't even realize you never once mentioned his name. (It works, because I do it all the time.)

Honesty, however, is always the best policy. Just admit the name has slipped your mind. Generally, you will be forgiven.

Give Your Own Name Quickly

Don't make people who have forgotten your name suffer while trying to come up with it. If you are talking to a friend when another person joins the group, and your friend doesn't make a move to introduce you to the newcomer, chances are your friend has momentarily forgotten either your name or the newcomer's name.

Save the situation. Put out your hand, give your name, and the other person will return your salute with his own name. Your friend will be grateful!

If you are a women who has kept her maiden name after marriage, make sure that people who meet your husband do not call him by your family name. I learned long ago when going to parties with my husband to introduce him to people he has not met by giving his name loud and clear. "This is my husband, *Bob Hollensteiner.*" Neither he nor I want to hear him called "Mr. Baldrige." It's up to the woman in this situation to make it very clear.

Calling Someone by a First Name
(*See also* Showing Deference)

If you have to stop and think about whether or not you should use a person's first name when you greet him, the answer is you should not.

Familiarity does indeed breed contempt. No one likes to be addressed by his or her first name by someone who doesn't have the right to do so. In some parts of America—small towns, farming communities, and rural areas—everyone is automatically on a first name basis. In larger cities and often in larger companies people are more formal. But, in any community, of any size, there is a right time and a wrong time to start calling people by their first names.

A young person should wait for an older person to ask him to call him by his first name. An executive should wait for a more senior executive to ask him to call him by his first name. It's a question of understanding deference.

If a senior executive calls a junior executive by his first name, that does not mean the junior person should indiscriminately call the senior one by his first name. For example, if the senior executive approaches with an older, distinguished client, it is much better for the junior executive to nod, smile, and say, "Good morning, Mr. Smith," rather than call out, "Hey, Sam, how's it going?"

Using Nicknames in the Workplace

An unflattering, ugly-sounding, or just plain comical nickname has no place in a conservative business situation. This kind of informality is fine in an art director's office but not in the office of the vice-president for corporate finance. Besides, a nickname is often a put-down of the person.

Some people have the misfortune to grow up with their childhood nicknames firmly attached—"Chuckles," "Bubba," "Pepper," "Pooch," "Pits," "Spritz," etc. Friends who insist upon calling an executive by this kind of nickname should be kindly reminded by the executive: "Look, I'm not called that anymore. I'd appreciate your calling me Bill."

Everyone has the right to be addressed by a dignified name in the office, one that is neither silly nor deprecating. If your nickname is a pleasing shortened version of your name (such as "Charlie," "Bob," "Dick," etc.), there is no problem. But if Charlie wants to be called "Charles" in the workplace, all he has to do is keep reminding people to call him that. Once his proper name is fixed in other people's minds, he will become "Charles" to them forever.

The head of an insurance company recently circulated a memo to his company executives decreeing that "names, not nicknames will be used in this office." He added, "I happen to love dogs, but dogs, not their owners, deserve the nicknames."

Greeting Others

The way in which you meet others—what you do with your body and your voice—shows the kind of person you are. If you meet others with interest, showing good manners, they will respond immediately to you. (Remember, you never get a second chance at making a first impression!)

When someone is introduced to you and you remain seated, you are telling that person, even if you don't mean to, that you do not wish to be bothered. Your body language denotes lack of interest.

When being introduced, it is important to:

- Rise
- Step forward and smile, or at least look pleasant
- Give your name
- Shake hands
- Repeat the other person's name and say something like "Delighted to meet you, Mr. Adams" (or "Bill," as the case may be) or "Nice to meet you, Mr. Adams." Even "Hello, Mr. Adams" will suffice.

Hugging, Kissing, and Air-Kissing in Greeting

We Americans are one of the most demonstrative people in the world. But when we are abroad or when our foreign business friends visit us, we should *not* give them the warm embraces and hugs that we would normally give old friends from this country whom we have not seen in a long time. We should not be overly demonstrative even to our friends in business in this country. Here are some thoughts on the subject:

- Business colleagues who have not seen each other for a long time but who have a good relationship can always shake hands warmly, and grab each other's right upper arm or shoulder with their free left hand. This makes a half-hug, a gesture perfectly appropriate for the office.
- Shaking someone's hand and putting your other hand over the two clasped hands is another sign of warm affection that does not entail embracing.
- Men and women executives should not kiss each other in public. A "brother-sister greeting kiss" is often misconstrued.
- Nothing is more phony, in my opinion, than the fad of air-kissing, which entails puckering up one's lips and putting one's cheek alongside someone else's cheek, then repeating the inane gesture on the other cheek. One sees a lot of this in the so-called "upper strata" of society, between two women or between a woman and a man. It is not a warm gesture, but a very awkward, artificial one.

The Handshake

It may be a sign of inhibition, but Americans shake hands less frequently than people from any other country. It's a pity, too, because it's an important contact—a physical link—between two people. Many people feel they can "take the measure" of another person by his or her handshake. When a business person shakes hands easily, often and graciously, he actually influences his peers to begin handshaking more often.

A good handshake is one that:

· Is made with a firm and not a bone-crushing or fish-limp grip
· Is held for about three or four seconds, not so long that the other hand feels caught in a vise.

The times at which you should shake hands are these:

· When you are introduced to someone and when you say good-bye
· When someone comes into your office from the outside
· When you run into someone outside your office
· When you enter a room, are greeted by those you know, and are introduced to outsiders also present
· When you leave a gathering attended by people from the outside

If your hands tend to be clammy, remember to keep wiping them inconspicuously with your handkerchief at a social-business gathering. If you have been holding an iced drink in your hand, your handshake will feel equally icy and wet, so when someone puts out his hand to shake yours, quickly wipe your hand on the side of your jacket or skirt and apologize: "Sorry for my wet, cold hand." You certainly wouldn't want anyone who didn't already know you to think the warmth of your personality matched that of your hand! (Of course, this problem doesn't arise if you learn to keep your drink in your left hand.)

When You Visit Another Executive's Office

Arriving executives should act with self-assurance and good manners the minute they cross the threshold of the office they are visiting. To make a good impression:

· *Arrive on time*—and ahead of time if you expect to use the restroom before your appointment.
· *State your name clearly,* as well as your company name and the name of the person you have come to see: "Dick Friedman, president of Avantage. I have an appointment with Sally Fay at two o'clock." It is smart to hand your card to the receptionist so that she can handle your name and company with ease.
· *Wait to be shown where to hang your coat,* or ask where you may conveniently hang it.
· *Sit down and wait quietly.* You never know who is going to pass through the reception area.
· *Do not hound the receptionist with questions.* ("When do you think Ms. Fay will be ready to see me?")

- Once inside Ms. Fay's office, *extend your hand in a firm handshake,* sit in the chair motioned to by your host, put your briefcase neatly on the floor close by, and sit in a comfortable but attentive manner. Refrain from smoking or fidgeting.
- If more than one person is present, *shake hands first with the senior, most important person in the group* (if you have been summoned to the meeting) *or with the person with whom you made the appointment* (if you requested it), then proceed to shake everyone else's hand.
- If you requested the meeting, *lead off with three or four minutes of pleasantries, then get down to business.* If you were summoned, your host takes the lead.
- *Watch your host's time commitments.* After greeting him, ask how much time he has to give you. Don't make him run over. (He will think highly of you for that alone.)
- *When it is time to leave, stand, thank your host, shake his hand, and take your leave.* Thank his secretary and receptionist on your way out.

Good Manners in Sports

Since so many business relationships are forged in the locker room and on the tennis court, the golf course, and playing fields, an executive's manners in sports are of great importance. His partners and opponents will judge what kind of person he is in business by his behavior in competitive sports. In the eyes of most people, a person's ability as a team player in sports and in the office are interrelated. Aggressiveness, speed, relentlessness, and determination are assets in both sports and business. Meanness, cheating, and boorishness are not. *Good sportsmanship is an essential part of a good executive presence.*

The following points of etiquette comprise a very basic code of behavior that should be followed:

- Be on time and never hold up anyone else's play.
- Don't cancel out at the last minute on a game, unless you have an incredibly good reason for it.
- Be neat in the changing rooms.
- Bring the proper equipment and clothing. (A person who never brings a can of new tennis balls is like the person who never picks up a check.)
- Be honest in advance about how good you are at the sport.
- Smile when you lose (you'll have a better spot in heaven some day).
- Never berate your partner nor complain about his or her playing.
- Don't complain about an opponent's play either.

- If you are big, don't use brute force to win points from a much smaller opponent.
- Know all the rules of the game you're playing.
- Be careful of the ground you play on, whether it's a court or a green, and leave it immaculate.
- Abstain completely from foul language and outbursts of anger.
- When you finish playing, shake hands with everyone, compliment their game, and thank them for letting you join them.

2

Men's and Women's Relations at Work

Until the 1960s the presence of women in the executive suite was largely confined to a man's executive secretary in the office and to a man's "corporate wife" at home, the latter with a schedule revolving around her husband, her children, and, most importantly, the company. The pre-sixties corporate wife enjoyed great status—her husband's. As his achievements multiplied, she reflected them; she mirrored his success. Quite naturally the corporation looked her over carefully before employing her husband in an important position. The company reasoned that, as his hostess, she would be present at all important business-social functions. Her behavior could make or break the company image. She therefore had to undergo lengthy interviews and checking before her husband was hired.

That kind of corporate wife does not exist today (except for older chief executive officers and their wives). Today, a corporation does not dare interview the spouse of either sex before employing an executive. Today's executive wife, even if she does not work outside the home, is often engaged in pursuit of her hobbies or the arts or involved in serious volunteer work in her community. Perhaps she is back in school. She is no longer on constant call for her husband's company.

This does not mean that she should not be ready to appear at her husband's side when it is important to him. The difference today is that *he* should be ready to be at her side, too, when it is important to *her* career. Companies today have new expectations of the corporate spouse, a simple request to "help out when you can" in business-social entertaining.

Today's Double Standard

The changes in the role of the corporate spouse over the past twenty or thirty years are minuscule in comparison to changes in what is perceived as "exemplary male executive behavior." As the women's movement of the 1960s rolled forward, the chivalrous male received signals to do an about-face on what seemed like everything he had previously been taught regarding the treatment of women. As a result, many well-mannered male executives follow a double standard of behavior. They treat women as colleagues during the day but treat their wives or loved ones at home in a different manner—more along the lines of traditional chivalry. Many women *want* their chairs pulled back, their coats put on, and their doors opened—at home.

There is a new kind of double standard. This time, it refers to a man's behavior in the office versus his behavior at home.

At the office, the polished executive foregoes the following rote behaviors towards a female colleague. He doesn't automatically

- Open all doors for her
- Hang up her coat when she arrives or help her on with it when she leaves
- Stand up when she enters the room (unless she is a visitor) and remain standing until she is seated
- Serve her before himself at table
- Help her with her chair
- Light her cigarettes
- Carry any packages in her possession
- Hail her taxis and usher her into them
- Order her meal for her in a restaurant and always pay for it
- Have her precede him in walking anywhere
- Walk curbside to protect her from being splashed
- Step back in the elevator car to allow any woman to exit first

With the arrival of women in the executive workplace, such chivalrous treatment has been replaced by a new set of manners, and by a new sense of *collegiality.* In other words, people are supposed to treat each other equally and act according to rules of protocol, not of gender; and one sex is supposed to come to the aid of the other whenever either needs assistance. For example, the polished executive:

- Moves quickly to open a door for anyone walking nearby who has his or her hands full

- Picks up whatever someone else has dropped who cannot retrieve it as easily as he can. (Walking down the corridor at IBM headquarters, I once saw the chairman take off on a run to help a messenger pick up a load of papers and files he had dropped.)
- Stands to greet a visitor to the meeting or his or her office
- Assists a colleague struggling to get in or out of his or her coat

Male or female, a senior manager should precede those junior in rank in moving through doors, in sitting down at the table, etc., except when filling the rank of host, in which case the host would usher guests ahead of him- or herself.

We are still in the developmental stage of the new manners. Witness the confusion, the hemming and hawing that occurred when Geraldine Ferraro received the Democratic vice-presidential nomination. It became a dilemma for Mr. Mondale and Ms. Ferraro to decide who should precede whom in mounting platforms, exiting from airplanes, etc. (Of course, Mr. Mondale, ranking first, should have preceded his female vice-presidential candidate partner at all times.) Also, they had to decide how they would greet each other when they met in public. A kiss on the cheek, like old friends? A handshake and a smile? A bear hug perhaps? Or should they not touch at all? (Actually, there's an easy rule to follow for this. To avoid any gossip, male and female colleagues can greet each other warmly with just a big smile and a firm hand-shake, fortified by the clasping of their free hand on the hand being shaken. No one could read any potential romance into that!)

Addressing Female Colleagues

A male manager's attitude toward a female colleague is an etiquette issue. And a first consideration is getting into the habit of addressing her politely.

The way men regard a woman newly arrived in the executive workplace can greatly influence her potential for success. Before she has even had a chance to prove herself, her career may be damaged by the way her male colleagues refer to her, even if simply in jest among themselves. The following are examples of inaccurate, stereotyped thinking that can damage a female colleague's career if expressed or implicit in male executives' attitude toward her:

- If she is assertive, she must be unfeminine.
- If she is soft-spoken, she is not tough enough for the business world.
- If she's unmarried, there's something wrong with her.
- If she is married but without children, she is denying her womanhood.
- If she has children, she'll neglect her work.
- If she is married, she shouldn't be considered for a promotion that might

require her to move from the city, because she would never leave her husband.

- If the company invests time and money to train her, she will become pregnant and then desert her job.
- She will complain more than a man about marriage troubles.
- If she's really good-looking, she'll only distract the men.
- If she's not good-looking, she will only detract from the office image.
- As a female, she obviously hasn't had the same opportunities to become as seasoned as her male peers.
- When it's time for her monthly period, she will inevitably show unstable behavior.
- When she is of the age for menopause, she will inevitably show unstable behavior.

Such prejudicial statements may seem exaggerated, yet they are heard with regularity when male executives deal with female executives. It is often obvious that women are measured by completely different standards than men. If a woman takes one drink too many on only *one* occasion, she may immediately be labeled an alcoholic, unlike a man in the same circumstances.

How colleagues address each other is also a point of etiquette. If a male manager wants to effectively irritate a woman colleague, all he has to do is call her patronizing names like "Honey," "Sweetie," or "Darling." A woman should firmly request that he not use those terms in referring to her (and remind him of her proper name). She should also help her male colleagues to use correct, respectful language when talking to her about other women. One can always write a friendly, amusing memo to someone who peppers his language with put-downs when talking about women. There is no need for a sermon, just a gentle reminder that when he discusses women in a denigrating fashion, he is really hurting himself more than anyone else.

I will never forget one memo sent to me from a senior officer in government during my White House days. I remember it very well:

Hey, sweetie-pie, what's with the Luxembourg mix-up? I should think that a babe with your intelligence wouldn't have let that happen . . .

I wrote him a return memo:

I would be very glad to discuss the Luxembourg "mix-up," as you refer to it, if and when you write a memo to me as a human being, and not as a female orangutan.

That was back in 1962. He wrote me a memo of apology, and I'm sure that today he addresses women executives entirely differently.

The Question of Our Sexist Language

There are so many terms in the English language containing the word *man* that it would be ridiculous to try changing them in order to make our language nonsexist—*man*hours, for example, or sports*man*ship, *man*power, *man*holes, *man*handling, *man*kind, and endlessly onward.

The woman executive should help keep our language simple by refusing to use new words coined to balance the use of *man* with *woman* on an equal basis. For example, *chairman* is a generic term, meaning man or woman. It is clumsy to have to refer to a woman chairman as "chairwoman" or "chairperson." And yet our language is full of exceptions to the rule. *Businessman,* unlike *chairman,* is a word that should be changed according to its gender. A woman executive is a businesswoman, not a businessman. A mixed gathering would be one of business people, not businessmen.

Certain professional designations have no gender—like *lawyer, doctor,* or *scientist,* for example. Others *do* have gender, such as *actress* versus *actor.* Other fields in the arts *no longer* have gender today. Now there are only poets and sculptors (women do not wish to be called poetesses or sculptresses).

Since there are so many exceptions to the rule, the confused executive will remain just that unless he or she memorizes the proper title in each field. A man is not going to know the proper title for women unless women peers graciously help teach him what is correct.

The Unprejudiced Male Executive's Good Manners Toward Women

Fortunately, there are male executives who feel that women deserve not only a fair chance but an assist when they enter the workplace. This kind of man perceives of his women colleagues' presence in terms of their value to the company.

- He judges a woman by what she can contribute to the company—to make everyone, including himself, look good.
- He regards her as a team member and includes her in all the team's activities.
- If he suspects her to be after his own job, he deals with her exactly as he would with a man after his job.
- He shows her the ropes during her early days with the company, including giving her valuable information on company politics. He assists her without patronizing her.
- As her supervisor, he is not unnecessarily tender in his criticism. He realizes that if he must moderate his criticism, she will never be able to

tell what kind of job she is doing. He knows that what she needs most is fair and accurate feedback on her job performance.

- He is not afraid to spotlight the achievements of women within his company.

One way in which a male executive can be most helpful to a woman is to admit her to the "Old Boys' Network"—make her part of those occasional lunches in which managers gather informally to discuss business and to share information and gossip garnered from various grapevines to which she does not have normal access. As Celanese Corporation Director Eleanor Elliott said in a speech, "Many of the businesswomen with whom I've talked—at Celanese and elsewhere—are lonely. Women on high levels in the company are spread far apart. They do not have the chance for casual interchange that men do, by dropping into each other's offices or going off to an impromptu lunch together. It's not the feeling of being socially snubbed that gets these women; it's the feeling of being professionally excluded."

When a woman is invited to join the men for lunch, she should be ready to contribute interesting information of her own to the group. It helps, too, if she sharpens her sense of humor for the occasion. It's a given that she does not let chivalry govern who picks up the check—she pays for her own lunch. (I once heard a businesswoman remark that there are only three occasions in a woman's life in which she should allow her male colleagues to pay for her lunch: if she has just given birth, if she has just won a Nobel Prize, or if she has just been nominated for the presidency of the United States!) And of course, a most important thing for a woman to remember after having been invited to join the "lunch bunch" is to say those two simple words: *Thank you.*

The Well-Mannered Female Executive

A harmonious working relationship between the two sexes certainly does not depend solely upon the male executive. A woman's good manners are as important as her work performance. Because of her sex, she is *supposed* to have good manners. That may be an unrealistic perception, but nevertheless many people still perceive it to be true. It's an old adage that women are "the keepers of the manners."

Certainly if a female executive has good manners, she will be easy to get along with at work. In relating to her coworkers, she should aspire to a very affirmative code of behavior.

- She should follow all rules of executive manners along with her male colleagues.
- She should be pleasant and agreeable to *everyone,* not just to the chiefs.

- She should always be on time.
- She should be well-organized, thorough in her preparation, and adamant about making her deadlines.
- She should possess a good sense of humor and know when to use it; she should know how to laugh at herself without being too self-deprecating.
- She should not be self-conscious about praising a male colleague's contribution to the company.
- She should know how gracefully to thank male colleagues for their assists.
- She should be compassionate in the womanly sense and not be afraid to show it.
- She should not be embarrassed by the traditionally female trait of intuitiveness but rather bank it as a useful asset to call on in the workplace.
- She should nourish a good self-image without being a braggart.
- She should understand the hierarchy of management and not attempt to skip over it to the top.
- She should keep her private life separate from her business and avoid wasting office time with excess conversation about either her family or her love life.
- She should make a special effort to be friendly to the wives of her male peers, so that she will appear less threatening to the colleagues' wives. (Occasionally the corporate wife is jealous of the women who inhabit her husband's life.)
- She should not complain of discrimination or sexual harassment unless there is full, just cause.
- She should refrain from using foul language (as should her male peers). In spite of our "equal world," bad language still sounds more offensive coming from a woman's mouth than from a man's.
- She should never blame others for her own mistakes.
- She should work hard to serve as a sympathetic mentor and an effective role model for the young women following behind her, keeping in mind her own early struggles.
- She should pay back a colleague with quality time and effort for any assistance given her in her work when she was absent because of a personal or family emergency.
- She should be mindful of any discrimination or unfair policies relating to other women in her office, whether her task is one of soothing over difficulties or supporting someone who has been unfairly wronged.
- In her conversation, speeches and articles she should never forget those who helped her. She should credit any teachers, bosses, or colleagues who patently gave her a career assist.

Special Problems of Female Managers

Unfortunately, women managers today must be better mannered and work harder than their male colleagues to prove they can do their jobs as well. It will be a pleasure to omit such exhortations once women have caught up with men in the workplace. Until that time, women must grapple, more or less succcessfully, with problems like these:

A Young Woman Boss and Her New Employees

Often a woman manager has an uphill battle if men report to her or if a much senior person of either sex reports to her.

If she is up-front with them from the very beginning and shows that she understands their dilemma, the relationships have a good chance to succeed. She should communicate her pride in having these senior and male employees on her team and show appreciation for their wisdom and experience. She should ask them to let her know when they feel things are going wrong in terms of their work and their morale, and she should carefully explain the goals toward which they will all be working. She should promise to make sure they are properly compensated for the work they do—and live up to that promise.

First meetings are very important. They set the style of management and the temperature of the working atmosphere. When the manager assumes her position of authority, an expression of admiration for her subordinates' qualifications and reputations, rather than any rationalization of her *own* superior position, will avert much of their possible hostility.

I watched a young woman on her first day as the head of a new section (the previous boss had been fired two weeks before). When the manager arrived at her first staff meeting, the tension in the room was readily apparent. People were gossiping in hushed voices; the men were frankly snickering. A man in his early sixties sat silent and glum, as though he couldn't believe his last years with the company would be spent taking orders from a young woman.

But she was ready for them. She walked in quickly, shook hands, smiled all around, and spoke each of their names. She asked them to be seated, then sat on the edge of a desk and talked to them for fifteen minutes in a charming, candid manner. She explained why she had been selected for the job (her credentials were impressive) and how much it meant to her personally to succeed. I watched the other people in the room loosen up. She addressed each person, one by one, saying nice, complimentary things about what she had learned from others concerning him or her. Her audience began to relax and smile at her friendly words. She then explained in a clear, professional manner what was expected of her staff and what they could expect from her in the coming year.

Everyone left the room with a pleasant expression on his or her face. The new boss had used her business polish to win them over.

Size Differences—the Amazon and the Doll

A woman who weighs only about ninety pounds may have a problem making men executives take her as seriously as she would like. A large, muscular woman may have a similar problem, since the men may be referring to her behind her back as a truck driver or football tackle.

One might think that the solution for a small woman would be to bristle twenty-four hours a day with crisp language and a strident sense of purpose, or for the large, strong woman to pretend she is helpless when men are present. Neither solution works.

There are all kinds of people inside those overly small or large bodies; those inside should try to forget their physical packaging and help others forget it. A sense of humor coupled with talent and competence makes the best antidote to problems of physical size. A woman should not be ashamed to ask for and to receive physical assistance. If a petite woman is approached by an overly solicitous man as she starts to carry a heavy load, she should thank him but announce she is perfectly capable of carrying it—if indeed she is. If the load is too big, she should gratefully accept his assistance. A big woman may suddenly find herself faced, just as any man, with too large a stack of materials to carry. She may give the appearance of being able to lift her own weight three times over, but she may have weak arms or a bad back. She should ask for assistance without embarrassment. So should a man in the same situation.

A man who makes disparaging comments about a woman's size, even in jest, should be answered with firmness laced with humor. People come in all physical sizes, and so does the nature of their tasks. Someone who is bigoted about matters such as people's sizes is no asset to his or her company.

A Woman Traveling Alone

A woman alone doesn't mean an available woman. A woman on her own is often afraid of being perceived as an easy pickup or, even worse, as a hooker. To some men, "alone" signifies "available," which is sexual discrimination in its worst form.

If you, a woman alone, are unpleasantly accosted by a stranger in your hotel who has the wrong idea, of course you tell him to "get lost fast." But you certainly don't need to spend your evenings imprisoned in your mustard yellow and poison green motel room because of an occasional unpleasant experience. You should summon enough courage to have your drink in the hotel bar as well as eat your dinner in the hotel dining room, if that's what you want to do. It may take a little practice to enter public eating and drinking places by yourself and, of course, they must be selected with care. After a few times, being alone in a restaurant on your travels becomes very natural.

There are some things to remember, of course. First of all, *you should look like a professional* at all times when traveling for your company. Your conservative, business image is conveyed by the way you dress as well as by the way you behave.

Enter the bar with your briefcase or some files (a symbol of your status in life). Hold your head high, with a pleasant expression on your face, and without any embarrassment tell the person seating you, "Yes, a table for one, please." After you have ordered your drink, shuffle through a paper or two, to further establish yourself as someone who is stopping in this hotel on business.

Look elsewhere if you find a man staring at you; don't put on an expression either of panic or of extreme distaste. Both are signs of uneasiness. If he comes over uninvited and seats himself at your table, call the waiter and ask, "Is there a free table for this gentleman?" The interloper should get the message and leave you alone. If he does not, leave the table and report him to the management; they will handle it from there.

If an attractive man comes over to your table and politely asks if he can join you, you may say yes, if you feel like it. Explain to him at the beginning, however, that you have only a few more minutes before you have to leave. This gives you a chance to desert him if you find his company less than satisfactory.

If he then offers to pay for your drink, it is proper for you to accept. If you both order a second round, make it clear that you are going to pay for *this* round. As for the third round of drinks, finesse it. This is the round that one (or both) will have been sorry to have ordered.

If your companion invites you to join him for dinner, if you wish to accept, make it clear that you will charge your dinner to your own bill and that you do not wish to leave the premises. By not becoming indebted to him, he and everyone else will know you are a no-nonsense woman who does not pick up men. Mention something like "Dinner will have to be a pretty speedy one, because I have a lot of work to prepare before the meetings tomorrow." With this statement you are emitting a clear signal that you will not continue through the night as his companion.

There have been some very unpleasant stories about what has happened to businesswomen who left their hotels or motels with strangers who invited them out to dinner. This is why you should stay where you are to dine. It is wise to be safe.

A woman often feels self-conscious dining in a good restaurant without an escort or a friend. Yet when she is on the road on business it is enjoyable to try out the restaurants for which that city is famous. If you wish to dine in a particular restaurant in another city, be sure to book a reservation beforehand. (Make certain your choice is not the night club–cabaret kind of place, because if you are typical, a woman sitting alone while a floor show is in progress can feel uncomfortable.) When you reserve your table, give your name, your title, and company. It helps impress management of the restaurant. If you are fussed over and shown special attention, remember to be generous with your tips when you leave.

On rare occasions a maître d'hôtel will discriminate against solitary woman guests. If this happens to you, ask for a better table. If you have booked a reservation well in advance and you arrive early in the dining hour, you should be shown to a good table, not to one directly in front of the kitchen, where you are in danger of being hit each time the door opens.

If you are shy about having others see you dining alone, you might pass some time by making notes in your office diary or by jotting down some notes on a pad. It doesn't look very nice—or appetizing—if you read your newspaper, because dirty newsprint means dirty fingers on a clean white tablecloth. An exception to this rule is of course the breakfast meal, when most people are too tired or sleepy to care about inky fingers, and the cuisine is not subtle enough to worry about what newsprint might do to the food.

You might take a small book to the table to peruse occasionally. Don't stick your nose in it the entire time, or others might think you have an inferiority complex and are afraid to be looked at. Glance up from your reading every so often; put a pleasant expression on your face. If you find someone staring at you, ignore it—unless you want to try staring the other person down (I've found it always works). You have a right to be there, to enjoy your meal and your surroundings without your privacy being invaded. Besides, it is much more enjoyable to dine alone than to share your meal with someone who is unpleasant or even boring. (Keep reminding yourself of this, and it will help you combat any possible shyness about being alone.)

One night a very attractive young woman traveling for Procter & Gamble was absorbedly reading a book through part of her dinner in a hotel dining room. An executive at a nearby table asked the waiter to find out discreetly what book was holding her interest so completely. When the headwaiter returned to give him the name of a book on Elizabethan England, the executive smiled broadly. He had written his college thesis on the subject. He had a very legitimate entree with which to begin a conversation. There was an immediate exchange of notes between the two tables; there were glasses of champagne shared after dinner; and there was a wedding six months later, which goes to prove that not all business trips are boring!

Rules of the Road for the Traveling Woman Executive

Many of the women on the road for business feel insecure about the do's and don'ts of business travel. The majority spend their days in meetings and their evenings unenthusiastically but safely, consuming a less-than-inspiring dinner on a tray in front of the television set in the room.

A woman doesn't have to hold all meetings in restaurants or hotel lobby bars when out of town. If a woman wants to use her room or suite for a business meeting, she can. She should make sure it is free of personal items— such as her clothing—before people arrive and should have anything left over from room service, like a breakfast tray, picked up before anyone arrives. If she has been smoking, she should air out the room.

A suite is by far the best arrangement for a meeting, but if one is unavailable or if her company cannot afford a suite, she should ask for a room with a bed that converts to a sofa. If that is not possible, she should pull up chairs and use the bed as a giant conference table, arranging papers, files, etc., on it. That will make the bed a very nonsexual object.

When people assemble for the meeting, she should offer them something nonalcoholic to drink. If the meeting is an afternoon one that drags on interminably, everyone might need a pickup, in which case a surprise tray of fresh fruit cut up into "finger food" and some glasses of iced soda water make a special treat. If the meeting is held in her room, she is the hostess, so to speak, and caring for the comfort of those sitting there should be considered part of her executive ability, not just a "womanly" gesture.

I asked one extremely attractive woman executive who is on the road every week and who has meetings in her hotel suite every time if she ever had any trouble from a sex angle. She laughed and then showed me a large double frame containing photographs of her husband and children. "I always put this conspicuously near the seating area of the suite," she explained. "No one would make a pass in front of my family!"

I might also add that when this woman arrives at whatever hotel she is using, she always tips the concierge, says hello to the manager, and tips the bell captain well, explaining who she is and why she is in this hotel. The service she receives is first class. She is given special attention rather than being treated as a second class citizen, which some women complain about.

Female Managers, Etiquette, and the Opposite Sex

From the time women first went to work in this country in the factories and sweatshops of the Industrial Revolution, men have flirted with, dated, and married women in the workplace. Today women are enjoying the fruits of their education, their new status in the business and professional worlds, and also their new ability to shape their own social lives.

If you are a woman executive who finds herself attracted to a business colleague, there is no reason you should not ask him to be your escort for a party, to accompany you to the theater, or to come to your house for dinner—provided:

- You know *for a fact* that he is not married.
- He is not a customer or client who might be "put off" by your invitation as being overly aggressive on your part.
- He is not someone in a much higher position than yours, which might lead him (and others) to feel that you are apple-polishing or being overly pushy.
- You make all the arrangements for the evening, as well as pay for them privately.
- You are not seeking anything more serious than a casual date. If you are looking for a real relationship, you would be wise to look as far away from your company and its clients as you possibly can.

On the other hand, if a male business associate or client invites you out for a date, be it a play, soccer match, beach picnic, or a foreign policy lecture, feel free to accept if you want to. Remember that person deserves to be thanked, not only verbally, but with a thank-you note. We often feel that our business colleagues are "family" and that we do not have to treat them in any way other than very informally. In actuality, it is discourteous to take anyone for granted. A little thank-you goes a long way.

How the Polished Female Executive Can Help Herself and Other Women

It's a known fact that one of the reasons men have done well in the workplace is that they have been engaged—for centuries—in "networking." They have used their schools, clubs, sports teams, and family connections to solidify their career successes. Women have not been privy to this environment, and yet the art of networking can be an important assist to them, too. It can help a woman executive by providing her with contacts, support, information, ideas, or even sympathy. The contacts made in the membership of a good professional women's organization can be invaluable in helping her enjoy and succeed in her job. Once again, if she is well-mannered, she will be well received by the other women in the organization. She also has a responsibility in accepting membership to attend meetings, serve on committees, help on programs, and help fellow members as well as draw assistance from them. There are many excellent national women's professional organizations, such as the "Committee of 100" (women business owners) and "The Women's Forum" (with chapters in major cities and a membership of the senior-ranked women in business, education, science, and the arts). Among other women's organizations that are helpful both in contacts and in programs are:

> Financial Women
> The Fashion Group
> The National Association for Professional Saleswomen
> The National Association of Bank Women
> The National Federation of Business and Professional Women's Clubs
> The National Home Fashions League
> Women in Communications
> Women in Advertising
> Women in Data Processing
> The National Association of Business and Industrial Saleswomen
> American Women in Radio and Television
> The Women's Economic Roundtable

There are many more. This is only a small sampling of the organizations listed in the *Encyclopaedia of Associations.* Important information is often disseminated at the meetings of these groups; sometimes social or political issues are championed; scholarship funds are often established. But mostly members use their associations for career development and for contacts. The woman who attends the meetings and whose manners are impeccable is usually the one who profits the most from them.

When top management encourages its young executives, male and female, to develop their potential through these memberships, and when it provides partial or full financial support of the memberships, the company benefits in the long run.

Helping Her Community

Women should never forget the institutions that educated them. Statistics show that women are paltry contributors to their secondary schools, colleges, and universities. There are religious institutions that helped shape their characters; there are community and national nonprofit organizations that need their talent, money, and volunteer time. Women in business should be energetic, diligent members of boards of nonprofit institutions. In short, with every measure of success a woman achieves, she should expend greater effort in her community. It is an important part of the responsibility of leadership; by assuming it, a woman sets an important example for the young women coming behind her.

Sex and Romance in the Office

As one young employee phrased it, "Self-control means you've got your head screwed on straight." There is no book of sexual manners in the office, because sex simply doesn't belong in the office. It exists, in lesser and greater degrees, but the greater the degree becomes, the closer the situation approaches disaster.

The vice-president for Human Resources can't very well issue a companywide memorandum stating "There will be no romance between any two of our executives." Like death and taxes, falling in love and establishing emotional relationships can and will happen. However, when it happens in the workplace, an inevitable whirlwind of gossip arises. Are they living together now? Will they marry? Are they both free to marry? Is there a good objection to their marrying? Just how good *is* their sex life? Is that what they're doing when they go out to lunch together? People will begin to think of them in terms of a love affair rather than in terms of how well they're doing their jobs. If the romance seems too hot to cool down, there will be talk and criticism. If they don't marry, more talk. If one of them is still married to another, the talk turns to scandal. Usually one executive then has to leave—usually the woman.

Talking About Your Sex Life

An executive's sex life should be kept out of the office before, during, and after marriage. If you feel the need to talk to someone about yours, whether to boast about it or complain about it, find a sympathetic and helpful source *outside* the office. There are professional counselors in this field. If you talk about it at work, others will perceive you as immature and thus unable to handle increased responsibilities. If you proceed to fascinate your peers in the office with tales of what happened last night, you are embarrassing them, even if they pretend otherwise. An office is not a gym locker room, nor a fraternity or sorority house.

Flirtation and Affectionate Body Language

If someone begins to flirt with you at work, a sentence or two should be enough to douse his or her efforts with cold water: "Look, this is *not* the place for that. I don't like it, and besides, I have work to do." If you allow the other person to continue, if you play along because you're embarrassed, it could result in your being fired or losing out on a promotion (even though you were the innocent party). So stop a flirtation before it is allowed to progress either in words or actions. Hopefully, you know how to distinguish between a real flirtation and a simple attempt to flatter and please you!

A public display of hugging and kissing on the lips is certainly not appropriate in the office, even if between two people who are married. Some people are naturally affectionate, ebullient, and demonstrative, even with people they do not know well. This kind of person hugs another as routinely as another person might give someone a brief handshake in greeting.

It is wise, whether you know a person well or not and whether you are very close to that person or not, to control your affectionate impulses. Others who don't know your motives may begin to gossip when they see you behaving in an affectionate manner. You don't have to go around feeling as though you're trapped in a box; just control your desire to put your hands on or your arms around others (until you get home at night).

Coping with Unwelcome Sexual Advances

It happens. Typically, a woman, sometimes at a business party in her home city but more often traveling with a male colleague from her own company, is unpleasantly surprised by a sudden overt sexual advance. It is usually instigated by something as simple as his ordering a third strong cocktail. Then suddenly the unwanted, unreciprocated pass is made—unpleasant and embarrassing for the woman. (Sometimes the victim of the advance is a man, and the predator is a woman colleague.)

If you are someone to whom this has just happened, try to reason with your colleague on the basis that it would be very bad for his career to have others talking in the office about his bad behavior when he's on the road. Explain that he is demonstrating a complete lack of professional respect for you. Tell him you know he didn't *really mean* to make that pass. Then leave, because you're in a no-win situation; further conversation is not going to help. Your colleague may now apologize to you, which in his present state could be quite humiliating, or he may become hostile and abusive. In any case, leave him and go to your room. When you see him the next day, act as though nothing has happened. Make no reference to it; he will be grateful for that. If he had been drinking a great deal, he might not remember any of the episode anyway, which would be the best for everyone concerned.

If he tries to keep you with him after making the pass, and if he is a married man, try using his family as a defensive weapon. Mention you're sure he's not serious, that because of his wonderful family he is not acting in a worthy fashion. If he follows you back to your room, intent on continuing his plan of action, threaten to report him back to headquarters. Keep reassuring him you know this is not his normal way of behaving. If he still persists, get help from someone in the hotel, even if you have to yell for it. (In this case, you must report the incident to your division head; the man in question needs help and should get it.)

When you return to the office, don't remind the person of what happened, even in an amusing, teasing way. As a single incident, it should not haunt either of you. Keep it to yourself; otherwise, your revelation of what happened could very well turn into a harmful kind of gossip that could backfire against you, the innocent person.

Men and women should forgive each other and forget unpleasant isolated incidents, like a single pass made under the influence of "old demon rum."

We are not talking here, of course, about actual sexual harassment, which is entirely different, because that type of behavior means repeated sexual advances accompanied by threats and bribes and must be dealt with in all firmness, without regard to diplomacy and tact.

Colleagues and Their Spouses

It's not easy to separate your friendship for a fellow executive from a friendship with his family, although some people manage quite successfully to lead a social life completely separate from their office life. In large companies, the harder people work, the easier they find it to organize their social activities with the people who are their peers in business life. The spouses often find it easy, too, to socialize with their spouses' associates, provided they are more or less of the same age, of the same background, and have the same interests. When something good or bad affects the spouse of a colleague, it affects his work and you feel the need to help. When something good happens to your colleague or to his spouse, you feel the need to reach out to congratulate them both. It is human nature to treat good and bad news that happens to one as something that has happened to the couple. Your thoughtfulness may manifest itself as a call to the spouse of your sick colleague to tell her how much you feel for her, or you might write a note of congratulations to the spouse of a colleague who has received a major promotion.

When a Colleague (or Client) Marries
(*See also* Wedding Gifts, in Chapter 16)

When a business associate marries, it is not necessary to mark the engagement announcement with a gift, but it is appropriate to mark the wedding with a present of a value commensurate with the importance of your friendship and the status of your wallet. The choosing of a thoughtful present, even one small in value, can cement a business relationship in a meaningful way.

If you are an intimate friend of a client or customer, the hosting of a party for an engaged or newly married couple is a gracious gesture. For this kind of party you could ask them to prepare a list of friends for you to invite or mix their friends with your mutual business associates, as well as two or three of your personal friends whom you feel they would enjoy knowing.

When a colleague returns to the office from a wedding trip, it is nice to have a "welcome home" bouquet waiting on his or her desk, or perhaps a bottle of champagne. When you share symbolically in someone's happiness, you become a closer friend, and your kindnesses are usually repaid later in some form or other, although that should not be your motivation in being nice.

Competition Between Spouses

When husband and wife have had the same kind of education and begin their careers at the same time, the quick success of one can become a major problem for the other. Good communication, an honest facing of the problems of competition, the ability to empathize, and the determination to build a happy family life in spite of an individual's success or failure can mean the survival of the marriage. If a corporation can help motivate its executives to this end, it will be well worth the money spent on professional joint counseling sessions for the couple. A spouse should never be forced to view the other spouse's firm or corporation as an adversary.

However, it is also important that a couple's friends and colleagues be sensitive to the whole subject of competition between husband and wife, whether they work for the same or separate employers. Friends should be able to sense if husband and wife feel the competition in the workplace too keenly; this is no time to joke, make fun, or even discuss "who is ahead of whom" in the career patterns of husband and wife. People show themselves blunt and thoughtless when in conversations with two executives who are overly competitive they ask questions such as:

- Does your spouse make more than you? Does this cause any problem with either of you?
- Does it hurt when your spouse bathes in the limelight and receives all the publicity?
- Are you both competing for the same job?
- How do you split the personal expenses, based on who makes more or what?
- (To the wife): Are you putting off having children because you feel you would fall too far behind your husband in your career?

- (To the husband): Do you wish your wife would quit and stay home and become a mother?

It is very thoughtless to tease half of a couple by intimating that the other half is doing much better. No matter how much love the husband and wife have for each other, if they are competing in the workplace, it is best to bring up the subject of one's great advancement over the other in private and to congratulate that person out of earshot of the spouse.

Colleagues and friends should be mindful of the fact that a married couple has two separate and distinct egos, both of which should be treated gently.

Be Nice to a Commuting Couple

There is a steady increase each year in the number of couples who hold important jobs in different cities and commute to spend weekends and vacations together. They certainly did not choose to be apart; usually one was offered a promotion or an opportunity that could not be rejected. At the same time, the other could not or would not leave his or her own position. Both have career goals they want to pursue. While this inevitably affects a relationship, many couples make a smooth adjustment to the changes that result. That's not to say it's an automatic, easy adjustment.

It's difficult to be a married commuter; it's also difficult to be married to one. There is the considerable expense, not to mention fatigue, of all that weekend travel. There is the expense, too, of two households, both of which are probably less than satisfactory. The worst part, of course, is the loneliness five evenings a week.

You can show kindness to a commuter colleague by inviting him or her home during the week to your family dinner or to join you in a restaurant for a meal, since your "batching it" colleague may very well not be eating properly. Invite the commuter to join you at a cocktail party of people he would find interesting or helpful in business. (Of course, you have asked your host first if it would be acceptable to do so.) You might provide a ticket for him to join you at a play, movie, or sports event, or you might simply ask him to join you at home for a beer and to watch television.

One caveat: In arranging for your commuter friend to join a group in the evening, don't fix him up with a date. No matter how innocent your planning may be, you might be providing fuel for gossip.

It's very gracious to give a party for the married commuter and his or her spouse one weekend when both are in your city. People will then be able to visualize them as a married couple, and they will begin to receive invitations on the weekends, when they will be in town together. They will start to put down roots in your city instead of being seen as gypsies, traveling from one place to another with no one aware of where they are.

Executives and Their Children

Pregnancy in the Office

When an executive informs her office that she is pregnant, she should do it quietly, without making it a *cause célèbre.* Her colleagues, for their part, have the responsibility *not* to bombard her with questions. ("Are you going to stop working?" "If you're coming back, when will you?") Someone on staff may be interested in obtaining her job, so invidious speculation about her future activities can be kept at a minimum if she announces as much of her plans as possible when releasing the happy news.

Senior management has a responsibility, too—not prejudging her ability to perform on the job, for one thing. Management should control the tendency to be embarrassed by having a pregnant woman representing the company. Pregnant executives working until the last minute are becoming more commonplace today; in a decade, no one will give it any thought.

Of course, the mother-to-be should refrain from discussing physical details of her condition in the office. (As one woman expressed it, "A daily report on gas pains and varicose veins is enough to put women back at least three thousand years!") Perhaps the pregnant executive's greatest responsibility is to make sure that others are not saddled with extra work during her pregnancy because of her condition.

The Unmarried Executive Mother

Along with the upswing in the number of births to professional people, there has also been an upswing of births to unmarried women, which throws somewhat of a curve ball into the workplace.

An unmarried office colleague who is not living with the father of her unborn child may suffer a great deal of shame and embarrassment in the executive suite. Her office colleagues should await a signal from her that she can be approached on the subject, then rally around her to give support. Naturally, if she has not announced her pregnancy but begins to show it, her colleagues cannot continue to pretend as though nothing has changed in her life. But neither should she hold an office press conference to announce to the world that, married or not, she has begun to knit booties while preparing her divisional budgets. This is a time for her close colleagues to approach her individually and privately to express their happiness at her news and to offer their help.

An unmarried pregnant lawyer shared with me a note a male colleague had discreetly dropped on her desk. She confessed that she had been coming into the office more times than not with swollen red eyes but proudly added that she never let any emotions show the minute she put her hand on the knob to open the door to the office. Her partner's written words of support were the first sign of recognition of her pregnancy—obviously everyone in the law firm had been too embarrassed to touch on the subject. The note read:

> I'm generally very unobservant, but if my eyesight doesn't deceive me, there's a certain roundness out front that hasn't been there before, and it seems to grow rounder every day.
>
> I told Marge [the writer's wife] about it last night, and since we both love kids, we immediately raised a toast to the unborn. We are rejoicing for you, but we also understand that these can be tough days for you, going it alone. I just want you to know that I'm around if you need any "fatherly advice," and Marge and I are keeping the car gassed up and the motor running, to get you to the hospital on time.
>
> Just remember, both of us are here, night or day. We *mean* it.

It was a small note, but its salutary effect on the recipient was immeasurable.

Congratulations for an Executive Mother
(*See also* For Special People and Special Occasions, in Chapter 16)

If a colleague with whom you work closely has a baby, some sign of congratulations is in order, whether it's sending flowers to the mother (or to the father, for that matter!), a small gift to the baby, or a hand-written note or studio card to the new parents.

A baby shower is a great help to expectant parents, and it is thoughtful of colleagues in the office (obviously female colleagues) to organize one. However, this is purely a personal activity and should not be organized during office hours nor take place in the office. Oohing and aahing over baby presents, no matter how much one loves babies, does not belong in the executive suite or anywhere else in the office.

When a Child Is Adopted

When an office colleague and spouse adopt a child, fellow executives should treat this happy news with exactly the same enthusiasm they would show towards a natural birth—including, of course, the extending of congratulations and giving of gifts. It is an occasion for joy all around.

Etiquette for the Executive New Mother

It's important to remember that a happy executive is a productive one, and although management may feel cheated of a certain amount of a woman's time prior to and immediately after the birth of her baby, or right after she has been granted an adopted child, when she returns to work she is usually a very hard-working, happy, well-adjusted person with a cheerful attitude that affects the entire office staff.

Though it may be difficult to control her joy and enthusiasm, it is important for the new mother to be able to focus her conversation on subjects other than her baby. The latest photos on her desk, a broad smile whenever the child is referred to, and a very short description of "how the baby is" are sufficient.

The woman executive returning to her job should be sensitive to the amount of work to be done, as well as to any extra work her absence may have created and any resulting hardship on her colleagues.

The Sending of Announcement Cards to Business Associates

It is not appropriate to send birth or adoption announcement cards to a business mailing list, except to those clients and customers who are close personal friends, too. To send a birth announcement to someone who is not an intimate friend is almost a hidden request for a gift, which is hardly the impression most new parents wish to give.

Diplomatically Handling the News of a Miscarriage or Abortion

When a woman suffers a miscarriage or chooses to have an abortion, it is important for close colleagues not to ask questions. The subject cannot be totally ignored, particularly by her women colleagues. The only kind of reference one can diplomatically make at a time like this is something along the lines of "We've missed you around here the last few days. I hope you're feeling all right," or, "I'd like to take you to lunch at a restaurant that specializes in good 'cheer-up' lunches." If during that lunch, you find yourself a sounding board and she confides in you, remember that your conversation is a confidence, not information to be shared with the office.

Whenever good or bad fortune befalls the children of people with whom you work, you should react in some way, even if only to write a note. It's cold to ignore news that has impact on an associate's personal life.

There are numerous kinds of small gestures one can make to welcome home men or women who return to the office after a heartbreaking incident. A tiny vase of flowers left on the desk, a pair of tickets to an amusing play, a funny new book of cartoons—these are all examples of gestures of friendship made for someone who may be feeling sad and depressed.

Divorce Etiquette in the Office

The trauma of divorce can, in addition to making the persons involved feel disoriented and depressed, also affect the quality of executives' work performance. As a result, companies are finding it cost-effective to pay for qualified counseling services for all employees who are dealing with divorce. It is generally agreed that work is the best therapy of all during an emotionally difficult time such as a divorce. Helping the person realize this is the responsibility of the company, and also of the person's colleagues.

Women in particular seem to suffer from feelings of personal isolation, failure, and fear for the future. Rap sessions organized for recently divorced women and supervised by a professional counselor have been found to be very effective.

When a person undergoes a difficult divorce, his or her office colleagues should rally around quickly. However, the person being divorced should remember that:

- He should not allow his work to suffer because of his emotional problems.
- Honesty is important. If he is only separated, he should make that clear; if a divorce has been filed, he should make that clear to members of management with whom he works closely and with whom he socializes. The longer he leaves his peers guessing, the greater the buildup of unnecessary gossip.
- Nothing is more boring than an endless lament. No one should be so consumed with his divorce problems that it is all he can discuss.
- Disclosure of very personal details shows a lack of taste. The person being divorced should not divulge the unfair terms of the financial settlement, the bitterness of the custody battle, etc. It only embarrasses the listener.
- He should not ask friends to "fix him up" with dates until his divorce becomes final.
- He should not insist that his colleagues cut off his former mate from their own lives out of loyalty to him—a sign of very unbecoming pettiness on his part.
- He can inform very close business friends who know him and his spouse socially and who live out of town by writing a short note about the divorce plans. (What is in extremely bad taste is sending out printed or engraved divorce announcements!)

The colleagues and business associates of the person being divorced should remember that

- He or she will need extra emotional support during this difficult time. But one should not treat the person as though he or she were terminally ill!
- One should not ask prying, overly personal questions, such as "Did you get custody of the children?" "How much alimony will you have to pay?" or "How much alimony did you get?"

- One should not try to be a matchmaker for a colleague until after the divorce is final and until he is ready to date once again. The nicest way of handling this is to invite the divorced person to dinner and ask, "Would you like us to invite someone for you?" "Would you like us to introduce you to someone nice?"
- Even in an attempt to cheer up someone, one should always avoid tasteless remarks at work, such as "You're free now; would I ever like to be in your shoes!"

When an Office Colleague Is Widowed
(*See also* Chapter 14, When an Executive Dies)

When a colleague loses a spouse, you should show your strong support not only at the time of the funeral but long afterward. The real grief of losing a spouse often hits hardest several months after death, at a time when most friends and associates have concluded that the bereaved "is doing okay now" and lessened their attention. The bereaved may not be doing okay. A mark of compassion and real friendship is to invite that person through the year to family occasions like dinners on holidays and weekend outings that fit in with his or her sports or cultural pursuits.

You can almost always tell when a widow or widower is ready to date again by being sensitive to signals in their conversation in the office. It may be time to have a few people to dinner and to invite someone you think your widow or widower colleague might enjoy meeting—or at least talking to for one evening. It's up to you to find someone who is suitable, eligible, and has a pleasing personality. Make the evening a relaxed one, with just a few good guests and good conversation, so that the two who have been paired off won't feel any pressure. Do not treat them as potential love mates but rather as two members of your group. Even if they never see each other again after your party, they will have enjoyed being there, and that is satisfaction enough. Try inviting someone else the next time if the first time was not a great success as far as their personal relationship was concerned. Gradually your friend will become accustomed to "getting around" again and to coping with the social aspects of dating and the single life, which he or she may have forgotten. After several years of marriage, dating is a learning experience all over again.

3
Executive Communications

The more computer terminals that pepper the office landscape, the more important personal communication becomes between one executive and another. The way we write and talk to each other, the sound of our voices, our choice of words, and the tone of our written communications can make or break our careers, companies, and negotiations with peers, subordinates, superiors, clients, suppliers, and the public—with everyone with whom we are in touch in our business lives.

The greater the technological advances, the greater the need for the human voice to be able to persuade, soothe, praise, and encourage. As an example, think of the way Ronald Reagan uses speech to sway others to his persuasion.

THE ART OF CONVERSATION

How You Sound to the Outside World

There can be no really effective presence without a cultivated voice. The way in which you communicate with others is almost as important as the context of your message. A letter should be written with the proper choice of words and with a nice hand (or neatly typed) on a good quality paper. A conversation should be conducted with the right choice of words and with a pleasing and appropriately modulated voice.

The manner in which you communicate verbally is an important part of your image and your executive presence. You may have an extremely high I.Q. and have graduated *summa cum laude* and yet not be able to sell your ideas successfully in the conference room to management and your peers. You may be extremely competent in handling your investments, to the point of having become very rich, and yet still be considered an undesirable dinner partner by the people you most admire if you don't have a repertoire of interesting conversational topics at your command.

Speaking in public is very painful for many people. One study reported on by Communispond Inc. (a company that trains executives to present themselves in public) showed that 19 percent of Americans surveyed feared death, while 41 percent feared having to speak in public. A good strong voice is an important managerial asset; it is also an important social tool. People make instant judgments when they hear you. They judge you on what you say and how you're saying it. It's wise to keep in mind the various elements that constitute the act of communication.

The successful communication of your message, whether you are making a speech or persuading someone across the lunch table to hire you or buy your company's product, depends upon

- Good quality of voice
- Careful use of vocabulary
- Good posture while you are speaking
- And, of course, clearness in your thinking

The Quality of Your Voice

You may not know how your voice really sounds. One way to listen to it is to make a tape of yourself talking—when you are not self-conscious about it. Put a tape recorder close to you on your desk and record some of your telephone conversations or conversations with staff. (Record your end only. Some people are sensitive to being taped.) Soon you will forget the recorder is there. Take the tape home and play it back when you are at leisure. If your voice needs work, you'll be the first to know it. Listening to a tape of one's voice is like gazing into a hard, cruel magnifying mirror..

Voice Should Match Professional Stature

The speech of an executive should match his professional dignity and stature.

The Voice That Does Not Match an Executive's Professional Stature	*The Good Voice That Matches an Executive's Professional Stature*
Has strong regionalisms, so that one instantly knows what part of the country he comes from	Is without a strong accent (the speaker could come from anywhere)
Has a harsh tone, which sounds strident and unreasonable	Is strong, denoting authority
Is breathy, denoting indecision and a lack of ease	Reflects proper breathing—with short breaths from the diaphragm, so that it is always well supported by oxygen
Has too high a pitch, so that the person sounds immature or overly nervous	Has a good low, comfortable pitch for almost everything the speaker says, making him sound completely secure in what he is saying
Projects in an unexpressive monotone, which is boring and distractingly dull	Has a warm tone expressing emotion, particularly when the speaker feels enthusiastic about something
Sounds tired	Sounds alert
Sounds nasal	Sounds distinctive
Sounds commonplace	Is easy to understand because the speaker enunciates properly
Is hard to understand because the speaker swallows his words	Has good pacing, which changes from time to time so that the speaker does not sound monotonous
Is paced too fast or too slow. When too fast, no one can follow everything the speaker says; when too slow, he loses his audience by making them impatient.	Has the proper volume
Is delivered too softly or too loudly	

The Relationship Between Voice and Vocabulary

If you think of another executive as having a good voice, you may or may not be aware that his choice of words also influences how you regard the sound of his voice. A good vocabulary helps a person to make good conversation and to communicate well; it also affects the quality of his voice affirmatively.

The English language has many beautiful sounds. An executive who uses a word like *mellifluous,* for example, must make an effort to pronounce it properly. It is a beautiful word, evoking a pleasant image. An enriched vocabulary sounds good to the ear and lends attractiveness to a voice. A person who uses distinguished words properly sounds distinguished and makes you *want to listen* to him.

A Cultivated Voice Implies a Cultivated Vocabulary

Contrary to what some people believe, a cultivated voice is not one with a phony "Eastern Establishment" type of accent. Someone who affects that kind of accent (partly British accent, partly muffled sounds and unfinished words) obviously feels insecure about his background. Locust Valley, Long Island, a place dotted with great estates and very rich people, has supplied the name people in the East have given this phony accent: Locust Valley Lockjaw. (Fortunately, very few people in Locust Valley speak that way.)

In reality a cultivated voice is:

- *Without a strong regional accent,* as noted
- One in which *only good grammar* is used
- Noted for the *absence of foul language.* I have heard construction men and miners use much better language than is heard today in many posh executive suites. Recently graduated MBAs seem to think it's perfectly all right to say "shit" or use "fucked up" every time they are slightly annoyed by anything. It's not perfectly all right. It tarnishes the image of their company and it's noise pollution at its worst.
- One in which *pejorative nicknames are never used* when referring to people of other nationalities or religions. People who use ugly, loathsome terms like *dago, coon,* and *kike* are practicing an insidious form of bigotry and discrimination. Their word usage will completely shatter any image they might have had of refinement, culture, or education.
- One in which *all words are properly enunciated*
- One that does not tediously feature *repetitious phrases* (for example: "Know what I mean?" "Isn't that so?" or just "You know?")
- One in which *common slang is absent.* For example, starting every sentence with *Like* is totally ungrammatical. So is "I'm *into* aerobics" or "I'm *into* cooking." Things should be called by their proper names. Liquor is liquor, not "booze." Money is money, not "bucks" or "moola." A woman is a woman, not a "broad."

    When parents emulate their children's slang (brought home from school or college), thinking it the young, hip, and with-it way to talk, the slang sounds far worse that it ever could in the mouths of young people. I remember so well when I began using our children's term *nerd* in my own conversation. Our eighth-grader, Clare, stopped me by remarking that it was "really gross for an older person to try to sound like a young person."
- *Devoid of "yeahs," "naws," "un-uns," and "uh-uhs"* as signs of agreement or disagreement. These words are not really slang, just perfect examples of improper English stemming from sheer laziness.

    One particularly annoying speech habit of young people is finishing every statement that is not a question with "okay." This repetitious "okay" has become a conversational tic in our language today; it is not part of cultivated speech.

Good Body Language Is Part of Good Conversation

You can't get away from the importance of your own body language, because it starts when you first meet someone and shake his hand.

Body language is a personal thing. A person who has a strong, aggressive personality will quite naturally lean over the conference table and make strong gestures with his hands to accompany his message. A normally shy, retiring person who suddenly leans over the table and begins to gesticulate emphatically gives a much stronger message.

There are certain aspects of body language that concern all of us, however. Here are a few:

- When you shake hands, the grip should be firm.
- When someone is talking, you should sit attentively and not slump.
- When someone is talking, you should watch his face and not let your eyes roam around the room.
- When you want to make a point, you should sit up straighter and appear more intent.
- When you sit down, you should keep your legs quiet and not continue to cross and uncross them.
- You should keep your hands from fidgeting and fingers from drumming.
- A woman should not sit in a provocative pose. (I do not have to explain what this pose is, because a woman who is sitting—or standing—in this manner is always aware of it!)

Body language in conversation is as important as it is in public speaking. Communications specialists help you when you are being trained to speak before an audience by reminding you to stand upright, not to lean on the lectern, and not to fiddle and fuss with your fingers, notes, eyeglasses, or a paperclip.

Your posture and body language in conversation sends signals to the other person that you are interested in him and want to communicate with him. Or the signals could mean exactly the opposite. If you slump down in your chair, your legs out straight, your hands folded on your stomach, you may think you are just relaxing in comfort; to the other person you are implying that he is not important enough to pay attention to what he's saying. Even if you are listening to every word, your body is telling the other person that you are not actively involved in the conversation.

Your voice does not sound right when your chin is caved into your chest. Your breath cannot support your voice tones if your body is not at least partially erect. If you do not sit up when you are talking to another person, your voice will sound wishy-washy, and your posture implies you don't really care about what you are saying.

If you are speaking to another person and trying to accomplish any goal, remember that the other person's attention will be deflected if you constantly shift position and if your hands are involved in some repetitive act or nervous mannerism.

When you sit up straight to talk (not rigidly, but comfortably) or when you stand up erect to talk, people listen to you because your posture tells them you have something worthwhile to say.

Finding Help for Voice and Speech

There are a tremendous number of resources in this country for those who need help in achieving a better voice or in being at ease in public speaking. The available specialists use all kinds of recording and sound analyzing equipment and videotapes as well.

For Voice Problems

- The American Speech, Language and Hearing Association offers a list of trained speech pathologists. There are over 35,000 speech pathologists in the United States at present, including the renowned Dr. Morton Cooper of Los Angeles, who claims that we commit "voice suicide" when we continue to use the wrong voice. He maintains that an executive can overcome many business problems by finding and using the right voice.
- Educational institutions provide workshops on the voice, offering information and good contacts to help people with voice problems.
- Some university professors in speech and communications also moonlight in private arrangements with executives who need help.
- Some members of local theater repertory groups are qualified to help people with speech problems.
- Some hospital staff speech therapists make the time to help private patients.

For Public Speaking

- Communication experts at local colleges and universities will sometimes accept private clients.
- There are large national communication consulting firms (such as Communispond Inc.) available for hire.
- There are freelance communication specialists in every large city who

help people prepare themselves, both in the content and the delivery of their presentation.

· There are television communications specialists (like Jack Hilton, in New York) who help prepare senior management to handle themselves in front of the electronic media.

The most important point of all, of course, in questions of the voice, is for an executive to know when he (or perhaps his assistant) needs help. The assistant's voice answering the executive's telephone is a mirror of the latter's own executive presence, so if that voice is less than good, he should tactfully suggest the assistant seek help for it, for his or her own good. If the company does not provide for this kind of help, the executive should pay for it himself. It is that important.

Sometimes all that an executive and his or her secretary need do is remember the admonition of Lily Lodge, a noted voice consultant in New York: "Think lower and slower when you talk, and you'll be all right."

Being a Good Conversationalist

A good conversationalist is not
one who remembers what was said but
says what someone wants to remember.
—JOHN MASON BROWN

Conversation is a very important part of executive presence, a natural cornerstone of executive communication. An executive who is at ease in conversation is an asset to the company, because that talent directly or indirectly contributes to profits. If he can artfully use conversation to explain, persuade, soothe, cajole, amuse, and motivate clients or customers, what is intrinsically a social grace becomes a tool for attracting and holding business.

When you make conversation is just as important as what you say.

In a business deal, conversation is like the frame around a painting. You should engage in the art of conversation at the beginning and conclusion of your business discussions, but during actual negotiations talk should be plain and simple communication. Business talk is not small talk. To be attractive, business talk should be articulate, clear, direct, forceful—and always polite.

This chapter is not about conversation during the actual transacting of business; rather it is about the importance of the social discourse that makes an executive a desirable person to be around—both in and outside of the office—during those many times when business and social occasions are mixed. The person conversationally at ease can use this tool to forge strong personal relationships within his business orbit; he has an advantage simply because he is someone people like to be with and listen to.

There are several ingredients basic to the success of every good conversationalist. One is the sincere desire to please. Another is a sense of humor, enabling a person to tease and laugh with others—always in a kind and gentle way—and to laugh at himself without any trace of self-consciousness. The ability to make people smile is a gift; the ability to make them laugh is also a business tool.

A good conversationalist is self-educated, a person who goes far beyond the intellectual demands of his job. He reads newspapers and news magazines, art magazines and design magazines. He may be a gourmet cook and able to speak on the subject of food and wine; he may be a haunter of museums and galleries or a fan of the opera or ballet. A good conversationalist is a person about whom no one would ever say, "The only thing he can talk about is his work." Clare Boothe Luce once defined a good conversationalist as a person who is "aware, witty, intelligent, and kind." Someone else described a good conversationalist as "the one who makes the trite and the mundane into the exciting and the wonderful." However you approach it, the art of conversation is a great gift to acquire.

Small Talk

When you've just met someone and you're standing there with no one saying anything . . . when you're tongue-tied with your dinner partner and he or she is, too . . . when there is a sudden cold silence while a group sitting around a conference table waits for a meeting to start . . . when you're in a car with your superior and the silence becomes uncomfortable—it's time to practice your small talk.

If you're with one person alone, think hard about something to say. If you have met the person before, bring up a mutual friend:

"The last time I saw you, you were lunching with Charlie. Have you seen him lately?"

Or, "Did you hear that Charlie Brown has been promoted to vice-president? Isn't that great?"

If you're at dinner, turn to your dinner partner and say something positive about the evening:

"The fact that we all made it in this snowstorm is a real compliment to our hosts, isn't it?"

Or "It's a real treat having crabmeat cocktail like this, isn't it?"

When you're in a car with your superior, mention something interesting you've learned about the competition:

"Did you hear that HeathCo has plans for five new plants?"

Or, "Our friends at Wesato are very nervous; there are signs of an unfriendly takeover. What do you think this implies?"

Or comment on a national news item in the morning press and solicit the other person's opinion.

If you have a total block and can think of nothing whatsoever to say, notice something the other person is wearing. "Nice tie. I really like it." Or a woman might say to another, "That's a lovely dress. I really could use something like that in my wardrobe. Can you recommend a place to shop?" (A discussion of clothes, however, is best saved for the dinner table when there is absolutely nothing else left to say.)

The Art of Listening

One of the great keys of diplomacy is to act interested in what someone is saying, even when one is not. The tendency *not* to pay full attention to the person speaking is a common form of rudeness in society today. Perhaps there aren't enough mothers saying to executives-to-be as they are growing up at home, "Listen to what he is saying. Pay attention!" In business it is not only rude but bad business practice when people do not listen.

If a speaker is considered boring or is too slow in making his point, or if what he says is not of particular personal interest, our own thoughts may become more important to us at that moment; we tune out on what we're hearing. A polite person, on the other hand, treats whoever is speaking with respect. He knows that by giving the speaker his attention, he may learn something of value; even in a seemingly unimportant conversation, he may learn something of import.

Executives who do not listen carefully to their superiors miss nuances and signals that could result in the loss of millions of business dollars. The good listener remembers all the major points of a conversation afterward and understands perfectly what is expected of him. The good listener subjugates his impressions of how the other person looks and sounds to an examination of the other person's ideas. If you need to make notes after an important conversation, your journal will become an invaluable tool for your success.

Senior managers claim they can easily tell if a young person has been listening *by the quality of the questions asked at the end of a meeting discussion* and by the accuracy of the young person's summation of the speaker's main points when this summation is requested. Many seasoned executives also say that the sign of real maturity in a young executive is when he can move easily from the role of speaker in a conversation to that of listener, and when he uses that listening time *to learn.*

Important Conversational Aptitudes

Many attributes characterize a good conversationalist, including being polite and caring about other people. Another strong requirement is a measure of intelligence. A good conversationalist:

- *Is well-informed and talks on a broad range of subjects.* The person who can talk only about his business bores very quickly even his own colleagues. A good conversationalist may be in the business of selling agricultural machinery, but he also knows how to participate, at least minimally, in discussing subjects like politics, science, and art.
- *Shows interest in what other people do for a living,* the conditions of their industry, and the new directions in which they may be heading.
- *Does not have tunnel vision but keeps abreast of the major news in the world.*
- *Is able to make a fast subject switch,* perhaps even from the status of the thrift industry to the philosophy of Zen Buddhism, or from shopping mall developments to the beauty of the Prince of Liechtenstein's art collection.
- *Adjusts to the person with whom he is talking,* whether you both are waiting for a meeting to start, waiting for a plane to depart, or waiting for the dessert course to arrive at the industry banquet. For example, a senior executive sitting with the young nonworking wife of a member of his staff should make an effort to talk to her about such matters as her children and the condition of schools in the area; in drawing her out, he will find subjects of interest to her, and if he's a good listener, he may even learn a thing or two.
- *Makes statements based on knowledge and experience, not just conjecture.* If he is not an expert on a subject, he should not pretend to be. One can easily join in a conversation without being an expert; what is important is not to exaggerate one's knowledge. If, for example, you are talking with specialists on rice growing in Texas, your best role would be that of an interested person. "Why is Texas rice gaining such a large share of the market? What's so special about it?" Never be afraid to admit you do not know something, and remember that people are flattered by having questions asked of them that they are able to answer.
- *Looks a person straight in the eye when talking to him.* Eye contact is very important in any kind of situation. If you don't look at a person when you're speaking to him, you're showing you're embarrassed or frightened or perhaps hiding something—hardly the executive presence you wish to project.

The worst kind of lack of eye contact is an odious form of social climbing, when one person talks to another with a roving eye to see who else is at the party or in the room. He's always looking over the shoulder of the person he's talking to, often watching the door to see who walks through it. If someone well known appears, you can bet that he will take off like a rabbit, abandoning you for someone who is of greater importance to him.

Do not feel bad. There is no question as to who is the superior person. A person of substance looks at *you* all during the time he is talking to you, whether it's in the conference room or at a business cocktail party. He gives you quality attention—the only kind that counts.

- *Avoids correcting another's grammar or pronunciation in public.* It is humiliating to people to have their personal errors pointed out to them in front of their peers. Real friends help their colleagues in private with any language difficulties. Someone with major speech or language difficulties should get help, either by taking courses at night in local colleges or universities or in private tutoring with an English teacher.

- *Shows genuine interest in good news about colleagues.* When you hear happy news about one of your peers, and you help spread it, you are demonstrating good team spirit.

- *Doesn't interrupt.* It is extremely rude to interrupt someone who's in the middle of a story or the exposition of an idea, even if that person is dragging on interminably, even if you *know* that what you have to say is more important, or at least more amusing.

- *Knows how to question a stranger in a friendly rather than prying way.* It's one thing to ask someone you have just met if his company has any plants abroad; it's another to ask how close he is to the presidency of the company. When you meet someone, he will be flattered by your interest in him, but keep that interest in a very general frame of reference.

- *Accepts compliments gracefully.* Nothing ruins the flow of conversation more quickly than refusing a compliment you have just received. Never disagree with something nice that is said to you or about you. If someone says, "Jan, you were brilliant in your presentation on the international markets this morning," don't reject the compliment. Don't say something like "Oh, I don't think I did all that well. I was too tense, and I forgot the best part of my introduction. I really could have done it a lot better." Your answer to a compliment should be, "Aren't you *nice* to say that! Thank you very much."

- *Knows how to pay compliments gracefully.* A compliment should provide a very "up" moment in the interaction of the people involved. It should cause people to smile. (When they smile, you'll note their voices become more animated.) Praise should be given in a sincere manner, without exaggeration, unless the person speaking chooses an inoffensively amusing tongue-in-cheek method of praise (example: "Bert did such a terrific job writing the chairman's speech, he's now been tapped to handle all of the chairman's daughter's wedding present thank-you notes!"). When someone in the firm does an excellent job on anything from producing the annual report to handling the typing of a complicated report, that person deserves a compliment. Give it to him when it will make him feel the best (for example, when a member of senior management is present to hear you pay the compliment).

- *Knows when and how to talk about nonbusiness subjects.* This requires understanding what is appropriate and also what good timing is. If you're talking to someone seriously engrossed in a particular business subject, you should not suddenly interrupt with a new subject that has nothing to do with business; the effect would be jarring and confusing. If the other person is wondering "how great a shortfall there will be in meeting budget this month," that is not the moment for you suddenly to start talking about this year's winner of the Heisman Trophy. However, if you are relaxing with that person over coffee after the meeting and you are discussing nothing in particular, it's perfectly proper to bring up this year's trophy winner (assuming he's at least something of a sports fan). It's an "up" subject that is pleasant to discuss.

- *Doesn't overdose on his own interests in his conversation.* Not everyone may be as interested as he is in the latest computer technology. The woman executive recently returned from maternity leave realizes that her conversation should not center solely on her new baby. The executive who races cars for a hobby realizes that he must not monopolize every nonbusiness conversation with a discussion of cars. In other words, one should treat one's own particular passions in life with intelligence and restraint.

- *Doesn't burst somebody else's balloon.* If someone has great good news to impart, do not try to dampen his spirits, even if you feel you have information that proves him to be overenthusiastic. If the person sitting next to you makes a strong positive statement about the economy and you disagree, don't throw a damper on him in front of everyone else. Wait to see him privately before telling why you disagree. In front of others you can always respond with some sort of statement that does not connote acceptance but is not hostile or accusatory either: "I certainly *hope* you're right."

- *Addresses everyone within the group, not just one or two people.* If everyone is listening to you, be aware of all members of your audience. Don't have a conversation that shuts out others sitting or standing with you. Glance at each person every so often as you talk; don't discuss something with one person in the group that has no relation whatsoever to any other member of the group (for example, a party to which only the two of you have been invited).

- *Knows how to make a shy person feel part of the group.* Sometimes, it just takes one question to bring a shy person into the group. For example, if there is a chemist who has not opened his mouth, probably out of shyness, throw him a substantive question on chemistry that would interest the others, too. In other words, give him a chance to shine in front of the group.

- *Is aware of when he may have begun to bore his audience.* Even a person who can talk about his job in a fascinating way can overdo it. A good conversationalist senses when this happens. If he sees the attention lagging, he should change to someone else's profession or project. It's not difficult to make that abrupt change. You can say something as simple as "Listen, you've all heard more than enough about my trials and tribulations in the new merger. I'd like to hear about Harry's company's new mining detecting equipment that just went on the market. Is it true, Harry, that . . . ?"

- *Steps in to fill an embarrassing void in the conversation.* We have all suffered through uncomfortable moments when all conversation suddenly ceases simultaneously and no one seems to know how to start it going again. Several pairs of eyes stare at the floor or out the window. If you make a joke or say something corny ("Listen, I'll give five bucks to the first person who can recite all of the state capitals in five minutes!"), you'll become an instant hero. You will have broken the tension, and the conversations will begin again.

- *Is diplomatic when he has a lot of work to do on a trip and is seated next to a person who insists on talking.* When you have a great deal of work to do on the airplane but there's a "Chatty Kathy" of either sex next to you, it's a time to call on your self-control and good manners. Respond politely but tersely to this person's questions—"Yes, you're certainly right about that." Keep your head bowed low in your work, and by the fourth interruption explain your dilemma. Show your seatmate all of the material you must study; explain all of the deadlines you are facing. Then apologize that this heavy work load is going to deprive you of the pleasure of chatting. Lend your seatmate a book or magazine to read that might be enjoyable. And during the service of the meal, show you are not an ogre by making some pleasant conversation. After all, it's very hard to concentrate on your work when attacking the airlines' standard chicken with rice.

Subjects to Avoid

There are some subjects a good conversationalist does not discuss.

- *Your health.* No one is that interested in the results of your annual physical or in the state of your allergies. If someone asks you how you are, answer "Fine," rather than giving chapter and verse about your gum surgery, conjunctivitis, and the wart on the bottom of your foot. Your diet is even a more boring subject.
- *Other peoples' health.* People who have serious diseases, such as cancer, atherosclerosis, arthritis, etc., usually do not want the ailment to be everyone's focus of conversation. Don't greet a business acquaintance who has been ill with a worried frown when you see him. If he is back at work, even part-time, take it for granted he is going to get well and be fully productive. Treat him like everyone else, not like someone who can't function. Don't keep reminding him—and everyone else—of what he has been through.
- *Controversial subjects when you don't know where people stand.* I once tried hard to stop a young woman executive from giving a vehement lecture on the subject of a woman's right to choose abortion; we were standing with her boss, and what I knew that she didn't know was that the boss's wife was the vociferous head of the state's pro-life movement. Unless you're on sure ground, it's better not to bring up subjects that people feel very emotional about—and that includes religion, genetic meddling, and nuclear warfare.
- *How much things cost.* A person whose entire conversation keeps returning to how much things cost, how much money so-and-so makes, and what kind of net worth everyone has is afflicted with the grossest kind of materialism. It's no one's business how much someone paid for his house, car, or fur coat. The person whose conversation is peppered with "How much?" makes everyone around him extremely uncomfortable. The general reaction of most people is to feel they would not want to have to make a deal with him.
- *Personal misfortunes.* Don't keep bringing up with a colleague some great loss he has suffered, whether it's a death in his family, the destruction of his house, the loss of his possessions in a robbery, etc. Of course, if the victim brings up the subject himself, then give him all your sympathy and listen for as long as he wishes to talk. But don't take on the role of reporter just to satisfy your own curiosity.

   Often the best kind of conversation to have with someone who has been through a traumatic experience is to let him do the talking—as much as he wishes to. This goes back to a basic rule of how to be a good conversationalist. *Be a good listener!*

When you are discussing business, try to refrain from inserting your personal misfortunes into the conversation. That puts others in a difficult position. They don't know whether to take time out to commiserate with you or simply say "too bad" and then get on with business.

- *Trite and overdone subjects.* Always bring up topics of conversation that people enjoy discussing, not something that is overexposed and already past its prime as a national or international story. If an industrial disaster has been overplayed in the media for a couple of weeks, don't bring it up unless you have some news on the subject no one else knows. Stay away from subjects that might cause others to groan inwardly, "Oh, no, not *that* again!"

- *Stories in questionable taste.* Off-color jokes may be great to hear in the locker room, but they are rarely successful when told in mixed company, or even just with members of one's own sex in public. The tendency is to regard executives who constantly tell dirty stories as people fighting their own insecurities and need for attention in a very unattractive way.

- *Gossip that is harmful.* There are too many opportunities in the business day to instigate or repeat harmful gossip that might seriously affect some-one's career. Think before you participate in gossip, either by adding to it or by reinforcing it, even if you believe it to be true. The executive who defends a colleague—even with an innocuous statement such as "Look, I don't think you're being fair"—shows leadership qualities.

If you want to defuse gossip, be ready with an interesting topic of conversation you can use to redirect the group's attention. After all, an executive's entire career and position in the community may be at stake.

Questions That Are Too Personal to Ask

Don't ask

- Your friend if the rumor is true that he lost his job
- A person who has just been diagnosed as having a feared disease (like cancer) if he would like to discuss it with you
- A person who is obese how much he weighs; a person with big feet what size shoe he wears; an overly tall or small person how tall he is
- Anyone if he or she is wearing a wig or toupee or if the hair is dyed
- A divorcing colleague for personal details, such as alimony payments, agreement on property settlements, child custody, etc.
- Anyone over thirty his or her age
- Anyone what his or her religion is
- Anyone if he or she is homosexual
- If a person is undergoing therapy
- If that person has had a facelift
- About anyone's sex life

Conversation When the Young Executive Is Alone with a Senior Executive

Most young executives dread being alone with the big boss in his office, while both are waiting for a plane at the airport, or when riding a considerable distance in the company limo. Instead of dreading it, they should realize that this is an opportunity and seize the opportunity, not only for self-aggrandizement but also to bring to light the things that never seem to be brought to senior management's attention.

A young person should "play it cool" and not force the conversation. The senior person may be tired, want to think, or prefer to read or work. A bubbling, enthusiastic young executive may be just the kind of company the senior executive is *not* seeking at that point.

There are obvious cues the younger person should notice. If the senior person seems distracted, lost in his thoughts, it is best not to disturb him. If he answers questions perfunctorily, that means he is not in the mood to talk. At a certain moment the senior executive will probably put down on his lap what he is reading and address a question to his younger companion. That is the time for the latter to answer with clarity and sincerity. If the senior person wants him to continue, he will give another cue, directing further questions to his companion, a signal that he is now ready to listen.

If the senior executive is ready for light talk—something not too serious—the younger person should be ready with some amusing stories of what is happening in the office or interesting news of competitors or of anyone associated with the business.

The young executive should follow his boss's lead as to whether he should talk about what is happening within the company or in his job in particular or whether he should talk about anything *but* business. He can tell by the kind of questions asked of him. If his boss asks about his squash game, it is not the time to talk about new information systems that are not working as well as they should.

Business and Small Talk

Small talk in business is exactly that—unimportant conversation, a filler for those cracks in substantive discussions when people want to relax and pass the time without intellectual strain. A person who knows how to make small talk has a useful talent. He can use it to fill embarrassingly silent moments, to put people at ease when they don't know each other and are trying too hard to size each other up, or to break tension in a conversation. He can use it to charm someone, flatter someone, or show off his own sense of humor.

If you have been talking commodity trading all morning and someone at lunch brings up the hockey skater who made three hat tricks the night before, that's small talk. When a group has been going over the final draft of the budget and at the break one executive teases another for "looking more like Prince Charles every day with your brown suede shoes, regimental tie, and double-vent back," that's small talk.

It is helpful to keep your own data bank on people you meet—your impressions of each person, built up from the way he looks, what he is wearing, what he said, and what others said to him. You can glean a great deal of helpful information when you meet someone. Another person in the group might mention their mutual college reunion, and you now know the newcomer attended a certain college. He might mention his children, his new project assignment, a business trip he just took. You keep adding data to your memory bank. Then, if you have occasion to talk to that person at a future date, you can introduce subjects of mutual interest with ease.

The more at ease you become in conversation, the better at small talk you become. It's a good way to survive common sticky social situations like being seated at dinner between two people whom you have never met, don't care about ever meeting again, and have absolutely nothing in common with except that you happen to work in the same company or industry as one of them. When you go into a situation like that, be ready to draw from a large group of topics, one of which *must* strike a responsive chord. Be sure these are topics on which you can lead a discussion during an entire meal course. Almost anything is appropriate for small talk; for example:

Gardening
The latest corporate takeovers
New developments in science
Favorite new parlor games
The next Olympics
Ways to stop smoking
Women astronauts
Famine control
Fitness and nutrition programs
Fashion fads
Landlord and real estate trends
Bestselling books
What you'd put in a time capsule today
The changes in women's and men's relations
News about local performing arts
Pets
Environmental issues

Gourmet cookery

Current museum shows

Favorite travel spots and experiences

Most people like to offer their opinions on the latest films; television shows and performers; national issues; trends in their/your industry; solutions to local problems such as waste disposal, housing, schools, zoning; the arts; sports; and other topics about which most of us have thoughts and preferences.

Listen carefully for clues to your lunch or dinner partner's interests (do some research ahead of time if possible), and lead by offering some provocative (but not overly challenging) opinions yourself. If most people have been watching a television series or a major sports event, you are probably safe in leading into a discussion about that. Out of the comments that follow, you will get cues about the further interests of your partner to guide you into a full-blown conversation.

Far from being trivial, small talk is a way to get to know others. It helps you gain popularity and intimacy with your colleagues and move up the ladder just a little faster.

The Immorality of Eavesdropping

Because the business world is really a small one, there is frequent opportunity to eavesdrop in airports, restaurant lounges, on suburban trains, etc. To eavesdrop is to break both the code of ethics and the Golden Rule.

If you happen to be sitting near people whose voices you hear clearly and they are discussing something sensitive to you and your company, stop them—quietly, politely, and quickly. Explain that you are with such-and-such a company and that it would be preferable for them to lower their voices or change the subject. They will always be grateful to you.

Someone who eavesdrops is usually caught at it one way or another. This is a situation in which a sense of morality should prevail. A conversation you should not overhear should be stopped, or you should move away.

Party Talk and Table Talk

In business entertaining, the role of conversation waxes and wanes according to the purpose of the gathering. A few generalizations are appropriate.

At a cocktail party, since it is noisy, always moving and full of interruptions, no one expects you to have a substantive conversation. Brush up on your small talk. The best your conversation can do you probably is to help instigate a meeting or a lunch date in the future during which you *will* be able to discuss a business matter seriously.

At a business breakfast, there often is only forty-five minutes to spend together. The conversation can begin immediately on business topics, once the first cup of coffee has been brought by the waiter or waitress.

At an hour-long lunch, with no outside people and with a problem to solve or a plan to discuss, it should be all business as soon as the food orders are taken. With outside guests present, if there is a business pitch to be made, ten minutes of chitchat and small talk are sufficient. Then get down to business (but always *after* the food order has been taken). As the host, for example, you might wait until there's a logical point in the conversation to start business talk. Always smile and joke about the business part of your meal, so that the other person is not made to feel uncomfortable. "Well, now that we've settled the entire future of the Chicago Bears, let's get down to business."

At a goodwill dinner in your home or in a restaurant, try to keep mundane business topics at a minimum so as not to bore the spouses of the people you are trying to impress. Sometimes you can forge a much better business relationship with a client if you confine the business part to office appointments and business lunches, and confine the "getting to know you" and the socializing to the dinner hour with the spouses present.

At a prearranged business dinner, a half hour of socializing and small talk are desirable. A dinner is much longer than a business lunch, so you should move into the "heavy stuff" later rather than sooner. Everyone is probably tired and needs to relax. The person who comes on with business topics like gangbusters is not welcome here. Remember, it's the host's role to begin the business discussion at his or her lunch or dinner table. Wait for his signal.

There is nothing more irritating than a person who can talk only business when he sits down at a meal. He is considered overly aggressive, and boring, too. He is looked upon as someone who is "unpleasant to do business with." Equally irritating is the person who will make only small talk and refuses to get down to business until it is too late and the meal is practically finished. This person is considered a lightweight and a time-waster. He ignores his host's constant signaling for the business talk to begin.

The Host's Responsibilities for Meal Conversation

If you are hosting a meal, regardless of whether your guests consist of senior management, peers, people whom you supervise, clients, customers, vendors, VIPs, or colleagues and associates, it is *your* task to keep the conversation flowing. Several responsibilities should be kept in mind.

Make certain that everyone is properly introduced to one another. Give each enough facts in the introduction to enable them to talk with comparative ease, even if these people have not met before (*see* The Art of Introducing People, in Chapter 1).

Give a clear signal to begin the serious business discussion: "Well, ladies and gentlemen, I guess we'd better get to the discussion of the business at hand, or they'll have to throw us out of here to make way for the dinner guests. Jim, why don't you start with the view of things from the comptroller's office?"

Break the pace if the business discussion gets too demanding, intensive, and draining. Sometimes you need to insert a topic of conversation in a much lighter vein, to break the tension in the air or to help tired brains to refresh themselves. You might ask how everyone thinks the local professional football team is going to do this season, or did everyone see the story in this morning's paper about the local television star being sued for bigamy? The time to insert a light topic is when the waiter comes to the table to clear away a course or to take the order for the next one. That is already an interruption, and sometimes to talk off the subject is the best thing to do.

You may notice that someone in your group has been consistently left out of the conversation, either because that person is shy or because that person has not been part of the subject being discussed. Make him feel good by bringing him into the group. Direct an interesting question, something in line with his or her own expertise: "Amantha, you were involved in the production of that new miracle arthritis drug before you came to us, weren't you? What do you think of the doctors' comments in this morning's newspaper story about that drug?" Directing a question like that at the person who is "out" of the group, quickly pulls him "in," where he can enjoy occupying the center of attention for a while.

If you as host have invited ten or more people, you would do well to invite two good conversationalists to operate at each end of the table. (Perhaps you are good enough yourself to hold down one end of the table.) In this way a good conversational flow is almost guaranteed.

The Tradition of Switching Conversation Partners at Large Dinners or Lunches

Since the early nineteenth century, the great hosts of Europe and members of the diplomatic corps have solved the problem of a guest's being "stuck" throughout an entire meal by inaugurating a system in which guests switch conversational partners as each new course is brought in. The system assures that a guest gives equal time to the person on his left and on his right during the meal.

When a corporate host gives a large party and pays no heed to how the conversation is going around the table, there are inevitably awkward results, with certain guests left with no one to talk to for a long period of time. What usually happens then is that the guest left alone begins talking across the table to another guest left alone; it becomes a shouting match over the din. When a host sees this happening, he should straighten out the conversational traffic and jokingly direct the partner of the guest left alone to please turn in the right direction.

To illustrate, consider a dinner for eighteen given by Mary Smith, a manufacturer's representative, and her husband for Mary Smith's top customers. When the guests are seated, the soup course is brought out, and Mary, as the host, turns instinctively to the guest of honor on her right (her biggest customer). Conversational pairings should then continue to form to the right on around the table. (Mary's husband, Jeff, will be engaged with the woman guest on his left, because the pairings initiated by Mary will first pair him with the person to his left.) When the meat course is brought in, Mary turns to her guest on her left, and everyone on around the table switches accordingly. And so it goes with each course.

EXECUTIVE TELEPHONE MANNERS

How your telephone is answered says a lot about you and your company. The manner in which a company telephone is answered gives strong signals to the caller on the corporate character of that organization. The answering voice may express an affirmative, positive attitude, a negative attitude, or perhaps a don't-really-care attitude.

It's a good idea for a member of top management to call his own company incognito once in a while, posing as someone who doesn't know the extension of the person he's calling, as someone trying to reach a person whose extension is always busy, or as someone trying to get through to the company president. Management should be aware of what happens when John Q. Public calls for information. You might try to find out if there's a job available or where a certain product is sold. How is the person who telephones for an annual report treated? A person who has a complaint to make against a company product, service, or employee? If an executive disguises his voice and calls his own marketing division "cold," pretending to have a "terrific idea" to pass on to management, he might be surprised to see how he is treated.

Management should be aware of how the telephone is handled throughout the company in order to know what kind of employee manners are on display and what kind of attitudes are being projected to the general public. Of course, the voices of those in charge of handling calls anywhere in the company are important, too. The telephone voice should be warm and pleasant, welcoming the call. The diction should be clear and the words easy to understand. If the person who answers the company telephone does not have this kind of voice, he or she should receive training from a voice coach (*see* How You Sound to the Outside World at the beginning of this chapter) or be transferred to a job that does not require telephone skills.

Good telephone manners within an organization are properly a matter of concern on three levels. First, the company should care about the subject. Next, every boss should care about how his telephone is answered and maintain constant surveillance of the quality of this communication. And third, the person who answers the telephone should care about his individual responsibility in this regard. If everyone consciously pays attention to his own telephone manners, this important aspect of business communication will be handled graciously, productively, and profitably.

The person calling into the company has a responsibility, too. If the caller is telephoning with a complaint, for example, he should remember that he is talking to another human being. No matter how justifiably angry he may be, his call will be effective only insofar as he makes his message clear and keeps his composure. It is very difficult to display good telephone manners oneself if the caller is unreasonable and out of control.

If you have an unreasonable caller on the telephone, and if there is some merit to his anger, you may either

- Suggest that he talk to someone higher up in the organization, and tell him that you will arrange for that person to call him in a few minutes. (Use those few minutes to explain the situation to the higher up executive.)
- In a very polite manner ask him to repeat everything he wishes to say but to do it slowly so that you can take down every word. Tell him that you want to have this matter resolved, so he must tell you all the points carefully and slowly (this often defuses part of the anger).

Deciding How Your Telephone Will Be Answered

If you are a professional or an entrepreneur, you would probably answer the telephone or have your telephone answered with the name of your company, partnership, or practice. The dilemma usually arises when the extensions inside a company are answered individually. If yours is a large organization, the way in which a phone is answered may have been the same for decades; however, it should be a part of the daily operations that management keeps adjusting according to the times, pressures, and activities of the organization.

The following are some personal observations on the options in answering telephones:

<table>
<tr><td>

When someone on staff answers your phone

Announcing an extension only is poor manners. It's too abrupt and impersonal.

"Richard Parker's office"—fine

"Mr. Parker's office"—fine (more formal than above)

"Contract Sales"—fine, if your name is not important

"Contract Sales, Richard Parker's office"—okay, but seems long

"Mr. Parker's office, Miss (or Ms.) Williams speaking"*—okay, but seems long

"Mr. Parker's office, Debbie speaking"—terrible (A secretary should never answer with her nickname; it is demeaning to her status.)

</td><td>

When you answer your own phone

Giving an extension only is poor—too abrupt and impersonal.

"Parker speaking"—poor (too abrupt)

"Dick speaking"—poor (too informal and it doesn't communicate properly)

"Richard Parker speaking"—fine (formal)

"Dick Parker speaking"—fine but . . . (informal, seems to lack authority)

"Richard (or Dick) Parker, Contract Sales, speaking"—too long

"Richard (or Dick) Parker, Contract Sales"—better

</td></tr>
</table>

The Heroes of the Business World Answer Their Own Telephones

Everyone, even the CEO of a major corporation, should be able to handle with grace a telephone call from an unknown person, but this kind of accessibility is rare today. An important executive who answers his own phones or instructs his secretary to put through his calls automatically achieves instant fame and popularity in today's world. Executives more commonly seclude and protect themselves from having to deal directly with the public. An important person who answers his own telephone is someone who wants to know what's going on around him, including the nature of complaints from the outside. However, he does not have to hang on the line if the call is not productive. Dispatching a call without insulting the caller is one of the fine arts of diplomacy.

One morning I watched a woman company president answer all her calls, and I marveled at her tact. She explained to me that taking her calls saves her from writing letters and keeps her abreast of what's going on in the world. While we were talking, an office systems salesperson she had never met called

---

*It may be necessary for an important executive's secretary to communicate her last name when she answers, even if it does slow up the business transaction.

her to make a pitch. She explained that the company had absolutely no plans at the present time to upgrade the system, but "when we decide to do something, I promise to call you back, and I always keep my promises." She made a note of his company name, his name, and the telephone number. She then thanked him for calling before he could interrupt and added she knew how much he must "enjoy working for a company with a superior product." Then she hung up before he could answer. She had said no to him but had left him feeling proud of his job. Her next call came from an officer of another company whose mission was to persuade her to accept the invitation from a nonprofit institution to join the board. She first told the caller how honored and grateful she was to have been singled out for this invitation. She explained that her overextended schedule made it "absolutely impossible to devote the quality of time necessary to fulfill the responsibilities attached to the board position." Then she praised the work of the organization in the community and told the caller she was writing a check that day to send him for the charity. The person who called had received a quick and polite no that was a yes in another form: a donation. If she had refused his call, but later, knowing of his request, had written him a letter declining the invitation, it would have taken a lot longer than the four-minute telephone call. Also, she would not have had at her command the lovely warmth of her voice, which had the power to make a no seem less disappointing.

How You Train Your Secretary Is Crucial

Staff contribute in a major way to the successful management of the company through their dexterity in telephone skills. Handling telephone calls graciously does not result from secretarial training so much as it results from the individual's own sensitivity and intelligence in complement with the training given by a sensitive boss.

Here are a few points you might include in your own personal training program:

- The secretary should be taught to answer the ring of your telephone at once. (First ring is best; third ring is sloppy.)
- No one should ever be left on hold for more than twenty seconds. If you can't get on the phone within that time, your secretary should get back on the phone with your response or a gracious "Mr. Dexter will call you back shortly."
- A good secretary will help you return all your calls by giving you a neat list and by helping you get through it: "Miss Jones, may I get Ralph Blacksmith now for you, since you have a few minutes before your next

appointment?" This can help you earn that coveted reputation of being someone who always returns his calls promptly and politely.

- If you are not in the office, the caller should be told this before he is asked for his name. How much better *this* sounds:

"Mr. Jones' office. No, I'm sorry, Mr. Jones won't return to the city until next Monday. May I ask who's calling, please?"

than this:

"Mr. Jones' office. Who's calling, please? No, I'm sorry, Mr. Jones is out of town."

- Encourage your secretary to refrain from making and taking personal calls in the office that are not important or urgent. It ties up the line; it distracts her from her work. And if someone is waiting to see you and is privy to her conversation, your office makes a very bad impression as a place where there isn't much work going on.

Screening Calls

The best advice one can give on screening calls is not to do it. When your secretary asks a caller, "May I ask what this call is about?" there is always disappointment and often hostility on the other end of the line. The caller feels as though he is deemed inadequate, unimportant, and unworthy of speaking directly to the person seated in splendor behind his executive desk.

You can teach your secretary to screen your calls most effectively if you first patiently explain your business, the politics of the hierarchy within your organization, and the priorities in your business and personal life. It will help considerably if you provide:

- A list of people who must be put through to you at once, such as members of the immediate family (who should also be cautioned not to call the office unless it is truly important); anyone in senior management; a member of the board of directors; an outside consultant (legal counsel, accountant, etc.) who says it is important; or anyone from the outside who is of obvious importance
- An understanding of what constitutes an emergency situation about which you must be notified at once—a call from anyone in the company who is "in a jam" of any kind; a call from one of the children's teachers or the family doctor; a reporter who is checking up on hot company news; etc.
- A list of the kinds of people whose calls should be returned within the same day, such as your stockbroker or banker or someone within the organization who needs assistance of any kind

- A list of close personal friends who should be put through at once, if it is at all possible
- An explanation of the type of caller who can be referred elsewhere, which a smart secretary will sense in talking to the caller and asking what the purpose of the call is
- An understanding of the kind of calls the secretary can handle personally

The executive should furnish the secretary with the exact language he wants used in screening his calls, whether it's a brisk "May I ask what this call is in reference to?" or a more gracious "I'm really very sorry that, because Mr. Wilson's schedule is all jammed up, he is not available to accept calls at the moment. Can you tell me the nature of this call?" When asked the reason for the call, a caller might respond, "Oh, this is a personal call," to which the secretary should reply, "I will give him your name and number the next time he opens his door, and I'm sure he will get back to you as soon as he is able to. However, I must tell you that he is involved in a priority company matter right now." Or, "I hope you'll understand. I'm really sorry things are so hectic in this office right now. I promise to see to it that Mr. Wilson knows you called today, and that he sees your letter when it reaches this office."

Call-screening is pretentious for a young person or an executive who is not on an upper rung of the ladder. At best, it is an unpleasant experience for the caller and for the secretary who has to cope with the caller's anxiety at not getting through. It requires expert handling by a "pro."

Transferring Calls

The most delicate part of call-screening is transferring a caller to a different party and doing it so deftly the caller is grateful the action was taken. Any caller who is transferred hither and yon aimlessly loses any good feelings he may have had about the company; when he is misdirected, it wastes his time and the company's time, too.

A boss should train his secretary how to transfer calls effectively. The act of transferring requires tact but also a thorough knowledge of the organization, of the different divisions' duties and responsibilities, and of the names of key people who will handle the call properly when it is transferred to them. There are points the inside person must handle before he or she transfers an incoming call.

- The caller should be given an explanation as to why he is being sent elsewhere.
- The caller should be given the name, title, division, and extension number of the office where he is being transferred, so that if there is a disconnect, the caller can easily find his way back to the right party by calling again.

- Before the transfer is actually completed, the secretary should make the caller feel everything is going to be all right: "It was a pleasure talking to you . . . I'm sure Mr. X will settle your problem *very* satisfactorily . . . I'm really sorry I couldn't help you, but I'm sure that Mr. X will know exactly what to do."

A really competent secretary follows up during the day on calls of importance that were transferred, with calls to the appropriate sources to see if the caller was ultimately properly handled.

How Good Are Your Own Telephone Manners?

What about *your* manners when you yourself place calls or transact business through the telephone after your secretary has placed the call for you? How good are your telephone manners when you receive business calls at home?

- To begin with, don't make a business call unless there is a good reason for it. A telephone call is an interruption, an intrusion into a busy person's day. You should always have a definite purpose in making it.
- Some people love the telephone and use it constantly. You can call this kind of person at home without fear, provided you call in the morning after 7 A.M. or in the evening before 10 P.M. The majority of people do not like to be called at home on business matters when it is something that can be handled during the office day.
- If you dial a wrong number, always make a sincere apology instead of rudely hanging up abruptly.
- When you have your secretary call someone for you, either be on the line as that person is about to pick up or have a signal (such as a double buzz) worked out with your secretary that gets you on the line the second the person called says "Hello." One of the worst faux pas a young executive can commit is to have his secretary call a more senior executive and then not be on the line when the senior executive picks up.
- Think about your diction and your quality of voice when you begin to speak into the telephone. Sometimes just thinking about how you sound makes you sound better. (*See* How You Sound to the Outside World, at the beginning of this chapter.)
- Don't be upset if you can't get through to someone right away. It happens to everyone, including the CEOs of the top ten companies in the world.
- Get quickly to the point in any business call (the other person will appreciate it) and be brief. If you have to break into the conversation, do so apologetically: "Janet, I have a department meeting starting, so would you mind if we made this a quick call?" The average person does not have

time to chitchat in his or her office; chitchat also makes it look as if you don't have a very important job.

- Explain your business to the secretary if the person you are calling is not available and if it is urgent. Forget your ego; the secretary is probably perfectly capable of relaying the message. Indeed, if you furnish all the facts and explain the urgency (assuming the details are not confidential), the secretary will probably go to bat for you and get whatever action you need and questions answered more quickly than if it were left in the boss's hands. (Naturally, you would not use a secretary as your emissary in an important deal with another senior executive.) In watching the various White House administrations at close hand, I have noticed how the wise petitioners, even those who are close personal friends of the President and the First Lady, know that the way to get things done quickly is to go through the staff rather than asking the President and First Lady personally.
- If you must ask a favor of a very busy person, ask the secretary what would be a convenient time to call to discuss that favor. This is smart politics.
- Don't remain silent while the other person continues to speak. This is very unsettling for the other person. You should react to his or her conversation, even if just to say "Yes," "I agree," "Isn't that terrible?" or some such comment to prove that you are alive at your end of the telephone.
- Don't eat or chew into the mouthpiece. The sounds are greatly magnified and that much more unpleasant to the other person's ear. It also signifies you are not paying close attention to the conversation.
- Don't allow background noises to penetrate the mouthpiece (such as a television or radio playing in the background). It may not distract you, but the sound is magnified and makes it difficult for the other person to hear you.
- When you are talking to someone on the telephone, give that person your attention. Don't make side remarks to a staff member who may be in the room. It's very unsettling for a person with whom you are speaking suddenly to hear the sound of your voice engaged in conversation with yet another person on another matter. If you can't help the distractions, telephones with "mute" buttons are available to overcome this problem.
- If you placed the call and you are disconnected, it's *your* responsibility to call back immediately, even if the call is long distance and even if the disconnect responsibility lies with the other person's office.
- When you have a visitor in your office, don't take any calls unless they are genuinely urgent.
- If you happen to be on the telephone when a visitor who has an appoint-

ment arrives, quickly terminate your call or tell the person to whom you are speaking that you will call back later. Someone with a fixed appointment has priority over the person with whom you're talking on the telephone.

· If you're visiting someone else in his office and an urgent telephone call for him interrupts you, offer to step outside so that he will have privacy. If he insists you stay because it "will just be a minute," study something in your briefcase, read the paper, or gaze out the window—don't stare at him. If his conversation takes a sudden emotional or overly personal turn, get up and quietly go out into the waiting room, making a sign that you'll wait out there. He will appreciate your sensitivity.

· End your telephone conversations on a pleasant upbeat note, but refrain from using that tiresome cliché "Have a nice day." The person you say that to may be facing an IRS audit or a tooth extraction. Use *anything* else: "It was nice talking to you." "It was nice hearing your news." "Thank you for filling me in—I appreciate it." If you know the person's family, it is always nice to refer to them before hanging up: "Give Em and the children my best."

· If you enter a colleague's office to speak to him, and you find him on the telephone, step right outside again, unless he motions you to come in. If you have an emergency and must speak to him at once, inform him: "Joe, emergency." Joe should finish his conversation at once.

The Hold Button: A Necessary Evil

In my opinion there is only one thing worse in telephone manners than being put on hold, and that is being put on hold with music playing in the background.

Being put on hold when you're calling an airline or a department store is one thing; if customers and clients are constantly put on hold in your office, it is quite another matter. If you are talking and a second line rings, apologize to the first caller and say you will return instantly; put him on hold and tell the second person, before he has a chance to say anything, "I'm sorry, I must come right back to you." Then return to the first person and try to finish your call. If it is not possible to finish the first call that quickly, apologize to him once again, put him on hold, and return to the second call to say you're sorry but you will call that person back in a few minutes if he or she will give you the name and number.

The first call always has priority, unless the second call is something like a station-to-station call from another country, in which case you should explain to the first caller why you must hang up and get back to him in a few minutes.

The important thing to remember is never to leave anyone on hold for more than a few seconds. Talk to him quickly, apologetically, and make him understand why you must call him back. Just the words "I really hate to leave you on hold" pour balm on the wounded caller. And remember your promise *to call back right away.* Don't forget it!

Cutting a Telephone Call Short

When you wish to cut a person short on an undesired conversation, there are ways of doing it that are more kind than blunt.

- Explain that your secretary has just announced an urgent call from a member of senior management.
- Prepare the other person for your finishing the call by saying something like "Jane, before I have to hang up, I wanted to mention that. . . ."
- Suddenly remember your next meeting: "George, I see by my watch that I'm due in the Conference Room in one and a half minutes. I'm afraid we'll have to continue this another time."
- Interrupt the other person's ramblings by sounding very pressured: "Look, Barbara, I have to finish the chairman's speech, and a press release in addition, this afternoon. I'm afraid I have to go. Forgive me."
- Long distance calls serve as useful excuses: "Jim, my secretary just put a note on my desk saying that there's a station-to-station call from Manila waiting on my other line."
- Hold out hopes of a time in the future to talk things over: "Jennifer, we have a lot to talk about. We should have a quiet time in which to discuss that properly. Let's wait until we can talk it over face to face some time."

The Art of Taking Good Messages

The person who takes messages for others efficiently and pleasantly is an asset to any organization. (My guilt shows here, for I have the terrible habit of scribbling messages on the back of used envelopes, restaurant match covers, or even blank checks!) The minute you answer a telephone that rings, you are assuming a responsibility to handle that call properly, even if it is directed to someone who is not there.

The easiest way to take a message is to use a printed pad designed just for that purpose. Otherwise, use a clean piece of paper (no writing please on the edge of newspapers or an available file folder). The message should contain:

- Name of the caller (If you don't recognize the caller's name, don't be embarrassed to make him repeat it and spell it for you.)
- Telephone number, extension, and, if applicable, area code

- Name of the caller's company
- Date and hour of the call
- Your name or initials (in case the person called needs to ask you more about the call)
- A request to call back immediately, if the call was an urgent one

Because of the lack of good clerical help and the resulting increase in the use of direct dialing telephone systems, the problems of message-taking are growing more acute. A good telephone answering machine is one solution. Certainly companies should experiment with some kind of recording device so that there will not be a symphony of "ghost phones" ringing aimlessly throughout the company when staff members of a direct-dialing office are not at their desks.

The Answering Machine: An Aggravating Necessity

If you really hate having an answering machine rather than a human being take your call, you will find consolation in the fact that as you make more calls to more machines, it becomes easier to handle and less irritating. The machine is, after all, a more satisfactory option than a telephone that rings incessantly and is never answered. It is also an invaluable tool for anyone who works at home, whether full- or part-time.

Before recording your voice on your own machine, practice what you're going to say (from a written script). Listen to playbacks and keep recording it until it is pleasant to listen to and until your voice sounds enthusiastic and upbeat. (If you record in what you consider a normal manner of speaking, it may sound as though you're announcing a funeral.) For your office, your message might be something as simple as this:

> "George Jones of Hammon Fastenings speaking. Please leave your name, company, and telephone number when you hear the signal. I will return your call as soon as possible."

If you are able to state the hour of your return to the office, do so:

> "I will be in the office all afternoon" (or, "I will probably be able to return your call before the end of the day.")

On your home business answering machine, for security reasons, the less detailed information you give, the better. Don't even give your name or your telephone number, so that a person who calls you by error won't get ideas for staging a robbery. This is all you have to record:

> "Hello. After hearing the signal, please leave your name, company name, telephone number, and message. Thank you."

When you leave a recorded message on someone else's machine, forget about being clever or amusing. Jokes left on others' machines usually fall completely flat or, at best, sound terribly tired. Also, they waste the time of the other person, who may have many messages to plow through. If it is someone who receives a lot of calls, the machine may run out of tape if too many people take up too much space and time, so be succinct.

Dealing with an Answering Service

If you use an answering service in your business, the first thing to remember is that the service is only as good as the instructions you give the service personnel and, second, that the people handling your calls are human beings who deserve to be treated like human beings. Answering services do slip up occasionally, particularly at very busy times when all of the clients are receiving calls at once. This is when callers are put on hold for too long and when messages occasionally are taken inaccurately. Losing your temper at your service personnel will not rectify a mistake already made. Usually the answering service gives you good service, and cares about the success of your business. Treat all of the people who work there with kindness and consideration, and you will see results in the way they treat you, even though they may never lay eyes on you.

The people I know who receive the best service from their answering services are those who know all of the people at the service by name and who acknowledge their importance by sending them boxes of candy or fruit at Christmastime.

THE PERSONAL SIDE OF BUSINESS LETTER WRITING

Business correspondence may touch very personal matters, not just the making of money. A considerate executive uses the mail to express friendship for his or her colleagues and associates in a human way. A letter is an important reaction to someone's good—or bad—news. A letter may be a means of refurbishing an old relationship that has grown musty. A letter of friendship pleases the recipient and may incidentally result in unexpected business, just because the writer has pleasantly brought himself once again to the recipient's mind.

Letters of friendship in the business world are exchanged between old friends, newer friends, and even people who meet only briefly for the first time. A letter takes only a few minutes to write and dispatch; its influence may be lasting.

Every time you add a personal sentence or two to a letter that is strictly business, you turn that letter into a personal-business letter. Every time you write a business letter that also touches on a personal subject, such as asking a personal favor of an executive, you are writing a personal-business letter. The volume of this kind of mail in the business world is massive.

Many times it's much easier to write what you feel or what you have to say than it is to tell it to a person face to face. In a world peppered with computer jargon and littered with business forms and form letters, a well-composed letter is like a ray of sunshine arriving on someone's desk. The person who sent it feels good about it; the person who receives it feels even more so. The writing of certain personal-business letters should be an automatic reflex for an executive. He should not need to be reminded to write these letters.

This section deals with the personal side of business letter writing. Not only is there structure, form, and etiquette inherent in this activity, but a good writer of personal letters uses the heart as well as the pen or typewriter keys to communicate the message. The information that follows covers the kind of letters that simultaneously please other people, perform an efficient function, and indirectly affect the image of the letter writer in his business milieu. It doesn't matter if he's running a farm, a factory, or a bank.

The range of this kind of business letter comprises everything from wishing someone well in his new business venture to explaining to the head of an advertising or PR agency why he didn't get the account and from writing a condolence letter to the office receptionist whose husband has just died to introducing a fellow executive to business friends in Rio de Janeiro.

The ability of a good letter to influence is considerable. I have seen many examples of this. A CEO passed around his organization a thank-you letter written by a young woman executive in his company who had attended a boiler-plate industry banquet as a guest at the company's table for twelve. No one else at the table had thought to thank the host afterward in writing. He circulated her letter as a subtle hint that his executives should send letters like that all the time—to outside clients and customers in particular. The writing of a good letter that is personal in nature but that is business-related is not only the right thing to do and the nice thing to do, it is the *smart* thing to do.

Anyone who feels devoid of inspiration on the subject of letter writing has only to go to the public library and spend a bit of time perusing famous collections of letters to be inspired. (A tip: Read all of Strunk and White's classic *Elements of Style*—Macmillan, revised edition 1959. It pays to know how to use the English language properly.)

Proper Form of the Business Letter

Your letters should always look professional and well-executed. After all, they represent *you.* To begin, select stationery that suits the occasion (*see* Good Visual Communication, Chapter 7). Don't try to write a long letter on a correspondence card. Don't send a thank-you note on a printed office letterhead when you have engraved stationery, but don't waste engraved stationery on interoffice memos either.

Be sure that the addressee's name is spelled properly and that the proper title is given. And always be neat throughout, regardless of whether your letter is typed or handwritten. Don't allow letters representing you and your company to go through the mails full of typos, misspellings, and strike-overs.

Overfamiliarity in the salutation of a letter can get things off to a bad start. Young executives in particular should be careful about using first names in the salutation, especially in letters to people in other countries, who already consider Americans excessively informal. Here are some guidelines for salutations:

The Circumstances	The Proper Salutation	Comment
You meet someone who is more or less a peer, and by the end of the meeting you are calling each other by your given names.	"Dear Joe"	
You have just met an executive and do not feel quite right about using his first name. Use both names in your salutation—a sign you do not wish to be stiff or overly formal.	"Dear Joe Williams"	Most likely he will respond using your given name—"Dear Alice"—a signal to you to use his given name in future correspondence. However, if he does not address you by your given name in his return letter, continue to call him by his last name.
You are a young executive who meets an older, senior one. Do not use "Dear Joe" as your salutation. That is too aggressive and overly informal.	"Dear Mr. Williams"	Even though he may respond with a "Dear Alice," you should continue to write him as "Dear Mr. Williams" until he requests that you use his given name.

Some people are known for their very stylized complimentary closings in their letters. For people in business, all that is necessary is a choice of either "Sincerely" or "Sincerely yours." For a letter addressed to the President of the United States or a high church official, "Respectfully yours" would be a suitable complimentary close.

If your signature is illegible, and if your name and title are not on the letterhead, a typed signature block is necessary. Always remember to sign your letters before they go out (or have someone sign for you). Too many letters arrive today without a signature, a sign of gross carelessness. If you do not sign your letter yourself, the signee should include his or her initials after your signature, with or without the phrase "(signed in his/her absence)."

The Etiquette of Who Signs the Letters

If a junior executive drafts a letter of importance, the protocol of who should sign it requires attention.

- Junior executives certainly should sign letters addressed to people who are more or less their peers.
- Junior executives' letters addressed to senior people outside the office should be signed by someone of a higher level working on the same project, i.e., a person closer in rank to the recipient of the letter. Once the first basic letters on the project have been exchanged, it is perfectly appropriate for a junior executive to sign his or her own letters to the senior executive on the outside, provided the latter understands that the junior person is in charge of those aspects of the project.

The Office Letterhead
Is Meant for Business Matters

A corporation should enforce strict regulations, both for employees and management, on the use of the official company letterhead for correspondence that does not pertain to company business. Only members of senior management (chairman, president, senior and executive vice-presidents) should use the company letterhead for purposes other than business, and even they should do so with discretion.

Here are times when *not* to use the company letterhead:

- For political or charitable fund-raising
- For sending controversial letters of opinion (as to the "Letters to the Editor" section of the local newspaper)
- For personal money-making activities not connected with one's company
- For matters concerning a lawsuit in which one is personally involved
- For purely personal matters (for example, a love letter)

Handling an Executive's Mail
in His or Her Absence

When an executive is away from the office for a period of time, a large amount of mail inevitably accumulates. Coping with it upon his return adds to the increased pressure of handling other deferred duties that also require attention. Yet it is a very important part of good manners to attend to all correspondence promptly. It is therefore advisable for a secretary or staff assistant to acknowledge all the executive's incoming mail as it arrives, immediately answering what can be answered or explaining why there will be a delay in a response to something requiring his personal attention.

Here is an example of the kind of interim response that will afford the executive a temporary reprieve in answering the writer:

> . . . I am acknowledging on Mr. Hendrick's behalf your letter to him of June 8th. He is away for a few days; your letter will be brought to his attention as soon as he returns.

If the staff member knows the writer of the letter well, the tone could be more informal:

> . . . I am acknowledging on Mr. Hendrick's behalf your letter to him of June 8th. He's fishing in Canada for two weeks and is evidently having a "good-catching time." I know he'll get in touch with you as soon as possible when he returns.

In this case, Mr. Hendrick's secretary obviously knows both boss and correspondent well enough that news of the fishing trip can freely be shared with him.

If an executive is ill, the secretary should refrain from mentioning that in answers to his mail, unless the illness is well known and has already been acknowledged by the company. Rumors fly with unreasonable speed. Before the secretary knows it, the executive's illness will become industry gossip.

If the executive's illness is serious enough to be threatening, and it is a known factor, the secretary should still be noncommittal in the letters sent in response to the executive's mail:

> I know how much Ms. Jones will appreciate hearing from you. She will answer your letter as soon as she is feeling better.

Or, if the executive's condition is very serious:

> Thank you for your prayers and for your concern. I know how pleased Ms. Jones will be to learn of your letter.

Proper Content of the Informal Business Letter

- *A good informal business letter should be brief.* The shortest I ever received came from a supervisor who was trying to teach me to shorten my presentations. When I finally accomplished this feat, he sent a letter to my home address that was exceedingly brief, but I cherished every little word. The message was, "Dear Tish, That's it!"
- *A good informal business letter is thoughtful, honest, simple and prompt.* Sometimes timing is more important than content.
- It is usually appropriate to drop something informal and personal into your business letter right after the salutation:

   . . . It was very pleasant running into you at the game yesterday. You looked in great form, and it reminded me that I had never sent you the article I promised . . .

   Or, in the last paragraph of the letter:

   . . . I wish you, Serena, and the children a very happy Easter. After this winter we've had, I certainly hope you'll be in some warm and sunny place.

   Or you may hand-write a personal note at the bottom of your letter.
- If you have something serious to impart, either enclose it on a separate piece of paper or send a separate letter containing just the business news. Your business letter can then be circulated throughout the recipient's office without any of your personal comments included in it.
- *A trace of humor and a trace of praise* of the recipient of the letter are two constant success factors in letter writing.

   . . . Next to the remaining Rockefeller brothers, you must be the most secure executive in the United States by now. Your success has been phenomenal!

- *Refrain from using foul language in a letter,* even if you think it will emphasize your main point. An unattractive word or expression always stands out in exaggerated form in print. It degrades the text.
- *Make sure that the first paragraph of the business part of the letter clearly reveals the purpose of the letter.* Don't make the recipient of the letter go on a scavenger hunt, trying to find the real point of your writing.
- Before you write the letter, make a list of all the points that should be covered in the letter, and let the list be a guide in the construction of your paragraphs, point by point. Here's a sample list:

   Compliment your correspondent about his recent golf game.
   Explain your new line of products and why they would be good for him.
   Mention their exclusivity.

Explain when he could get delivery and how.
Refer to price.
Give him news of your classmates.
Sign off.

- *Don't exaggerate in order to persuade.* It lessens your credibility. It's all right to exaggerate your good wishes—"Here go a million good wishes for your new enterprise"—but it is not all right to say "everyone of your competitors has taken our new product line" if that isn't so.
- *Write simply.* Malcolm Forbes' advice is to "search out and annihilate all unnecessary words and sentences—even entire paragraphs." My brother, Mac Baldrige, created a furor when he had all of the Commerce Department's word processors programmed to reject trite, sometimes grammatically incorrect business jargon (e.g., *to prioritize, bottom line, impact* used as a verb, etc.) This was one of his first steps as Secretary of Commerce in the Reagan administration.
- *Write interestingly.* Read the advice of wordsmiths like *New York Times* columnist William Safire, so that you learn to use figures of speech correctly to add variety to your writing.
- *Carefully edit any important letter.* Rewrite it, if necessary, in order to make sure it is clear, that it fulfills its purpose, and that it contains no "distracting garbage." This applies to informal business letters as much as to strictly business letters.

The following are the kinds of letters that people in business should know how to write. Of course, everyone has his or her own style of writing. I am not trying to put my words into your mouth, but showing how I would write the letters. Note the form and tone; use your own words, keeping in mind what is and is not appropriate.

Letters Pertaining to Favors

It is easier both to ask and decline a favor in writing, rather than face-to-face. When you put someone on the spot in person it can negatively affect your case.

Letter Asking a Favor

Opening paragraph: a personal message	. . . It was a great pleasure seeing you and Marge at the reunion. We're not growing older, just wiser, mellower, and much more exercised both in body and mind than we ever were at college.

Favor asked is stated clearly up front, as well as an acknowledgment that it might not be possible to grant the favor.	I have a big favor to ask, which may be out of the realm of possibility. (Text should follow, stating succinctly all the necessary information, including timetable, etc.)
Innocuous personal closing	Again, I understand perfectly if this is not an appropriate gesture I'm asking you to make. In any case, it was good to see you, I hope our paths will cross again before too long, and Jennie joins me in wishing you both the very best in the New Year. . . .

Letter Declining a Favor

Inability to perform favor is mentioned up front.	. . . It's tough not to be able to grant a favor, but not to be able to help a really good friend is doubly difficult.
Short, clear explanation is given of why it did not work.	I immediately called Pete on receipt of your letter of January 3rd to see if I could get the deal back on the track again. (Etc.)
Exchange of wives' greetings. Letter ends with hope for another reunion and a promise to be of assistance in the future.	Marge sends you and Jen her love. We'll have to get together very soon and not wait for another class reunion. And I hope the next time you write, Pete, I'll be able to act with the speed of Superman. I had to let you down this time, but I hope that I can make it up to you in the future.

Thanks for a Favor, However Small

When someone does you a favor, it's wise to go on record immediately with your thanks, before you forget about it. If you become known as someone who jots a line to say thanks, you will also become known as someone who is thoughtful and well-mannered. People will be more inclined to extend you extra consideration, seeing that you value their willingness to be helpful and are ready to reciprocate.

The note takes very little effort—perhaps five minutes of your time from the moment you set pen to paper to the moment you throw it in the out-box. Only a few words are required.

> . . . Your lending me your car this morning in the company garage when I couldn't start mine was a *lifesaver.* I made it to Aetna's headquarters on time for the meeting, and it was important that I be there on time.
>
> I really owe you one. Thanks!

Letter Informing a Person Why He didn't Get the Job or an Agency Why It didn't Get the Account

A serious contender for an executive position goes through a very harrowing experience of interviews, telephone calls, and endless waiting to hear if he or she will be chosen. So does the team of an advertising or PR agency, an architectural firm, or any kind of service agency going after a contract or an account. Sometimes, even though polite inquiries are made, nothing is heard for months. When leading contenders hear via "the grapevine" that someone else got the job or, even worse, when they read about it in the newspaper, it is a very debilitating kind of rejection. Corporate America is very tough about getting everyone to submit proposals and make their pitches promptly and in great detail. Unfortunately, corporate America is also very careless about thanking people and letting the contenders know when they do *not* have the job or the account.

There is a tremendous selfishness among companies in the way in which they handle people who are competing for their business. It takes very little time to make a telephone call to each "also ran" to inform them of a decision (the very day the decision is made). *It should be followed up with a letter,* with as much face-saving for the recipient and his team as possible, since people often don't retain what is said to them on the telephone in times of emotion.

Letter to a Person Who Didn't Get the Job

Someone else got the job.

Reasons why someone else won out.

... As I told you on the telephone today, the position for which you were being seriously considered was given to another lawyer, a women with over fifteen years experience in our field of entertainment. We decided that this aspect of her background gave her a distinct advantage over the other highly qualified candidates.

Compliment the person's self-presentation.

I am particularly sorry in your case, because your credentials are excellent and you presented yourself in a very fine manner. We were all greatly impressed by you and would like to keep you in mind in case you are interested in future job openings.

Wish the person luck and thank him.

I'm sorry things didn't work out the way we thought they would. I hope your search for a position as legal counsel will be successful right away. My associates and I thank you and wish you all the best for the future.

Letter to an Agency That Didn't Get the Account

Another agency got the job.

Reasons why the other agency won out

... As we discussed on the telephone today, the chairman selected Agency X to handle the account. He had a very difficult decision to make, and in the end selected the other agency because of its strong international experience in the marketing field.

Compliment the agency's presentation.

We all know you would have done a great job, and we appreciate the amount of agency time and creative work that went into your proposal. The content of the presentation was excellent, the creative ideas were impressive, and your efficient approach to company planning was invaluable in giving us new insight.

Thank the agency and wish them good luck.

I have a feeling this is not the last time we will be approaching a project together. Please thank the team who put together your presentation, and I send you my best personal wishes for a successful year ahead.

Letters of Reference and Recommendation

When you are asked to write a letter of recommendation for a business colleague, keep the following in mind:

- *Write the letter immediately after you have agreed to do it,* preferably within twenty-four hours. Otherwise you may forget it, or you may do it in such a big rush your letter will be counterproductive.
- *Include the person's resume or curriculum vitae* so that you won't have to waste precious letter space going into the details of his or her background.
- *Before composing the letter, write down a list of the person's affirmative points;* be sure to cover them in the letter.
- If you're writing to the board of an apartment house in which your colleague is trying to purchase an apartment, *remember to mention your colleague's "fiscal reliability."*
- If you have had a figurative gun put in your back, and you have to write a recommendation for someone when you do not wish to, *you can write a lukewarm letter* that sends immediate caution signals to the recipient (see the example that follows).
- When you have sent a reference letter for a friend, *don't send* him a copy of your letter unless it is dripping in hyperbole. Do, however, send him a note saying that you dutifully sent off an enthusiastic reference letter in his behalf, and tell him the date you sent it.

· Remember to include all necessary information in your letters of reference.

> The person's full name
>
> His business title and business address
>
> His home address, if pertinent
>
> The names of his family members and his children's ages, if pertinent
>
> The name of the seconder or others providing endorsement letters, if proposing someone for membership
>
> Any athletic prowess, if proposing someone for a club with athletic facilities

Letter Introducing Someone Moving to Another City

. . . Joe Doakes and his family are moving to Akron next week, where he will be opening a new office for his company, The Academy Marketing Group, of which he is a founding partner. His office address is 1300 Lake Street, Akron 00000, and his telephone is 000-0000. Joe tells me they were fortunate enough recently to find "the perfect house," which they have purchased, at 34 Shoreacres Road, 00000.

You will notice in the enclosed biography that Joe has gone very fast in his career for a forty-year-old. His wife, Jeannie, is very bright and attractive, and so are the children, Joe Jr. (16) and Clare (12). They are not only close personal friends but Joe is an important investor in one of my new projects, so I would greatly appreciate anything you might do to smooth the way for them. I have asked Joe to call you some time next week.

We are all well. My last two will be out of college in a year, thank the Lord. Susy and I send you and Michele a great deal of affection. . . .

Letter Recommending Someone for a Club Membership

. . . It is an honor to propose the John Boyton Wright family for membership in the Rolling Hills Club. The following information is submitted for the consideration of the Membership Committee:

John Wright, aged 38, has just moved to Tennessee with his wife, Gloria, and their three children—Amy (12), Russell (10), and Nils (7). John is vice-president of the Erie Cement Company and has been transferred here to establish a Tennessee headquarters. He and his wife are both graduates of the University of California at Berkeley. The family presently holds memberships to the Erie Country and Downtown Athletic clubs.

John is a first-rate tennis player and was captain of the Berkeley squash team. Gloria is an excellent tennis player herself. She has headed the women's board of the largest hospital in her area for the past five years.

All three children are budding athletes, and the entire family is attractive, bright, and full of charm. The Wrights have also assured me that they would use the club facilities for entertaining—something which John, in his new position, will have to do frequently.

In the attached business biography of John Wright, you will find his addresses and telephone numbers.

Seconding and supporting letters are being written by George Humphries, Janet Wilkerson, Tim Wright, Dick Jones, and Neil Gallo.

I am honored to propose the Wright family for membership in the Rolling Hills Club. . . .

Lukewarm Recommendation for Membership to a Club

. . . In response to a specific request, I am addressing this letter to the Membership Committee of the Hopeful Executives Club on behalf of a colleague, John Doe, who is very anxious to join.

I have known John casually for several years, and have enclosed his biography, which will furnish the important details of his background.

I would be happy to discuss with anyone on the committee his qualifications and his suitability for membership . . .

Recommendation for Membership in a Professional Organization

To the Chairman of the Membership Committee of Women's Forum

The purpose of this letter is to propose for membership in the Women's Forum Ms. Jane Marston, vice-president of Cable Network CYC Sports.

I have known Jane for fourteen years and have watched her career flourish as her accomplishments have multiplied. Her attached biography details her numerous awards in the television field, as well as her membership on the boards of several nonprofit institutions. She has made outstanding contributions in the field of drug abuse, and has a reputation for being a person in the communications industry who cares about her community and *does something about it.*

Jane is a wife and mother of two. She has managed to juggle her family and a distinguished career with a sense of expert balance. I know of no one who would make a more suitable member of the Forum, and I hope the Membership Committee will look kindly on this proposal for membership. . . .

Letter of Reference for an Executive Who Has Been Let Go

When you must let an executive go for reasons other than incompetency or theft, give him a good letter of reference by a senior member of management. A letter of reference addressed to "To Whom It May Concern" would contain the following:

To Whom It May Concern:

Dates she worked for the company and in what capacity

Give reason for the termination.

Ms. Anne Garrison worked for Atkins & Boyd from September 1, 1982, to September 1, 1986, starting as an executive secretary and functioning as an account supervisor since 1984. Due to a reorganization of the executive staff and company-wide budget cuts, we are forced to terminate her services.

Explain what she accomplished and what her special skills are.

During her four years here she proved to be a loyal, bright, resourceful member of the executive staff. Her rapid promotion from secretary to account supervisor was well merited. She "learned" the company quickly, was interested in the company's goals, and helped us work toward them. She has strong people skills and is also adept at outlining projects and in writing proposals for new business.

She has a very creative mind and is able to articulate creative ideas in a practical fashion. She is a good writer and a good team member. I recommend her highly as a hard-working, able person.

Offer to talk to any prospective employer.

I would be glad to answer any questions on Ms. Garrison's service with this company.

Letters of Resignation

In most cases of resignation, it's wise for the person resigning to go on record with as affirmative a letter as he or she can muster. Whether you resign by choice or by force, your letter will remain in the files, to be seen in the future by people who may have some influence over your life.

Letter of Resignation from a Contented Executive

Gives reason for resignation

. . . It is with great regret that I submit my resignation from Seafarb as of February 9, 1986, after eight very happy and productive years of service. The reason for this decision is a personal one—my wife's deteriorating health. Her doctors advise an immediate move to a warmer, drier climate and her health is a top priority in my life.

Compliments management and employees

I have watched with pride Seafarb's growth from a company with $2 million to one with over a $100 million in sales. In these past months I have often reflected on what I am going to miss most in leaving this company, and the answer is always the same: the people. I'm going to miss not only management but also the employees, who have given me friendship and support during these wonderful years.

I wish you and every member of the Seafarb team a brilliant, happy future. . . .

Letter of Resignation from an Unhappy Executive

It's important that an executive's file not reflect an overly bitter and rancorous departure. You don't want a record of hard feelings to haunt you afterward.

An explanation of what the executive is unhappy about is in order. However, that should be given without any derogatory statements about staff or the company.

My resignation from Seafarb is submitted as of August 15, 1986, after six years as assistant vice-president and vice-president of the firm.

Explains why he is resigning

My resignation is submitted in protest over lack of senior management support for the much-needed plan you assigned me to devise for tightening up the management functions of this company. I have attached a copy of my final report to be filed with this letter. The report represents several arduous years of research and planning, so it was particularly difficult to accept the fact that I was not allowed to finish the job I was hired to do—and one that is desperately needed for the good of this company.

Mentions proudly what he accomplished

I am proud of the fact that during my six years I managed to effect a dramatic increase in both gross sales and net profit margins within my division.

Ends with an "up" note, wishing the company well

I have enjoyed knowing the many fine people in this company. Seafarb is a first-rate organization, and I wish it well for the future. . . .

Letters of Acceptance and Regret in Answer to an Invitation to Join the Board of a Nonprofit Institution

Letter Accepting

. . . Your invitation to join the Board of Trustees of the Melton Illiteracy Institute is a great honor, one I accept with pleasure.

I have watched the enormous strides the Institute has made in the community and throughout our state in combatting the growing problem of illiteracy. Under the leadership of Dr. Melton, I hope to be able to join you in contributing to the activities of the Institute. I will also search for ways in which my corporation can be of assistance in your work.

I am looking forward to working with you, Dr. Melton, and the staff of the Melton Illiteracy Institute. . . .

Letter Regretting

. . . With great regret I must decline your invitation to join the Board of Trustees of the Melton Illiteracy Institute.

I have long admired the excellent work carried on in combatting illiteracy by the fine people of your Institute. Your program has commanded national attention—and admiration.

The reason I must decline this honor is that I am already overextended with two other board positions. I am also overseeing changes in my company at the present time and must decrease, rather than increase, my outside activities.

I will certainly remain a steadfast supporter of the Institute, and I hope you will call on me for advice and help with contacts at any time.

All good wishes for a very successful year in your wonderful work . . ."

(*Note:* If a donation check accompanies a letter of regret, the blow to the institution will be lessened.)

Letter Declining to Endorse or Praise Anything for Commercial Purposes

You can acknowledge having received something without endorsing it in any way.

Thank you so much for sending me Daisy Mendendorf's new book. It looks very impressive, and I will enjoy perusing it the minute there's time in my hectic schedule for such pleasant relaxation. . . .

Or,

How very nice of you to send me a sample of your latest product. I will certainly try it when time permits. Thank you for thinking of me. . . .

Complaint Letters

Composing Letters of Complaint

It takes time and reflection to write a really effective letter of complaint. When you first write it, don't mail it, because it probably shows your emotions of anger too revealingly. Look at it again objectively the next day, tighten it up (including the grammar), and remove any vestige of emotional tone. Remember that a lot of people might be shown your letter. Remain polite. Action is usually taken faster in response to a letter written with a cool hand than to one written with a sense of hysteria. Also, cut the sarcasm in your letter. (When I am the injured one, I tend to slather sarcasm all over my complaint letters like catsup on a burger, and it *never* helps.)

A Sample Letter of Complaint

Dear Mr. Jones:

The invitations printed by your company have arrived, exactly two weeks behind schedule.

We engaged your company to print a very important invitation for this company's 50th Anniversary dinner. You were given a great deal of information on exactly how we wanted these invitations to look. I enclose a memo to me from our Director of Special Events, Mr. Ronald Smith, detailing the many errors in printing, layout, and color separation. The invitations delivered to us are unacceptable and certainly not in keeping with the image of this company.

This leaves us in serious difficulties. Since we cannot mail these invitations and cannot wait for new ones to be made, we will have to send Mailgrams to our guest list—an expensive but unavoidable step.

I would like to suggest that we meet as soon as possible to discuss the mutually agreeable steps we must take to reach an agreement on the payment of your bill. I know that your company has a long history in this community, as has ours, so I am certain we will be able to settle this matter equitably.

Sincerely,

cc: R. A. Smith   Helene Jenkins, Executive Vice-President

Fielding Complaint Letters

The President of the United States, desiring to know what's on his constituents' minds, as part of his official function periodically checks on the thousands of letters addressed to him weekly at the White House. Heads of corporations should care equally about the nature of the complaint mail arriving in their company's mail room—not just to see what the complaints are but also to check on how they are being answered and what follow-up action is being taken.

When management attends well to complaints about the company's services or products, it can often save the company millions of dollars. (It is also an executive's responsibility to write a careful letter of complaint when outside services his company uses prove inferior.)

Some companies receive thousands of letters of complaint every year. These are answered by form letters as much as possible. The fact that a form letter is used should not mean that management gives the complaint a low priority. Rather it should simply mean that management has advanced, sophisticated technology with which to answer high volume mail.

A computerized word processor that can automatically respond to about thirty different kinds of letters makes the logistics of answering mail fairly easy. One strong asset of such a computer is that the answer to any one letter may be duplicated in several copies. The original of the response letter would be marked with the names and titles of the other executives within the company who should receive a copy of the response. The recipient thus knows a lot of people will now be aware of his problem with the company. It's impressive and very good for the ego of the writer of the complaint letter.

The facet of advanced technology that must never be forgotten is the human side. No system can invent true kindness and thoughtfulness, so word processors can't be good guys automatically. A human being has to program them that way.

Even if a letter is impolite, the company answer should "keep its cool." The task of responding to critical mail in a small company should be given to someone who is gifted with words—and tact.

In general, a substantive letter of complaint should be answered within two weeks' time. If it is a small matter, the letter may be answered within a month's time. Keep in mind that the longer you wait to answer a letter of complaint, the more furious the writer may become. It is best to defuse a potentially unpleasant situation as soon as possible.

Letter in Response to Receipt of a Complaint

Dear Ms. Jenkins:

Your letter, which just reached me by messenger, deserves an equally rapid reply by messenger.

I agree that the invitations that reached you today were two weeks late, but you failed to mention that your own staff did not return the signed, approved design dummy until eight days after we had submitted it, nor did Mr. Smith, the Director of Special Events, release the printer's proofs until ten days after their delivery, so we are hardly responsible for the delay in delivering the invitations.

The person in my company whom I appointed to direct this rush job for you has answered, point by point, the objections raised in the memo you enclosed from your Mr. Smith, and I think you will find them clearly answered, one by one.

I am leaving the city in one hour on an emergency trip, but upon my return in two days, I will come to your office at a mutually agreeable time to discuss the entire matter.

I am very sorry that you are unable to use the invitations we printed, but I also feel that a fair study of the matter would show us not to be entirely responsible for your displeasure with our services. I look forward to discussing this with you in person.

Sincerely,

Henry Jones, Vice-President
Speed Printing Services

Encl: Memo on invitation job from
job supervisor

Acknowledging a Compliment

If someone writes you or the company to say something nice about you, the company, its products, or its services, an answering note signed by you or by someone in senior management should be mailed within two weeks of receipt of the letter.

Make sure that the writer of the original letter knows that everyone mentioned in a complimentary way within the letter will have seen that part: "I have shown Ms. Hawkins your letter so that she could read the delightful comments you made about her. She is very pleased." "I have circulated your letter through the entire corporate communications division, and everyone is grateful for your kind words of praise."

You can always sign off your acknowledging letter with a phrase such as this: "It is certainly nice to come across something as pleasant as your letter in my large pile of austere business mail. It makes my job a lot easier."

The Interoffice Memo

How you write memos provides a clue to your style of management as well as to your personality. A good memo can serve offensive or defensive purposes. It gives you the opportunity to capsulize or summarize everything important in a lengthy meeting or presentation. A good memo reveals your sense of humor, if you have one, and it certainly reflects your writing ability. What the memo is about should be immediately apparent and clearly expressed—and what response, if any, is expected. For example, if you write a memo intended to prompt action somewhere and your memo indicates

Who is to do what,

What should occur,

To whom it should occur, and

By when it should occur,

then you have written a useful memo.

A new executive in the company should be shown by Personnel or Human Resources (or a well-trained staff member) what the procedures are in writing and distributing memoranda within the organization.

These are some general guidelines to remember:

- A manager may criticize an employee in a memo, but it is preferable not to criticize one's fellow executives in a memo. Those criticisms are better made verbally than put on the record, where they might appear overly harsh or even unfair.
- It's wise not to complain about how much work something required. Management is not interested in the problems you encountered, but in the results, listed simply and explicitly.
- If you've been seriously delayed in taking action and someone is waiting to hear the results, memo that person about the delay, stating the reason for the delay and providing a new timetable. A memo is an efficient way to update another executive.
- If circumstances provide you an opportunity to praise someone, do so in a memo. This shows you are a secure and fair person and the object of your praise will not likely soon forget it: "Anderson really clinched the deal in those last few moments." "Jenkins was brilliant in shooting down their objections." "Agnes came forward with the compromise that saved us." "Henry softened him up perceptibly beforehand."
- Don't be known as a person who "manages by memo." Some individuals find it difficult to confront others in person; they hide behind the printed word rather than talk to a colleague or subordinate. A memo cannot replace a face-to-face meeting.
- A touch of humor is almost always a welcome relief, but don't let it distract the recipient from the real purpose of the memo.

- Don't write a flurry of memos just to justify your presence in a job. Generating a flood of unnecessary paper is criminal in any business office.
- Although a memo is a brief form of communication, good manners are still important. Phrases such as "Thank you very much for . . .", "I would really appreciate it if . . .", and "I'm sorry to have caused all of this extra work" are as necessary in a memo as they are in a formal letter.
- When you must criticize someone in a memo, say something nice before you say something that the recipient will not be pleased to hear. End the memo with a "thanks"; it softens the blow.

> . . . The presentation went well this morning for the most part. However, I had the feeling that the budgetary aspect could have been explained much more clearly, succinctly, and even interestingly. Perhaps audio-visuals would help. I hope you will give this your priority attention before the Florida presentation. Show me the changes as soon as possible, and thanks very much.

The Form of a Memo

There should be a definite policy on the form of interoffice memos sent by company people. For example:

July 2, 1987

MEMO FOR: Harriet Coe (Marketing)

Copy everyone who should be copied.

      cc: John Harrison (Marketing)
           Anthony Mendes (Personnel)

Put the message in the first paragraph . . . Praise is always welcome.

Your request for an additional staff member has been granted. Frankly, you prepared a terrific case for needing this person.

Sign off not too abruptly.

Proceed right away to find someone suitable. I look forward to talking to him or her when you have final candidates.

/s/ David Schellkopf
VP, Marketing

Communicating by Memo with a Person Whose Name You Don't Know

We are used to writing "Dear Sir," "Dear Madam," or "Gentlemen" when communicating with someone whose name and gender we do not know. There are three options for avoiding addressing a letter to someone by a title that does not correspond to his or her sex.

Straight Memo Form

MEMO FOR: Name of company to whom you're writing
                Address of company
                City, state, and ZIP
ATT: Section or Division
RE: Subject to be discussed
                (Text of memorandum follows.)

                Your signature and title

Simplified Letter Style

Name of company
Address of company
City, state, and ZIP
ATT: Section or Division
(Text of memorandum follows.)

Your signature and title

Memo-Letter Style

Name of company
Address of company
City, state, and ZIP

Ladies and Gentlemen:
(Text of memorandum follows.)

Sincerely,
Your signature and title

Letters of Friendship in Business

Many letters exchanged by business executives today could as well be called letters of friendship, because they are really reactions to something of a nonbusiness nature. Their mission is to please in some manner.

Letters to Congratulate or Mark Special Occasions

Be sure that you don't ruin a happy letter with bad news. When you are relaying good news or congratulations to someone, don't throw in negatives that could effectively destroy the cheer you meant to communicate. Avoid adding lines like "Did you know Spud is desperately ill and isn't going to make it?" or, "I think it's a shame Bill and Aggie are splitting on the eve of their fifteenth anniversary. They say that the kids are very upset."

Good News in a Colleague's Family

You must be some proud father! The first thing that hit my eye in this morning's paper was the announcement that Rufus Jr. has won the Stanford Alumni Club scholarship.

Your whole family must be celebrating. Even our family has declared a national holiday in honor of Rufus. Of course, he has done a lot on his own, but I think you will agree with me that his parents must take no little credit for his accomplishments. . . .

Congratulating Someone You Know Well

. . . Great news! You are climbing the ladder of success so fast that I'm dizzy looking up and trying to keep you in view. We're all celebrating for you.

Congratulating Someone You Don't Know Very Well

. . . Your new position is certainly a recognition of your contributions to this company during the past few years. No one is more deserving of the promotion and the added responsibilities it brings. We all wish you great luck.

Complimenting Someone on a Speech

. . . I was in the back of the ballroom today, so you probably didn't see me. Not only did you deliver your speech with a lot of punch, but what you had to say was important. I had no idea our Foreign Service career diplomats were in such need of support from us.

Congratulations on a first-rate job. I am ready to fire off cables to Congress!

Congratulating a Person on a Personal Triumph

. . . You won! All your old friends in this office really rejoiced when the final election results were announced and our favorite dark-horse colleague had won.

I wish I could have videotaped the reaction here at corporate headquarters. We'll miss you like crazy, but our loss is Washington's gain. Here's wishing you every success in your new life—but some fun in it, too. . . .

If you don't have time for a letter, two lines are sufficient:

Charlie,
I was there.
You wowed 'em. You're terrific!

An Executive Thanks His Staff for a Job Well Done

. . . Your group should feel proud of a job beautifully done and a thoroughly professional performance. The hard work and the polish clearly showed.

I hope you will express my personal thanks to everyone who pitched in to make our presentation a success; save a big vote of thanks for yourself, will you?

To an Employee on an Important Anniversary of Service

. . . This may be a proud day for you, but it is one for us, too, in this company. You have worked twenty-five years with *Monarch,* and during all of them you have given of your talent and worked hard. People with your enthusiasm and dedication are what has made the company the success it is today. You are as important as the management that runs this company and the products we sell.

Congratulations. I am proud to have you on the team, and here's wishing you another happy, healthy, productive twenty-five years with us.

Letters to Consolidate a Contact

You meet someone interesting who will be coming to your city on a business trip. You feel you would like to maintain the contact and develop a friendly, closer relationship.

. . . Just a quick line to say how much I enjoyed meeting you at the conference and exchanging experiences in this crazy business of ours. Let me know well in advance of your next trip to St. Louis. My wife and I will take you to dinner and show you this town's culinary distinctions.

All the best to you,

Letters of Encouragement

A letter written to someone who has just come through a very difficult time always means a great deal to the recipient. A colleague may just have been through a very messy court case, have returned from a tough rehabilitation program, or finished a long hospital stay. A note of encouragement is really appreciated.

If you know the person well, include a warm, personal compliment.

. . . Welcome back to us. You were missed for many reasons. First, because you're such a wonderful person, and second, because you're so good at what you do, no one around here can begin to replace you. We've all been sailing at half mast.

You have no idea how nice it is to have you "home" again.

If you don't know the person well, however, leave it at a simple statement that reflects a sincere sentiment without hyperbole:

> . . . Your return makes everyone in this office feel better. I hope you feel good as new. You were certainly missed by all of us.

Letters for Difficult Circumstances

Condolence Letters

Never hesitate to write a condolence letter, whether you are a very junior or a very senior member of management and whether the person who has lost someone in death is a very junior staff member or a very senior member of management. The two examples below may seem opposites in a way. One letter is from an executive to a young receptionist whose mother has just died. His letter is circumspect but warm. The other letter is from one executive to another who is a very close friend, on the occasion of the friend's wife's death. The same guidelines apply to both.

	To an employee who has lost a member of her family	*To a colleague who has lost his wife*
Explain how badly you feel about the news.	. . . Elsa has just told me the terrible news, and I want you and your family to know how sorry I am that you lost your mother.	. . . I don't know what to say, except that my heart is breaking for you.
Praise the person who has died. If you have some personal anecdote about the deceased, mention it.	I have heard from several sources that she was a wonderful woman and we all knew how close you were. These will probably be among the toughest days of your life.	Ginny was, quite simply, "the best of the best." Wife, mother, real estate agent, volunteer, she did everything with a careful, loving hand. The last time I saw her I marveled at her juggling abilities as she sold a client an apartment and three dozen Girl Scout cookies for little Ginny at the same time!

	To an employee who has lost a member of her family	*To a colleague who has lost his wife*
Make a concrete offer to be of help.	Your friends in this division are all thinking of you and wishing there was something we could do to help in this time of your terrible loss. Please call on us—for anything. . . .	We are all wandering around the office in a state of shock. We are actually suffering for you and waiting for your telephone call to press us into service. We are ready to answer phones, cook your meals, and handle any detail that needs handling for the funeral.

A Letter of Sympathy When There Is Bad News

I just heard the awful news that Ginny lost the baby today. What a terrible blow for you two to have such an occasion for joy turn into such an occasion for sorrow. I know it won't change anything, but you ought to know that all of your colleagues here are grieving right along with you.

When Someone Loses a Job

Your letter should take a positive approach. Talk about action in locating the new job. Don't just commiserate.

I just heard the bad news. It may be pulverizing to you right now, but think about all that talent and experience you have amassed. You'll probably find something you like a great deal more, and in a company where your talents will be fully appreciated.

To me you are a winner. This is a temporary setback only. Why don't you call me to tell me when you and Jean can come for dinner, so we can talk about your future in a leisurely fashion? I've got some ideas, and I'm sure you do, too. . . .

Letter of Apology

Apologies rarely come easy. It's always uncomfortable facing up to the fact that you've inconvenienced, embarrassed, or offended someone. You'd just as soon forget it. The difficulty is that not acknowledging your failing or error in a given situation is only likely to result in ill feelings hardening against you. Biting the bullet and expressing your sincere regret, on the other hand, will often regain you whatever goodwill you might otherwise have forfeited.

Here's a sample apology for a particularly inappropriate behavior. Note that a lack of intention to give offense is not really an adequate excuse. The apology here is for an unintentional racial slur delivered in front of a person of the race mentioned.

> . . . This is probably the hardest letter I have ever had to write, because I've never been so wrong or acted in such a shameful way.
>
> My remark this morning was reprehensible, uncalled for, and totally unforgiveable. But I'm asking you to forgive me anyway. I hurt you, but I hope you will show me all of the mercy I seem to lack myself.
>
> I promise never again to think, much less express, a remark like that. I hope you are big enough to forget my lamentable behavior.

Letters Marking a Time of Transition

Mergers and company reorganizations often create upset or apprehension among executives and lower echelon staff members. In a time of emotion like that, acknowledging the pain of transition can mean a great deal to the recipient. This is especially true when a company is merged out of existence.

The following is a letter sent to all of the trustees and executive staff members of the New York Bank for Savings when the bank was merged out of existence in the spring of 1982. The writer, Charles J. Urstadt (chairman of Pearce, Urstadt, Mayer & Greer Inc.), was for many years a trustee of the bank.

March 30, 1982

Trustees and Executive Staff
The New York Bank for Savings
1230 Avenue of the Americas
New York, N.Y. 10020

Dear Friends:

Last Friday a great institution quietly disappeared. It was both a significant and sad event and to me it was a great personal loss because of many enjoyable years I had spent as a small part of it.

We will probably not get together again so I would like to take this moment to express to each and every one of the trustees and to the staff and, in particular, to Gene Callan, my gratitude and admiration for the relative ease and lack of pain which this transition entailed. I have been a party to many small and less momentous liquidations and none have gone as smoothly as this one. It is a great tribute to all concerned.

I also want to express my gratitude to all of you for the many enjoyable constructive meetings which we have all shared. It was great to be part of this institution and its leadership team. It has been a time I will always cherish.

My deepest and best regards to each and every one. I hope our paths cross in the future.

Sincerely,

(s) Charlie Urstadt

Letters of Acknowledgment and Thanks

Many people feel that a word of thanks on the telephone is sufficient acknowledgment for a favor, gift, or invitation. This definitely is not so. A hand-written (or typed) note is a hundred times more effective and more appreciated than a telephone call. It is not only a permanent record of thanks from the sender but something that can be passed around and enjoyed by others, too. If you make a telephone call, you may be intruding at the wrong moment on the other person's privacy. The person you are trying to thank may be in the middle of an important meeting or, if you call him at home, in the middle of cooking, taking a shower, or trying to relax over a cocktail for the first time that day. Your telephone call may suit *your* schedule, but often it will not suit the other person's schedule.

It is well to remember when writing an acknowledgment that:

- It should be written on proper stationery, not just on any piece of paper and a mismatched envelope.
- It should be hand-written if your penmanship is good; otherwise it should be typed.
- If more than one person at the receiving address should be thanked, ask the recipient to convey your message to the others. Mention them even if you don't know the names: "Please tell your secretary how indebted I am for all her hard work on the project. . . ."
- *Thank-you notes should be kept brief and without hackneyed phrases.* James T. Mills, president of the Conference Board and a prodigious note-writer, emphasizes this strongly. "Thank you very much" should be said only once in a letter. I remember well the letter that Ezra Zilkha, the New York financier and director of a big insurance corporation, wrote to thank Ralph Saul, the insurance company's chairman, for the special gift of a wood and bronze plaque engraved with the name of every director who had sat in the historic chair now occupied by Ezra at board meetings. Careful research had been done to ensure that all the directors who had used that chair since 1792 were included on the plaque. Ezra's note was characteristically brief:

Dear Ralph:

I received today the plaque engraved with the names of the various occupants of my chair at INA. It made me think of the number of times we have talked of the "legacy." Just looking at the plaque reminds me that as directors we are there in a transient manner, making sure we will improve in the future what the past has created. Thank you.

- A "canned" acknowledgment is appropriate for an excessive amount of mail.

There are times when a company or an individual within the company receives hundreds of letters from friends, stockholders, and the general public. When this occurs, a "canned" acknowledgment letter may be sent. The recipient's name, address, and the personal salutation are typed into the word processor, but the same form letter is sent to each individual. When an executive dies, the company may send in reply (to mail, flowers, and other expressions of condolence) either a letter or an engraved or printed card of acknowledgment.

The personalization of these letters and cards is still an important factor. By personalization I mean a short hand-written phrase across the bottom of the letter or card. For example, an executive might write (remembering always to sign his initials afterward, even though he has signed the letter):

> *On the occasion of the death of a fellow executive:* "You have no idea how much your good wishes to mean to us. . . ."
> *On the occasion of an important company anniversary:* "How nice of you to write. We are all very proud of our company."
> *When he has been raised to a very senior level in the company:* ". . . Of course, I feel very proud, happy, and challenged, too. . . ."

- *Don't sneak a favor request into your thank-you letter.* A letter of thanks is supposed to be an expression of gratitude. If you ask for a favor or a donation or anything that requires the recipient of your letter to take positive action, you have ruined the impact of your thank-you gesture. (Any favor you wish to ask should be expressed in a different letter sent at another time.)

Thanking a Colleague Who Defends You

. . . I heard what happened in the Boardroom this morning—that you stood up and supported my views on the Wallace report, regardless of the criticism I have received in the past few weeks.

It is difficult to express my gratitude in words, because if you hadn't said what you did, my association with this company might be in great jeopardy.

Some day I hope I can return this act of friendship. I am most definitely in your debt.

Gratefully,

Thanking Those Who Volunteer on a Major Project

There are many industry-wide projects that require one person to supervise others in the same business but not necessarily in the same company who volunteer their services. It may be a benefit for charity, a sports tournament staged for the good of the employees, social events at an industry meeting, or something similar. It is important for the person managing the event to write thank-you letters—the next day—to the manager of any division (or company) that donated its time and talent:

> . . . Our awards banquet would never have taken place if you and your staff hadn't pitched in to save the night for me. Your group provided me with brains and brawn, all sorely needed. I will never be able to thank you enough.
>
> My staff and I really enjoyed working with you, because, quite miraculously, everyone's good nature, sense of humor, and imagination never stopped functioning, in spite of all the crises. You were my great White Knights, come to the rescue.
>
> I owe you several lunches, Mike. I'll be in touch. . . .

Thanking for a Job Interview

A letter to the person who interviews you should go out no later than twenty-four hours after seeing him; if you are a "hot prospect," have it delivered by hand.

Note to the Interviewer

> . . . You were very nice to see me today in the middle of such a full schedule. It was profitable for me to listen to your comments on the direction of J. H. Cutter & Sons. I hope I will be seriously considered as a candidate for the position we discussed, because I feel I have the necessary experience, incentive, and drive to do a great job for the company in that slot.
>
> The atmosphere in your offices, the company's widespread reputation for quality products, and the obvious dedication of everyone I met there make me even more enthusiastic at the prospect of joining the company.
>
> I will wait to hear from you with a great sense of hope.

Note to the Person Who Arranged for You
to Have the Interview

. . . Mr. Reinhardt and I, thanks to your miraculous intervention, spent over an hour today discussing the position at J. H. Cutter. It is a job I want *very much,* not just a little.

It was your call that did the trick in getting me in to see him. It was because of your call that he did not settle on another person whom he had "on hold" for the slot. I am now playing the waiting game, hoping to hear affirmatively. If I do get the position, I'm going to invite you to a victory celebration worthy of my esteem for you—which means it will be *some* celebration!

Writing a Journalist After an Interview

Following your appearance on a television or radio interview show, either the show's producer or the interviewer deserves a note of thanks for having given you the opportunity to communicate your message. The rare people who do write to thank the media are always remembered.

Thanking a Broadcast Journalist

. . . You were very kind to invite me to appear on the "Afternoon Show." You and Elena Enriquez make an excellent interview team, and you handled my subject with great intelligence and taste.

I appreciate your letting me give my side of the story. The fact that you are successful was proven by the number of people who told me that they saw the program the day I was your guest, and that they watch it regularly.

I enjoyed being your guest. Thank you.

Thanking a Print Media Journalist

Your story was on target and very well written. I congratulate you for presenting the subject in an accurate, interesting, even humorous manner. The occasional negatives you mentioned were fair. Thank you!

Thanking When You Have Been Treated Unfairly

. . . I appreciate the fact that you took so much time and effort to profile this company in your story. However, in fairness to me, your readers, and the public, I must point out some grossly inaccurate statements that were made: (List them)

I have the greatest respect for you as a journalist, so I hope that with this revelation of inaccuracies, you will be able to publish some kind of retraction. I thank you for anything you might be able to do. . . .

Thanking for a Meal

If someone buys you lunch, a short note of thanks is in order, whether you had lobster in an expensive seafood place or a fruit salad in a tearoom. Even if the person who took you to lunch was trying to negotiate a business deal with you or was paying you back for a favor rendered, you still have an obligation, manners-wise, to write a thank-you note.

The old tradition decreeing that it's the wife's sole responsibility to handle all thank-you notes no longer holds true in this era of supposed equality. For meals in which spouses are not present, the executive obviously thanks his host himself. For meals in which the couple is present and both people work, either spouse should write the thank-you note. It does not matter if the executive or his wife (or the executive or her husband) writes the host or hostess to say thank you on behalf of the couple. What *does* matter is that the letter be written and sent within three or four days of the meal.

A Good Friend Takes You to an Informal Lunch

. . . Many thanks for the nice lunch yesterday. It was great catching up with you, and your new position sounds perfect. Congratulations on landing it!

I know it won't be so long before we lunch again. I'll call you in a few weeks to set a time and place. . . .

Someone Who's in Your Business Debt
Takes You to Lunch

. . . Lunch was very pleasant yesterday. I'm glad you got our account, because the presentation you and your team made was better than anyone's. I know we can expect great things from you.

A Colleague Invites You Home for Dinner

This requires a much more careful note.

. . . Amy and I enjoyed ourselves thoroughly last evening. What a superb dinner you gave us! Amy said she has never seen such pretty lilacs. I concentrated more on the lemon souffle for dessert. We particularly enjoyed meeting those attractive children of yours.

One of the nice results of having been transferred here are the new friends we have made and the warm welcome we have experienced. We both want to thank you very much for last night. . . .

Thanking Management for Gifts

Corporate America seems to think it is entitled to free gifts of products, tickets to evening charity events, tickets to the company box at the opera or the baseball game, etc. Many executives consider these as regular perks to which they have every right. As a result, when a thank-you letter is written to senior managers, they usually pass it around, partly in pleasure, partly in shock at having received it! Here are some sample letters management would enjoy receiving:

For the Annual Christmas Gift

. . . Our whole family greatly enjoyed the plump, juicy turkey at our traditional Christmas lunch. The company gift has become a much-loved tradition in our family, so I thank you and the officers of the company on behalf of my family for a most welcome holiday gesture. . . .

For Free Tickets to the Game

. . . You are most definitely the hero of the entire family, particularly since the Cubs' victory yesterday was such a spectacular one. Our seats were excellent; for the first time the kids were able to identify the players by their forms and faces, not just by their numbers. It was a day of great excitement.

Helen, Toby, and Warren join me in thanking you for a very special gift. . . .

For Tickets to the Benefit

. . . Your benefit tickets were well used by us last night. Roland James, our dates, and I represented the company last night at the Premio D'Oro dinner at the Remington.

The operatic solos were absolutely magnificent. The dinner was excellent (and so were the wines), and we got to meet the Mayor and his wife. We also did a lot of dancing.

Thank you for giving us the company tickets. We had a great time—and the cause was certainly a worthy one, too.

Thanking for a Corporate Giveaway (However Small)

. . . The new *Treatco* calendar has just arrived, once again in time to mark all of my business appointments, and my New Year's resolutions, too.

Thank you. I look forward to this nifty calendar each year. Always keep me on your mailing list, and have a wonderful new year yourself!

Thanking for a Gift of a New Product

. . . The new water gadget is first-rate. We immediately hooked it up to our faucet and it works! It was easy to install, it is easy to use, and it does a very effective job. I'm sure your company has a winner with this one. Thanks so much for remembering us this Christmas, and for letting us be one of the lucky ones to try out the new product.

Have a wonderful holiday, and good luck with the launch. . . .

Thanking a Colleague for a Personal Gift

If a colleague gives you a gift—for a reason or just for friendship's sake—you should not just thank him on the spot or on the telephone. Write him a note. Tell him how or when you are going to use it:

> . . . The Swiss chocolate you brought back from Zurich has turned not only me but my entire staff into chocoholics. The box was so enormous I had to share it with them, although I am now rather sorry I did. There are furtive glances and footsteps creeping into my office during the entire day, as they try to snitch some more.

> I marvel at how nice you are to have lugged that huge box back on the plane. I guess you knew that, next to winning the state lottery, I love the taste of chocolate best!

Thanking for an Inappropriate Gift

There are times in life when we might receive a very inappropriate gift from a business acquaintance—such as something for your garage when you don't have one, or a sprinkler for a lawn you don't have. It's better to thank the person and *not* return the gift. (Give it to a good friend.)

The following is a sample letter from a recovering alcoholic to a person who sent a case of liquor:

> . . . It was a pleasant surprise to receive the nice gift from you and the company this holiday season. I appreciate the thought and send you and your family every good wish for the holidays. . . .

Politely Refusing a Gift

At times you may be in the position of not wishing to accept a gift from another executive. Great tact is called for in returning the gift. That is, after all, a very tough rejection for the sender. Phrase your response in a positive tone. (*See also* Giving and Returning the Inappropriate Gift, in Chapter 16.)

> . . . You were so kind to think of me this Christmas. Your gift was much too generous, however. There is a strict company policy governing the acceptance of gifts, and everyone of us has to comply. I must therefore return your wonderful present. I know how much thought you put into obtaining it.

> Thanks for the thought, and I wish you a healthy, happy successful New Year.

Thanking the Boss for a Present Marking a Major Occasion

	When the Executive Writes	When the Executive's Spouse Writes
Mention what the gift is, how pleased you are and how you are going to use it.	. . . Rowena and I are delighted with the handsome leather frame you and Mrs. Winfield sent us for our wedding. It is ideal for our big colored wedding picture. The fact that our joint initials and the wedding date are embossed on the frame makes it all the more special.	. . . Malcolm and I consider your wedding present one of the greatest we have received. The frame with its good tooling is the perfect size for our formal wedding portrait, and it looks very impressive on the hall table. In fact, when you open the door to our apartment, it's the first thing you see.
Explain why it is so useful.	You could not have chosen anything that was more needed, since we do not possess one frame! And even if we had looked hard, we never could have found one as handsome as the one you had made for us. I hope we can get our apartment in shape so that one day you will come visit and see how we are using your wedding present.	I hope it won't be too long before we can have guests. I have a job to do first in bringing order out of chaos, but I did want you to know how much your beautiful wedding present means to us. I look forward to meeting you both.
Express the hope that the giver will come to call one day to be able to see how well it looks.		

Retirement Letters

The occasion of retirement calls for an intricate exchange of letters, many of which are put in the retiree's scrapbook and handed down to posterity:

- Letter from the retiree to his or her superior, expressing his love for the company and his sadness at leaving
- Letter from the retiree's supervisor to the retiree, expressing everyone's sadness to see such a valued team member depart
- Letter from the retiree to his successor, wishing him happiness and success in the job
- Letters from the retiree's personal friends, wishing him well
- Letters from the retiree to everyone who wrote him or sent him a gift

Here are some examples:

From Retiring Employee to CEO

. . . AXCO's observance of my retirement was one of the nicest things that ever happened to me. The reception in the Executive Dining Room came as a total surprise. I still can't believe so many people turned out to honor me.

The handsome leather scrapbook will be the perfect sentimental reminder of all my years of service. It will take me a long time to place all of my pictures, clippings, and mementos in the book. I look forward to the task.

This letter is a very small expression of my gratitude to everyone responsible for making my retirement such a special occasion. My memories of this company and of everyone connected with it will be cherished for as long as I live. . . .

From the Retiring Senior Manager to the CEO

. . . It's hard for me to realize, much less accept the truth: that the time has come to go. I keep telling myself that retiring from this company is not retiring from life, and yet it is difficult to separate the two in my mind.

I have enjoyed my eighteen years with Aquarius for so many reasons, it would take me a book to list them all. Mainly, I will miss the people around here, all working enthusiastically for a common cause under your leadership. I will miss the feeling of camaraderie, the joy of watching the efficient interaction of our divisions on major projects, and the total satisfaction of a feeling of individual accomplishment.

This company is the best. Its management is the best. Its employees are the best. Its customers are the best. I will miss it every day of my life. . . .

CEO's Response to the Above Letter

. . . If your retirement is difficult for you to accept, let me assure you that it is *impossible* for me to accept! You were the backbone of your group. I wonder if we'll know how to grow another one. I hope you will think of us, floundering and wondering which way to turn while you're pondering your next shot on the 10th hole.

You deserve to be on that golf course, and Ruth deserves to have you with her after all those years of spending all your time working your way through our problems. Her gain is our loss. I hope you'll always remember that.

Your sad friends bid you farewell.

Letter from a Personal Friend to the Retiree

. . . The time has come to sleep that extra hour in the morning and not worry about whether the ice scraper for the windshield is in the glove compartment—and not panic when Miss Sidwell's word processor goes on the blink. Now you can finally read all those books on growing herbs you've never had time to read. In fact, you can start actually growing those herbs instead of just talking about them!

It's a big change in your life, sure, but it also means your friends like me will have more of a chance to see you, so as far as I'm concerned, it's a change for the better. . . .

4

Dressing
for Business

There is an art to dressing well in the workplace. In a sense each business has its own dress code, a framework within which an executive can be as creative as he pleases as long as it is appropriate for that business.

The appearance of an executive is more important in some businesses than in others. Someone engaged in handling people's money, for example, should be carefully, conservatively dressed; someone engaged in solely creative work can dress for action and comfort, not image. I overheard a lawyer giving one of his young colleagues a lecture on his unkempt appearance. "Only an eccentric worth over ten million can afford not to care," he said, "and you've got a long way to go before you get there. You'd better clean up and dress up if you're going to be a member of *this* firm!"

The way a person dresses for work is more formal in some places than in others. In southern California, Florida, and Texas, many business people dress casually, while a place like New York, according to *New York Times* reporter Enid Nemy, "is so subtly attuned to nuances that a see-through plastic handbag carried by a woman or a pair of white socks on a man without a tennis racket can put a major crimp in a promising career."

Dressing Sense

There are countless subtleties in knowing how to dress, and many of them are learned only through personal experience and close observation of what seems right as opposed to what seems slightly off or totally inappropriate. *Right* is when a man appears in a dark blue suit for a cocktail party, and *wrong* is when a woman appears in a black silk crepe dress with a sequin trim at an afternoon event. *Right* is when you wear your favorite tailored shirtwaist cotton dress on the golf course or shopping at the supermarket; *wrong* is when you wear that dress to a lunch in the city. *Right* is when you show up at a six o'clock business cocktail party in your best silk dress; *wrong* is when you show up in a heavy tweed sport suit. *Right* is when a man wears a yellow linen coat and white ducks at a summer resort cocktail party; *wrong* is when he dresses like that for a summer cocktail party in downtown Chicago.

There is no doubt but that a young executive who does not know how to dress will be held back in his or her career. It's unfair that something so artificial should be so important, but it's a fact of life. A person dressed quietly in fashion, in what is obviously quality clothing and appropriate for his or her business life, projects a strong quality image for his or her business.

Before buying apparel, an executive should ask three questions of him- or herself:

- Considering my job and the company for which I work, is this appropriate for me to wear?
- Is it good basic fashion or is it faddish?
- Is it a good style for my kind of body?
- Does it fit properly?
- Is it right for *this* season?
- Are the fabric and the cut of top quality, so that it can stay in my wardrobe for several seasons?

Every time you dress for a business situation you must go through the decision process all over again. You must choose, combine, and accessorize so that you will arrive at your destination properly dressed and feeling confident.

Where to Go for Help

The logical resources for fashion assistance are the fashion magazines and the fashion sections of the newspapers. Don't use television as your authority.

Fashion publications help you understand contemporary trends, but you must still "edit" the material yourself for your age, figure, and position before blindly barging ahead and buying whatever is shown in the photographs. For example, you might find a five-page spread in *Vogue* on a hot new Japanese designer's work, with everything done in a wild, exaggerated way. That spread is meant to show you future trends, not what you should wear to the office.

These are some other sources of help in dressing wisely:

- The on-staff fashion consultant in a department or specialty store
- A free-lance fashion consultant who will charge you by the hour or by the half-day to take you shopping and advise you
- A friend who has obvious fashion sense and whose clothes and "look" are admired by everyone

A Few Basic Do's and Don'ts

- A man should be careful not to apply too much fragrance in a conservative office, because a little goes a long way. (The application of after-shave lotion, of course, is accepted everywhere.)
- If you were to ask people what aspects of a person's appearance upsets them the most, you would find a surprising number who say:

  > When a woman's slip strap shows or she has a bad run in her stocking
  > When a man's hairy leg (or unhairy leg, for that matter) shows between the top of his sock and the bottom of his trousers

- People should be very wary of dressing in clothes that are too tight. If you gain weight, either lose it or have your clothes let out. If you wear something that is too small, your weight problem is visually magnified several times.
- Men or women who wear running shoes to parties after work are, in my opinion, insulting their hosts. When they wear them in the office, they are insulting their bosses.
- No one should brag about the famous designer label in his or her clothes. Half the time the people you brag to will not have heard of the designer anyway. It is much better to let fashion-conscious people "discover" who the designer is.
- Women should avoid wearing dressy fabrics to the office that are really only suitable for evening—e.g., satin, brocade, cut velvet, lamé, etc.
- Nothing is more attractive to both men and women than a rancher dressed in his own Western clothes. But when a city dude insists on wearing to his office a Stetson, cowboy boots, a fake rodeo prize buckle, and a string tie, he looks ridiculous rather than authentic.
- As a general rule in non–summer resort areas, put away your white shoes and handbags the day after Labor Day, and don't bring them out again before late May.

Jacket Etiquette

- A double-breasted jacket on a man or woman is meant to be left buttoned, and not hang open (it looks very awkward and bulky if left open).
- A man who often works without his jacket in an office should never wear short-sleeved shirts. The latter are meant never to be seen. Long-sleeved shirts look much better, even when they are rolled up to the elbows in the heat.
- If you are working without your jacket in the office and you go to see the big boss, put on your jacket. The same goes, of course, if an outside client or customer comes into your office, or anyone of importance from the outside. It's a sign of deference.
- A woman who has doffed her jacket in the office should put it on again in the very same circumstances that govern when a man should put his on again.

Grooming

Grooming is the cornerstone of a good appearance.

Grooming Kits

Executives should keep grooming kits somewhere in the office, to use for freshening up during the day and in preparation for after-office social events. A grooming kit might consist of the following:

For Men	*For Women*
Toothbrush and toothpaste	Toothbrush and toothpaste
Mouthwash	Mouthwash
Comb and brush	Comb and brush
Hairspray	Hairspray
Razor	Makeup paraphernalia
After-shave cologne or fragrance	Fragrance
Shoe buffing kit	Shoe grooming kit
	Sewing kit
	Extra hosiery

Grooming Checklist

If you want to be master of this important subject, post a grooming checklist in your home. Refer to it in the morning before you leave for the office. After you are dressed and ready to leave, check out what people will see when they see *you.*

HEAD-TO-TOE MORNING GROOMING CHECKLIST

	For a Man	*For a Woman*	*For Men and Women*
Head	Well-shaven After-shave applied Beard and/or mustache well trimmed	Makeup carefully applied Eyebrows plucked Earrings and/or necklace polished and clean If wearing a scarf, it is unspotted and pressed	Hair well brushed, well combed, well cut, clean Face well washed Ears clean Neck washed
Body	Clean shirt Collar and cuffs checked for fraying Spotless well-tied tie	Fragrance applied sparingly No makeup on top of dress, blouse, or sweater Slip does not show	Body well washed Deodorant applied Underwear fresh Clothes spot-free and well pressed No buttons missing Clean handkerchief Check for dandruff "fallout"
Hands		Nail polish in perfect condition Hand lotion applied	Hands washed Nails clean and in good shape Rings clean and free from soap film Watchband in good shape
Legs and Feet	Clean socks pulled up high Laces on shoes or tassels on loafers in good shape	Pantyhose run-free If seamed, seams are straight	Shoes well-polished and free of scuff marks Shoe heels in good shape
Handbag and/or Briefcase			Leather clean and polished Hardware polished
Gloves			Clean

Hair

When someone looks at you, one of the first things they notice is your hair. No CEO wants the company image affected by its executives' avant garde hair styling—unless, of course, it is in the business of making rock stars' video albums!

Your hairstyle can be in fashion without being flamboyant. A man with long hair or an exaggerated Afro looks as though he is fighting the establishment instead of working for it.

Beards and mustaches come and go in fashion. Many senior executives do not like them but suffer in silence over their middle managers' tonsorial peculiarities. There is something nicely nondistracting about the direct gaze of a man who is clean-shaven and whose facial characteristics are clearly visible instead of being hidden by hair. Again, it is important to distinguish between a creative or intellectual environment, such as teaching and writing (in which an abundance of facial hair is fashionable), and a conservative business environment (in which facial hair is considered distracting).

A woman with long straight hair down her back, "flower child" style, may give the impression she is clinging obsessively to her youth, which immediately makes her seem much older. A woman who frizzes her hair all over and wears it "tangled jungle vines" style may look to others like an oversized scouring pad. A woman who teases her hair to the maximum should realize that the style is passé and improper for the office. A woman should be remembered for what is *inside* her head, not what is growing on top of it!

Here are some other hair grooming points for women to consider:

- *Keep your hair neatly combed or brushed at all times,* but don't fix it in front of others.
- Don't overdose your colleagues with the fumes from your hairspray.
- Make an unbreakable promise to yourself *never* to be seen in public in hair curlers.
- *Keep your hands off your hair.* Constantly stroking the ends of your hair or pushing it back from your face are nervous, very distracting habits. It is particularly important not to touch your hair in a restaurant. I will never forget lunching with a lawyer in a restaurant in full view of a young woman constantly combing through her long hair with her fingers. The lawyer mentioned that there was something unappetizingly analogous between what she was doing and what he was trying to do, eat his way through a plate of thin spaghetti with a fork.

Hair Coloring, Wigs, and Hairpieces

Whether someone dyes his or her hair was considered a forbidden subject until about 1950. Until that date, it was something "one really didn't do," except that people did it anyway, in secret—having their hair color applied in curtained booths and even making their appointments under assumed names. The only men who one assumed dyed their hair before that period in America were aging movie stars and gangsters.

Today hair dye and wigs are universally popular. In spite of their popularity, one should still remember points such as these:

- No matter how common the practice is, it is still rude to ask a person point blank about his or her hair dye, hairpiece, or wig.
- A woman executive who wears a wig should keep it styled in a conservative manner, again so that someone doing business with her will pay attention to the business at hand and not to her curls, bangs, and waves.
- A woman executive should refrain from wearing wigs of different colors or drastically changing her own hair color from time to time. This confuses people. It makes her seem somewhat schizophrenic to them.
- It is better for a man *not* to wear a hairpiece than to wear an inexpensive one, one that doesn't fit, or one that is obviously completely artificial. Before a man starts wearing a toupee, he should remember that it's a turn-off to many people. If a market research study were to be made, with questions asked of his friends and associates, the chances are that the majority would say they prefer his baldness to his hairpiece. It is, however, a man's choice and not his friends' to make. If he feels strongly that he looks younger and better with a hairpiece, then he probably does.

Makeup

Cosmetics undoubtedly enhance a woman's appearance. When deftly applied they disguise faults and highlight attributes, but when applied with a heavy hand, they accentuate faults and disguise attributes. The face that is excessively made up becomes distracting.

A smart woman realizes that for her office life "less is *truly* more." She never wants her makeup to be the first thing one notices about her. She therefore uses less makeup at the office than she does in her leisure hours.

The same rule governs cosmetics that governs wearing jewelry to the office. Put on what you please but, before going out the door, subtract something. Check your face with a critical eye, and then remove something, lighten something, or blend whatever is exaggerated.

The maximum amount of makeup needed for the office would be:

- Moisturizer
- A foundation that is either colorless or that exactly matches your own skin tones
- A light dusting of powder
- A light application of blusher to the cheekbones
- A very thin eyeliner, not too dark, applied so that others are not really aware of it (which means no bright colors in eyeliner)
- Eyebrow pencil (lightly applied, following the contours of the natural brows)

Eye shadow and thick mascara do not belong in the office. Neither do beauty products such as false eyelashes, gold-tinted powder, artificial beauty marks, and other attention-getters.

Business women should automatically blot their lipstick before a meeting or meal where liquids will be served. There is nothing more unattractive than a glass, mug, or cup emblazoned with a ring of greasy lipstick—suddenly the woman's seriousness is erased. If she blots her lips beforehand with a tissue, her lipstick will stay on her mouth.

Nails

Clean, well-shaped nails and a healthy cuticle are as important to a man's appearance as they are to a woman's. Hands are on constant view and are an important part of one's executive presence. Dirty, bitten-down nails give a strong negative impression.

A woman who wears nail polish should use a quiet color—again, the antithesis of distraction. Long sharp nails covered in bright red or "passionate purple" are a magnet for everyone's attention. A woman who is proud of her overly long nails should balance her career development against her personal preferences in fingernails!

Fragrance for a Woman

Perfume belongs in an office only if subtly applied, so that the people who sense it are only slightly aware of it.

There aren't any "businesslike perfumes." Buy what pleases you, but remember:

- Buy good perfume and cologne; the "cheap stuff" is worse than a cheap cigar.
- Apply fragrance sparingly and in private. (It's as personal an act as combing your hair.)

A Male Executive's Wardrobe

Here's a listing of a suitable wardrobe for the young manager beginning his career and for an established mid-manager (we assume that their bosses have learned what their wardrobe needs are as they have climbed the corporate ladder):

Young Manager	*Mid-Manager*
3 winter suits (perhaps a dark blue or dark blue pinstripe, gray flannel, and lighter glen plaid)	5 winter suits
3 summer suits (perhaps a lightweight pinstripe, a tan and a navy poplin, or a seersucker)	5 summer suits
1 lightweight navy blazer, to wear winter and summer	2 navy blazers (winter and summer weight)
1 tweed sports jacket for leisure wear	2 tweed sports jackets
2 pairs odd trousers, one of which is gray flannel	2 pairs odd trousers
3 pairs casual trousers (jeans, khaki, corduroy)	4 pairs casual trousers
3 pullover sweaters	5 pullover sweaters
12 pairs daytime socks; 4 pairs athletic socks	14 pairs daytime socks; 8 pairs athletic socks
1 topcoat or overcoat, depending on climate	1 topcoat and 1 overcoat to wear in any climate
1 raincoat	1 raincoat
12 business dress shirts	24 business dress shirts
8 sports (or polo) shirts	12 sports (polo) shirts
12 ties	20 ties
3 belts (black, brown, striped sports belt)	4 belts
2 pairs daytime shoes (brown and black)	4 pairs daytime shoes
14 sets underwear	14 sets underwear
3 pairs summer weight and 3 pairs of winter weight pajamas	5 pairs of pajamas
1 dressing gown for travel	Bathrobe and travel dressing gown
1 pair bedroom slippers for travel	2 pairs bedroom slippers (winter and summer)

Young Manager	*Mid-Manager*
Action sports clothes for his sports, including winter sports	(the same)
Jogging clothes and summer warmup suits, shorts, and T-shirts	(the same)
Athletic shoes for his sports (running shoes, ski boots, etc.)	(the same)
Hiking or work boots, if appropriate	(the same)
Boat moccasins or another sports shoe	(the same)

Black-Tie Requirements

Lightweight dinner suit

2 evening dress shirts

2 black bow ties

Suspenders (or braces)

1 pair black patent laced shoes (or pumps with bows)

2 pairs black evening hose

Suits in the Office

An executive should invest in a minimum of three well-cut suits made of a top quality fabric. (An expensive suit looks better and lasts longer, so it is a better investment.) Obviously, the higher he progresses in his career, the more suits will be hung in his closet.

If when ordering a new suit he feels unsure about fashion trends (such as shoulder shape, one or two vents in the back of the jacket, a change of width of the lapels, trousers to be cuffed or not cuffed, etc.), he should seek the advice of a well-dressed peer.

A single-breasted jacket is slimming and looks good on everyone; a double-breasted one looks very good on a well-proportioned man who is not too heavy. The three-piece suit, of course, is the most formal daytime look of all, but is worn much less now by older executives (who feel it is a badge of young executives trying to look older).

A lightweight navy blazer worn with gray trousers is an important ingredient in an executive's life away from the office. This combination may be worn in the summer in large cities, often in place of a business suit, as well as in resort cities in any season.

A person with a weight problem should remember these factors when selecting his fabric for a new suit:

- Dark solids are the most slimming.
- Subtle patterns are much more slimming than big, bold ones.

Shirts and Ties

The way a man assembles his shirt and tie should not be haphazard exercise. It should be carefully thought out as to color and pattern coordination.

The Shirt

· May be a button-down or plain pointed collar style
· May have button cuffs or the much more formal "French cuffs" (which require cufflinks)
· May be a "town shirt," with contrasting white collar and cuffs—worn around the clock by the Eastern establishment, but only on dress occasions in many other communities
· Should have sleeves long enough so that the cuff extends about an inch beyond the jacket sleeve

A view of a man's undershirt (T-shirt) when he is relaxing with his shirt collar open is as unsightly as a woman's slip strap showing. A man who wears a high T-shirt should keep his collar buttoned; if he wears his collar unbuttoned at home, for the sake of everyone else present, he should wear an undershirt low enough not to show at the neck.

The Tie

The four-in-hand tie should be chosen according to how it will coordinate with the suit and shirt already selected for wear in the morning. The man with a sense of color and an observant eye can be creative in mixing his shirt and tie colors; otherwise he should stick to the tried and true color combinations.

The width of men's ties varies with fashion changes. If an executive has a closet full of wide ties, and the current fashion is slim ties, he can have the wide ties cut to a narrower width. If he has a closet full of narrow ties, he should save them until they come back in style again. A man who has no fashion sense should just use his eyes to notice what width of tie all the men around him are wearing (plus look at the men's fashion magazines, particularly at the advertisements for shirts).

A man who is very tall should buy extra-length ties at a big man's store or have his ties custom-made for the proper length. A man who is very small can have his ties shortened to the proper proportion for his body.

The "cutesie tie" with the funny message or design printed on it is amusing and appropriate only for an executive's leisure hours. In the office this kind of tie looks juvenile or just plain silly.

A bow tie makes a man look young and sometimes whimsical. If worn constantly, it becomes a kind of trademark for that executive—others describe him "as the one with the bow tie." If a man wishes this kind of trademark, there's nothing in the rules of dressing that says he should not adopt it.

The Conservative Look

Banking and finance are business areas that call for conservative dress. A man who deals in trusts and estates, for example, should wear conservative shirts and ties in combinations along the following lines:

- A white shirt with a quiet tie (somber colors, quiet stripes and patterns that are not strong)
- A subtly striped shirt with a solid tie or a quietly patterned one

The Young Manager's Look

A younger person in another kind of job does not have to be as conservatively dressed as above, unless he is in an ultraconservative business. With his suits he might wear these combinations:

- A pale yellow shirt with blue and yellow striped or foulard pattern tie
- A pale blue shirt with a blue pattern tie or a red, white, and blue pattern
- A pale pink shirt with a tie in which the predominant color is red
- A brightly striped shirt (candy stripe) with a very quiet tie (preferably a solid color like black or dark blue)

Only a really sharp dresser knows how to mix patterns in his suit fabric, shirt fabric, and tie fabric. Therefore, it is best to avoid mixing stripes, checks, and plaids. (On weekends a man may mix anything he wishes, but in the office his combination might be considered too loud.)

Shoes

Since an executive's feet are almost always in view, his shoes should always look right—that is, be of good quality and in good condition. Expensive shoes will stay in shape for years if they are resoled and reheeled regularly, brushed and polished daily, and kept with shoe trees in them at night. The condition in which a man keeps his shoes is as important as their style.

The laced shoe (wing tip or cap toe) always has been the conservative choice, but loafers and leather slip-ons are now accepted everywhere. The shoe-boot style is *not* an establishment look. Men who wear colored shoes are demanding foot attention, which is not an advantage in most businesses.

Socks

The only kind a man should wear to business is the mid-calf length or full-length (the latter are held up by garters). When a man wears anklets, he is bound to show the skin of his leg when he sits down, a vision that ruins anyone's perception of him as a man of refinement.

Here are some general rules about sock colors:

Color of the Socks	Appropriately Worn With
White	White suits in summer Athletic shoes, boat shoes and loafers in leisure activities
Black, navy, or dark gray	Business suits
Brown	Brown or khaki suits
Pastel-colored	Summer suits of poplin, khaki, and seersucker (for "sharp dressers")
Bright colored and Argyle	Blazer or sports jacket with gray flannels, or with corduroys or khakis for leisure wear only
Black sheer	Black-tie suits

Hats

Until the 1950s, a man's hat was an essential part of his attire; it was also a means of greeting other people. When introduced to a lady on the street, a man would remove his hat as a sign of deference. Upon seeing a friend, he would tip or touch his hat as a gesture of recognition. In the presence of a lady in the elevator, no gentleman would have been seen wearing his hat.

Today hats are only occasional additions to some well-dressed men's wardrobes. A man may own a fur hat to protect his head during the harsh winter, or he may own a tennis hat to guard him from the sun in summer. If he looks good in a hat, he should wear one—a fedora in winter and a town straw hat (such as a boater or rough straw), complete with a colorful hatband, in summer. Outsized and colored straw hats are for summer resort beaches, not for the office.

Jewelry

Many people today still agree with the pronouncement made by Walter Hoving, the former chairman of the New York jewelry store Tiffany & Co., when he banned the sale of diamond rings to men in his store. He felt that the only kind of ring a man should wear is his family's gold signet ring or a college ring.

Many senior executives are also uncomfortable when their junior male executives wear gold neck chains or bracelets. If the business is a flamboyant one, it does not matter how the executives dress, but otherwise a man should wear a minimum of jewelry in the business world. (What he does on his own time is, of course, his own right.)

A watch is usually a man's first important jewelry purchase; cufflinks to wear with French cuffs come next; then finally, when and if he needs evening clothes, studs and matching cufflinks for his evening shirt.

"The well-dressed man," to quote my well-dressed New York friend Edward Russell, is "someone whose jewelry you don't really notice, but when you finally do see a flash of something, it is always something of great quality and very quiet."

A Female Executive's Basic Wardrobe

The female executive who thinks that she needs a closet full of severely tailored mannish suits, complete with a man's shirt and string tie or necktie for each, is, in my opinion, making a mistake. Women look attractive in appropriate dresses in the office, and in soft, feminine skirts and blouses, sweater-and-skirt combinations, and suits cut along soft lines. A female executive who is proud to look like a woman, instead of imitating men's fashions, makes the men around her much more comfortable and therefore easier to work with.

A female executive should buy with quality instead of quantity as her guideline. She should be sure that everything *fits*. She should accessorize her costume each day with care. She should know where the hemline of the skirts should fall on her leg. (It depends on her legs and her height.) She should know what is appropriate for her age and body as well as her occupation, and she should keep her wardrobe in spit-and-polish condition, so that it works as a plus in her career.

Here's a listing of a suitable wardrobe for the young female manager beginning her career and for an established mid-manager (we assume that senior executives have long since learned their wardrobe needs in their corporate climb):

Young Manager (for winter and summer)	*Mid-Manager* (for winter or summer)
2 daytime suits	4 daytime suits
6 blouses	8 blouses
3 sweaters (appropriate for office)	3 sweaters (appropriate for office)
3 skirts	5 skirts

Young Manager (for winter and summer)	*Mid-Manager* (for winter or summer)
3 daytime dresses	5 daytime dresses
1 basic black dress (for cocktail parties and dinner)	2 basic black dresses and 1 dressy cocktail dress in color
2 well-cut coats, one winter, one spring weight	2 well-cut coats, one winter and one spring weight 1 fur coat (obviously for winter)
Fashionable raincoat	Fashionable raincoat
3 belts	6 belts
3 scarves	6 scarves
Several sets of underwear; 3 nightgowns	Several sets of underwear; 4 nightgowns
1 bathrobe	Winter bathrobe; silk dressing gown
8 pantyhose	12 pantyhose
2 pairs of flat or medium-heeled shoes	4 pairs of flat or medium-heeled shoes
2 pairs of dressy sandals or pumps	4 pairs of dressy sandals or pumps 1 pair evening slippers
1 long dinner dress	1 long dinner dress 1 ball gown 1 evening skirt with 2 tops
2 pairs of pants	4 pairs of pants
2 pairs of sports activities slacks	4 pairs of sports slacks
4 polo or sports shirts	6 polo or sports shirts
2 sweaters for sports	4 sweaters for sports
2 bathing suits	2 bathing suits
Active sportswear for her particular sport	Active sportswear for her sport
Athletic shoes and socks	Athletic shoes and socks

Accessories

Accessories are personal fashion statements that differ greatly from woman to woman. A woman who does not understand how to accessorize her wardrobe with ease is probably better off buying few accessories and buying those only with the help of a fashion-wise friend or a shopping consultant. In the office, accessories should never be overly conspicuous in their color, shape, or sound. Again, *fashion in an office is wrong if it is distracting.*

Hats

Hats are a tremendous plus for a woman who loves them and knows how to wear them. They can wake up a drab dress or suit; they can add a dash of youth to a costume; they can hide hair that needs attention. A woman who wears hats should choose them carefully to coordinate with her topcoat and the dress or suit beneath.

She should take off her hat in her office while she is working (although when she is visiting a client or customer outside, she may leave her hat on).

Handbags

The average woman needs two handbags—a sporty one large enough to store the necessities of her working day and a smaller cocktail bag to carry for dressy evening events. Both should coordinate in color with her other accessories.

Some feminists preach that women should learn to live without purses and handbags on the job, because a woman who carries one, particularly a large one, seems "always to be fumbling inside in a most unprofessional way, thus distracting and irritating any man in her presence."

The solution to the fumbling problem is proper organization of your handbag, so that you know where everything is. Put all your personal grooming items like compact, comb, lipstick, and blusher in a small zippered purse inside the handbag, so that you always know how to find them quickly. Put your keys on a keychain with a large, light tag attached, so that you can always find them without difficulty. Keep your eyeglasses in a case so that you can find them easily in your handbag and protect them. Put your notebook, pen, address book, and checkbook in one specific part of your bag, so that you can easily find them also.

Handbags need grooming. A leather handbag requires an occasional saddlesoaping and polishing. A suede bag needs brushing with a suede brush; the hardware trim on a handbag needs polishing from time to time.

A woman should *not* leave her handbag on her desk or on the conference table when she is in a meeting, or put it on the table during a meal in a restaurant. One's handbag should always be stowed away out of sight.

Jewelry

Wearing jewelry requires fashion know-how. The perfect touch may be something as simple as a large pair of earrings, an unusually shaped bracelet, or a necklace of an unusual material. The perfect touch may be a trio of slender gold chains with small pendants that carry their own stories. It may be a piece of Art Deco jewelry or something that came from great-great-grandmother in the nineteenth century. It is *never* a lot of things at once.

What a female executive should remember about jewelry:

- Jewelry should be completely noiseless in the office. Noisy jewelry is irritating and distracting to anyone near you.
- Long, dangling earrings are an evening look as a rule and don't really belong in the work environment.
- A pearl necklace may be worn with anything any time of the day, either by itself or in conjunction with other jewelry. A pearl necklace and earrings always look right.
- If you wear a small elaborate piece of antique jewelry or a piece of real jewelry (like a small brooch of diamonds set in platinum), don't mix other jewelry with it. Let it be the only accent.
- Gold jewelry items and silver items often do not mix. Knowing how to combine them requires a strong sense of fashion. If you have a bracelet, however, that is both silver and gold, then you may wear something else of either metal.
- Choose your watch carefully. You would be wise to invest in more than one watchband, so that you will have a watch for sporty occasions, your life at the office, and an evening look.
- Don't wear rings on all your fingers. It is very distracting and unbusinesslike.
- Big, bold costume jewelry makes a great accent, but after you have put it all on, look at yourself in a full-length mirror and start taking it off, piece by piece, until you are wearing only one striking piece or two small items.

Jewelry for the Woman on the Dais or at the Microphone

A woman who is speaking at a lunch or a dinner or who will be sitting on the dais is usually one of only two or three women in a sea of men. Since she is conspicuous, she should take pains with her hair, makeup, and clothes to look her best in representing not only her company but other female executives, too. Since the audience will see a woman on the dais only from the waist up, she should not wear too fussy a dress or too severe a suit. A soft bow-tie blouse worn with a suit helps soften the effect. A dress with huge shoulder pads looks distorted from a distance. Too much makeup is exaggerated from a distance, and too much jewelry makes a woman sitting on a dais look like a chandelier.

If a woman executive is making remarks into the microphone, she should not be fussing with a stole, shawl, or scarf. She should wear a simple dress that needs no rearranging of its neckline or its accessories. Otherwise, the audience will accuse her of being overly nervous. (If she is a necklace fingerer or a bracelet clutcher, she should not wear jewelry on the day of her presentation.)

The Fancy Leg

Lacy stockings and pantyhose embroidered with flowers, birds, polka dots, and such should not be part of a woman's personal daytime dress, because they are conspicuous and draw constant attention to her legs. They are perfectly suitable for an evening business-social party, however, because they are designed for dressy evening purposes.

Shoes

A woman's shoes are often the focus of other peoples' attention. That is why they should be kept polished and clean, with the heels in good order.

A woman who wears toeless sandals, bright polish on her toenails, and sheer stockings draws everyone's eyes to her red toenails. If her footwear is an unusual color or a startling style, they become even more conspicuous.

If she wears shoes of an unusual color, she should wear a very quiet, solid-color dress or suit with them. Her handbag should either match her shoes or coordinate with them.

A woman who wears overly high heels to the office cannot walk gracefully; she also emits a signal that she really doesn't mean to do work that day that is too demanding. A woman who wears handsome, well-made, good quality shoes with medium or low heels shows that she is ready for action and can go anywhere.

Dressing Casual

When a host writes in the lower right-hand part of the invitation the command "Dress Casual," the signal given is confusing at best. To be casually dressed is one thing in one region of the country, quite another in another region.

It's really up to the host to spell out what he means, and not to use that ambiguous directive "Dress Casual." It's also up to the guest to call the host if he doesn't understand how he should dress. The host would be wise to include a small memo sheet (with its information duplicated so that there is one for each invitation) giving specific information if he wishes his guests to come dressed in a manner other than what they normally wear to the office: "Wear slacks and sports shirts." "Bring your tennis gear." "Jacket and tie needed in the club dining room." "Please wear boat shoes" (for an invitation to a party on a boat). Etc.

When you attend a party in a place like southern California, where the men dress casually in the evening, *don't equate informal dressing with sloppy dressing.* Your slacks, jeans, sweaters, and sport shirts should be of quality materials and designed in the latest fashion. Your shoes must be shiny and clean. Too many people who live in large cities take "Dress casually" to mean "Come in any old thing." To assemble a properly accessorized outfit of sportswear requires effort and a sense of fashion.

When Your Customers Are in Work Clothes

I regularly receive questions from young managers asking whether or not they should "dress down" for customers who are out supervising projects in the petroleum, agricultural, mining, and construction fields. The answer is yes and no. *Yes* when an executive is young and new in his selling game. If he approaches the supervisors dressed in work clothes as they are, he will probably find them more at ease with him than if he appears in his most preppy Brooks Brothers best. However, if he is a snappy dresser, he will probably find that after a long trial period, once he gets to know the men well, he can begin to dress as he prefers to in his city life, and they will respect him for it. One senior sales manager told me that if he were to show up dressed other than in his city best, the men in the field would feel let down and disappointed. His pinstripes are an object of great good-natured teasing; his Wall Street appearance is his trademark, and the men love it. (Obviously, a manager should not go on a selling mission wearing good clothes if they will become dirty on the job site.)

Changing Your Style to Suit the Occasion

If the style in your office is casual dress (such as in an office that makes films or in the creative director's office of an ad agency), your clothes should be as well coordinated and as good quality in material and cut as the clothing worn by financiers and heads of major corporations. Sweater and slacks should make a fashion statement in texture and color. Shoes—loafers or whatever—should be well-shined and in fashion, too.

If your natural uniform for work consists of a pair of jeans and a sweater or sports shirt, you would be wise nevertheless to call on clients and customers in the more conservative businesses dressed as they are. In other words, a woman should put on a dress and a man a suit and tie before going to a Wall Street firm, a Texas bank, or a Hartford insurance agency.

Resort Wear Fashions Change Quickly

Dressing mistakes occur far more often in a man's leisure wardrobe than they do in his office wardrobe, because business wear fashions are more stable and slower to change. When leisure time is spent in a company activity—such as a convention at a resort or a meeting in a resort town—then the company image is involved in the way the executives dress and appear in public.

Resort wear fashions change mercurially. What is very much in vogue one year may be completely out the next (bleeding Madras plaid trousers and the Harry Truman Hawaiian flowered shirt are cases in point).

Certain resorts and beach clubs are very conservative, and a man wearing a skimpy swimming brief there would be criticized. He needs to know what kind of swimsuit most men wear in that place. If he's going to be swimming on the Riviera, he can show up in a G-string and no heads will turn, but he will be criticized if he wears that same garment to the Lawrence Beach Club on Long Island, where longer bathing trunks seem to be *de rigueur* (without anyone's having published it).

The best thing for an executive to do before going to an important meeting at a resort is to ask advice from someone in the know, and then avoid glaring fashion errors by updating his leisure-time wardrobe.

Knee Socks and the Sockless Look

In very hot weather in certain tropical cities around the world it is appropriate for an executive (*if* he has good legs) to go to his office in long Bermuda shorts with white, beige, black, or gray knee socks and a coat and tie. In major urban areas, however, this look is currently not appropriate in summertime.

When a man is on vacation in a summer resort, he should wear either white athletic socks or no socks at all with his loafers or boat shoes (dock siders), whether he is wearing shorts, slacks, or jeans. The sockless look is fine for a vacation's daytime or evening wear. It looks a lot better, however, if the wearer's ankles are tanned.

A Female Executive in Pants

Fashion keeps bringing pants and pantsuits to the foreground and then returning them to the closet. One factor remains constant, however: Some women look great in pants and some don't, and the latter should wear them as seldom as possible.

A woman should not wear pants on the job unless she can meet all of these criteria:

- She has a great figure for pants.
- She has good fashion sense and knows what kind of top to wear with them.
- She can afford good quality fabric and well-cut pants.

Some men simply don't feel comfortable with a woman wearing pants; the woman may unconsciously be threatening to her male colleagues. To me, this is reason enough for female managers not to wear pants in the office.

A Female Executive in Shorts

A woman on a social outing involving business should wear shorts only at an outdoor leisure occasion and *only* if her legs and figure are perfect. (That eliminates the majority of women!) A woman who wears shorts around her business colleagues is like a woman who wears a low-cut dress. She is asking to be looked at in a sexual way.

A Woman and Her Bathing Suit

When a woman is with clients, customers, or senior management at a convention resort or health club, she should wear a fashionable swimsuit (like a one-piece maillot) but certainly not one that is almost nonexistent (like a cutout one-piece suit or a miniature bikini). If her figure is terrific, it will be highly visible anyway; if her swimsuit is a flashy signal, it could reflect in a negative way on her own career management.

Dressing for Various Kinds of Parties

Men do not have the same problems women do in deciding how to dress for an event; this is quite obvious from the charts below:

FOR A BREAKFAST, LUNCH, TEA, OR EARLY (5 P.M.) COCKTAIL PARTY

	A Woman	A Man
Summer	Dress (not décolleté) or suit of a summer-weight fabric, such as pure linen, silk, or cotton Dressy shoes (but not made of an evening fabric)	His best dark summer-weight suit His favorite tie His nicest business shirt His dark shoes in the best condition
Winter	Dress (not décolleté) or suit with a dressy silk blouse or a winter-weight fabric Dressy shoes (not made of an evening fabric) Any winter color or prints are appropriate	The same as above, except that his dark suit would be of a winter-weight fabric

FOR AN EVENING BUSINESS PARTY
(COCKTAILS AT 6 P.M. OR DINNER AT 7 P.M.)

	A Woman	*A Man*
Summer	Black or dark solid-colored or print dress Summer or glittery jewelry Evening pumps or sandals Small handbag Regular or dressy hosiery	His best dark summer suit His favorite tie His best dress shirt Black shoes in good condition
Winter	Dress or theater suit in velvet, brocade, satin, faille, lamé, etc. Dark and jewel colors appropriate Glitter jewelry Evening handbag Regular or dressy hosiery	The same as above, except that his dark suit would be of a winter-weight fabric

FOR AN EVENING BLACK-TIE PARTY (AT 7 P.M. OR LATER)

	A Woman	*A Man*
Summer	Short, three-quarter, or full-length evening dress of a cool or filmy fabric (cotton, chiffon, organza, etc.) Glitter jewelry Evening bag Evening sandals Evening hosiery (sheer or embroidered)	His summer-weight black-tie suit Dress shirt Black hose Black patent leather shoes
Winter	Short, three-quarter, or full-length evening dress of a winter evening fabric (satin, brocade, sequins, lamé, heavy taffeta, etc.) Glitter jewelry Matching evening bag and evening sandals Evening hosiery (sheer or embroidered)	His black-tie suit for winter Dress shirt Black hose Black patent leather shoes

Wardrobe Changes to Make in Going from the Office to an Evening Party

It is a good idea, if you will be going directly from the office to a party, to dress in a special way that day.

In the following charts, two fashion-conscious, meticulously groomed managers, John Doe and Jane Doe, dress in the morning for the office on a day that will end with a cocktail party or an informal dinner. They carry a minimum of extra clothing with them to the office. These are the changes they will make in either summer or winter:

In the Summertime

John Doe wears to the office	*Jane Doe wears to the office*
Navy tropical worsted suit	Cream-colored cotton knit dress with plain neckline
Yellow (or any pastel) button-down shirt	Chunky coral necklace and earrings
Navy tie with small yellow pattern	Cream-colored rope belt; large rope handbag
Black tassled loafers with lightweight navy hose	Cream-colored low-heeled calf pumps,

At 5:30 they change at the office before going to the party.

Same suit	Same dress, but changes belt to a narrow gold one
Clean white shirt with French cuffs and cufflinks	Changes jewelry to pearl, gold, and rhinestone
Pastel, solid-colored shantung silk tie	High-heeled cream-colored sandals
	Changes to small cream-colored bag

In the Wintertime

John Doe wears to the office	*Jane Doe wears to the office*
Dark gray flannel suit	Black wool Chanel-type suit
Striped button-down shirt	Red silk soft-tie blouse
Coordinating dark silk striped tie	Black calf pumps (medium low heels)
Black shoes and black socks	Beige pantyhose
Dark wool topcoat or well-cut trench coat	Gold button earrings
	Large leather handbag
	Loose, well-cut winter coat in black and white tweed

At 5:30 they change at the office
before going to the party.

Same dark gray flannel suit	Same black wool suit
Clean pale blue "town shirt" with white collar and cuffs and cufflinks	Changes to gold lamé blouse
	Adds pearls and gold chains (necklaces)
New tie—navy with a small blue, red, and white pattern	Changes to gold-toned evening pantyhose and black satin opera pumps
	Changes to small black satin handbag

The Successful Female Executive's Evening Persona

- Her handbag and evening slippers should match.
- She wears long gloves *only* at a ball, a white-tie occasion, or something very formal.
- A nice touch: short or bracelet-length white kid (not cotton) gloves
- If she does not have a full-length fur or fur jacket to wear in the winter, she might buy or have made a long wool-lined coat or cloak of velvet or satin.
- She can cover up a bare party dress for a business-related party with a jacket of velvet, silk, or brocade, with a jeweled sweater, or with a stole or shawl (a nonslippery one that sits comfortably on her shoulders).
- She should save her daring low-cut dresses for her private life and private parties.
- Less is more in wearing jewelry, real or fake.
- She makes a mistake if she wears a completely different and bizarre hairstyle in the evening. Chances are her colleagues much prefer the woman they see in the office.
- She makes a mistake if she appears with long false eyelashes and an overdose of colored eye shadow. Her business associates might suddenly see a different side of her—one that is *not* business related!

Different Ways of Dressing for Black-Tie Evenings

A black-tie event is something special, out of the ordinary, so the hosts request their guests to take special pains to dress. When people wear evening clothes, there is an unmistakable added air of festivity.

A man's attire is traditional, almost ritualistic. A woman has many options.

Black Tie for a Woman

*For a Business Dinner in a Private
Home in the Country or in the City on
a Weekend*

Covered-up floor-length sheath, or
Caftan or djellabah, or
Long skirt with blouse, or
Long skirt with evening sweater, or
Party pajamas

For a Large Dance or Ball

Beaded floor-length sheath, or
Strapless satin gown with full skirt and
matching stole, or
Flowing chiffon dress, or
Anything that is very formal and that
moves gracefully

*For Dinner in the Executive Dining
Room, a Restaurant, or Any Public
Place*

Evening suit (floor-length skirt and
matching jacket of a dressy fabric),
or
Evening dress that is beaded or made
of an evening fabric (either short,
three-quarter length, or long—to
the floor), or
Long bare, décolleté sheath with a
jacket of dressy fabric (which is
not removed at a business event,
only a private one)

Black Tie for a Man

A man's evening attire for a black-tie occasion calls for the classic black dinner suit (or tuxedo). If an executive has only one in his wardrobe, he would be wise to buy the light to medium weight kind that he can wear everywhere.

The jacket of a dinner suit is cut single- or double-breasted, sometimes with a single- or double-vent back. The collar, made of satin or faille (never of velvet, please!) may be a shawl type, or it may have peaked or notched lapels. The width of the lapels changes with the fickleness of fashion. A jacket made of a nontraditional fabric, such as a colored brocade, really looks too theatrical and obvious.

The white (or off-white or very pale pastel) evening shirt is often pleated; *it should not be ruffled or embroidered.* The understated look is the right look for men's evening clothes. The evening shirt has small pearl buttons (or a man may wear his own studs). The cummerbund and bow tie are properly black or occasionally bright red or a tartan plaid or velvet. During the winter a brocaded or needlepoint cummerbund may be worn.

An evening vest is often worn with a dinner suit. It is usually made of black silk damask, satin, velvet, or faille, with small buttons covered in the same fabric. The vest holds the shirt neatly in place and, if well-tailored, can give an illusion of slimness to a man's figure. A double-breasted dinner jacket, of course, obviates either a cummerbund or a waistcoat, but again, a double-breasted jacket should not be worn by an overly heavy person.

Evening trousers, with black satin stripes down the sides, either have self-belted waists or are held by suspenders (braces), which are buttoned or clipped onto the waistband.

Some men like to wear "trews," very tight-fitting evening trousers made of a clan tartan. They also have black satin stripes down the sides. A person of Scottish descent is often irritated at seeing someone with "no right to wear the clan tartan" in trews. However, a more serious mistake is made when a portly rather than slim man wears them.

Black dress hose are worn with black patent leather shoes (with laces) or black patent leather "dancing pumps" with black grosgrain bows. While many men wear black patent loafers with their dinner suits, *it does not look right.* Velvet or needlepoint lounging slippers are appropriate only when worn at a black-tie dinner at someone's home or club; at business dinners and at public events they look rather foppish. So does a velvet smoking jacket worn with black trousers. This handsome ensemble belongs at a black-tie dinner in a private home, not in a public place. In my opinion, a damask or fancy fabric dinner jacket belongs nowhere.

In cold winter weather, a man should wear gray gloves with his black tie; if he wears a hat, a gray or black fedora (with a black band) is appropriate. (Of course, if he has a black derby, he should have the courage to wear it—it can provide a dashing touch.)

Summer Black Tie

For a summer black-tie event in town, an executive should wear his black dinner suit.

For a summer black-tie event in the country or at a resort, he has these options:

- His black dinner suit (black tie, white shirt)—*always right*
- A white dinner jacket with black evening trousers—not as elegant as the black dinner suit
- A bright solid-colored or patterned jacket with black trousers
- A black jacket worn with bright solid-colored or patterned trousers

A Man's Evening Accessories

A white or colored evening handkerchief, arranged in points and tucked into the left breast pocket of a dinner jacket, adds a touch of style to the dinner jacket. Sometimes the handkerchief is a patterned silk foulard. To look proper for evening, a man's wristwatch band should be either gold, silver, platinum, or plain black.

Cufflinks and studs should be on the small side. (When they are oversized and flashy, they are of questionable taste, even when they are made of gems or semiprecious stones.) Cufflinks may be of gold or platinum with pearls, mother-of-pearl, enamel, semiprecious stones, or small gemstones.

A black bow tie with a dinner suit is appropriate for all seasons. The material of the tie is either satin, faille, or velvet. While a bow tie may be ready-tied, most men prefer to tie their own ("one of the first acts a true gentleman learns," according to a well-dressed friend).

Although small bow ties worn with a wing collar are often featured in fashion magazines and now worn by young men all over America, I agree with John Duka of the *New York Times,* who wrote in 1983 that a man who wears a cummerbund and bow tie with a wing collar "looks like a waiter and not a guest." In the opinion of many, a wing collar should be worn only with a white bow tie on a white-tie-and-tails occasion.

A White-Tie Event: A Late Evening, Very Formal Occasion

The most formal of all occasions is a white-tie evening. Before World War II it was a common event in the social lives of business and civic leaders; today it is almost an endangered species, except for an occasional wedding *"Men look so absolutely smashing* in their white tie and tails," The Princess of Wales was quoted as saying. (Actually, women have been saying that since the mid-nineteenth century!) White tie and tails are still worn today to certain White House dinners and receptions, to some debutante balls, and at some traditional events, such as the opening night of the National Horse Show in Madison Square Garden, opening night of the San Francisco Opera, the Swan Ball in Nashville, and the Al Smith Dinner, held annually at the Waldorf Astoria in New York.

White tie and tails can be rented in every major city in America. Along with the black wool-and-silk tail coat, a man wears a starched white shirtfront with a wing collar, studs, a white pique tie, waistcoat, black socks, and black patent shoes. For dancing, a man wears soft white leather gloves—no sweaty palms when wearing *this* male plumage!

Women wear their most elaborate ballgown and jewels and furs (their own or borrowed). This is the time for a fancy coiffure; long white gloves are optional.

The "White Tie" dress stipulation is written at the lower right-hand corner of the invitation. White-tie events are not held from mid-June to mid-September, simply because of the heat—the outfit is *very* warm to wear.

A white-tie wedding begins no earlier than eight P.M., and usually includes dinner and dancing after the ceremony. The groom, the fathers of the couple, and the ushers wear white tie and tails, and as many of the male guests as possible. (If it is too difficult to assemble such formal regalia, a male guest may wear black tie.)

Dressing for International Business

There is a very simple solution to dressing appropriately while on business in another country: *Ask before you pack.* Ask your foreign counterpart what your schedule will be and what clothes you should bring. Find out what the dressing customs are in that country, either from someone who is a national and working here or from a diplomat or businessman who has recently returned from a long stay there.

There are many customs and taboos you should be aware of in certain countries. Here is a sprinkling:

- In the Peoples' Republic of China, don't wear white (the symbol of mourning).
- Wear a lightweight dark suit in the Arab countries. (If it is exceedingly hot, you may remove your necktie.)
- Women should not wear pants in Arab countries—or anything that could not be described as "covered up" (long-sleeved, below-the-knee, etc.).
- Dark-colored suits and somber ties are the most appropriate wear in the Far East.
- In the Philippines a man may wear a *barong* (an embroidered long over-shirt) with his trousers day and night. A woman executive should not try to wear one, however (until she gets home and wears it as a summer shirt at the beach).
- A man or woman wearing a wild, flowered pattern (like that on a Hawaiian shirt) is too conspicuous in any country abroad. An American in another country should be "toned down" and as physically inconspicuous as possible.
- In the Far East and in Arab countries you may be asked to remove your shoes before entering a shrine or mosque; therefore, make sure that your hosiery is in good condition!
- A person in mid to senior management may very well need evening clothes in Western Europe. Be prepared, even if a black-tie event has not been put on your schedule.
- In Israel total informality is the word. You won't need a tie and sometimes not even a jacket. However, as a general rule of thumb, if you go on the assumption that every other country is *more* formal in its business practices than we are, you will probably be correct.

5

International Business Manners

When you go abroad on business, whether for a short trip or to work out of a foreign branch office for a number of years, you carry with you the flags of both your country and company. You are conspicuous in your behavior abroad at all times. Arriving in another country and knowing *nothing* about it is an automatic insult to the people of that nation. They will feel you hold them unworthy of bothering to find out who and what they are.

The key to success in your business dealings and personal relationships in a foreign country is thoroughness of preparation in learning about the country and a sincere desire to fit in with the new and different culture. As a business executive you should want to be a good citizen of the host country, just as you should want your foreign contacts to be good citizens of America when they are here on our shores. Some Americans feel that since we are the strongest country in the world, we can throw our weight around and dominate the situation wherever we are. They affect an irritating but-why-aren't-you-like-us? attitude in other countries when things don't go exactly as they do at home.

A sensitive American in a foreign country makes hundreds of friends and does an incredibly effective public relations job for the United States of America. The unfeeling American (or even the unfeeling spouse or child of the American business person) can undo in one hour what the sensitive American took many months to accomplish. On occasion one sees American business people and their spouses making scenes in airports, hotel lobbies, restaurants, and shops. Inevitably, when Americans are bad mannered—whether it's not bothering to excuse themselves when an apology is called for, or whether they're raising their voices, complaining about the country, or berating a subordinate—the scene is witnessed by numerous people and remembered by all of them forever. Our entire nation can become "ugly American" in foreign eyes, all because of the actions of one or of a very few.

It's as easy to be a "beautiful American" as it is to be an "ugly" one. There is always something good to say about any country, and if you are living in another country with your family, it's wise to seek out the good at once and to concentrate on it. If you *will* a desire to get along with the people in another country, you will succeed in doing so.

I hope this chapter imparts a sense of *awareness* of how important it is to be sensitive to cultural differences. This is the key to success and productivity, as well as to happiness, for the executive and his family who are living abroad or for the executive who travels abroad a great deal.

Once an executive realizes that what he considers to be the height of civility may be considered the height of rudeness in another country, he will understand the importance of preparing himself before dealing with people of another country. He will learn to ask questions and obtain good information about the *people* and not just concentrate his attention on financial spread sheets.

First and foremost, it is important to remember that no matter how perceptive an American executive may be, if he cannot speak the host country's language with a certain ease, he himself never really will be at ease.

We Americans tend to have trouble not only with foreign tongues but also with our own. We should watch what we say every second of our waking hours in another country, because in blundering ahead with a conversation we think is humorously teasing, we may actually be insulting our foreign hosts. I watched a Greek official get up and walk out of a conference room when a young executive who was trying to be humorous said to him, "You know where all of the Greeks are in the U.S., don't you? They're right here in New York, making sandwiches in the delicatessens." I also sat in a dining room in Stockholm and heard a senior American executive become obnoxious after two martinis and one schnappes. He first addressed himself to our distinguished elderly hostess: "I bet you Swedes are proud of the fact that you brought free love to the world, aren't you? I mean free sex started here, didn't it?" In his next sentence he remarked about "your lousy socialism in this country." (Although some in the room may have agreed with him politically, politesse dictates that he had no right to make such statements.) Then he began attacking Sweden for remaining neutral in World War II and compounded it by hurling insults at his host. With this, another American and I, although we did not know our drunken compatriot very well, rose from the table, put a figurative muzzle on his mouth, and took him back to his hotel room. Our Swedish hosts and the other guests were grateful to us. That executive and his company will never again enjoy a good reputation in Stockholm, because word of that evening traveled fast.

Preparing Yourself for Business Abroad

Cross-Cultural Training

There is help available for executives, managers, and technical personnel and their families who wish to supplement their own study programs of a foreign country to which they will be assigned. More and more companies are sending executives who are destined to live and work abroad to any one of the excellent cross-cultural training centers, such as the twenty-seven-year-old Business Council for International Understanding Institute (BCIU) in Washington, D.C.; The American University in Washington, D.C.; the Key Man Course at the Thunderbird School in Phoenix, Arizona; and The Monterey Institute of International Studies in Monterey, California.

Copeland Griggs Productions, of San Francisco, markets a very general series of films on the subject of international business training. Actors portraying Americans in business are shown innocently blundering into situations in which they embarrass or insult their foreign colleagues. This is a recommended film series for the unseasoned international business person.

Cross-cultural training programs include a discussion of the history, values, customs, and work ethics of a foreign country. As of this writing, a three-day program at BCIU costs $4000 per family unit, and a fourteen-day course costs $8000 per family unit. An additional person (such as an unmarried executive) costs his or her company $250 per day. However, the sessions are cost-effective when one compares them with the expense of failing overseas. As explained by Gary Lloyd, director of the BCIU Institute, "It can cost between $47,500 and $355,000 to return a manager or technician and his or her family to the United States. If a company can reduce its failure rate of returning or ineffective employees by one percent, it would cover the cost of putting all its personnel through training before they go abroad."

Since one untrained, unfeeling person abroad on a ten-day business trip can quickly destroy any good business-friendship relationships that may previously have been established between the two countries, a company should seriously consider giving its executives cross-cultural business training, even if those executives will not actually be living in a foreign country, only traveling frequently. The BCIU Institute conducts one-day programs in-house for companies throughout the United States and overseas.

A manager's spouse and children certainly should not be neglected if the family is moving abroad, and the BCIU Institute has special programs for them as well. They should be motivated and trained in their new roles as representatives for their country (like it or not). They must learn how to cope with the tough cultural differences between the two countries. It is particularly difficult for teenagers to leave their friends and their very special American lifestyles behind them. This is why the training and development programs are so important for the entire family, and not just for the business person.

Debriefing a Newly Returned Business Person and Other Sources of Information

A major source of information for executives and families going abroad is a recently returned American executive and his or her family. Each member of the executive's family who will have to adjust to new conditions in living within peer groups in another country can gain invaluable advice from those who have just been through it.

If you are headed for another country, take each opportunity that presents itself to question intelligent people from that country. It is a good way to gather helpful information; even small nuggets gleaned at a social function are useful.

For example, at a luncheon given by Secretary of State George Shultz for President Mitterand of France, I asked one of my lunch partners, a senior French businessman who resides in Paris, what bothered him most about doing business with Americans in his country. He answered without pausing, "Doing business at breakfast!" He shuddered. "In France we like to eat our breakfast and read our papers in peace in the morning. You Americans with your endless meetings at the breakfast hour—it kills us!"

"Does that mean," I asked, "that in France one should not discuss business at lunch or at dinner until the food has been consumed?"

"Pas du tout," he replied. "After ten in the morning one is perfectly capable of eating and talking business at the same time. But in the morning at the hour of the *petit déjeuner*—never!"

I asked the same question of an Italian industrialist last summer when I was in Rome on business, namely what bothered him most about doing business with Americans. "The length of your cocktail hour before dinner," he replied. "I meet my American friends in a restaurant, and they keep ordering drinks before we can order the meal. It exhausts us all. One cocktail before dinner is enough; otherwise no one makes sense in our discussions."

A foreigner is impressed by an American's enthusiasm to learn about his or her country and to adapt to the local culture. The foreigner usually goes out of his way to make entry to his country smoother for the American, including providing personal introductions, a kind of bonus for the homework the American has done.

If you talk to a member of a foreign consulate who has only recently come to this country from his own, you are in a good position to ask questions about the life in that country. You will be able to get the names and publishers of good books that have been written recently on the country. The Industry and Trade Division of the Department of Commerce in Washington, D.C., is an excellent source of information for material on the country you will be living in or visiting frequently. Commerce will send those who request it material called "Background Notes" (which is actually prepared by the State Department), which helps explain the people of that country, its government, history, economy, and geography. Commerce also distributes "FETs," brochures that report on economic trends around the world.

If you are going to live abroad, you might find reading the State Department's *post report* on that country of interest, even though it is targeted at foreign service personnel and not business people.

What You Should Know Before Leaving on a Business Trip Abroad

Before going on a business trip to another country you should:

- *Learn a few key phrases in the country's language,* including "Good morning," "Good evening," "Thank you," "It's a pleasure meeting you," and "Excuse me."
- *Become familiar with the code of dress in that country,* so that you pack the proper clothes
- *Familiarize yourself with any religious taboos* that are important
- *Know basic information about the country,* such as who is the head of state, the name of the political party that person represents, and the name of the United States ambassador to that post
- *Know how to greet someone properly,* whether that means shaking hands and giving your name or immediately offering your card or whatever is the usual protocol in that country
- *Know what kind of gift is appropriately given to whom and when.* For example, should you bring or send flowers to your dinner host? What kind? (*See* International Gift Giving, later in this chapter.)
- *Learn about punctuality in keeping both business and social engagements.* Should you be on time, slightly late, or quite late? When you are the guest of honor at dinner, should you leave first, and if not, who should? At what time should you leave?

- *Know the way people refer to their own country.* For example, the Soviets want you to say "the Soviet Union," not "Russia." East Germans want you to use "the German Democratic Republic," not "East Germany."
- *Be cognizant of the names of the major newspapers and magazines* and their political stance

What You Should Know Before Going to Live and Work in Another Country

Know all of the preceding, plus:

- Acquire more than a rudimentary knowledge of the language, in order to be able to ask and answer simple questions and read the daily newspaper. (You should make speaking the language fluently a number one priority and build language training into your daily schedule on the job from the very first day.)
- Know what the country's great problems are and be sympathetic to them
- Be knowledgeable with respect to the cultural life of the country—its authors, singers, dancers, artists, museums, symphony orchestras, opera companies, and great universities.
- Find out who the sports heroes and movie and TV stars are.
- Learn the metric system, if it is used in that country.
- Make sure that your spouse and children are enrolled in any courses that may help them adjust to a new culture. Anything that can be done to smooth a family's adjustment to a new way of life in a foreign country should be encouraged.

What to Give a Colleague Who Is Going Abroad
(*See also* For the Traveler, page 490)

Along with all of the helpful kinds of gifts there are on the market to assist a traveler in coping with a foreign currency and a foreign language, one of the best gifts you can give a colleague is the kind of *standard medical kit* that some companies provide for their executives. Finding a pharmacy in a foreign city is difficult enough; finding one open on an emergency basis in the night or on a weekend (or on one of the constantly occurring national holidays) is impossible. The Chase Manhattan Bank's medical kit for its executives, to give an example, contains items like aspirin, a decongestant inhaler, throat lozenges, a gentle laxative, an antacid, and small bandages. These are all over-the-counter items; when one needs such an item in a foreign country, it is very nice to find it stashed away in a compact kit, a gift from a friend.

Another gift—very time-consuming at best in its preparation—is a gift of research for a close friend who will be spending a considerable amount of time in another country. This involves the preparation of a notebook filled with information on the country: interesting articles clipped from recent publications; a list of top government officials (supplied by that country's consulate); a list of national holidays; the major museums and cultural institutions; the major sports teams; the names and addresses of leading hotels and restaurants; the top stores and hairdressers; the names and telephone numbers of English-speaking doctors (again, obtainable by doing research at the consulate or by writing the American embassy in that country). This kind of personally compiled resource aid can be invaluable to the traveler.

The Importance of Speaking the Language

I cannot emphasize enough how important it is to know the language of the country you will be living in. In using a foreign language in your work, you'll find yourself in possession of a skill that puts you well ahead of others. You will be translating letters, communicating with important foreign visitors, and in general filling a great need within your company. It will make you look very good. When you are in a foreign country, people automatically warm to you when they find you have learned to speak their language, whether you're dealing with the concierge of your hotel (who usually speaks seven languages) or with a foreign peer on the other side of the desk. When you know another person's language, you can sense the nuances of his behavior (very important in business dealings); you can also enjoy his country's theater, films, books and newspapers, even television shows. You'll be tuned into the local gossip; you'll be a participant in lively exchanges of conversation instead of a perplexed spectator. You'll be able to bargain in shops, understand jokes, recognize political prejudices, and become a much more fascinating person yourself in the process.

Someone else may be more computer literate than you, but if you know a foreign language and he doesn't, his computer knowledge will not help him abroad when his car breaks down or when he loses his passport or has to find an emergency dental clinic. He'll need *you* at that point.

Part of the secret of learning a foreign language is learning to laugh at your own bad mistakes. Hundreds of Americans have refused second helpings during large meals in France by saying, *"Non, merci, je suis pleine"* (thinking that to mean "I am full"; instead it translates to "I am pregnant"). The American woman who says *"Je suis pleine"* is quite forgivable; a corporation that makes a major blunder in translation of an ad is less so. General Motors Corporation once poorly translated its "Body by Fisher" trademark in Belgium into the Flemish equivalent of "Corpse by Fisher"—hardly a slogan destined to sell cars!

Of course, executives who travel constantly to different countries cannot possibly master all of those languages. Sometimes an American businessman develops an inferiority complex because of not knowing a foreign language. Such a complex is unjustified—as long as he makes certain that there is a competent interpreter working with him at all times and that his letters and all written communications are properly translated.

When a Translation Is Essential

Efficiency and courtesy go hand in hand in dealing with business people in another country. What is most efficient is usually also politest. For example:

- Your business cards should be printed in English on one side and in the host country's language on the other side. You should offer your dual-language card with the native language side showing.
- Your first letters to the host country are much more effective if they are written in the host country's language, particularly if the recipient has a limited command of English. It is far better for you to retain an excellent translator in whose abilities you have absolute confidence than to have the recipient of your letter find his own translator—one who may not properly translate your thoughts and thus perhaps ruin a deal.
- For the same reasons, the promotional literature or visuals you take to another country should be in the language of the country.
- Don't correct a foreigner's English unless he or she specifically asks you to, and then, when everyone is tired of all the corrections, just let the other person speak uninterruptedly.

Several years ago graduate students from the Bilingual Studies Office of East Texas University, aware of the tensions created by people who are unable to speak the language of the countries with which they do business, wrote guidelines for Americans in connection with the use of a foreign language. These guidelines are paraphrased here:

- If you speak the language of a non-English-speaking foreign guest who is visiting you in this country, introduce your American colleagues and guests to him while speaking his language. Explain what they do and what their titles are; it will mean a great deal to your guest.
- Make sure the interpreter you retain for the meetings understands the purpose of each meeting and the nature of your business. The interpreter should be familiar with the jargon that will be used. Sometimes foreign students in business school are available for interpreting.
- If you yourself are making an important business trip to another country, have a business colleague in that country engage a proficient interpreter for you.
- If you are hosting foreign guests, provide a bilingual program or agenda for those who do not speak English.
- If no interpreter is present and your foreign guest is not completely fluent

in English, stop every so often to make a brief, clear, slowly spoken summary in English of what has been happening.

· Never tell dirty stories or relate risqué anecdotes (even those almost all Americans would think very funny) and never use profane language in front of someone who does not understand your language or who, if he or she did understand, might find it offensive.

Treating an Interpreter with Consideration

If two people in need of an interpreter are not of high official rank, the interpreter should be seated between them at the table and be treated as courteously as every other guest. He or she should be trained to sit in an unobtrusive position and to lean back at the table when whispering into either person's ear. The two protagonists should always be able to see each other clearly and be able to communicate with body language, even though the interpreter is sitting between them.

I have seen some pretty thoughtless handling of interpreters in my business career. I have seen interpreters spend an entire evening working, exhausted from hours of concentration, without ever being offered a drink or something to eat. On the other hand, I have seen interpreters not properly briefed about the dress code beforehand, with the result that they arrive unsuitably dressed and very conspicuous. If your guests are formal in the way they dress, tell your interpreters to wear jackets and ties or, for the women, dresses instead of pants. If it is a black-tie event, instruct them to come in evening clothes.

If the event is a top-level one, such as a dinner meeting between heads of major corporations or one including high-ranking officials and diplomats, the interpreter should sit in a small chair placed between the two main protagonists but slightly in back of their chairs, so that he or she can translate but the two protagonists will still be sitting close together. In this case the translator does not eat the meal but remains quietly poised to translate the two languages being spoken. (Be sure to have any interpreters you retain given a meal before or after their work stint.)

Handling Tough Questions with Tact

It was a wise executive who told a group of young people about to go overseas for the company, "Remember, never criticize the people in that country to their faces; even refrain from criticizing them behind their backs. It's not that we're better or that they're better, just that we're all different."

It's true that the more at ease you become in the host country's language and lifestyle, the greater target you become for tough questions about your country's policies and your own opinions on controversial issues. U.S. embassy personnel are not the only Americans who have to be able to answer these questions; Americans in the business community and their families are under just as much scrutiny as the American diplomats are in that country.

If you are a totally committed Democrat in a Republican administration, or vice versa, learn to temper your attacks on the party in power in your country in the presence of your foreign friends. If you keep your emotions in check and make calm, fair criticisms, everyone around you will feel comfortable. If you explode with rage about your country's president and make exaggerated accusations, you can make those in your presence feel uneasy and upset about what's happening in our country.

You should watch your accusations, too, about the party in power in the country in which you're posted. Negative remarks about that country's head of state, no matter how justified, can hurt the feelings of that country's nationals. Remember that outsiders who criticize the regime are often resented and distrusted. You can make others turn against you and your company by attacks on the government of their country—even if they don't like the government themselves. Most serious of all, your negative remarks may get your foreign friends into trouble. When a political argument goes unchecked and becomes very heated, your wisest move is to attempt to change the subject or, failing that, to withdraw quietly from the group.

If the United States is harshly attacked by your host country's nationals in your presence, stand up for it in a calm, firm way, correcting any inaccuracies or falsehoods being bandied about. If, however, the rhetoric becomes inflammatory, there is probably nothing you can do except quietly withdraw.

You can't very well defend your country if you do not keep current on what is happening within it, so you should keep yourself well informed by reading periodicals, books, magazines, and newspapers on foreign policy and current events. Most American embassies have a library and information service (called USIS) where you can have access to American foreign policy statements. Arrange to have a copy of the daily State Department news briefing material routinely given to the local journalists picked up or mailed to you, so that you will be able to defend your country's foreign policy with intelligence. An American abroad, even if he doesn't agree with his country's foreign policy, should make sure he knows what it is.

Charles T. Vetter, Jr., has written a helpful book called *Citizen Ambassadors—Guidelines for Responding to Questions Asked About America* (published by the David M. Kennedy International Center for Brigham Young University, Provo, Utah 84602). Vetter wrote this book to prepare Americans for their life abroad in business or academia, and to help them answer tough questions on U.S. actions or policies, many of which are played up in a most negative manner by the foreign press. The "emancipated American woman," for example, is a subject of much derision on the part of many Europeans and Asians. The traveling businessman must be prepared for questions such as, "Is it true that the American wife runs the husband and that the children run the mother?" Or "Is most of America's divorce, juvenile delinquency, and unemployment caused by women working outside the home?"

Many foreigners attack the U.S. position on human rights as hypocritical on the grounds that "Americans discriminate against blacks and other minorities." In many countries the people believe that a person can't go anywhere in the United States without being mugged. If a business person is prepared for such questions, he or she will be able to discuss issues in an informed manner, thereby toning down any exaggerated reporting. It is a definite art to be able to discuss an American foreign policy issue fairly rather than just to dismiss it as something you know little or nothing about.

Business and Cultural Differences Are Intermeshed

We Americans (as well as people from some of the Mediterranean and South American countries and from the Philippines) tend to touch other people of whom we are fond—perhaps kissing and embracing them or taking them by the arm or patting them on the back. In many other countries, such familiarity is totally out of place, particularly among business associates. We Americans also are inclined to frank criticism when something is going wrong in a business relationship. In many other countries both parties must engage in a long and intricate face-saving minuet before criticism can be handled. In Latin America business people will often say "no" when they really mean "perhaps" or "let's talk about it again." In Spain most executives are extremely casual about the hour at which they arrive for appointments, whereas in Japan people are either strictly punctual or arrive ahead of time.

We Americans tend to regard the wasting of time as something akin to bubonic plague. We jump into the business at hand swiftly, after completing the groundwork; then we press hard for quick decisions. This method is totally alien to the culture of people like the Arabs, for example, They will not change to adapt to us; it is we who must change and adapt to their ways when we are in their country.

We tend to make instant judgments and to be ready to begin talking business almost immediately with someone whom we don't really know but about whom we have heard good reports. Many other nationalities go slowly, insisting upon knowing a person well before doing business with him, regardless of that person's reputation. For politeness' sake, allow your foreign business colleague sufficient time to size you up and try to understand your style of doing business. Take the cue from him on when it is time to begin serious negotiations. Americans need to learn the ancient Middle Eastern and Far Eastern tradition of *patience.*

Relationships with one's peers and subordinates within the office abroad are also sensitive points. In Sydney, Australia, for example, managers treat workers as equals. When riding in a taxi, for example, a manager who is alone will not ride in the back seat but will sit up in the front seat with the driver, so as to appear more democratic. In a country like Spain, the philosophy is exactly the opposite, as one American corporation discovered when members of senior management donned chefs' aprons and *toques blanches* (tall white chefs' hats) in order to serve the employees hot dogs at a "real American" company picnic. The Spanish employees were extremely embarrassed at this "demeaning" behavior on the part of their chairman and president.

An American executive should learn the proper protocol to follow when meeting foreigners, whether in the United States or in their own countries, as well as how to introduce them properly to his colleagues. The first impression is usually lasting. An American should learn the foreign country's style of personal greeting, whether that is a pumping, up-and-down greeting handshake, as in Germany; a bow, as in Japan; or a palms-together salute, as in India. If a German with an engineering degree is used to being called by his business title coupled with his last name, the American in Germany should use the engineer's title with his last name. If an Italian who has graduated from college is accustomed to being called "Dottore" (or, in the case of a woman, "Dottoressa") in Italy, then the American should address his colleague by that title in combination with the family name. Even if a French nobleman does not use his title of *comte* (count) in the United States, the American should be sensitive enough to know to use it when he sees that person back in France. (*See also* Chapter 10, Proper Forms of Address.) Things like this are seemingly small nuances, but they show a foreign person how sophisticated, knowledgeable, and polite an American business person is—or is *not.*

A Glance at Some Behavioral Signposts

China

Leave your wild-colored clothing at home before going to China. Dress conservatively; you will be conspicuous enough by virtue of being a Westerner. Don't embrace, hug, kiss, or pat a Chinese; they do not like body contact with strangers. Your group should always conduct itself with restraint, for noisy, obstreperous behavior is very offensive to the Chinese.

In Chinese the family name is given first. Thus Wang Fuming would be known as Mr. Wang. You should be ready to exchange business cards early in your meeting. You would be smart to have your own card translated into

Chinese on the back (you can get this done in Hong Kong if you have not done it in the States).

If in your travels the people in the streets applaud you, smile and applaud them back. (You will receive a lot of nice warm smiles wherever you go.)

Your business hosts or the organization sponsoring your trip will undoubtedly offer you a banquet. Arrive punctually but also leave rather quickly after the meal is finished. (As the guest of honor, no one else can leave until you have left.) Your host will probably raise a toast to you early in the meal. Wait a few moments, and then toast him back. Your host may rise from his chair and come over to you with his plate in hand to put some food on your plate. This may be because he has found a particularly choice morsel he feels should have been given to the honored guest, not the host.

Since this banquet is a gift to you, you should give one in return, and you must give a banquet equal in stature to the one given you. (There are four classes of banquets.)

When you meet with Chinese for a business discussion, you will probably be served tea—several times during the day. This is a firm part of the ritual; you must always accept. Learn to enjoy it. There are usually interpreters present to help with the business discussions; however, don't launch into business right away.

Tipping is prohibited. Be sure to thank personally all of the people who served you, from the head of the hotel to your chambermaid. If you feel you really should give someone a gift, ask someone in authority if it can be arranged and, if so, how. (You might work out an arrangement whereby you are making a gift to an organization, not to one person.) When you return home, you should write a letter of appreciation to the manager of the hotel and have it translated into Chinese before sending it to him. If you do this, you will never be forgotten by him or the staff.

Greece

Refrain from making the okay sign (thumb and forefinger touching in a circle) in Greece, for this is an obscene gesture there. Don't try to be more Greek than the Greeks and be the first to crash the crockery during one of their famous heated dances. Leave that to the local experts, who know their timing, the owner of the restaurant, and the value of the crockery that must be paid for.

Holland

If a business colleague in Holland offers you a drink at any time of the day during a business discussion, take it. You can always feign drinking it; with the Dutch, the offering and taking of a small drink is an essential part of their business hospitality.

Iron Curtain Countries

The main thing to remember is never to bring books and magazines with political overtones with you. And be aware that anything you say or do that derides their government, even in a joking matter, might cast suspicion on the people with whom you are doing business. If you feel someone has bugged your hotel room, don't say so.

You will greatly please the people in these countries if you know their glorious national history and if you are familiar with their great works of art, their museums and palaces, their winning soccer and ice hockey teams, and their film stars.

Israel

Israel strictly observes the Sabbath (from sundown Friday to sundown Saturday). Don't smoke on the Sabbath (unless you are in someone's home and your hosts are smoking) or ask for butter for your bread or milk for your coffee if you're eating meat in a kosher restaurant. Dietary rules are followed very closely in Israel. (*Kashruth* rules prohibit the mixing of meat and dairy products.)

Japan

Although it is impossible to list all of the do's and don'ts of any particular country in this book, a brief review of the customs of this country with which Americans do an inordinate amount of business is worthwhile.

Japan is an excellent example of a country whose customs are very different from ours, whose people are extremely well-mannered, and whose people appreciate the American business person's effort to understand their country's culture.

Theirs is a country of intricately structured rituals that have evolved through centuries. The people act within a framework of gentle manners based on well-defined traditions. Everything a Japanese does, including the way he greets people, entertains them, offers his business card, enters a room, exchanges gifts, and drinks his tea, is done according to prescribed rules. Americans would do well to emulate the inbuilt Japanese custom of always saying thank you for a favor or a gift; an acknowledgement is made immediately by letter or by telephone, and it often includes a personal visit.

You would be wise to do as the Japanese do and have your business cards printed in English on one side and Japanese on the other side. Carry around a large quantity of these cards with you, for you will find yourself exchanging them constantly. (If you go into a meeting with twenty people, all twenty of them might offer you their cards and expect yours in return.) If you are with a group of Japanese who are all of lesser rank than you, they may shyly wait for you to make the first move with your card.

Overfamiliarity

The Japanese react strongly in a negative way to people who are noisy, wear flashy clothes, and are overtly familiar. One should not kiss or embrace a Japanese upon meeting him. The younger Japanese, of course, are less formal; one even sees an occasional pat on the shoulder among them.

Since tipping is frowned upon, give money only to someone who serves you well privately, such as the maid who does extra work for you, and wrap the yen in paper or in an envelope so as not to make her lose face by openly receiving money. You will find that the Japanese go out of their way to help you when you need directions in their country. They will help you with everything from carrying your heavy baggage to searching for a lost contact lens; to tip them for such gestures of hospitality would seriously offend them. At a Japanese inn (as opposed to a hotel), you are expected to give the maid who serves you tea a tip of money wrapped in paper when you have checked in and are shown to your room.

The Bow of Greeting or of Departure

The Japanese have become accustomed to shaking hands with foreigners, but they themselves live in a society of bowing, based on the importance of the individual to whom one bows. A Westerner is not expected to know the subtleties of Japanese bowing procedures, but if one does learn them, it is greatly appreciated. At the very least, you should observe certain rules in the art of greeting.

A Japanese makes a lower bow for the more important individual, a lesser bow for his peer or a person of less importance. For a standing bow of respect, a Japanese bends forward at about a 30-degree angle, lowering his hands, palms down, down the sides of his body or down the front of his thighs almost to his knees. After a short pause, he lifts his head. It is an act that is performed quietly, conveying respect. As a Westerner, you should learn to make at least a light bow (15 degrees) while nodding with your hands at your sides. Count to three before finalizing the bow.

A junior person stops first and bows to a senior person. If you, for example, were to meet someone of senior rank on the street and you happened to be carrying a briefcase or packages in one hand, you would make a slight bow, putting your free hand close to your side. You will find a junior Japanese making a deep bow to you at the beginning of a business day, but then he or she will make a lighter bow to you every time you pass by during the day. (It can become amusing when a junior person bowing to someone more senior raises his head and discovers the senior person still bowing; the junior person must bow again and make sure the senior person is upright before he finishes his bow.) A junior person will also wait at the left for you to precede him in a narrow hallway; when approaching a staircase, he will always wait for you to precede him. Even if you are a young person, you are given great honor as a foreign guest, so if someone makes a motion for you to enter a room ahead of the others, even senior, older Japanese, take the cue and enter the room quickly.

Removing Your Shoes

If you are taken to a sacred shrine or into someone's home (the latter is a rarity), you will be expected to remove your shoes. You may or may not be given slippers to wear. At the shrine, follow the lead of your Japanese host. Water may be presented to cleanse the hands. If your host goes to the shrine and makes a bow, you should follow him.

When you are visiting a Japanese home, remove your shoes right inside the door and place them neatly facing the door (a Japanese custom, so as to make the departure of the guest more efficient). If you are given slippers to wear, upon your departure be sure to place them neatly together on the floor, facing inside the house this time, to be ready for the next guests. The Japanese remove their shoes for the sake of cleanliness, but also to protect the tatami mats on the floors.

Visiting the Japanese at Home

If you should try to do as the Japanese do, and sit in a kneeling position on a tatami mat, it's easier to accomplish if you rest one big toe on top of the other behind you. Women are supposed to keep their knees close together; a man keeps his knees three to four inches apart. A man sits with his hands on his thighs, while a woman's are clasped lightly in front of her.

If you find this difficult to do, you can sit with your knees turned out, or with your legs angled back to one side, Western style. However, if older people come into the room, you would look too casual, so you should try to sit Japanese-style for the time they are present in the room.

Don't try to master the Japanese art of sinking down and rising gracefully from the kneeling position. However, if you live in Japan for a long time, you will do your host country proud if you do indeed learn the very graceful motions. (If you have arthritis in your knees, forget it!)

If you are offered a twisted moist towel, use it for your hands. In hot weather, your host will urge you to use it for your face, neck, and arms. After using the towel, refold it neatly and replace it in its container.

Stay only for half an hour to forty-five minutes if you are a guest in a Japanese home. You will probably be served tea and cakes during your visit. When you leave, you will be urged to stay longer, but you should say that you really "must leave." (Your hosts will be relieved.) Be sure to pay your respects first to the older or more senior people in the room when you leave.

You should entertain Japanese in your own home in your own Western style, always remembering, of course, to show great respect for seniority and age.

Eating in Restaurants

First class Japanese restaurants (or Western ones, for that matter) are extremely expensive. The surroundings are luxurious, and the food and service are superb; this is why most Japanese prefer to entertain their Western guests in restaurants rather than in their homes, where they might not be able to entertain as smoothly.

Sometimes you will find yourself in front of the *tokonoma* (alcove), which is the seat of honor; your host and hostess, contrary to Western custom, will sit together at the opposite end of the table. (Remember if you are the host to place your honored guests in the *tokonoma*.)

You will probably be served five entrees and rice and soup at a first class dinner, but don't think this is anything extraordinary. For hundreds of years a business dinner entailed anything from seven to ten entrees! It is only recently that the number of dishes has been reduced.

Remember when paying a restaurant bill that there will probably be a service charge of 10 percent added to your bill, and you do not tip more. Tipping openly is demeaning to the recipient, so if you wish to show your appreciation to the staff for doing your party so perfectly for you, fold money in an envelope and hand it secretly to the head waiter, who will distribute it to the proper staff.

If you stop at a fast food restaurant, eat your food inside rather than on the street. Adults of "class" do not eat on the streets (nor do they do so in the United States, for that matter).

Table Manners

It makes a big impression if a Westerner learns to say a couple of words in Japanese, such as *Itadakimasu* ("I shall begin eating"), said with a slight bow to one's host, and *Gochisosama* at the end of the meal, meaning "I have eaten well."

Learn to handle chopsticks with ease. It may be embarrassing for your host (and at times logistically difficult) to obtain a knife and fork for you in a restaurant. Remember never to leave your chopsticks in the bowl (as gauche as a Westerner's leaving his soup spoon inside his soup cup), and remember never to leave your chopsticks crossed. They should always be placed neatly, side by side. (There is a chopstick rest provided at your place, upon which to rest your chopsticks when they are not in use.)

If you are right-handed, you always hold your chopsticks in your right hand and your bowl of soup or food in your left hand. You will find that practice makes perfect as you learn to use these implements and to keep the bowl under your chin to prevent spilling. If you are the host of the meal, remember to pour sake for your senior guest first, and then for the others before pouring your own cup.

If you learn how to manipulate your rice and soup bowls properly, you will already have mastered enough table etiquette to greatly impress the Japanese with your sincerity in trying to understand their culture.

Since rice is Japan's principal food, the talents of the cook are often based on his or her ability to make good rice. The preparation of the soup is a great art, and if a guest praises it, these are most welcome words.

You will find your rice bowl on your left (remove the cover with your left hand and place it face up next to the bowl), and you will find your soup bowl on your right. (Remove the cover with your right hand and place it face up next to the soup bowl.) When the food service begins, you will be given a tray on which to place your rice bowl (use both hands to put it on the tray). The server will fill your bowl with rice, return it, and you should replace it on the table on your left. Never start eating from the bowl immediately—first replace it on the table in a ceremonial gesture. Pick up your chopsticks in your right hand, your rice bowl in your left, and eat a couple of mouthfuls. (While holding your rice bowl, refrain from putting your thumb inside to anchor it.)

Now take the soup bowl with your right hand and place it in your left. Taste the contents, express appreciation, and then drink some of the soup. Now you should begin alternating between mouthfuls of rice and sips of soup and tastes of any other dish, always holding the container in your left hand while you eat. If there is a dish of pickles at your place, leave them to the last, as they are very strong in their taste and could overwhelm the taste of the other dishes you are enjoying.

According to old tradition, if you wish a second helping of rice, you should leave a bit in your bowl, which signals that you wish more. If you do not wish any more, tradition says you should not leave a single grain in your bowl. Young Japanese do not adhere to this custom all the time.

The Wedding
(*See also* Ideas for Gifts, later in this chapter.)

If you are invited to a wedding reception, it is a mark of honor. (The ceremony is private for the families.) You should send a congratulatory letter with your response card. As in the West, you would send a nice present before the wedding day (unless it is impossible to do so, in which case you may bring the gift, carefully carded, to the reception.) A gift for the newlyweds' home is perfectly appropriate, just as in America. (You will receive a gift of lesser value back from the bride's family in time.)

Do not say *sayonara* when leaving the reception, as it signifies parting and is bad luck for the occasion of a wedding.

Funerals

When a Japanese business associate dies, or a member of his or her family, if you are away from Japan, you would send a telegram of condolences or arrange to have flowers sent by your office in Japan.

If you are in Japan, you would call promptly upon the family, bringing flowers but preferably a gift of yen in a special funeral envelope, as well as the flowers.

The funeral services are private, for the family only. If this was a close business friend, you might attend a "farewell ceremony" before the burial. You would enter the room where the coffin is kept, bow to the close friends of the deceased lined up on the left of the coffin, then bow to the coffin and pray, and then bow to the family and the "chief mourner," who are lined up on the right of the coffin.

The Arab World

Arabs are generous hosts and will be insulted if you refuse their offers of hospitality. Accept an offer that is made, after gracefully protesting that you don't want to inconvenience your host.

At all times, use your right hand for holding, offering, or receiving materials. If you write with your left hand, apologize to your host for having to do so. (The left hand is used for handling toilet paper.)

Be careful not to expose the soles of your feet when sitting, and never point at or beckon to an Arab (they use the latter gesture to summon dogs). On the other hand, be prepared for an Arab to stand quite close to you in conversation. Avoid even the mildest of expletives, and never use the word *God* in any context.

Arabs are intensely private about their women and families; it's considered rude to inquire about an Arab's wife or family if you have not personally met them. Soccer is a safe subject for small talk.

In general conversation you will be pleasing your Arab friend very much if you allude to their ancient history and the many contributions they have made to world civilization. The American who is familiar with the architectural ruins and art treasures of the Islamic world is considered a person of learning and culture.

However, don't praise their possessions in their homes and offices, for they may feel compelled to give you what you admire (including a large oriental rug!), and you would have to give back an equally handsome present.

Praise the interior in a general manner, without referring to a specific object, and you'll be all right.

An Arab is easily offended, so if you are the kind of person who teases those with whom you feel relaxed or if you are the kind of person who enjoys jumping into an intense argument on international affairs, control those impulses.

Appropriate dress for Western male executives is dark but light-weight clothing, white shirts, and lace-up shoes. Female executives should cover their arms from shoulder to wrist, avoid clothes that reveal body contours, and avoid slacks.

The Arabs are becoming more used to women executives. Dealing with a woman in business is against their natures, but the more sophisticated ones realize that the role of women has changed in the outside world, and they must accept the women leaders from other countries. More and more of their own women are being educated in the Western world, too, and are assuming jobs of importance in that world. American women who are doing business with the Arabs should dress very modestly, never act in an overfamiliar manner, and should block any impulse to discuss the women's movement or the position of the Arab woman.

Egypt

You'll get used to waiting in Egypt, for promptness is not a part of the Egyptian way of doing business. Remember to tip heavily here, for the tips in the service business are a way of life and often the workers' only source of income.

Saudi Arabia

The business person in Saudi Arabia should be sensitive to the country's strict religious customs and manners of dress (*see* Dressing for International Business, in Chapter 4). Don't insult a Saudi by trying to schedule a business trip during Ramadan (the annual month of fasting and prayer from sunup to sunset). No business may be transacted on Friday, the Islamic holy day. A foreign businessman who tries to pressure an Arab to meet with him for business on one of these days may find himself without a deal.

You must have patience in an Arab country. Patience is not a virtue; it is a necessity. Take the constantly offered little cups of mint tea or overly sweet black coffee and engage in small talk until your Arab counterparts are ready to talk business. A Saudi wants to know the person before he does business with him. Nothing happens quickly in this country—decisions are made with aggravating slowness—but it is rude, unfeeling, and counterproductive to try to hurry things along.

Most Saudi businessmen have been educated in English and American schools. They therefore speak English, but if you learn a few Arabic words— even something as simple as "thank you very much"—they are delighted.

Don't try to bring liquor into the country, because it will be confiscated by customs and you will be starting off with a black mark on your record. Don't smoke, either, unless your Arab host does.

Stay loose with your schedule when you go to Saudi Arabia. The Saudis are anything but punctual; in fact, if you have a meeting scheduled for a certain day, you may have to wait over another day in order to have it. You may very well find yourself joining a cast of characters in a meeting room full of people waiting to see the same person you are. This custom derives from the ancient conventions of tribal life in tents.

The high-powered business person simply has to shift into lower gear in this country.

The best way to learn how to entertain someone important from another country is to study how he himself entertains important Americans. It's very tough to keep up with the Saudis. Arab watchers are always fascinated when a member of the royal family visits the United States, because the Washington-based Saudi diplomats, at the royal family's command, stage a proper feast for the Americans. In February 1985, when King Fahd bin Abdul Aziz from Saudi Arabia visited President Reagan, His Majesty gave a return dinner party for several hundred people at his Washington ambassador's mansion. During the cocktail hour, the non-alcohol-consuming Saudis served a number of fresh fruit drinks, including freshly squeezed juice from guavas, oranges, grape-fruits, tomatoes, mangos, and pomegranates. A mountain of fresh caviar was on hand, as well as hors d'oeuvres made of baba ghanoug (an eggplant dip), falafel (ground, fried chickpeas), hummus (chickpea dip), and a giant sculp-ture of fresh shrimp. The Saudis also served a typical Arab sweet dessert: boxes made of chocolate and containing chocolate truffles, chocolate-covered strawberries, and other sweets.

An "oasis" was created for this party, with hundreds of palm trees brought into the house and on the grounds. The royal seal, massively sculpted in flowers (measuring twelve feet by twelve feet!), served as a backdrop for the receiving line. An American official commented that in order for President Reagan to emulate that party, he "would have to move the Grand Canyon to Jeddah, have the U.S. presidential seal sculpted (twenty-four feet by twenty-five feet) in oranges and grapefruits, and fish every Maine lobster and Florida stone crab right out of the sea."

Scandinavia

If you are hosting a meal in one of the Scandinavian countries, remember to *skål* your guests almost immediately, so that they can then start *skål*-ing you and each other, and everyone can get on with his drinking. In Sweden, remember to be scrupulously punctual for your business meetings and social events. People tend to be dressy in the evening in this country, so bring your dinner clothes with you. The honored guest at a Swedish meal sits to the host's left rather than to his right. In Sweden do as the Swedes do, and arrive at your host's home for dinner with a bunch of unwrapped flowers or a box of chocolates. If you're in a group in which no one has introduced you, take the initiative to introduce yourself to everyone. Swedes are reticent, and they appreciate someone else breaking the ice for them.

Thailand

In Thailand one should speak softly and never use swear words. Don't pat children on the head (or adults either, for that matter), which may be a sign of affection in the United States but is a strong negative in Thai eyes.

Being Courteous to Visiting Foreigners in Your City

When you are hosting foreign business people and their spouses in your city, there is a great deal you can do to make them grateful for the creativity and thoroughness of your hospitality. Anyone can reserve a luxurious suite like Chicago's Drake Hotel Presidential Suite, but not just anyone will plan ahead to make life as easy and as pleasant as possible for tired travelers. The hotel will stock the suite or the reserved room with all kinds of niceties, but it is the foreign guest's host who should apply the *really* personal touches. For example, this is what an American executive and his wife did for a Japanese executive (a close associate) and his wife when the latter spent a week for both business and social reasons as guests of the American couple.

In their hotel suite the travelers found the following items:

- A new can of tennis balls, a borrowed tennis racket, and a note to the Japanese man stating that the pro at a nearby club was waiting for his call in order to set up a good game for him at his convenience. (Needless to say, the American was aware of his colleague's great love of the game; he had also written him in advance, advising him to pack his tennis whites for the trip to the United States.)
- Bottles of his favorite scotch, bottles of her favorite soft drinks, with a bottle of champagne also tucked into the small fridge
- A basket of fresh fruit with plates and fruit knives (this was left by the hotel)
- A large flowering azalea plant
- A teapot, strainer, and two tins of Japanese tea left in the tiny kitchenette
- Two small pocket dictionaries (Japanese-English)

- A tin filled with the American wife's homemade cookies
- A list of needed telephone numbers, one copy for him and one for her
- A confirmed schedule of appointments for the Japanese businessman for the entire week, with both social and business engagements marked, with a copy also provided for his wife
- A copy of a special social schedule for the wife, plus a list of places to go shopping and exhibitions to see

The American wife arranged to have an interpreter present when she entertained the Japanese wife at luncheons and teas, so that making conversation with strangers would not be so difficult. The American wife had heard her Japanese friend mention how her children loved Michael Jackson, so the American host purchased some new cassettes and T-shirts for their friends to take home to the children. (The Americans and the Japanese subsequently exchanged but did not open their gifts, as is customary in Japan.) The Japanese couple wrote back later to their American hosts that one of the things that was most appreciated was the collection of colored candid photographs that had been taken of them during their various activities during the week. Small glossy prints of their activities had been placed in a small photo album to send to Japan, a wonderful souvenir of their unusual trip to America.

Another gesture made by the American wife which proved most helpful to the Japanese was a collection of all the American names and addresses of everyone of importance, so that they would have an excellent reference file, to use immediately for sending thank-you letters, as well as to use in the future.

Don't Importune the Traveler with Personal Requests

One of the most exasperating things you can do to anyone is to burden him down with a package you want delivered in another country or ask him to run an errand in another country. The traveler usually has a difficult enough time coping with his own baggage and packages; when you hand him something in addition, it may cause him great hardship. Don't forget that he also has to cope with your package in customs.

The errand you ask him to run for you may take a lot of time and cause hardship for his staff, too. So think before you ask someone going abroad, either an American or a foreigner, to execute a favor for you.

International Gift Giving
(*See also* The Art of Business Gift Giving, Chapter 16)

Gifts, while an integral part of the American business scene, are even more important in the case of business relationships between Americans and people of other countries. Sometimes foreigners tend to generalize that

Americans are crass and materialistic. Small gifts showing taste and imagination can help change that perception. Sometimes we Americans are accused of being a spoiled people. We can show we are *not* by being thoughtful and creative in our gift-giving practices.

In gift giving you prove that you think about someone other than yourself. A well-chosen gift showing some obvious research encourages a feeling of trust in the recipient's mind.

- If you are not familiar with the gift-giving customs of a country, ask the advice of someone knowledgeable, such as:

    A business colleague who is familiar with the culture of that country

    An official in the local consulate of that country

    A business person from that country now living in the United States
- Your gift should never be too costly, or the recipient will consider it a bribe. While your intention was to please someone, you will have done just the opposite.
- Your gift should be tastefully wrapped—presentation is very important in other countries.
- The most flattering gift is one that has been secretly researched by talking to the recipient's secretary or associate to find out his interests. You might bring a welcome addition to his stamp collection or start a subscription for him to a publication for horse breeders; you might add to his porcelain collection or bring a gadget for his new automobile.
- A gift relating to his profession is always meaningful. For example, you might find an antique lawyer's sign for an attorney or an old book written by a journalist to give to someone in the media.
- A gift relating to both countries is particularly precious. For example, for a French colleague, you might find a reproduction of a map used by Lafayette in the American Revolution or an antique box painted with the head of that great French gift to America, the Statue of Liberty.
- A gift dominated by an oversized corporate logo will seem like an advertisement, not a present.
- Your foreign colleague will appreciate something bought in your own country more than a gift bought in his.
- You should be reticent about giving gifts to people you do not know well. Don't bring a gift to your first meeting, for example, or you might give the recipient the impression that you are pressing too hard to close the deal.
- If your gift is sharp or pointed (such as a bar knife or letter opener), send or present it with a cork placed on the sharp point. This will counteract any vestige of the old superstition that a gift with a sharp point is meant to be driven into the recipient's heart. (You can always explain why you are sending the cork on your gift enclosure card.)

Follow the Gift and Flower Customs of the Country You Visit

If you are going to send flowers to your hosts when you are in a foreign country, ask about the etiquette involved with certain flowers. The gladiolus, so loved in Italy, is the symbol of mourning in many other countries. In Germany red roses are the symbol of lovers, while in the Far East white flowers are symbolic of mourning. In America a potted plant makes a very suitable gift to someone who is ill; in Japan, if you send one under those circumstances, you are wishing him to be "rooted in his illness."

Here are some other traditions and superstitions:

Argentina

Never give an Argentinian a set of knives, as it signals a desire to cut off the business relationship.

India

Never give a Hindu a gift made of cowhide, since the cow is considered sacred in the country of India. In my White House staff days, I made all of the arrangements for Mrs. Kennedy's state gifts to the officials of India during her visit there. Without giving the matter a thought, I ordered six dozen custom-made blue leather frames, each embossed with the presidential seal. Since the frames were made from cowhide, if we had presented them to Hindu officials, it might have caused an international incident. When my error was discovered, we were fortunate enough to be able to have silver frames quickly made as a substitute!

Britain

Don't give a Britisher a striped tie. An Englishman wears only his own regiment's tie; to wear another's would be considered very bad form.

The Iron Curtain Countries

When business executives from Soviet bloc countries come to this country, the best present you can send to their hotel room is a bottle of liquor. However, if you visit their country, it may not be possible to pass the liquor through customs. It is better not to attempt it.

Gifts pertaining to the arts are very appreciated in the Soviet Union. Record albums of classical music have always been popular, but country music and folk music are also passionately loved by them. It is wise not to give them rock albums, although the young people love rock; sometimes the design of a far-out rock group's albums are considered "too degenerate" for the customs officials to allow to enter.

Coffee table books on art or photography or sports make nice presents. So does a conservative tie for a man and a scarf for a woman. A piece of art is appreciated; so are books of photographs of dancers in action.

Because of health regulations, you are not supposed to bring food into the Soviet-bloc countries. However, a sealed tin of cookies or chocolates will often pass through customs.

The Arab Countries

Arabs are extremely generous gift givers. Your Arab colleague should be the first to present a gift. When you reciprocate, you should try to match his in elaborateness and cost.

As previously mentioned, do not bring gifts to an Arab's wife and children unless you know them extremely well. If you do bring presents, toys and scarves would be appropriate.

Do not bring an Arab liquor or wine. It would be confiscated by customs, since alcohol is illegal in an Islamic country. Do not bring food either, since it can be construed as a criticism of your host's hospitality.

If you plan to buy a gift for an Arab, select a gift from a recognizable store, such as a piece of sterling silver or porcelain from Tiffany & Company, a globe from Neiman Marcus, a crystal bowl from Steuben, linens from Pratesi or Porthault, the latest "do everything" calculator from a major American technology company, etc. A "name" gift pleases them.

China

Gift giving is difficult in China. A present given by a foreign visitor to a Chinese in his own country must be offered with great tact, and certainly in private, since the law prohibits him from accepting a personal gift. To give a Chinese a gift in front of others would embarrass him terribly, and he would most likely have to embarrass you, too, by giving it back.

There is even less tipping in China than in Japan. If you wish to reward anyone who went to a great deal of trouble to serve you in your hotel, for example, you would have to put the cash in an envelope and make the person take it when no one was looking.

The Chinese are very culturally inclined; if you give an art book, a lithograph, or a framed print, and if you offer it as a gift for the host's organization, it might be accepted.

Never give a clock to the Chinese, since it is a symbol of death.

Japan

No one practices the art of gift giving more enthusiastically than the Japanese. Twice a year, in December (Oseibo) and July (Ochugen), the Japa-

nese exchange gifts with their business contacts, either to express appreciation or to repay an obligation. Since this is a costly, time-consuming custom,
younger Japanese managers are trying hard to stop it.

The Japanese talent for gift giving is legendary. Jack O'Dwyer, writing in
his national public relations newsletter of July 19, 1984, used as many words
to describe the gift involved in the signing of a working arrangement between
two major agencies (Hakuhodo and Daniel J. Edelman) as he did on the news
story of the agreement itself. The gift was nothing more than a silk-covered
album of photos, but the way in which it was presented and the beauty of the
ritual greatly impressed the Americans present. We Americans could learn
many things from the Japanese in thoughtfulness and creativity. When I was
making arrangements to travel to Tokyo to lecture on behalf of the big cosmetic company Shiseido, I mentioned to one of the executives that I wanted to
learn a few phrases in Japanese before my departure. Shortly thereafter a
cassette of English phrases translated into Japanese arrived in my office,
which has endeared the Shiseido company to me forever.

The Japanese customarily open their gifts in private, but if you open your
gift in front of your Japanese colleague, he will undoubtedly do the same, so as
not to make you uncomfortable. Notice how he always carefully rewraps a gift
he has opened so that it looks untouched and unopened. (As someone who
always tears any gift wrapping to shreds, I am fascinated by this skill.)

Gift wrapping has many traditions and symbolic gestures related to it in
Japan, including matters of how the paper is folded and the choice of the cord
and the style in which it is knotted. The Japanese are most apt to use colored
wrapping paper and fabric. In the ancient tradition, a wrapped gift is then
presented in a silk scarf (a *furoshiki*), which is the final wrapping.

When a Japanese presents you with a gift, the nice thing to do is to thank
him and make a small bow in appreciation.

It is considered rude for an executive traveling on business to surprise a
Japanese colleague with a gift. It will make him lose face, and he will feel
compelled immediately to buy a return gift. Let him be the first to give the gift
when you are in his country. If you reciprocate, your gift should be slightly
less expensive than his.

It is redundant to give a Japanese colleague a gift that is readily available
in his own country (such as a digital watch or a tape recorder). Give him
something American. Like the Chinese, he cherishes a gift of art—a painting,
weaving, sculpture, or ceramic by an American artist. The Japanese also
appreciate ties (somber colors) and scarves and handbags for the women,
particularly if they have trendy designers' names attached. And, of course,
liquor is a very welcome present.

Never give a Japanese a present in front of others unless you have gifts
for everyone present. Always send a thank-you note within a couple of days of

receiving a gift, or the giver may feel you do not like it. If you are fortunate enough to be invited to a Japanese home, either bring a gift with you or send one immediately after. It should be something understated, such as candy or food that can be shared and enjoyed by the entire family.

Ideas for Gifts

- With the exception of the Islamic countries, *a gift of liquor* is always a popular one. Until rather recently, it was considered unbecoming of a female executive to bring liquor to a male executive, but that is changing now. One should not worry about what the recipient drinks; it can always be used for entertaining in the office or at home.
- *The latest American gadget* is usually cherished by a foreigner. If you decide on an electrical item, be sure to find out what the import tax will be and arrange to pay for it. It might be necessary to include an adapter to change the current and voltage to the other country's standards. If the wall plug is different in the other country, let the recipient worry about it.
- If your business associate abroad is fluent in English, *a best-selling book on American foreign policy,* on the President and his cabinet, or on American business practices will be of interest.
- *Pen and pencil sets* are always popular and appropriate. If they bear the corporate logo, it should be small in size. Remember to include refills as part of the gift (if they are needed).
- A box of *fine stationery* is always a welcome gift. (For a man, choose a conservative color, such as white, gray, or tan.)
- A gift involving *music* (tapes of classical music, American jazz, folk, country, or rock) is usually a good idea for any age.
- *Food,* well-packed in tins or sealed containers, is a good family present—nuts, candy, cookies, gourmet crackers, preserves, etc.
- *A gift of clothing* is often very welcome (but *know* the size, don't guess at it).
  Blue jeans and all Western wear
  American sweaters
  Running shoes
  Ski caps (with American ski organizations and team names)
  T-shirts with amusing sayings or representing famous American sports teams
  Designer-name accessories (scarves, ties, belts, etc.)

Especially for Children

It will please a foreign colleague if, when you go to his home for a meal, you bring presents for the children. Do not bring the children gifts, however, unless you have met them or their parents have spoken of them in your presence. The exception to this rule is in the case of a newborn baby. An infant six months old or less in the house where you are being entertained signals a present, no matter how small. It is politic, of course, when bringing a present for a baby, to bring something small like a box of candy to the other children in the family, simply because of sibling jealousy.

A handsome but expensive gift for an infant might be a sterling silver mug engraved with the baby's name or initials and birth date. However, I was there when a very expensive ($250) silver mug "bombed" as a present because it was engraved with an oversize corporate logo that far outshone the baby's initials. The beautiful present was regarded as a commercial statement. Less expensive gifts in silver are a spoon, rattle, food pusher, or bar-bell teether. Linens for the crib make nice gifts, as do colorful mobiles to place in the nursery, stuffed animals, amusing night lights, and books for a baby (such as pop-up fairy tales or "touch and feel" books).

Toys made in America are popular presents, particularly those that are the big fad in the States at the present moment. Whether it's the latest album, doll, or space toy, the word seems to pass around among children very quickly between one country and another.

Teenage girls who are allowed to wear makeup always appreciate gifts of American cosmetics (choose lighter colors), skin care products, and nail polish. They also like the latest American fads in belts, handbags, scarves, or costume jewelry.

Female Executives Giving Gifts

An American woman executive should refrain from giving gifts to her foreign colleagues until she knows them fairly well, simply because the position of women in most other countries is far less advanced than in our own. She should wait until a foreign colleague first gives *her* a gift (unless she knows him extremely well, or unless she is the honoree of a party he is giving).

If she has met the wife of a foreign colleague, she may certainly bring her a small gift when she goes to that country on business, for that is something easy for a male executive to accept. Cosmetics, nylons, a designer perfume, or costume jewelry make great gifts to a woman whom you have met previously. Travel cases, a good looking tote, and an umbrella make suitable gifts from one woman executive to another, even if they have *not* met previously.

If a woman knows her foreign colleagues well, she must still be careful to refrain from giving anything of a personal nature (such as a bathrobe). A clock, except in China, makes a suitable gift for a man; so does any kind of desk accessory. One woman I know scored a big success when she sent each of her foreign colleagues a handsome American leather picture frame after her return to the United States. Her gift card suggested that the frame be used to hold a family photo. That suggestion immediately made her gift a suitable one, not an overly personal one directed at the man alone.

A woman executive who brings gifts of food is also on sure grounds in the art of gift giving abroad.

A Special Gift for a Foreign Guest Speaker

When you sponsor a program that features a foreigner as guest speaker, you should give that person a memento commemorating the occasion. If the speaker is not receiving an honorarium, you might give him a piece of luggage or a briefcase, something of good quality made in America. If your speaker is receiving an honorarium, it is still a nice gesture to send him a small gift, such as a book. You might enclose your business card or a correspondence card with this kind of message: "Your address was unanimously well received. It was substantive and well-delivered. Thank you from all of us."

PART II

BUSINESS
PROTOCOL

When executives in a corporation are familiar with and at ease with the rules of protocol, they are a shining asset to the organization. Understanding and becoming familiar with protocol in business is like using a good road map to arrive at one's destination without stress or delay. One first must know what good protocol is before being able to practice it (this is a major problem in business today). The chapters that follow deal with the corporate manners that show a company knows how to do things properly.

Corporate protocol covers everything from office stationery to posting the flags properly for your company's civic function in a hotel ballroom. It defines what is appropriate rather than improper when giving gifts. It is based on the philosophy that there is a great deal more to successful business entertaining than merely having caviar and champagne on the menu.

Companies like IBM are regarded as class acts, and not just because of their financial successes. Behind the "class" lies a lot of hard work, training, attention to details, and an insistence on maintaining the polish on the company image. Corporate protocol also concerns itself with the individual executive's behavior as an aspect of the company's image. The two work with or against each other.

A company can become expert in corporate protocol first by caring about the subject, then by learning about it, and finally by insisting on following proper procedures. The tenets of protocol do not stifle creativity in the corporate culture; rather, they enhance it greatly.

6

Meetings, Conferences, and Seminars

$\mathbf{A}$merica is a nation of meeters. Our system of business uses the meeting as one of its basic tools, whether for the purpose of selling, informing, instructing, critiquing, planning, or exhorting. A small business owner adds three people to his staff, and suddenly the staff meeting is born; it is inevitable. A staff meeting may take place with three people sitting in their offices, calling to each other through open doors, or it may take place around a beautifully polished burl conference table, with everyone sitting upright in leather swivel chairs. Besides the many thousands of office meetings held every day, there are approximately 750,000 corporate meetings organized formally in the United States each year, and another 50,000 held on an international basis under the sponsorship of the participants' states or regions. And that is not to mention seminars and conferences staged by educational companies, institutions, and business organizations.

Since Americans are already the most meeting-afflicted people in the world, executives should make an earnest effort to hold meetings *only* if necessary and then to make them as physically and psychologically comfortable as possible.

It is the meeting chairman's responsibility to manage meeting comfort factors. I have observed that *every well-run meeting invariably has a combination of a chairman with good manners and participants with good manners*—it's like an excellent symphony conductor, who needs an excellent

191

corps of musicians in order to make truly beautiful music. Good manners, smooth management, and efficiency all seem to fit together, resulting in a meeting that is productive, pleasant to attend, and finished either on time or early.

An office meeting may be called for any number of reasons, but it will not be productive unless the need to call the meeting is properly communicated and unless everyone leaves it understanding the signals and the lines of responsibility and takes appropriate action as a result.

Behavior in an office meeting should not differ from behavior at meetings outside the office, and that includes conventions, sales meetings, conferences, and seminars in which each of us represents our company to the community at large. Of course, since we are on show in public—a different kind of show from that in our offices—we should not only demonstrate the same consideration we do in our office meetings but make an even greater effort. Social animals that we are, the more we practice, the more automatic the correct responses become, and the easier and the more natural good manners become.

The manners of the individual attending a meeting are important; those of the organizers who stage the event are equally so. The whole feeling—the ambiance—of a large meeting really depends upon the professionalism, efficiency, creativity, and caring attitude of those in charge.

A large gathering can be a warm, personal experience for its participants. I have, for example, the warmest of memories of a three-day seminar I attended in the Montreux Palace Hotel in Switzerland for Dean Witter Reynolds (a major financial services company) at which I was one of the speakers. All attendees were sent several mailings of material before our departure so that we arrived in Montreux thoroughly briefed on the company's program, the country, the history of the hotel, and options for what we could do in our free time. Our suitcases were tagged with large bright-colored tags, which made them readily identifiable in airports. When we checked into the hotel, we each found a beautiful packet of Swiss postcards, all stamped with Swiss air mail stamps, ready for us to send back home. Each night a little gift was left in our rooms by the meeting manager. One night it was a small box of chocolates, another night an embroidered Swiss handerchief, another night a basket of fresh fruit.

Since this was an international meeting, protocol was strictly followed; every dinner was properly seated; all Swiss and American business people and government officials were properly introduced to each other, with names and titles correctly given. Every little detail was "just right," because a great deal of advance planning had gone into it. The Dean Witter Reynolds meeting manager had beautiful manners; he was very conscious of the image his company was trying to project, particularly since so many thousands of dollars were being spent on its projection.

However, even if your meeting is in Room R-4 on your office floor rather than at the Montreux Palace in Switzerland, remember the old saying: It *is* the little things that count!

Interoffice Meetings

The Effective Meeting Chairman

There is no situation in which an executive's managerial skills are more visible than when running a meeting. In order to make sure that meeting behavior is completely correct, the meeting chairman should keep a copy of *Robert's Rules of Order* (by H. M. Robert; published by Fleming Revell; paperback, $3.95) at his or her desk.

In addition to following correct rules of order, the polite chairman:

- *Is thoughtful about when he schedules the meeting,* knowing that most people are at their best and freshest in the morning. He does not schedule meetings on Friday afternoons, when people are trying to get away for the weekend. He does not schedule them on the eve of important holidays, when out-of-town participants will have difficulty returning to their home cities. He does not carelessly schedule meetings on important religious holidays.
- *Informs participants as far ahead as possible of the date*—two weeks ahead of an in-house meeting, if possible, and four weeks ahead for participants who have to travel from other cities.
- *Is apologetic if circumstances force him to call a meeting without a proper lead time,* because he realizes he may have greatly inconvenienced the people who must attend.
- *Invites people to his meetings on a selective, carefully thought out basis,* realizing that only those who *must* attend should be invited. He is aware that many meetings do not have to be called at all. He includes those who have direct responsibility for the business at hand, as well as those in training who would find it useful to be there. He invites people from other areas of the company whose expertise will be needed, so that he will never have to say to himself, "I *should* have asked so-and-so to attend today." However, he keeps remembering that valuable management resources must not be wastefully tied up in meetings.
- *Distributes the agenda well in advance,* to give invitees the time to think about the subjects at hand.
- *Makes sure that pertinent material is in the participants' hands* well

before the meeting, to help in their preparation but also to avoid wasting time reading the material during the meeting.

- *Determines how long to wait for missing people before starting.* One executive I know will not wait one minute beyond the scheduled hour for *anyone,* including the CEO. When he begins the meeting, he starts a tape recorder and makes anyone who is tardy stay behind afterward to hear what he missed.
- *Introduces all newcomers to the group in a complimentary manner* and introduces the others to the newcomers with their names, titles, and responsibilities.
- *Shows the younger executives that he is approachable and human,* not only by his sense of humor but by allowing the younger people (or new-comers or visitors) the opportunity to show what they know and to contribute to the discussion. In other words, he orchestrates the proceedings in a way that permits them to establish their knowledge and expertise before their peers.
- *Is aware of any tension and nonverbal communication that flows in a hostile way around the room* and talks it over afterward with anyone involved. Sometimes, of course, there is open hostility, which must be dealt with on the spot. I will never forget being present in a meeting of two sharply opposed factions. The chairman, a senior executive, had trouble keeping order as managers argued vehemently on two sides. Finally he rose from his chair and walked over to the light switch on the wall. Suddenly fifteen emotionally upset executives were plunged into total darkness. There was no sound in the room; it was as though a cool wet blanket had been wrapped around a steaming room interior. A few seconds later, the chairman switched on the light. It worked. The discussion continued in a calm, rational way; the disagreement was settled, and the meeting came to a close.
- *Keeps one eye on the clock and one on the agenda* and thereby avoids delays caused by people rambling and talking off the subject.
- *Does not smoke if smoking is not permitted in that room.* He is considerate of nonsmokers and discusses with management whether to have Smoking and Non-Smoking sections of the room or whether to have smokers sit clustered together around the conference table.
- *Handles the "meeting hogger" with agility.* Shuts off with kindness and firmness the person who tries to dominate the meeting.
- Sees that the meeting place is comfortable—that it is:
    Clean
    Well lit
    Aired out (stale air makes stale minds)
    Cool in temperature

          Equipped with comfortable seating
          Equipped with ice water and glasses
          Equipped with pads and pencils

- Calls a seventh-inning stretch for participants every hour and a half of a very long meeting, to allow them to stretch their muscles, talk to colleagues, make a telephone call, etc.
- Gives credit to everyone who gave presentations but also to everyone who helped prepare the meeting, including those who prepared any graphs, slides, and/or audiovisual presentations that were used.

The Art of Good Meeting Behavior for the Young Executive

The manners of the chairman of the meeting are not the only important protocol consideration; the participants' manners are equally important. The successful, well-run, decorous meeting is definitely a two-way street, and there are many ways in which a participant can demonstrate efficient good manners.

- *He arrives on time,* even several minutes before the meeting is scheduled to begin.
- If he's on new turf of his own or on someone else's turf, *he introduces himself* in a friendly, informal manner to anyone also waiting. If he is the outsider, he explains to the others who he is and why he's there. This is also the time for him to hand out his business card—if the executives with whom he is talking ask him questions about himself and his company.
- As a newcomer, *he does not take a seat* until someone who knows why he is there motions for him to "take a seat anywhere," or perhaps to "sit over there, next to Ann Smith." It would be bad politics to plunk himself down next to the meeting chairman. The seats to the right and left of the chairman are for that person's peers or honor guests.
- If the meeting is delayed for some reason (such as the late arrival of the chairman), he should turn to someone on either side and launch into a conversational topic (unless that person is studying the papers in front of him). He might ask a question about current events ("What did you think of the incredible upsets in yesterday's primaries?") or perhaps bring up the meeting itself ("I'm anxious to hear the presentation of the new campaign, because I hear it's a great one.").
- *He arrives prepared for the meeting* with all his homework carefully done.
- *He has rehearsed his own remarks well if he is to do a presentation, and has asked the manager to let him try out any audiovisual and electrical equipment* needed for an audiovisual presentation, to make sure it works properly. In other words, he is *ready.*

- He receives permission from the chair before using a tape recorder.
- *He makes careful notes of the discussion and the criticisms* that are put forth on his own ideas and makes careful notes, too, of his own criticisms of others' ideas.
- *He doesn't slump in his seat,* an action that denotes boredom, which is the exact opposite of the impression he should be trying to create.
- *He does not doodle,* another very distracting gesture. (True, United States presidents have been known to doodle in cabinet meetings; when the junior executive gets to be President of the United States, he can doodle, too.) He also refrains from other "conference table tics," such as bending paper clips into endless combinations or rolling bits of paper into tiny balls.
- *He avoids interrupting whoever has the floor,* instead making a note of what he wanted to say at that moment. Particularly in the case of large, formal meetings, he awaits a timely moment in which to interject his comments. He obtains recognition to speak by calling out the name of the chairman and half raising his hand, as though he were in school getting the teacher's attention. The chair will then nod in his direction or call out his name, signifying he may now have the floor.
- *He resists the temptation to monopolize the proceedings* at any point, even if he is qualified to do so. (He remembers how his classmates felt about the student who perpetually had his hand up first every time the teacher asked a question.)
- *He has the courage to ask for clarification* of an unclear point. Probably there are several others in the room just as confused as he is. He knows that there is wisdom in admitting one does not understand, rather than trying to bluff through it.
- He is relaxed about showing his positive emotions but careful to control any display of negative emotions if in violent disagreement with something that has just been said. There are degrees of showing disapproval; "violent" disapproval is rude. He can evince his disagreement by shaking his head and making a quiet comment after the other person has finished speaking. If the chair does not call upon him to elucidate further, he should keep quiet and voice his opinions only after the meeting.
- *He uses the editorial "we" instead of "I"* when talking to the group. "We" signifies he is part of a team; "I" sounds egocentric, as if he refuses to grant credit to the others working on a project (even if their role is very small).
- If shyness overcomes him when he has something to say, he knows *he can put his thoughts in a memo* sent to the chairman and to whoever else present at the meeting should receive it.
- *He thinks before he speaks* and does not present his comments in a

sloppy, disorganized fashion. He also sticks to the subject, so as not to waste everyone's time.

- He knows perfectly well that if smoking is permitted in the room, that does *not give him license to light up either a cigar or a pipe* without unanimous permission. (If he's the chairman of the company, of course, everyone else is out of luck!) If he does have permission to smoke a cigar or pipe, he should do so only if he sits next to an open window and exhales through it.
- He pours any canned soda he is offered into a glass; he *never* drinks from a can at a business meeting.
- He says a quiet "Thank you" to the meeting chairman as he leaves the room at the conclusion of the meeting.
- He later congratulates anyone he meets who performed exceptionally well in his or her presentation.

Thinking Before Speaking

A young executive often has a tendency to project creative ideas at meetings based more on enthusiasm than on substance, feasibility, and logic. I am grateful to Ely Callaway, who was once my boss as president of Burlington Industries, at that time the world's largest textile company. He chaired a meeting that I attended in my new capacity as the company's first woman senior executive and first Director of Consumer Affairs. At one point in the crowded conference room I seized the floor and became inflamed with the passion of my own remarks. Ely very quietly slipped me a note, which I managed to glance at while on my feet still talking. "Tish," it read, "enough is *enough.*" He had sent me a signal to stop, for my own good. I finished quickly and sat down, my cheeks flaming red.

He explained afterward that I had not been communicating properly to the group. I did not have the *sense* of the group. When I thanked him for tipping me off, he urged me to have a little more patience. He explained that a newcomer first has to gain the respect of old-timers before suddenly interjecting a whole stream of new ideas. "Prove first that you're a professional," he advised, "before trying to change the world." Then he chuckled and said, "But, Tish, you gave quite a performance!"

Rules of Decorum for the Board of Directors' Meeting

This is the kind of meeting that should—and usually does—take top priority in a chief executive officer's life. He is answerable to the shareholders through this board. Service on the board is usually an aspiration, both for inside directors (whose presences signify that they are the company's leaders) and for outside directors (for whom this service is an honor, a challenge, and often a financially remunerative plum).

The board of directors is supposed to be a counterbalance to all of the yes-men surrounding the CEO, so their meetings rank at the head of the list in importance and prestige of all meetings held inside the office. The board meets monthly in most large corporations, from two to four times a year or more in small companies. The composition of this group should ideally include minority representation but seldom does, except in larger companies. The directors should serve conscientiously, not only for the company's sake, but also for their own, since there is a great potential for shareholders' lawsuits. Their liability is a serious matter—the directors' liability insurance taken out by companies and institutions is often inadequate to cover damages that might have to be paid.

Outside directors are supposed to communicate to senior management what the public and the company shareholders are really saying about the company and how it's being run. Outside directors are *not* supposed to rubber-stamp the CEO's actions. Ideally the board should be comprised of people who are excellent in their various fields and who bring a wealth of experience and talent to bear on the issues discussed. They are often heads of other companies, as well as lawyers, accountants, and people conversant with finance, technology, product development, insurance, marketing, public relations, or any other important aspects of business as it is conducted today.

The Importance of Good Communications

A productive board is a well-informed one; necessary materials should be sent out and studied by directors well *before* the meeting. If management understands the importance of advance communication and has put the material into each director's hands in advance, the work process should flow smoothly, and the directors will feel better about handling their responsibilities toward the company.

The following summarizes the contents of the monthly packet that should be sent by the corporate secretary to each outside director four or five days in advance of a board meeting.

- A full agenda of the upcoming meeting, as well as the announcement of the date, time, and place for it
- The standard report material (most importantly, the financial reports)
- The full minutes of the preceding board meeting (which, if read and found to be without error, can then be quickly approved at the board meeting)
- Special presentations dealing with policy, procedure, budgets, and/or committee reports

- The full minutes of committee meetings (except for those committees that meet the same morning, in which case there will be an oral report by the committee chairman at some point during the meeting)

When a Director Attends His First Meeting

When an outside director arrives for his first meeting, there should be extensive introductions made. The new director should be introduced personally to everyone in the immediate executive office, but it's productive and courteous if, after the meeting, the CEO also takes him around as much of the company as can be covered within an hour's time for brief introductions.

The new director's photograph and biography should be published in the house organ so that everyone at every level will know about the newest management team member.

When Division Heads Appear Before the Board

It is very helpful if the CEO schedules on a regular basis a brief appearance before the board of various mid-managers and division heads. This enables the outside directors to understand the company better, and it provides the entire board with the opportunity to scout good potential senior management candidates.

Since it is obviously a very important moment in the division manager's career, he or she should be as well dressed (and as conservatively dressed) as possible, show respect for the board, and display a polished set of manners. This includes paying attention, not interrupting a director when he speaks, answering directors' questions carefully but succinctly (so as not to waste time), and thanking the board for the opportunity to present his division's case.

The Directors' Manners

The directors should be careful always to mind their manners, because they are highly visible within the company. They should be considerate of the company's administrative staff and not take for granted staff efforts to keep the directors informed and to make their lives pleasant at board and committee meetings. The directors usually have good reason to say "thank you" all the time.

Outside directors should request to be led through the various manufacturing processes on the line. Workers in plants like to see the big brass, and it's important for the directors to understand how the company's products are produced.

Company "perks" should not be abused, either. There is always the occasional director who asks the company to get tickets for him to a popular play and then does not pay for them, who changes his plans about using the limo but does not bother to inform the person who ordered it, or who foists his student son or daughter on the company for a summer job even when there is no summer hiring. On the other side there is always the occasional director who sends all of the secretaries in the executive office Christmas presents or who has breakfast in the company cafeteria and sits down to talk to the employees instead of being served breakfast with the directors in the chairman's dining room.

Most important of all, of course, directors should do their homework diligently, make sure they understand every issue and its implications, and ask questions and speak out if they disagree on how an issue is being handled.

A Photograph of the Board

It is a nice gesture to have a good group photograph made of the board of directors and to give each director a print, handsomely framed. Most shareholders want to see what the board looks like, too, so the same photograph makes a (usually) welcome addition to the annual report.

Good Manners at a
Routine Meeting Outside the Office

Both junior and senior executives' actions are conspicuous when they attend meetings outside their own offices. As a visitor, an executive is very much on parade.

- If he is a casual dresser, on the day of the meeting he should dress up, and conservatively.
- He should arrive *on time.*
- He should not ask to use the telephone of anyone present, nor should he ask anyone's secretary to make a call for him or run an errand for him during the meetings. (He should have done all of that previously, using a pay telephone if necessary.)
- If no one in the host group introduces him before the meeting, he should extend his hand to those near him and give his name and company. He should also introduce himself to the meeting chairman when the latter arrives. In this way the meeting will begin on a friendly note.
- He should wait to sit down until someone has waved him into a seat or until the chairman has asked everyone to be seated.
- It is the host's duty to offer the group refreshment, like coffee, tea or soda, but if nothing is offered, the visitor should not request anything.
- An absence of ashtrays in the room is a sign that he should not ask to smoke.

- It is wise for him to hand his business card to the person taking the notes of the meeting, so that the note-taker will know his name and affiliation immediately when he contributes to the discussion.
- He should make a special effort to remain alert and look interested throughout the meeting, even if he is acutely bored.
- He should personally thank the meeting chairman for his hospitality at the meeting's conclusion.

Large Meetings Out of Town

Holding a meeting or event in corporate headquarters, whether yours or your client's, is simple in comparison to holding one at a conference center or hotel. When the meeting is in another city and attended by a large number of people, sometimes from other companies based in other cities, then the logistical planning for the sponsor becomes very complicated.

A first class company should hold its meetings in first class facilities. A facility that is close by and easy to reach may not be worth the convenience; one that is "really cheap" may be a total waste of money rather than a saving of it.

A meeting out of town is usually worth the planned expense, because changing the scene instigates fresh ideas. If the attendees are well taken care of, they usually regard attendance at the meeting as a cherished executive perk.

The Person in Charge

The CEO's executive secretary or an administrative staff person can make the arrangements for small meetings held on company premises or in other cities. When a large, complicated meeting is to be organized, either at company headquarters or in another city, it may be time for the CEO to retain the professional services of an outside company that specializes in developing an entire scenario for the meeting, including dealing with the hotels, negotiating with the airlines, setting up the programs, the banquets and the entertainment, deciding on the menus and the decor, making arrangements for office and audiovisual equipment needed at the meeting, running the sports programs and, as one wag expressed it, "holding hands and wiping noses."

Large corporations often have a meeting planner (or meeting manager) on staff, whether they use outside professionals or not. This person, sometimes referred to as the Coordinator for Special Events, has the full-time responsibility for arranging the company's meetings, entertainment events, and seminars and conferences—both on home base and around the world.

The person directly in charge of the meeting may take care of the physical atmosphere, but the psychological atmosphere at the meeting and the objectives to be achieved are the responsibility of senior management.

Picking a Conference or Seminar Location

The objectives of the company's meeting should dictate what type of facility is used. Sometimes a resort is appropriate, so that business may be combined with sport and recreation; sometimes the aim is primarily a "working meeting," and then a comfortable hotel in a city with excellent meeting facilities is appropriate.

If a meeting manager has been told by senior management to find a suitable resort facility, he usually contacts first the known, proven hotels, such as the Broadmoor in Colorado, the Williamsburg Inn and the Homestead in Virginia, the Greenbriar in West Virginia, the Breakers in Florida, the White Mountain Inn in New Hampshire. Sometimes the famous places are fully booked, or he may not be able to make the right deal. When it comes to booking an unfamiliar newer facility, he can find out how good it is very quickly by checking with the person in charge of a large group that recently used it—the reputation of the establishment spreads very quickly by word of mouth. When it comes to signing up with one of the older establishments, he should check with someone who recently used that particular facility, too, because the facility can change quite drastically from one year to the next.

Alternatives to Hotels: Clubs and Conference Centers

Meetings may be held in facilities other than hotels—for example, *private clubs* and *conference centers.* Although almost everyone enjoys going to a private club, inviting people to a meeting in a place that would exclude them from membership because of their sex, race, color, or religion may be counterproductive. Women executives, for example, usually chafe at an invitation to a business meeting in a private men's club where they must use a special entrance, stairway, or elevator.

A favorite kind of facility for executives away from their home cities is the conference center, usually located in an idyllic setting and offering meeting and recreational facilities in an atmosphere of peace and quiet. At a place like the Executive Conference Center in Tarrytown, New York, for example, you find no tourists, parties, dance music, or traffic sounds to disturb what is usually a week's stay. There is no room service or television in the bedrooms. Conference centers do not have the staffs large hotels do.

Sharon L. Hassinger, of the Hotel Hershey and Country Club in Hershey, Pennsylvania, advises meeting planners to book well in advance, to be as specific as is humanly possible (with valid numbers on sleeping accommodations needed), and to *confirm all arrangements in writing,* whether it's the responsibility of the meeting facility or of the meeting manager. She urges meeting managers to be extremely clear about the company's billing require-ments, since "nothing can ruin a well-coordinated conference more effectively than billing problems that arise afterward." She also urges complete feedback from the meeting manager afterward, because the only way a facility can improve its services is to know what problems the client company may have had. Constructive criticism is essential, not just a "nice thing to give."

Other alternatives to holding the meeting in a hotel or resort catering especially to business organizations include:

· A chartered cruise for a "conference at sea"
· A meeting at a ski resort in the mountains, even if many participants don't ski
· A meeting in a health spa where those who wish may eat at special diet tables (one group of 135 executives recently lost a total of 518 pounds in four days!)

Negotiating for the Site and Services

Often senior management has no idea of how important the job of the meeting planner or meeting manager is. A good manager proficient in the art of negotiating can save his company hundreds of thousands of dollars in meeting expenses. This person needs experience on the job. He needs to keep himself constantly informed; he needs to gain information through the networking possibilities offered by the various meeting managers' associations. Before any written confirmation is made reserving a conference site, or before an entertainment contract or a deal on group fares on the airlines is concluded, a meeting manager has to go through a delicate series of negotiations. He is truly performing an important management function.

A good planner does not settle for the first price quoted on anything. He either tries to get the price down, or he tries to get additional services added for the price quoted. He should negotiate:

· Room rates (perhaps getting lower prices on smaller rooms or rooms without views or rooms next to noisy areas)
· The entertainment (for example, obtaining a special price should one orchestra play for four functions during the meeting)
· Banquet facilities (for example, getting special prices if the Grand Ball-room will be used for lunch and two dinners consecutively)
· Use of the recreational facilities
· Gratuities paid as a percentage of the total cost

James E. Jones, former president of Meeting Planners International, sug-gests in the "Meeting Management Series" (published by Bayard Publications,

Inc., 500 Summer Street, Stamford, CT 06901; $19.95 plus $1.95 shipping and handling) that the host company promise to pay all meeting-related charges either in cash or by company check, thus saving the hotel, resort, or conference center the fat percentage earned by credit card organizations. This incentive may well prompt a price reduction somewhere in return. Remember, there is nothing ungentlemanly or unladylike about the phrase "Let's make a deal."

Every final decision worked out with the hotel or other suppliers must be confirmed in writing, including:

- Agreed-upon prices
- Agreed-upon times of delivery for all products and services

Tips and Gratuities

Some planners find it economically advantageous if each attendee tips as services are rendered and then is later reimbursed by his home office. If this is the plan, each attendee should receive a memo in advance of his departure for the meeting explaining the tipping system, so that he will be properly prepared.

If a meeting planner decides to provide "blanket gratuities" for his group, he will pay anywhere from 15 to 22 percent of the total facility charge (minus bar tips, always paid for by the attendee himself). The planner should make sure that the tips go to the right people by specifying to the hotel manager those members of the staff who were particularly helpful and under great stress (such as beleaguered telephone operators; the maître d' hotel in the dining room, and the main bellmen). Unfortunately, some unscrupulous hotel managers take the gratuities and hide them in the hotel's monthly profit statement rather than pass them on to the staff.

If service was excellent, a corporation should tip very generously—an investment in the future, so that when it returns to that facility it will be greeted with open arms.

If service is poor, it's the meeting planner's job to demand from the facility management that an immediate improvement be made. (Threatening to omit the gratuity payments usually works.) As an extra reward, on the last day of the meeting some planners carry with them envelopes containing $5, $10, and $20 bills to give those who worked extra hard to give the group good service.

The worst thing that can be said about a company when it leaves its meeting facility is "Those people are cheap." Courteous treatment should be expected by a paying customer, but it should also be rewarded!

The Annual Sales Conference

One common type of "away" meeting is a company's annual national sales meeting, which provides an excellent forum in which management can observe executives' interactions with both their peers and with their seniors. The purpose of such a sales conference may be to present a new line of products or to motivate the sales force to push harder with the old line. In either case, this coming together serves as the perfect time in which to pep up the attendees, to recognize their individual contributions during the past year, and to provide fresh assistance and ideas for attaining the company goals. The atmosphere at a good sales meeting inspires the staff, raises everyone's morale, and provides them with a lot of new and helpful information at the same time. It's a time for motivating, learning, explaining, questioning, planning, renewing old friendships, getting to know senior management better, and incidentally having a good time. It's a time for senior managers to be more available and friendly than circumstances permit them to be at the home office. But along with all the camaraderie, management's aim for the meeting should be inserted clearly, concisely, and *often* throughout the proceedings.

It helps, too, when the meeting is run in a warm, personal way with an occasional touch of humor. I remember being in a ballroom at a company's final banquet meeting one night, in the middle of 350 people who were all fired up watching a slide film with an accompanying musical sound track. The film consisted of clever candid photographs taken of the participants at the previous year's meeting. There were some very funny shots; everyone laughed, hooted, and applauded all the way through, particularly at the end when all five screens used in the presentation showed different views of a popular sales manager fast asleep in his chair, his head down on the table, during the CEO's final banquet speech.

The head of a company usually judges this kind of conference a success if:

- The objectives of motivating the sales force were achieved.
- The executives understood the new technology presented in the training sessions and are eager to begin working with it.
- Everyone received a nice pat on the back.
- Those who had fallen short during the past year were encouraged and are now willing to try harder.
- Those who had excelled were properly recognized and felt sufficiently rewarded.
- Everyone perfectly understands the plans and the new products and is eager to get going.
- All participants came away with increased respect for the company.
- Everyone had a good time.

Ensuring the Achievement of Objectives

Sometimes management has to help meeting participants gain the benefits hoped for. They may send memos to participants before they leave for the meeting, defining their meeting goals, then explain the goals at the opening talks during the conference. Some, like the Proprietary Association (a trade association, headquartered in Washington, representing the over-the-counter drug companies), will include written advice in their registration kit. One year the Proprietary Association included the following message for annual meeting attendees:

> . . . The Association realizes the success of the meeting depends not only on the programming, but also on the attitudes of the attendees. To make sure that members get the most out of their attendance—information, contacts, etc.—the Association makes the following suggestions:

> - *Do your homework.* Summarize beforehand (mentally or in writing) the things you would like to get out of the meeting—questions and problems that you wish to have answered. Then you can systematically go about getting answers from other members, speakers, and staff.
> - *Take the initiative.* Don't wait to be drawn into conversations or discussions. Get your questions and ideas into the arena. Introduce yourself. Your badge gives you the right to approach new people, most of whom will be pleased to get this attention. If you associate only with people you have met before, you cut down your chances of getting some fresh ideas which, after all, is the chief reason you are at the meeting.
> - *Read the program thoroughly.* Study every session speaker and social function and be sure you don't miss the ones that could help the most.
> - *Meet with someone different at every meal.* Meals are a perfect opportunity for informal conversations and shop talk with others who share mutual concerns within the industry.
> - *Ask questions.* The Association staff, for example, will be more than happy to make suggestions, provide information, and be of any assistance possible.
> - *Keep notes.* In the rush of activity it's easy to forget names, sources, and tips. Write them down while they're fresh in your mind.
> - *Keep in touch.* Use your Attendance Book (which is designed so you can jot down a person's room number beside his name) to make contacts while at the meeting. Follow up on questions and acquaintances by telephone or letter after the meeting. Your fellow members will be glad to hear from you.

The Meeting Manager's Notebook:
An Executive Diary for the Meeting Planner

(*See also* Organizing a Large Social Function:
A Checklist, in Chapter 8)

The consummate tool for anyone in charge of meetings is his or her notebook. The first thing one learns to do in this business, in order to survive, is "to write it all down," including having all the questions written down before the necessity arises to ask them. The quality of the checklists, charts, and information—kept neatly filed and always updated—can spell the success or failure of any operation of this kind. The information contained in the meeting manager's notebook should cover everything from the kind of beds requested by the VIPs to the quality of the air-conditioning in the meeting rooms. For an in-house meeting, there are few pages required for the notebook, since the logistics of the conference room or auditorium are a "given." However, when a meeting planner utilizes a facility outside company headquarters, the number of pages grows quickly.

A meeting, conference, or seminar is a success not only because it is well-organized, but also because of the considerate attitude of the special events staff in charge, all of which reflects very positively on the company's image. Disorganized, sloppy individuals usually are not well-mannered. They don't have time to be thoughtful and to think of others; they spend all their time trying to muddle through their responsibilities. The following pages represent the way one meeting manager who is *not* sloppy and disorganized goes about managing his company's large events. He has different colored entry sheets for different types of meetings and events:

First-Page Entry

Event:

When:

Where:

Why:

Company Sponsoring Division:

Divisional Contact:

Budget

Management-approved budget $_____ Date_____ Authorized by_____
Negotiated cost for use of facility—rooms, meals, meeting room rental, etc._____
Transportation total costs_____
Entertainment (including music, entertainers, lighting, sound equipment)_____
Flowers and decor_____
Gifts and prizes for registrants_____
Audiovisual extra costs_____
Speakers' fees and expenses_____
Sports programs_____
Spouse program_____
Printed materials_____   Duplicating_____
Extra help (registration desk, press room, hospitality suites, etc.)_____
Photography_____
Press room telephones, rental of typewriters, etc._____
Hospitality suite telephone, rental of typewriters, etc._____
Contingency fund_____

An Evaluation of the Facility

Facility Name: Facility Address: Tel. no:
Manager's Name: Secretary's Name: Telex no.:

Location's proximity to: Airports_____ Train_____ Bus depots_____
Weather conditions at time of meeting_____ Mean temperature_____
Negotiable price of:
    Meeting rooms_____ Banquet rooms_____
    Bedrooms: (double)_____ (single)_____
    Suites: (1 bedroom)_____ (2 bedrooms)_____ (3 bedrooms)_____
No. superior rooms (quiet, good view)_____
No. inferior rooms (noisy, no view)_____
Condition of facility when last used_____
Who recommended_____ Tel. no._____ Date of their last visit_____
Athletic facilities either on the premises or very close by:
    Bikes for rent_____ Outdoor pool_____ Indoor pool_____
    Squash courts_____ Paddle tennis_____ Outdoor tennis courts_____
    Indoor tennis courts_____ Court tennis_____ Handball courts_____
    Croquet_____ Ping-pong tables_____ Volleyball court_____
    Badminton_____ 18-hole golf course_____ 9-hole course_____
    Skiing_____ Fishing_____ Horseback riding_____
    Ice skating_____ Trail hiking_____ Skeet shooting_____
    Video game room_____ Movies_____ Health club_____
    Sauna_____ Gym_____ Weights with supervised instruction_____

Exercise programs such as aerobics & calisthenics_____

Quality of food & beverages_____

Quality of general service_____ Quality of room service_____

    Tel. service_____

Cleanliness_____ Quality of heating_____ Quality of

    air-conditioning_____

Computer capabilities_____ Audiovisual capabilities_____

Availability of word processor rentals_____

Facility's transportation_____

Nearby hospital and medical services_____

Staff attitude_____

Shopping availability for spouses_____

Tour guide availability_____

Restaurants in the facility for "nights off"_____ Nearby restaurants_____

Condition and size of Hospitality Suites_____

Refrigerators with drinks & snacks in rooms_____

Banquet facilities

Name of Room	Capacity	Type of Facility
_____	_____	_____
_____	_____	_____
_____	_____	_____

The Invitation

Traditional Printed	Engraved	Issued by telephone	Issued by letter	Signed by whom	Issued by Mailgram	Signed by whom
_____	_____	_____	_____	_____	_____	_____

Who is responsible for text_____

Who will print or engrave invitations_____

    (Name, address, tel. no.)

When to be delivered_____

How many ordered_____

Who is responsible for invitee list_____

Who will sign off on finished proof_____ Date_____

Who will address envelopes_____ Hand-stamped or metered?_____

Date to be mailed_____

NOTE: Invitations should be issued three to four months prior to a meeting to which people will be coming from the outside, to allow participants the chance to clear their schedules for it. Invitations to senior management should be issued six months prior to an intra-city meeting, particularly one that will last two or three days.

It is important, when inviting people to a conference or seminar, to list the guest speakers, their titles, and credentials.

Invitation List (Alphabetized) and Responses

Guest's Name	Title	Address	Tel. No.	Accepts	Regrets
George Abell					
Jennifer Anderson					
Gregory Apgar					
Jonathon Arthur					
Giorgio Attuno					
et cetera . . .					

NOTE: The meeting planner should put the date of receipt of the acceptance or regret in the proper column. Eventually the meeting planner will add another page after the guest list, in which just the acceptances will be listed alphabetically. This becomes the final working list.

Room Assignment Chart

(Copies to be given to the general manager of the facility, to all on meeting planner's staff, and to all hotel switchboard operators)

Attendee	Title	Office	Tel. No.	Hotel Room No.	Size	Arrival Date	Departure Date

NOTE: On this chart, under "Size" would be written: *S* for single; *D* for double; *ST* for suite. If an extra-large bed is requested, *K* is put in the "Size" column, to indicate "king-size bed preferred" and *TW* for twin beds in a double.

Room Setup Plans

The meeting manager should make a rough sketch in his notebook of how he wants each room or area set up by the facilities manager for each use. He would sketch one room per page, with instructions, and give a copy of each to the facilities manager. Following is a hypothetical page from a meeting planner's notebook, showing the kind of rough sketch and information needed by the hotel staff to prepare a room for one group's morning seminar, to be followed by lunch on another floor.

February 22nd—Morning Session and Lunch
for the Marketing Division

The Bristol Room—Mezzanine North

9:30 to 11:45 A.M. Seminar with slides
projected
80 people seated
auditorium style
Projector and screen
Head table with 6 chairs
Lectern at side

The Cheshire Library—off Lobby

12 to 2:00 Lunch service for 100 people
No head table
10 tables for 10 people
Lectern with mike at one side
Open bar
Piano in corner

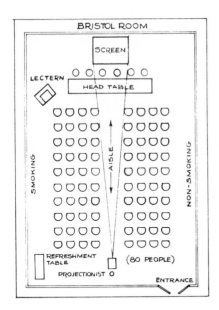

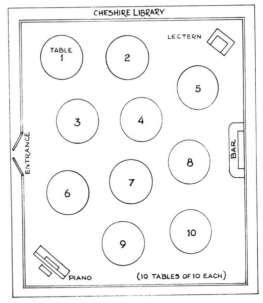

Transportation Checklist (page 1)

(Copy to be given to all on meeting planner's staff)

Name of in-house (or outside) coordinator for this meeting:_____

Agency handling:_____ Tel. no. or ext._____

Names of officials at airport or terminals to help in case of lost baggage:_____

    Tel. nos._____

Meeting Attendee's Name	Arrival Date	Time	Coming from	Mode of Transport	Departure Date	Time	Going to

NOTE: Mark *X* if attendee requires meeting upon arrival. Mark *Y* if attendee requires escorting on departure.

Printed Luggage Tags	Quantity	Supplier & Tel. No.	Date Delivered	Date Mailed to Attendees

Cars to be Rented

Agency Name	Tel. No.	Contact	Attendees Requesting	Dates of Rental	Car Model Special Request

Buses to be Chartered

Bus Company	Tel. No.	Contact	Dates of Usage	Times of Usage	Bus Capacity Needed

Limos to be Reserved

Limo Company	Tel. No.	Contact	Dates of Usage	Times of Usage	Attendees Needing Service

Registration Area

No. of desks or tables (covered with floor-length cloths)_____
No. of chairs needed_____
Flower arrangement ordered_____
Sign-in Book ordered_____
Jumbo typewriters ordered for those preparing badges_____
Checklist of items to be on tables for registrants
_____Registration kits
_____Badges
_____Information sheets
_____Press kits for press

Note on Badges

· A badge is best worn high on one's upper right shoulder. This is the easiest viewing point for right-handed people talking to the badge-wearer.
· Let the attendee select his or her choice of pin or adhesive-back.
· Gender titles should not be used on badges (Mr., Mrs., Miss, or Ms.), but professional titles should be (Dr., Lt. Col., Ambassador, etc.).
· When the meeting attendees come from several companies and cities, put their company names and home cities beneath their names.
· Spouses' given names and their spouses' names should both be furnished.
  Example: Mary Howard   or   Spencer Golden
            (John N. Howard)   (Mary Golden)

Information Packet (Registration Kit)

The meeting planner's notebook should specify the items to be included in the information kit given to all attendees. This packet is usually given to attendees when they register at the meeting, although some companies prefer to leave it in the registrants' rooms. When spouses attend the meeting, there should be two copies of the information kit, one for each.

· List of attendees, with home addresses and telephone numbers and giving attendee's facility room number
· The schedule, complete with speakers' names, speech titles, and bios
· Map of meeting exhibits
· Instructions on how to dress for sporting events and for meals
· Check-out instructions
· Transportation information

- Emergency instructions: what to do in case of fire, how to call a doctor, name and telephone number of all-night pharmacy
- Information on jogging trails and all sports facilities
- If there is an evening free, a list of good local restaurants, theaters, and movie houses
- If meeting goes over weekend, list of churches, synagogues, and services
- Names and telephone numbers of nearby hairdressers for both sexes
- List of notable local museums, historic spots, and famous attractions
- List of better stores in the area

Often a gift is attached to the registration kit. It may be a company product giveaway; it may be a T-shirt, hat, or some other item of apparel meant to be worn at "pep-'em-up" sales conferences.

Organization of the Hospitality Suite

- Make arrangements to have it cleaned three times daily if it will have extended use (and pay particular attention to the bathrooms).
- Sufficient telephones must be in place.
- If there is not enough closet space, set up coat racks and umbrella stands.
- Arrange for a large bulletin board to be set up, with thumbtacks provided (for telephone and other messages to be posted).
- Specify refreshments to be provided.

Snack Bar Setup

Check desired offerings:

Fruit juices_____ Kinds desired_____
Soda water_____ Soda brands and mixers desired_____
Wine: White_____ Red_____
Coffee: Hot_____ Iced_____ Tea: Hot_____ Iced_____
Milk:_____ Low-fat_____
Hot soup_____ Crackers_____
Sandwiches_____
Platters of hors d'oeuvres_____ Cheese tray_____
Liquor: Scotch_____ Bourbon_____ Vodka_____ Gin_____
Cookies_____ Pastries_____
Popcorn_____ Potato chips_____
Raw vegetables with dip_____
Bowls of fresh fruit_____

Signs for the Entire Event

Sign Maker:

Name_____Address_____Telephone Number_____

Date signs to be delivered_____ Consigned to whom_____

Address_____

Quantity	Purpose	Text	Dimensions	Color	Area to Be Placed	How Displayed
						(mounted on wall, easel-back on table, on stanchions etc.)

NOTE: Before ordering the signs for your event, be sure to check with the facility's management on their rules regarding signs in the public areas. Be sure all signs are well designed, worthy of the company's image, and complete in the information that they communicate.

Food to Be Served

There is a boring monotony to much of the food served at meetings. How many times a week should one have to face chicken in gravy? If you give a chef a challenge to make his roast chicken taste better plain than swimming in gravy, he will probably accept it.

There is often a sense of complacency in the food and beverage industry. It is much easier to serve the same set menus week in and week out to different groups. When the catering official says to the meeting manager, "Now, for a group like yours, we normally like to serve the following. . . ." that is the moment for the meeting manager to counter with, "We don't want what everyone else always has. We want something different."

One should never overtax a facility's kitchen with complicated new recipes at a busy time, but if you give a chef a few easy new recipes far in advance to try out at his or her leisure, you may book great success with your menus. Just think of how many executive stomachs you will delight if you use some imagination and enlist the chef's cooperation!

In the Food section of the meeting planner's notebook, all of the food and menus ordered for each day should be marked, one day per page, if possible. Nutrition should be the major factor in the selections. Following is a sample entry in the meeting planner's notebook for one day, with the number of people changing throughout the day:

Food

Monday, September 13

Breakfast (buffet setup) in Sun Patio (60 people)

Fresh fruit	Croissants
Juices: orange, grapefruit, apple	Bagels
Scrambled eggs	Buttered rye toast
Cheese omelets (to order)	Coffee
Bacon	Decaff
Sausage	Tea
English muffins	Milk (homogenized and low-fat)

Morning Meeting Refreshments (4 meetings of 20 people each)
Bring into Rooms A, B, C, & D at meeting break

Coffee (also decaff)	Cut-up finger-sized pieces of fresh fruit
Tea	Small cubes of hard cheese

Lunch (seated) in the Baroque Room (125 people)

Mixed green salad with hard-boiled egg yolk and oil and vinegar dressing	Coffee
Fresh broiled fish with vegetables	Tea
Fresh melon with cookies	Decaff

Afternoon Meeting Refreshments (4 meetings of 35 each—total of 140)
Bring into Rooms A, B, C, & D at meeting break

Cups of hot consommé	Tall glasses of soda water over ice
Crackers	

Cocktail Party (open bar) on the Sun Patio (200 people)
(See attached on Nonalcoholic drinks)

Hot: Stuffed mushroom caps
    Melted cheese on melba rounds
    Bacon broiled in brown sugar, served
      on toothpicks

Cold: Giant shrimp or crab claws served on
      ice (for high budget)
    Endive leaves embellished with pâté
    Tiny chicken salad sandwiches on
      brown bread
    Tiny rare roast beef sandwiches with
      a dollop of mustard
    Platters of crudités, including raw
      carrots and broccoli, with dip

Dinner Party in Grand Ballroom (200 people)

Unlimited budget	*Tight budget*
Fresh crabmeat cocktail	Consommé Julienne
Roast pheasant with wild rice	Roast lamb with new potatoes
Fresh asparagus with Hollandaise	Carrots and peas
Green salad	Green salad
Individual chocolate soufflés	Butterscotch parfait
Demitasses (coffee or decaff)	Demitasses (coffee or decaff)

Nonalcoholic Drink List
(all to be served over ice)

Cranberry juice with sparkling water_____
Pineapple and orange juice (floating cherry)_____
Ginger ale with strawberries floating_____
Grapefruit juice with fresh mint_____
Sparkling water with small fresh peach slices floating_____
Apple juice with slice of apple on side of glass_____
Limeade, made with water or sparkling water, with lemon slice on side of glass_____
Lemonade, made with water or sparkling water, with lime slice on side of glass_____

NOTE: Smart meeting planners set up nonalcoholic bars where cocktail guests will find the prettiest glasses, the most ice, and the most carefully prepared and best-looking drinks available. Anything that can be done to cut down on the consumption of liquor at meetings deserves special consideration.

Program

Key: Blue—Business Meetings
      Green—Meals with Guest Speakers
      Red—Social Events for Executives and Spouses
      Yellow—Spouses' Special Program
      Black—Leisure Time/Sports Activities

	Monday	Tuesday	Wednesday
7 A.M.			
8 A.M.			
9 A.M.			
10 A.M.			
11 A.M.			
Noon			
1 P.M.			
2 P.M.			
3 P.M.			
4 P.M.			
5 P.M.			
6 P.M.			
7 P.M.			
8 P.M.			
9 P.M.			
10 P.M.			

NOTE: There are many ways in which a meeting planner can chart out the meeting's activities. On this page he uses blocks of color to denote the kind of activity and organizes the activities by the hour of the day, giving the name of the place in the facility where each will take place.

Checklist for Handling Speakers or Entertainers

(Use a separate page in the meeting planner's notebook for each speaker or entertainer appearing at your event.)

SPEAKERS AND ENTERTAINERS CHECKLIST

Name_____

Address_____Tel. No._____

Date of Program_____Where Held_____

Lecture Bureau or Agent's Name, Address & Tel. No._____

Program or Speech Title_____

Date Contract Signed_____Date Bio & Photos Requested_____

Length of Program_____Hour to Be Given_____

Amount of Fee_____How and When to Be Paid_____

Expenses to Be Reimbursed_____

Arrival & Departure Times_____

Who Is Making Reservations? Air_____Hotel_____

Will Parking Facilities Be Needed?_____

Date Info Sent Speaker on Type of Audience_____

Date Info Sent on Any Dress Requirements_____

Rehearsal Necessary?_____Dressing Room Necessary?_____

Special Sound & Lighting Requirements?_____

Can Speech Be Taped? Videotaped?_____

Can We Arrange TV and Newspaper Interviews?_____

Will He Sign Copies of His Book?_____

Will Speaker Accept Dinner Invitation for Night Before His Program?_____

Names and Addresses of Any Special Guest(s) Speaker Wishes Invited:_____

_____

_____

_____

There are four ways in which to handle a speaker that will make him love the host company forever.

- Schedule him lightly, so that he does not have to talk to too many people before his appearance or answer too many questions and risk straining his voice. He should be given a place in which to rest and time expressly for that—an hour before he should appear.
- Treat him graciously at all times, including introducing him properly.
- Express immediate appreciation for his efforts, ideally in a letter "written" by the CEO the day after the presentation, telling him how great it was, thanking him, and congratulating him on a job well done.

- *Pay him promptly.* This is very important. If he has an agent, the latter usually gets the money immediately, removes his percentage (often 10 percent) and then sends a check to the speaker for the rest. If there is no agent, the nice way to pay the speaker is to hand him an envelope with the check inside as he leaves to catch his plane or train. Mention that his out-of-pocket expenses will be reimbursed immediately upon receipt of a list of expenses and receipts.

Every speaker likes to be treated this way.

Audiovisuals Checklist

Date of event_____

Place_____

Division requesting_____

Division executive in charge of event_____ Tel. no._____

If handed by outside professional:

    Name of company_____ Tel. No._____

    Company coordinator_____

Names of people handling projectors_____
_____

Staff handling light cues_____

Staff handling room-darkening draperies_____

	AV Needs	Time of presentation
Speaker_____	_____	_____
Speaker_____	_____	_____

(Et cetera)

Name and extension of house electrician_____

Number of outlets_____

Extension cords needed_____

TV monitors required_____

Projectors: Types_____ Stands needed_____

           Number_____

Extra projector bulbs_____

Pointers needed_____

Portable screens needed_____

    Sizes_____

Microphones: Types_____

            Number_____

Lectern: In place_____ Bring_____

    Needs corporate shield_____

    Check light and mike_____

Easels needed_____

> Floor plan of room

Blackboards needed_____ Chalk_____ Erasers_____

Corkboards_____ Thumbtacks_____

Other_____

Inventory of Office Supplies for Meeting

A list of supplies needed for each room of the facility should be prepared in advance. When supplies are packed, they should be put in boxes marked with the room number. The list should be packed inside each box. The inventory list could include any or all of the following:

Typewriters; word processors___

Paper and supplies for the above___

Duplicating machine___

Paper and supplies for the above___

Computer software___

Blank tapes and cassettes___

Calculator___

Dictating machines with tape___

Copies of the agenda___

Extra copies of press material___

Message pads___

Pens and sharpened pencils___

Pencil sharpeners___

Paper clips___

Staplers___

Masking tape___

Cellophane tape___

Cord or string___

Postage meter or stamps___

Rubber bands___

Scissors___

Portable blackboards and chalk or corkboards and tacks___

Staple gun___

Company stationery___

Steno pads___

Mailing envelopes (indicate sizes)___

Rulers___

File folders___

Notebooks: lined and unlined fillers___

Legal pads___

Expense voucher forms; petty cash slips___

White bond paper___

Flower Inventory

Florist_____Contact_____Tel. No._____

Reception area arrangement_____

Bouquet(s) in Hospitality Suite_____

Bouquets for rooms of senior management_____

Bouquets for rooms of visitor VIPs_____

Dais arrangements

   Banquet #1_____ Banquet #2_____ Banquet #3_____

Centerpiece arrangements:

   1st day lunch_____   Banquet #1_____

   2nd day lunch_____   Banquet #2_____

   3rd day lunch_____   Banquet #3_____

   Spouses' lunch_____

Decoration of the stage: Flower arrangements_____ Plant rental_____
Flowers to decorate receiving line area at reception_____
Boutonnières needed for staff_____
Flowers sent to speakers' and performers' homes after meeting_____

NOTE:
- The florist should be given a firm budget before starting to work and use table centerpieces more than once.
- The florist should keep in mind the color of decor in the room to be decorated.
- Dais flowers should be kept low, so the audience can easily see dais guests.
- Tall plants and flowering trees in tubs may be rented to disguise an ugly stage or other unsightly area.
- Never send a woman speaker a corsage; send flowers to her home.

Post-Meeting Evaluation Report

	Evaluation	*Comment*
Noise:		
Condition of the rooms:		
Condition of the bathrooms:		
Baggage handling:		
Room service:		
Telephone service:		
Service at meals:		
Condition of the Hospitality Suite:		
Condition of the Press Room:		
Audiovisual support:		
Computer capabilities:		
Front office cooperation:		
Air quality in the facility:		
Air-conditioning or heating sufficiency:		
Condition of sports facilities:		
Professionals and trainers in sports facilities:		
Quality of the food:		
Quality of the drinks:		
Condition of the grounds:		
Parking facilities efficiency:		
Facility bus and shuttle service:		
Other:		

NOTE: A good meeting manager fills out his or her post-meeting evaluation immediately, because details are forgotten every day that goes by. This report will be helpful when considering whether to reuse the facility, or in giving a favorable or unfavorable recommendation to another company that may wish to use it.

Thank-Yous

This page should be reserved for the meeting planner to write the name, title, and address of everyone connected with the event who did a good job and who deserves a letter of thanks, which in reality is also a letter of recommendation for that person. (Commendations of special employees are usually recorded in their files and can result in faster promotions and greater job security.)

On this page the meeting planner should write down not only the name of the person to be thanked and praised but also the date on which the letter was actually sent.

Prompt thank-yous can also lead to a warm welcome upon return to a meeting facility. The owners and staff of a hotel, conference center, or other meeting site judge a company by the behavior of its employees, but most particularly by the manners of the meeting manager and his staff.

Letter to General Manager of the Facility

This page should contain a copy of the letter sent to the general manager of the facility, in which he or she is thanked and complimented, but in which constructive criticism is also offered. The recipient of this letter needs this information in order to do his job better and to make more companies return to his facility. Good criticism is the best favor you can pay the head of a facility.

Meeting Manners Away from Home

A company shows its class—or lack of it—by the way it organizes and invites people to events under its sponsorship, whether it's a lecture, workshop program, or seminar. Those attending these meetings, conferences, and seminars also show their class—or lack of it—in their behavior, in the way in which they interact and by the way in which they follow both the prescribed rules of the meeting and all the subtle "unsaid" rules. The latter involve attitudes toward noise, litter, tardiness, lack of cooperation, and generally selfish behavior. For example, a conference or meeting is no place to drink to excess and to use drugs. The use of controlled substances (including pot) or an excess of alcohol may lead to the damage of hotel property as well as physical damage to the person; it may also completely sabotage the objectives and goals set by the meeting's sponsors.

The company minds its manners by having a staff that is meticulous in its planning and production of the meeting; the attendees show their manners by their behavior during the meeting. But a third factor also comes into play in the making of a successful event—the attitude and performance of the facility's management staff. If all three factors are well in place, the meeting will be a sure-fire success.

When Mates Come Along

If mates are present, and if the meeting will last three days or longer, it is very wise for the sponsoring organization to schedule special activities for them. In a resort situation, with sports available, it is only necessary to organize one activity, preferably early in the morning. A good speaker is always a plus; exercise classes and sports tournaments for women are usually successful (male spouses are usually excused from an activity, if they wish to be, when they are very pronouncedly in the minority). The days of "the little woman" programs, doing such things as making lace valentines together, are gone; women today, even if they do not work outside the home, are usually involved in major projects and do not enjoy being patronized by a silly program. If a fashion show luncheon is planned, it had better be a good one—fast-paced and with the fashion part of the program done quickly and very professionally.

What is important for the spouse is to be allowed to sit in on as many sessions as possible with his or her mate, particularly when the guest speaker is someone with an important message. Also, it is usually extremely important to an executive's career to have his or her mate understand the company's business and its problems and to be able to speak knowledgeably about it and offer support—as well as good ideas whenever those would prove helpful.

A spouse who remains aloof from the rest of the crowd is not doing his or her mate any good at all; the executive becomes the innocent victim of a snobby mate who acts "too good for the rest of them," a situation hardly likely to help in one's career. I have a good piece of advice for the spouse who is bored by his or her mate's conventions and meetings and consequently does not wish to participate with enthusiasm: Stay home.

As for "friends" who join executives—their apartment mates, lovers, or just dates—they have a responsibility, too: to act in a discreet fashion and to play the game along with everyone else. No one should be discriminated against at meetings in which spouses participate just because they are single. When recreation and entertaining are a major part of the agenda, a single person should be allowed to bring a date, but both people should watch their comportment. For example, their friends won't care about the fact they are sharing the same bedroom, but the wife of the chairman of the board may care very much. The way to prevent gossip that could become malicious and harmful is to check into two separate rooms, even if that means the executive will have to pay for his or her friend's room. It should not be difficult for a couple to occupy two rooms during the meeting. After all, they have 363 other nights they can spend together.

The Annual Shareholders' Meeting: A Company's Most Important Large Meeting

The annual meeting of a publicly held corporation is traditionally held when the year-end accounting is complete, when the directors are voted back into their seats on the board (or not, as the case may be), and when the stockholders have the opportunity to propose changes and to criticize, question, or applaud management's decisions during the preceding year.

Even the CEO of a small company should look upon his or her annual meeting as an important opportunity to communicate in person with the company's most important audience—its owners, the shareholders. The meeting is an opportunity to present management as a strong, competent, no-nonsense group of executives worthy of the shareholders' trust—as well as their money.

Sometimes when a company has a big story to tell, a little "show-biz" is called for—perhaps photographic blow-ups in the entrance to the meeting, a short film, a slide presentation, or even a fashion show (if the business is related to fashion). An effective graphic or audiovisual presentation impresses stockholders and influences their support of company plans *if* it is well done.

Time and Place of the Annual Meeting

The annual meeting is held once a year by law, often in the spring, within a reasonable time after the close of the fiscal year. It may be held at any hour, but the most popular time for a publicly held company is in the morning or early afternoon, in order to allow the press sufficient time to write a thorough story before the newspaper goes to press with the next day's news. The company's charter or by-laws set the place, date, and time for the meeting. All stockholders are invited to attend this meeting. Many companies with stock plans for the employees give those employees time off to attend the meeting. After all, they are shareholders, too.

The meeting may be held *anywhere*—in the headquarters office or in a factory, ice skating rink, hotel ballroom, or football stadium.

Many companies take their "show on the road," away from their corporate city headquarters and into an area where they have plants, subsidiaries, or just a large aggregate of retired shareholders. Attendance is always high in cities where there is a large proportion of retired stockholders.

The company should make very certain that its image is projected well when it goes on the road—that it demonstrates away from home that it is an efficient, well-run organization. It should also be ready to prove that it has a strong social conscience, which can be demonstrated in its handouts, displays, and speeches from the podium.

Communicating the Details

The CEO of a publicly held company must send out a notice of the annual meeting to all shareholders a minimum of three to four weeks beforehand to allow for a good response on proxy returns. (The president of a privately held company obviously is not as limited as the CEO of a publicly held one. The head of a private company can change the date of his annual meeting simply by telephoning his board—usually close friends and family members—and arranging another time.)

Accompanying the notice of the meeting is the proxy statement (a disclosure document announcing where and when the meeting will be held and what proposals will be voted on), plus a proxy voting card for the stockholders who will not be at the meeting. Everyone should fill out and mail back the proxy voting cards at once. When there are written comments on these voting cards, management should note them with care, for they often reveal which way the wind is blowing in terms of feeling toward management. The proxies can also hint trouble that might occur at the annual meeting, such as demonstrations by dissident factions against company policies.

A successful corporation is a responsive corporation. It listens to the voice of its shareholders.

If the place where the annual meeting will be held is difficult to locate, it is wise to include a map with the proxy material. Some companies also include a program of the meeting; some even give the lunch menu if this meal will be served free to shareholders!

Mailing the Annual Report

A corporation's annual report must be mailed in advance of the meeting. (It is sometimes sent along with the notice of the meeting.) There is usually tremendous deadline pressure on the staff charged with the responsibility for producing the report, professionals on both the inside and on the outside. Last-minute changes are inevitable. The CEO should be compassionate about these pressures on the staff. Gestures such as arranging to have a catered dinner brought in for the late workers and sending them home late at night in taxis, if they don't have cars, are very much appreciated by everyone working on the report.

Another person who deserves consideration at this time is the corporate secretary, whose job involves tremendous responsibilities. The annual report must reflect that he or she is fully conversant with the laws of the state in which the corporation is incorporated, with the requirements of the stock exchange listing the company's securities, with the board of directors' standing resolutions pertaining to the annual meeting, with the company's by-laws and articles of incorporation, and, of course, the rules and regulations established by the Securities Exchange Commission. One top industrialist, who serves on five major boards, personally selects a Christmas gift each year for each of the corporate secretaries of the companies he serves; with each gift goes a hand-written note of thanks.

Ensuring Security and Comfort

Security is a prime factor in selecting the place for a large corporation's annual meeting. The company should assure that only stockholders and invited press are admitted. The mailing of tickets to stockholders when they request them is one method of controlling the situation. It is better to have two registration areas for a large meeting when admission tickets are used—one for stockholders who brought their tickets and one for those who forgot or who didn't bother to write in. It takes time to check their identification and find them on the stockholders' list. Someone from the legal staff should be standing by at the "No Tickets" desk, as well as company representatives who are gifted with an extra dose of patience and good manners. (Those who must be turned away from the meeting must be treated very diplomatically.) The company should use its most gregarious and well-mannered people to greet the shareholders, collect ballots, help register, and perform other duties at the meeting.

The quality of the lighting, ventilation, bathroom and first aid facilities are other important factors to consider when staging the annual meeting. The sound system is paramount. Nothing makes a stockholder more hostile than not to be able to hear what is going on. That is also why company spokesmen should speak up clearly when they are at the microphone. Directors who offer resolutions to be voted upon should turn toward the audience and address them in a clear, well-projected voice, so that everyone hears every word of the resolution.

The comfort of the stockholders tends to affect their attitude toward the company. One CEO told of the air-conditioning breaking down completely on the day of his annual meeting—the hottest day of the year. A quick-thinking employee rushed to several stores carrying oriental merchandise and returned with three hundred hand-painted paper fans. The CEO opened his meeting in rolled-up shirtsleeves, apologizing for the discomfort of the room. He told his audience to "strip as far as you dare," and removing his tie, he began to fan himself, chuckling audibly.

"I never thought I'd be using a fan showing maidens sipping tea by a lotus pond," he laughed, "particularly at a meeting with my shareholders!"

The audience had to laugh, too, and after inspecting their fans, began to fan themselves vigorously. The entire meeting progressed smoothly, in a general flickering of fans.

Keeping Order

The days have long since gone when publicly held corporations looked upon the annual meeting as a mere cut-and-dried series of approvals of the CEO's motions. The combative forces of social trauma seem to have joined the corporation permanently and refuse to evaporate either in good times or in bad.

Therefore, corporations cannot remain aloof from the social needs and aspirations of the public. Issues such as the handling of minorities, investments in controversial countries, and environmental considerations will always be raised in this era. When questions are properly asked, a company must be responsive, not antagonistic. The annual meeting is not a time for fuzzy deception. The CEO should be up-front; he and the stockholders should respect each other's views.

Most corporations now place a time limit (five minutes) on shareholders' speeches. If the company officers are well organized and professional about the way they handle the meeting, it will be orderly. Questions may have had to be submitted beforehand with the returned proxy statements, thus providing the CEO with enough time to ready himself with the proper answers. If a shareholder is unruly and unreasonable, peer pressure in the meeting generally disciplines him far better than the chairman could.

Sometimes a little creativity helps if the economic climate is hurting the company's and the stockholders' pocketbooks. One chief executive officer who has a good sense of humor concluded a particularly lugubrious, bad-news annual meeting with a smiling last word to the shareholders as they rose to leave: "I certainly don't want anyone here leaving this hall without feeling that our company smells like a rose." With that, the corporate staff pulled out great bouquets of fresh roses from beneath the check-in tables and handed each person a very sweet-smelling flower.

It must have worked, for they all came out smiling.

The Agenda

Most annual meetings follow a general pattern. The chief executive officer introduces himself, calls the meeting to order, and after introducing the company officers and directors, he gives a kind of "president's report," highlighting the main events of the past year.

A typed or printed copy of the agenda should be placed on the chair of each person before the meeting.

The following is a sample of a typical agenda:

AGENDA
ANNUAL STOCKHOLDERS' MEETING
(Give date and time)
(Give location, city, state)

1. Meeting called to order
2. Introduction of directors, directors emeriti, officers and others
3. Notice of Meeting
4. Roll of stockholders present or represented by proxies
5. Motion re affidavit of transfer agent pertaining to mailing of Annual Report, combined Notice of Meeting and Proxy Statement, and Proxy, and a copy of each, together with affidavit, made a part of the minutes of the meeting
6. Convene meeting, quorum present
7. Corporate secretary to read minutes of previous year's annual stockholders' meeting
8. Motion to be made (by a director) to dispense with reading of the minutes of previous year's annual stockholders' meeting
9. CEO's report
10. Viewing of film on new product
11. Inspectors of elections to be appointed
12. Directors to be elected
13. Proposed acquisition to be voted on
14. Proposed ratification and approval to be voted of the company's auditors for the forthcoming fiscal year
15. Any other business to be discussed
16. Questions
17. Adjournment

The Electronic Meeting: The New Wave

The newest kid on the block in the meeting world is video teleconferencing, or the electronic meeting. For those who can afford it, the system saves an executive travel time, hotel bills, and meal expenses, not to mention the hassle and stress of dashing to airports and driving a car great distances.

In August of 1979 Ciba-Geigy held an hour-long simulcast to transmit the "World Soybean Report" via satellite from the American Soybean Association meeting in an Atlanta hotel. Fifteen hundred people crowded into the ballroom to watch the U.S. segment of the four-way feed, the first ever attempted between four countries, even by the commercial networks. The public relations team that staged the simulcast was ready for the worst, such as losing the picture. (In the event that happened, they were prepared with still photographs of the participants to leave on the screen while the audio continued.) If the satellite audio, on the other hand, was temporarily lost, they were ready with telephone lines to carry the voices. History was made that day in Atlanta and, as one guest remarked, "all for a bag of soybeans."

In February of 1983 *Newsweek* made history when Jack Hilton, head of a successful New York–based video consulting firm, produced a seventy-minute video conference to mark the magazine's fiftieth anniversary. This time four cities on three continents were linked interactively (Washington, London, Zurich, and Tokyo) while the audiences of distinguished *Newsweek* guests watched on large screens, heard an address by President Reagan, and then asked questions on world issues of the *Newsweek* editors. The video conference was produced in a matter of a few short weeks, in spite of overwhelming logistical problems (such as having to cue the editors who moderated in the four hotel locations) and protocol and security considerations inherent in any situation where heads of state are present.

The video conference is a perfect tool for communicating a uniform message simultaneously to audiences in multiple locations. The chief financial officer of W. R. Grace, for example, makes an annual presentation via videoconferencing to securities analyst groups in nine northeastern cities. He spends only two hours before the camera to get the job done instead of rushing under pressure to appear in two different cities each day over a period of several arduous days.

Some corporations, like ARCO, use the system to facilitate internal communication within their network of offices and plants throughout the country. Others, like Ford Motor Company, use teleconferencing to produce a spectacular new product launch in the presence of journalists and dealers around the world. Unfortunately, because of the expense, a small business owner must look wistfully at teleconferencing today—the way a high school junior would when dreaming of a Rolls for his first car. There are several kinds of teleconferencing, ranging from audio only or audio with graphics to freeze-frame video or motion video. You may select a system offering a video hard copy, or one with interactive spontaneous graphics between the locations involved in the conference. Every year there is new advanced technology, but this technique will never replace the need for human beings to interact in the same room.

Robert Keiper (see *Corporate Design* magazine, May/June 1983) advises management to study the company's communications patterns, rather than its travel patterns, before deciding on the kind of teleconferencing system to be installed. Management should understand, for example:

· The cities most often visited
· Why those trips are made

- How many attend
- How many should attend but can't because of pressing work in their offices
- What kind of graphic materials are used
- What specific events could be considered true teleconferencing candidates
- Which traveling executives would make the best teleconference users because of the nature of their work.

How You Look and Act Through the Camera's Eye

Many business people find themselves adjusting how they present themselves to the camera after seeing how they look and sound in video replays. A person will notice that he should sound warmer and more sincere and that he should communicate more succinctly and effectively. When people look at you across the conference table they see one thing; when the camera takes a closeup view of you, they see another thing on the screen.

Conspicuous elements of attire are drastically magnified through a camera lens. A loud plaid suit will "scream" at the camera. A woman with spots of color in her makeup will find them looking clownlike on the monitor. A man who works in the southwest and never wears a jacket or tie to work, will suddenly realize that he must look overly casual to his counterparts in the north, who are sitting around the table uniformly clad in dark pinstripe suits.

Of course, any lapse in manners in a two-way audio-video conversation jumps right out from the screen. The person who interrupts too often, the person who raises his or her voice, the person caught making a sour face behind the back of the speaker, the person doodling in a bored manner—the camera catches and magnifies these actions almost mischievously. The camera also magnifies one's nervous mannerisms—studying the fingernails, stroking the hair, picking at fingernails, chewing on the stem of one's glasses, or, far worse, chewing gum.

The optimum impression of oneself glimpsed on a monitor is of a relaxed yet authoritative person, someone with a sense of humor. People who are unused to television are at first quite stiff and perhaps overly formal. Their voice may be forced or overly loud; their laugh may be very artificial. They may shift position constantly, which is quite distracting to viewers. After viewing themselves in replays and after practicing being relaxed, those same people find they can look good and act well on camera. The rapid increase in the use of video-conferencing will mean more and more business for television consultants who produce meetings and teach people how to relax on screen.

The increased use of electronic meeting techniques should not be considered a threat to the meeting manager's position but rather as a very useful tool to make his job easier.

Regardless of the role teleconferencing assumes in the future, it can never replace the importance of travel to a person's education and personal growth. Nor will it ever replace the importance of people getting together under one roof, not just to exchange ideas but to develop personal friendships as well. An electronic system will never be able to console, flatter, inspire, amuse, and play on the emotions of a human being like another human being!

7

Good Visual Communication: The Executive Stationery Wardrobe, Business Cards, and Announcements

$\mathbf{T}$he look of a company's graphics is something deserving of priority attention from management, whether the firm is a giant multinational or a very small local operation. A company's graphics comprise one of the most important aspects of its total image. The design of the corporate trademark, symbol, or logo; the choice of the typeface and colors in printed communications; and the way the logo is utilized on all outside communications together constitute the "company's public face." Good graphics help make a company a "class act."

In the 1960s America's major corporations, inspired by the early pioneers of good design in business (Container Corporation, IBM, Champion International, etc.), began to retain consultants (such as Paul Rand) and corporate identity firms (such as Lippincott & Margulies, Chermayeff & Geismar, and Anspach Grossman Portugal, Inc.) to help them decide on what their public faces should be. Faces must change with time as corporations diversify or expand. Graphics designers are kept very busy today with resulting design changes, which may be very subtle (such as a change of background color or a slight variation in lettering style); on the other hand, graphic changes may be all-encompassing, starting with a name change, such as when ESSO became EXXON and First National City Bank became Citibank. Graphics also change when companies merge. The logo design of a newly merged entity is one of the most important early decisions to make, because of its effect on image and on sales.

Once a company's logo has been designed, there is a great deal of implementation to be done. The new design elements must be worked into all of the visual facets of the company, which in a large corporation could include the giant signs atop its plants; signs on the sides of its corporate jets, trucks, and water towers; and design elements on letterheads, business cards, invitations, invoices, and telephone message pads.

The fact that a mid-manager of a corporation has no choice in the matter of his stationery—he is simply provided with the prescribed items—does not mean that he should feel removed from the importance of knowing good graphics. If he understands and appreciates good design, there will be moments all through his career when he can exert influence on decisions covering everything from new notepads to be ordered to the design of a company invitation, ad campaigns, mailing pieces. A mid-manager might even find himself part of his company's committee to commission and approve a new logo.

If he leaves the corporate world and opens a new business for himself, he will immediately understand the importance of a graphic image he must now project for the new company. In other words, consciousness of good graphic design, noticing its presence (or its absence!) everywhere in business, is an asset to any executive at any stage in his career.

Stationery

The more sophisticated a business becomes and the more successful an executive becomes, the larger his stationery "wardrobe" becomes. He starts out with the company's regulation printed stationery, then works his way up to a senior or executive vice-presidential level and begins using the same engraved stationery used by the CEO. If he's a lawyer or a banker, he may use engraved stationery at a lower level when dealing with important clients. In any case, if his company management is committed to good design, then all the office stationery is carefully prescribed according to a manual, whether the executive is working at the Omaha corporate headquarters or in a Singapore branch office. With the company's corporate identity program already decided upon and spelled out in endless memoranda, the junior executive has no decisions to make regarding company stationery.

When he reaches the ranks of senior management (when he is involved in community projects and has an important social life of his own), he should order (and pay for) his own personal-business stationery, the same used by the entrepreneur (*see* Start-up and Continuing Stationery Needs for the Entrepreneur).

Folding Material Properly into an Envelope: A Simple Exercise in Design

Part of the overall image of a company can be destroyed by something as small as the sloppy folding of the company's letters into envelopes. Unless there is an unusual design scheme, this is the classic way of folding a piece of paper and inserting it into a horizontal envelope:

1. Fold the bottom edge of the page up to a line approximately one-third of the way down from the top.
2. Then take the top edge and fold it down to meet the bottom edge of the bottom fold, thus dividing the page into even thirds, giving a shape that should slide easily from right to left into the back side of the envelope when that is held vertically toward you.
3. If you are inserting a more square piece of paper (like a card or a foldover note) into an envelope, slip it right-side-up into the envelope and facing the back so that when the message is pulled out, it can be read at once without even turning it.

FOLDING AND INSERTING STATIONERY

Stationery Should Properly Reflect the Company's Image

Anything mailed out by an executive strongly reflects him and his company, including:

- The quality of his writing and his articulation of the message
- The quality of the paper used for the communication
- The quality of the graphic design
- The neatness of the typing

A company should know what kind of image it wants and should strive to make all communications reflect that image. The following chart shows how stationery reflects image in three broad business image categories.

	A Conservative Business (Banks, pharmaceutical companies, insurance companies, stockbrokers, lawyers, doctors, accountants, textbook publishers, etc.)	*A Contemporary Look* (Automotive, computer, and home furnishings industries; design firms; ad agencies and communications companies; health clubs; restaurants, etc.)	*A Fashion Image* (Retailing, textile industry, men and women's apparel, hair salons, cosmetic and fragrance industry, etc.)
Paper	Good quality paper; no texture interest	Good quality paper; heightened texture interest	Good quality paper with or without texture interest
Colors	White or ecru paper; black lettering	Smoky colors (gray, tan, olive green, etc.) with deeper colors of lettering	Unusual colors or color contrasts (for example, pink paper with fuschia border or aqua paper with navy lettering)
Typeface	Traditional typeface, such as script or antique Roman	Very contemporary lettering, often unusual	Wide range of typefaces used; the fashion is in the color.

Start-up and Continuing Stationery Needs for the Entrepreneur

When you work for a large corporation, you receive the standard stationery offering to use, but when you start your own business or open an office, you must decide on what your basic stationery items should be. You must choose a designer—and in most major cities there are numerous good design firms and freelance graphic design consultants. Some printers have very capable designers on staff, but some do not and the results show it.

Among the decisions you will make with the designer of your stationery are these:

- The design of the logo, symbol, or trademark of your business

- The types of stationery you need (When you first start up a business, a minimum selection is wise.)
- The quality and texture of the paper
- The colors
- The sizes
- The process to be used for the lettering:

    Printing is the most widely used and is all that is necessary for a new business.

    Engraving is a luxurious, expensive process, requiring the making of a special steel die; one can feel engraved lettering on both sides of the paper. For a small business owner, it is a sign of success. In most companies only senior management is allowed to use engraved papers.

    Thermography is a heat process that causes the ink to rise slightly, giving a kind of engraved feeling to the letters. It is often referred to as "the poor man's engraving." Since it is neither fish nor fowl, I personally don't like it.

    Embossing the logo is something that is done to add a special feeling of luxury to any paper. A "bumped embossed" logo rises prominently from the paper. People like to feel it with their fingers. When there is no color used, it is called "blind embossing." Since embossing has a definite cachet of its own and can become a part of the logo design, some companies *always* have their logos embossed, even on paper and on business cards that are printed rather than engraved.

The *ne plus ultra* in the field of fine stationery is a true luxury touch: personally watermarked paper. A watermark is a translucent mark or design that is produced in the paper during its manufacturing process. You can see it better by holding the sheet of paper up to the light, but that state of near invisibility is part of its charm and mystique. Makers of fine papers like Crane have their company names watermarked on their stationery and bond, but when a business has its own name or symbol watermarked on its stationery, the company has reached the ultimate in snob appeal.

Anyone who custom orders his own good stationery must remember that once all of the decisions have been made, there is a long lead time required—often three months or more—before receipt of the paper. It is not easy to obtain quickly the desired combinations of color, weight, rag content, and texture of paper desired. There is only one consolation: The wait is worth it!

A Successful Entrepreneur's Stationery Case History

When you start in business, all you really need are some letterheads with matching envelopes and some business cards. As you succeed, other elements of stationery should be added to show you are a solid business, here to stay.

Here's a study of the evolution of the company stationery—and of the career—of an imaginary young woman entrepreneur named Mary Eammon, who has opened her own business designing, manufacturing, and selling clothing at wholesale for pre-teen and early-teen boys who are extra tall or big. She has decided to call her company Long Boy Enterprises, Inc. She has hired a free-lance Fort Worth designer who has used her favorite colors (green with a warm cream) to come up with an entire stationery program. She subsequently uses the green and cream colors for the interiors of her office and showroom, for her packaging, and for everything that represents her business. Her designer has conceived her green logo, combining the letters *L, B,* and *E* for Long Boy Enterprises.

Her Stationery Needs When the Business Opens

- *Office letterheads* (8½″ × 11″) with standard matching envelopes (see illustration, items 1 and 2).
- *Business cards* (approximately 2″ × 3½″) printed with information identical to that on the letterheads (see illustration, item 4).
- *Memo pads* (or routing slips or forwarding slips) to be used for brief internal and external communications. These can be of any size—one popular size is 4½″ × 6″ (see illustration, item 3).
- *Business forms* necessary for the business, which are ordered from a house specializing in forms. Having the company's logo and typeface printed on them in green is an additional charge, one that can be delayed until the business is solid.

The Next Step: Her Business Grows

She adds staff; they use the identical printed letterhead, but without their names and titles separately indicated. She now needs:

- *Engraved letterheads* (of an identical design, green on cream, but the quality of paper is better and the paper is smaller in size—perhaps 7½″ × 10½″), which connotes executive status.
- *Engraved business cards* (of an identical design). Her staff continues to use printed ones that contain their names and titles.

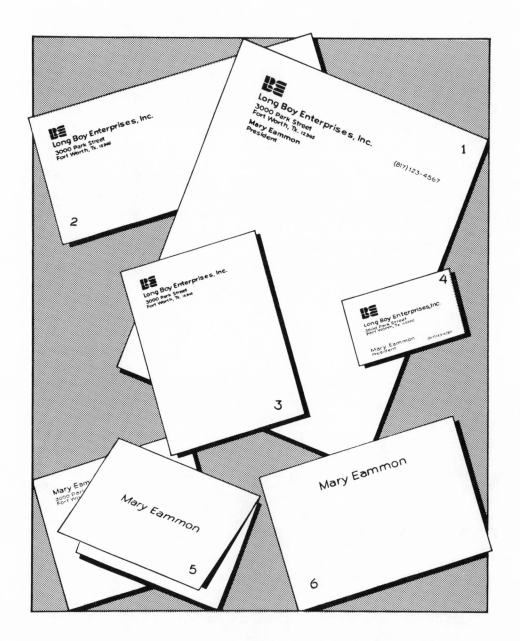

A STATIONERY WARDROBE FOR THE SUCCESSFUL EXECUTIVE

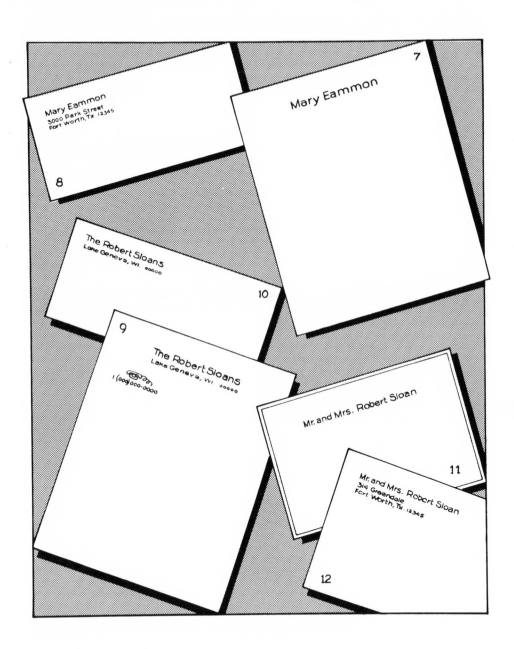

Her Business Continues to Grow and Prosper

She opens an office in two other cities. Her stationery is redesigned to allow for the branch offices to be included at the bottom of the letterhead.

She does an impressive amount of business-social entertaining and now needs personal-business stationery of a good quality to use for writing letters of thanks, congratulations, condolence, etc., to customers and business associates. She can also use this paper for gift enclosures and for hand-written invitations. Her options are these:

- *"Informals" or folded notes* with matching envelopes—4¾″ × 3½″ or larger (see illustration, item 5).
- *Correspondence cards* (one popular size is 4½″ × 6½″). These may have colored borders, with envelopes lined in the same color of tissue—an extra touch of luxury (see illustration, item 6).
- *Small-sized letterheads* with matching envelopes (one example: 6½″ × 8″; see illustration, items 7 and 8).

NOTE: On all three of these options, only Mary Eammon's name is engraved, not her company's. On the envelopes her name and the street address of her company are engraved. The exclusion of the company name is what makes this kind of business stationery very personal; the recipient feels "special." Men's and women's stationery of this kind is identical. Some prefer their personal-business papers bordered in color (which looks richer but costs much more, particularly when the borders are hand-done).

She Marries

Mary Eammon retains her maiden name in business but becomes Mrs. Robert Sloan in her personal life. She and her husband now need joint stationery: correspondence cards to use for personal matters in the city (see illustration, items 11 and 12) and letter paper for their summer home (see illustration, items 9 and 10). Mary Eammon does some business entertaining at home, involving her husband; it is important that the guests don't address him as "Mr. Eammon." That is why the joint stationery is important; it signals that when she is at home, she is Mrs. Sloan, not Ms. Eammon.

The Sloans use the correspondence cards to issue invitations, to thank for gifts sent to them both, and as gift card enclosures in important presents (again, possibly business related) they send as a pair.

Business Cards

The first really important graphic statement for most of us is our business card. Today's young entrepreneur and professional orders his or her business cards at the first flush of business. I've seen the cards of many entrepreneurs, including an eighth-grader in the plant seed business, a golf caddy, a college student who acts as a mime, a senior citizen who dog-sits when people go on trips, and a handicapped woman who has a flourishing seasonal home business sewing name tapes on the clothing and possessions of young people who go away to school or to camp.

Most of us remember our first business cards and how proud we were of them. Mine came from Tiffany & Company, the famous New York jeweler, when I began as the store's first director of publicity and public relations. I remember how proud I was of how beautiful my engraved card looked. The store's name was engraved boldly in the center; almost hidden in one corner was my name and title in tiny lettering. When I remarked about this to the president, Walter Hoving, half seriously and half in jest, Mr. Hoving addressed me sternly. "When you work for Tiffany," he said with a trace of a smile on his face, "the only thing that matters is the company. The individual is secondary." He taught me a good lesson that day, as he did every day during the four years I worked under him.

Your business card and how you handle it is a very personal part of executive communication. It's like a handshake that you leave behind you. You should give your card to someone in such a way as to make him *want* to remember you and *want* to get in touch with you.

There are three main uses for business cards:

· To give to someone to remind him who you are, where you are, and how to reach you
· To use as a forwarding agent when clipped to something like a photograph, the annual report, a clipping from a newspaper or magazine, or anything you promised to send to a particular person or you know someone would enjoy receiving
· To use as an enclosure for a present or flowers

A handsome card, properly presented, makes a tremendous impression. We should know when to present our cards, when to take the initiative; we should know how to exchange cards gracefully when someone else has taken the initiative.

Business Card Etiquette

It is particularly important for a young executive to learn how to present his or her card properly, so as to avoid being "pushy" or appearing maladroit.

· *Do not force your card on a senior executive you meet.* Wait until he or she asks for yours.
· *Don't offer your card early in the conversation to anyone who is a com-*

plete stranger and whom you meet by accident (for example, when sitting next to a person on a plane or at the lunch counter). Your overeagerness may be based on nothing more than youthful enthusiasm and may irritate your neighbor. (In addition, there is a possibility that if you knew the truth about the stranger, you would not want him to have your name, company name, and address!)

- *Don't scatter your card about in a large group of strangers.* People will immediately begin to think you're trying to sell them something, and they'll freeze you out. Learn to be very selective about the people to whom you give your card. Also remember that at a business-social gathering the best way to do it is so that others are not aware you are giving someone your card. It should be a private exchange between just the two of you, not a conspicuous gesture made in public, and particularly not at someone's private dinner.

- When you attend a meeting outside your office with people whom you do not know, *wait for the signals that may be given.* Let *someone else* begin the exchanging of cards among those who do not know each other. Often cards will be exchanged at the beginning of the meeting, sometimes at the conclusion. However, if you are giving a presentation, you have every right to distribute your cards in advance to those near you, so that they will know exactly who you are before you stand up to speak.

- *It is much better not to give out a business card than to give one that is defective, out-of-date, or soiled.* Carry your cards in your wallet or in a card case to keep them protected and fresh. If your remaining cards are not spit-and-polish perfect, throw them out. Apologize to people you meet for a sudden depletion of your cards, and then write the necessary information on a piece of clean paper to give those who wish it.

- *Women as well as men should carry business cards in the evening at social events* in case a good business target of opportunity presents itself.

- No matter whether you are dining in a fast food restaurant, at a black-tie dinner in a hotel, or in someone's home, *cards should never be brought out during a meal.* People should be discreet about talking business when they are having cocktails or dining either at someone's home or in a restaurant when the event has been billed primarily as social, rather than business-related.

- *The most important part of business card etiquette is knowing when and how to personalize your card.* "Personalizing" your card entails putting a slash through your name and writing something personal with a pen on the front (or on the back, if there is insufficient room on the front). For example:

> If you send flowers to your dinner hosts at their home, you would write on the back of your card something like, "Thank you for a

perfectly wonderful evening. I enjoyed every second." You
would sign with your first name only.

If you are forwarding some material, you would write something like,
"This might be of interest to you. All the best," followed by your
first name signature.

If you are introducing someone who has an appointment with a colleague of yours, attach your card to that person's resume or
brochure or whatever: "Know you'll enjoy talking with Ken,"
followed by your first name signature.

The Design of the Business Card

A business card is part of a large corporation's unified graphics program.
A junior executive's cards, like his stationery, are usually printed until he
ascends the corporate ladder to a height where engraved cards are supplied.

For the entrepreneur or professional, self-expression is possible, and
there are certainly many imaginative designs representing small businesses in
circulation. Anyone in a quality-image business should keep in mind that a
well-designed card on quality stock denotes a person of taste and importance.
When you "think cheap" without any good design advice on your cards, you
may very well look cheap to those who are left with your card to remember
you by. A person who looks on your card with disdain most likely will not
want to do business with you.

The standard size of a business card is 3½″ × 2″ or variations thereof.
Cards may be made in unusual shapes to represent certain types of businesses. (I have seen clever cards in the shape of a hamburger, automobile,
French poodle, and typewriter.) If you have cards of this nature made for you,
remember that what you gain in cleverness, you may lose in one respect:
People cannot easily put an odd-shaped card in their wallets or card cases.
Some designers cleverly use unorthodox sizes to make their cards memorable,
as do these renowned figures in the design field: John Saladino with his oversized card, Massimo Vignelli with his mini-card, and Lawrence Peabody with
his vertical, double-fold card.

The stock of the card may have a shiny or dull matte finish; it may be
thick or thin but must be strong enough not to tear when fingered or when
extracted from a card case. Managers often use both printed and engraved
cards, the former to use in mass mailings and the latter to use for VIP business. The colors of the business card should, of course, match the colors of
the company's stationery.

The information contained on the card should include the following:

· *The logo, trademark, or company symbol.* A small-business person may
  work with a graphics artist to find a symbol representing his or her work,

such as a bouquet of flowers for a florist, a market basket full of vegetables for a food consultant, a calculator with printed figures issuing from it for an accountant, a camera with printing in the lenses for a photographer, a mug full of cosmetic brushes for a person in the beauty business, a dressmaker's dummy with a scarf wrapped around its neck for a dressmaker.

- *The text,* including the following:

  Name
  Title (if pertinent)
  Company name
  Business address
  Telephone
  Telex number (if pertinent)
  Address of other offices in the country (if pertinent)

Some people who work out of their home as well as out of an office include their home telephone number along with their business number.

Proper Procedures on the Design of the Card

- If you own more than one business, it is preferable to have separate cards for each business.
- If you have offices in several places, you may certainly include this information on the card.
- Unless you have a professional title such as M.D., Colonel, Ph.D., etc., do not use a title (Mr., Miss, Ms.) on your card. The exception to this rule is when you have a name that could be male or female (Duane, Clair, Marion, Cameron, etc.). In this case you would be wise to put a Mr. or Ms. in front of your name.
- If everyone knows you by your nickname, include it with your formal name: "Marianne ("Buffy") Endicott, Vice-President."

Business Cards Abroad

(*See also* Chapter 5: International Business Manners)

If you do a considerable amount of business in a foreign country, you should have your cards printed in English on one side and in the country's language on the other. Some European business people print extra information on their cards, such as the type of products manufactured, the number of employees and gross revenues. This kind of business card is a mini press release of sorts.

The classic European business card is often larger than ours (3" × 4½"), leaving space at the bottom to jot a note if necessary.

In Japan the business card is more important than anywhere else. There is a ritual to how cards are printed and how they are presented. (One American businessman told me he distributes an average of fifty cards whenever he visits Japan on business.) An American should learn from a Japanese businessman before he goes over to Japan about the subtleties of when and how he should present his card; he should be prepared for a barrage of cards to be presented to him, to which he must respond with his own card. He should understand when he is given a card from a senior Japanese with no title beneath the name that it means everyone is *supposed to know* what that person's lofty title is. (*See also* A Glance at Some Behavioral Signposts—Japan, in Chapter 5.)

Business Announcement Cards

Business news may be communicated through a telephone call, a letter, a Mailgram, or the mailing of a business announcement card. A letter is, of course, the most personal way of imparting news; it also permits the inclusion of supporting material—brochures, press releases, newspaper clippings, etc. However, for a widespread mailing, it is expensive and cumbersome to send letters. The sending of Mailgrams to announce business news to a large mailing list is very expensive and should be reserved for only urgent news. For a large mailing, the best device is the printed, thermographed, or engraved business announcement card. A business announcement card reaches out in shorthand to a maximum audience of clients, customers, colleagues, associates, VIPs, potential customers, and friends.

It should be kept in mind that:

- The announcement card and envelope reflect the image of the company, just as its stationery does. Therefore, both should be of a good quality stock and well-designed.
- The card should not be so bulky in size that its weight exceeds the minimum first class postage requirement (or it will entail an unnecessary added expense).
- The names and addresses on the envelopes should either be typed, printed by a word processor, or hand-written—*not* done on labels!
- There should be enough, but not too much, communicated on the announcement. If the recipient is confused by the purpose of the announcement, the desired effect will be lost.
- It is acceptable etiquette to jot a short note on an announcement card to personalize it, if there's reason to do so.
- A printed announcement card is the least expensive way to communicate; an engraved announcement card is formal, expensive, and creates an atmosphere of "something special."

- If your company sends out many announcements on a continuing basis, like an insurance company announcing its new representatives, it's a good idea to keep in stock white cards or folded notes that contain the company logo already engraved or embossed and the announcement message already engraved or printed. Then the name of the person, his address, and telephone number can be filled in by hand.
- When you receive a business announcement in the mail, you are not obliged to acknowledge its receipt. However, if you are a personal friend of the subject of the announcement, it's very nice to send him or her a short hand-written, or even typed, acknowledgment conveying your congratulations and best wishes. This is a simple gesture and rarely forgotten.

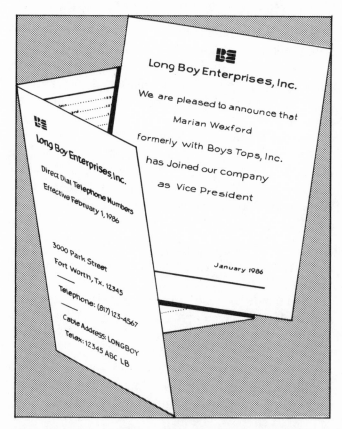

This particular announcement card serves two purposes:
- It announces the company's new direct dialing numbers and lists personnel alphabetically inside.
- It announces the appointment of a new company officer.

Formal Versus Informal

As with a company's stationery, business announcement cards should accurately reflect the company's image. The use of the same logo and typeface as well as colors of stock and printing helps reinforce the corporate identity; this holds true for a small business as well as a large one.

The wording of the business announcement should be carefully proofed before it is printed—a little mistake becomes a major error on a small card.

There are formal and informal ways of wording an announcement, as the following examples attest. The nature of the business governs which type of announcement should be sent:

Announcing a New Company

Formally

JOAN McINTOSH LEE
RONALD SCHULTZ
ANNOUNCE THE FORMATION OF
LECTON INC.
A MARKET RESEARCH FIRM
SPECIALIZING IN
FOOD SERVICES
3422 Contrad Street
Fargo, South Dakota 00000
(000) 000-0000

Informally

TIM MCCOY
HAS OPENED
TIM'S TINKER TOYS
A CHILDREN'S TOY AND BOOK EMPORIUM
AT 4TH AND HOWARD
MINNEAPOLIS
(000) 000-0000
Bring this card for a 20% discount on your first purchase.

Announcing a New Branch

Formally

KENYON, ATKINS & REYNOLDS
ANNOUNCES
THE OPENING OF THEIR FOURTH TEXAS OFFICE
3314 SOUTHWEST FREEWAY
DALLAS 00000
UNDER THE MANAGEMENT OF
MR. ALLAN E. ELKINS
VICE-PRESIDENT
DECEMBER 1, 1986
(000) 000-0000

Informally

HI-JINKS PREMIUM DESIGNS
145 Broadway, Newark, NJ 00000
IS SUCH A GREAT SUCCESS
WE ARE OPENING
TWO NEW BRANCH OFFICES

124 First St.	314 Palisades, 14-F
Naples, FL 00000	Canton, OH 00000
(000) 000-0000	(000)000-0000
Anne Cox, Manager	Ed Reed, Manager

Reasons for Sending an Announcement

A Change of Address (in a Party Invitation)

PLEASE JOIN IN CELEBRATING OUR MOVE
TO NEW OFFICES
MORGAN, LYMAN & BORNEMOUTH, P.C.
1345 SEAVIEW AVENUE
ATLANTIC CITY, N.J. 00000
WEDNESDAY, MARCH 27TH
COCKTAILS—5:00 TO 7:00 P.M.
RSVP: (000) 000-0000

A Group Departure for Another Firm

(Included in this mailing would be a separate card listing each lawyer and his
or her direct-dial number.)

WE ARE PLEASED TO ANNOUNCE THAT,
HAVING TERMINATED OUR RELATIONSHIP WITH
GORDON, REEVES & HOLLYWORTH,
WE WILL CONTINUE THE PRACTICE OF LAW
UNDER THE NAME
GOODWIN, O'MEARA AND KRAFT
WITH OFFICES AT 345 DECATUR PLACE
LINCOLN, NEBRASKA 00000
September 1, 1986   (000) 000-0000

Move of Offices

JONATHON P. FILLMAN ASSOCIATES
PUBLIC RELATIONS COUNSELORS
ANNOUNCES THE LOCATION OF
THEIR NEW OFFICES AT
et cetera

or

JONATHON P. FILLMAN ASSOCIATES
PUBLIC RELATIONS COUNSELORS
WISHES TO ANNOUNCE A MOVE TO
A NEW LOCATION AT
1415 STATE AVENUE
ATLANTA, GEORGIA 00000
MARCH 1, 1986   (000) 000-0000

or

JONATHON P. FILLMAN ASSOCIATES
PUBLIC RELATIONS COUNSELORS
ANNOUNCES THAT THE COMPANY HAS
MOVED TO A NEW ADDRESS AT
et cetera

A New Officer of the Company or Firm

COMPANY XYZ
IS PLEASED TO ANNOUNCE THAT
JOANNA S. BARKHORN
HAS BEEN NAMED EXECUTIVE VICE-PRESIDENT
JUNE FIRST

123 LA SALLE STREET
CHICAGO, IL 00000
(000) 000-0000
TELEX 00000

or alternatively

COMPANY XYZ
WE TAKE PLEASURE IN ANNOUNCING
THE APPOINTMENT OF
JOANNA S. BARKHORN
AS EXECUTIVE VICE-PRESIDENT

123 LA SALLE STREET
CHICAGO, IL 00000
(000) 000-0000
TELEX 00000

A New Division Within the Company

GEORGE LANOS, PRESIDENT
ANTIOCHTEK INC.
TAKES PLEASURE IN ANNOUNCING
A NEW LINE OF PRODUCTS
"LUMINOSO"
LAMPS, LIGHTING FIXTURES AND ACCESSORIES

Harold Wenzel, General Manager
"Luminoso" Division
134 EAST ERIE
DETROIT, MI 00000
(000) 000-0000

The Departure of a Partner for Government Service

AMES, CUTTER, McILHERNEY & JONES
ANNOUNCES THE WITHDRAWAL FROM
THE PARTNERSHIP
OF MARIO A. ANTONINI
TO BECOME
AMBASSADOR OF THE UNITED STATES OF AMERICA
TO THE REPUBLIC OF ITALY
APRIL 1, 1986
141 WATER STREET
MILWAUKEE, WI 00000
(000) 000-0000

A Return to the Firm

(The partners and counsels of the firm would be listed on the inside page of a double-fold announcement; or, if the announcement is on a single card, the partners would be listed on the back side.)

THE PARTNERS OF
MANNING, BABCOCK, WEISS, GREEN, KOE AND STAIR
240 UNION STREET
SAN FRANCISCO 00000
ARE PLEASED TO ANNOUNCE
THAT
THE HONORABLE WILLIAM A. GELLHORN
FORMERLY OF THE UNITED STATES SENATE
HAS REJOINED THE FIRM
AS OF
JUNE FIRST
NINETEEN HUNDRED EIGHTY-SIX

A Change in Senior Management

(For example, a senior officer retires but remains with the company in some capacity.)

PETER M. FINNERTY
CHAIRMAN OF THE BOARD AND CHIEF EXECUTIVE OFFICER
A. L. JOHNSON ASSOCIATES INCORPORATED
IS PLEASED TO ANNOUNCE THE ELECTION OF
WILLIAM S. PEASE
AS
CHAIRMAN EMERITUS
MAY 1987

Retiring and Becoming a Company Consultant

A. R. JONES
PRESIDENT, A.R.J. MANAGEMENT SERVICES INC.
ANNOUNCES THE RETIREMENT OF
JOHN J. FINN
AND HIS APPOINTMENT AS
CONSULTANT TO THE COMPANY
2000 HUNTS POINT
BOULDER, COLORADO 00000
(000) 000-0000

The Resumption of a Maiden Name

MARY BRIGHTON GRISWOLD, PH.D.
HAS RESUMED HER
MAIDEN NAME
MARY LOUISE BRIGHTON, PH.D.

The Change of Name and Company

ANNE DAVIS
ANNOUNCES
THAT SHE WILL NOW BE KNOWN AS ANNE WELDON
AND THAT HER COMPANY
WILL NOW BE KNOWN AS
ANNE WELDON AND ASSOCIATES
1034 STANTON DRIVE
AUSTIN, TEXAS 00000
(000) 000-0000

An Addition to a (Medical) Practice

SEYMOUR R. GRATIAN, D.D.S.
DIPLOMATE, AMERICAN BOARD OF PERIODONTOLOGY
ANNOUNCES WITH PLEASURE THE ASSOCIATION OF
PHILIP B. YORK, D.M.D.
IN THE PRACTICE OF PERIODONTICS
3422 STATE STREET   (000) 000-0000
DES MOINES, IOWA 00000

Different Sets of Promotions

WE ARE PLEASED TO ANNOUNCE
THAT THE FOLLOWING HAVE BEEN ELECTED
SENIOR VICE-PRESIDENTS
ANGELA H. NIZZI   DANIEL R. KOCH
AND
THAT THE FOLLOWING HAVE BEEN ELECTED
VICE-PRESIDENTS
RAYMOND P. BONE   CARLOS J. LIAS
SUZANNE CHURCH   C. AUSTIN OLLMAN
NICHOLAS DAMORTH   PLATO POULOS
MORTON LEE & CO.
320 HUDSON STREET   MEMPHIS, TN 00000
OCTOBER 24, 1986

Company Name Change

EDMUND A. SINCLAIRE, PRESIDENT
THE SINCLAIRE ADVERTISING AGENCY
ANNOUNCES
THAT AS OF JULY 1, 1986
THE FIRM'S NAME WILL BE CHANGED TO
THE SINCLAIRE GROUP
331 MAIN
BATON ROUGE, LOUISIANA 00000
(000) 000-0000

A Career Change

Formally

MARIANNE LINDSAY, A.S.I.D.
FORMERLY WITH THE INTERIOR DESIGN STAFF OF
MARSHALL FIELD & CO.
WISHES TO ANNOUNCE
THE OPENING OF HER OWN OFFICES

LINDSAY DESIGN CONSULTANTS

DESIGN CONSULTING BY THE HOUR
OR ON A PROJECT BASIS

1740 NORTH STATE STREET   (000) 000-0000
APT. 12-B CHICAGO, IL 00000

Informally

RICK SONDHEIM
FORMERLY OF "ROCKLAND"
HAS OPENED HIS OWN RESTAURANT
"FOOTLIGHTS"
AND GIVES A SPECIAL WELCOME TO FRIENDS
345 Mohegan Avenue
Providence, R.I.
(000) 000-0000

A Simple Announcement of a Merger

THE MERGER
OF TURNER REAL ESTATE
AND
BRENT PROPERTIES
HAS BEEN FINALIZED
THE COMPANY WILL NOW BE KNOWN AS
TURNER-BRENT PROPERTIES, INC.
1415 LAKESIDE
UTICA, NEW YORK 00000
(000) 000-0000

A Complicated Announcement of a Merger

When two companies merge, such as two law firms, all four sides of a double fold announcement are used.

Side one (the cover):	The announcement of the two firms having merged, the date of the merger, and the new name of the firm
Side two (left inside cover):	The name and address of one of the merging firms, the year it was founded; the number of lawyers "engaged in the general practice of domestic and international law"; the list of law specialties (such as "corporate," "labor," "banking," "real estate," etc.)
Side three (right-hand inside page)	The same information as on side two, but for the other firm involved in the merger
Side four (backside of announcement):	A list of the members of both firms and of the "of counsel" lawyers for both locations if two offices will be retained

8

The Art of
Business Entertaining

Business people spend a great deal of time at the table eating, drinking, and talking shop. As Brillat-Savarin, the nineteenth-century French gastronome, wrote, "The table establishes a kind of bond between the bargainer and the bargained-with, and renders the guest more apt to receive certain impressions." Business entertaining is a multi-billion-dollar industry today, because companies have found it's good business to entertain clients, customers, business colleagues, politicians, civic leaders, celebrities, and potential customers. It doesn't matter whether hamburgers and hot dogs are served during a picnic in a dusty meadow, or champagne and petits-fours at a reception in a palatial museum. The natural potential for creating goodwill is intrinsic in every business-social event. It's a way for people to get to know one another in a relaxed atmosphere; it's fertile ground for the germination of future business deals.

We entertain in business for the following reasons:

- We want to or need to repay someone for his or her hospitality.
- We realize this is a good opportunity to "size up" someone.
- There are favors to be returned and favors to be sought (i.e., we can say "thank you" and "please" at the same time).
- There is a reason to celebrate.
- A person or group or institution (maybe our own company) deserves to be honored.

- We need important new contacts, to bring in more business.
- We need to soothe old customers and impress new ones.
- We wish to embellish our corporate and civic images in our community.
- In rare cases, our company simply wishes to be nice!

Entertaining is a powerful business tool that must be wielded with care. Success demands planning, an efficient and effective staff, a creative spirit, and, most important, an attitude of caring about the guests. A perfunctory host ruins a good party faster than any logistical misfortune that may befall it. One has only to think back on the many times, for example, that attendance at a business cocktail party, overcrowded beyond belief, has meant being shoved about mercilessly in a smoke-clouded atmosphere, where any hope of a decent conversation, much less of a decent hors d'oeuvre, is a joke, and where getting a drink without fighting for it is a rare occurrence. Fortunately (for the host), at this type of party one may never know who the host is, never mind being able to locate him!

It is the attitude of caring that makes the host at a short business lunch treat his single guest with the same attention to his comfort and welfare that an important dignitary would command. It is the attitude of caring that makes the host of a large function aware of all the important little details, including everything from the way the invitation envelopes are hand-stamped to the presence of pretty guest towels in the restrooms on the night of the party.

How You Entertain

The ways in which you entertain are usually governed by:

- The time available
- The resources available
- The cost of what you wish to do
- The importance to your business objectives of the person you are entertaining.

The following are the most common forms of entertaining in business today.

Entertaining in a Small Way: The Options

By far the most popular form of business entertaining is that conducted on a one-to-one basis or in a small group and involving invitations to breakfast, lunch, or a drink after work (or, as is fast becoming a fad in New York, a cup of tea in the middle of the afternoon).

When you leave the office for another atmosphere removed from the distractions and interruptions of your home base, you can concentrate on the other person and on new ideas. You can relax and clear your head.

An executive should want to be known as a person who does things with style. That means knowing how to extend invitations and where to do his entertaining. The following are some of the options on the latter:

The Quickest Way to Entertain Someone While Talking Strictly Business

- Breakfast in a coffee shop or restaurant (45–60 minutes)
- Lunch ordered from a deli, eaten together in your office (20 minutes)
- Lunch at a nearby modest restaurant (60 minutes)
- Tea at a convenient spot set up for the service of tea (50 minutes)
- A drink after work in an attractive, nearby place (60 minutes)

When You Really Want to Please a Present or Prospective Client or Customer

- Lunch at a good restaurant (1½ to 2 hours)
- A game at your club followed by a quick lunch (2 hours)
- Dinner with spouses (or dates, if unmarried) at a good restaurant (2 to 3 hours)

When You Want to "Knock the Socks Off" Someone by Impressing Him

- Tickets that are exceedingly difficult to get, such as for:
    The World Series
    Opening night at the opera
    Preview of what will be a hit play
    The Rose Bowl, Super Bowl, Stanley Cup, etc.
  preceded by or followed by dinner in a superior restaurant (4 to 5 hours)
- Tickets to a very social black-tie (or even white-tie) dinner at which somone like the President is in attendance, or a famous star is entertaining (3 hours)

When You Are Really Close to Someone and His Family

- An invitation to the entire family to join you for a meal at home (or perhaps a club) and a family-oriented activity, such as ice-skating, a tennis tournament, softball game, or beach picnic

- An invitation to the executive and his family to spend the weekend with you.

Inviting Someone Home to Dinner

When you invite someone home for dinner, it is the nicest kind of compliment you could pay a colleague who is a good friend, particularly one who has been on the road for a long time and who is passing through town. It is, of course, an informal way of entertaining, particularly if it is last-minute and your family is included. However, there are some rules to be followed here, too. For example:

- Your guest deserves a *proper meal.* This is no time for a pizza or a frozen dinner. If you don't have a good dinner to give him or her, go out to eat.
- The table should be set for a guest (this means no paper napkins and plastic mats).
- The bar should contain the kind of alcoholic (or soft) drink your guest prefers.
- Although he will probably ask to help, the guest should not be allowed in the kitchen.
- The small children of the house should not be running underfoot the entire time. It is fine to have them greet the guest and stay for a short while, but an exhausted business person should not have to suffer through a noisy, hyperactive (it's always hyperactive when the children aren't your own) evening.

Inviting a Guest to Lunch at Your Office Desk

Many times there is no executive dining room to run to for a quick lunch when you are having a business discussion with outsiders, and you have a deadline and must work through the lunch hour. Sending out for a deli lunch is the obvious solution. If this happens often in your office routine, you should keep some things in your office that will elevate the deli lunch to a delightful repast, properly served. For example:

- If there is a refrigerator on the premises, keep washed, chopped raw vegetables in a plastic bag (slivers of carrots, broccoli and cauliflower florets, cherrystone tomatoes, fresh fruit, etc.), which dress up, both visually and, more importantly, nutritionally any sandwich or pizza that arrives for lunch.
- Keep a supply of attractive plates; glasses for the soda you will drink; "real" knives, forks, and spoons (to avoid having to use the ghastly little plastic ones supplied by the deli); and some large, good quality paper napkins (not the little scratchy ones supplied by food vendors).

Entertaining the Out-of-Town Business Guest

When you are entertaining a business colleague who has been on the road for a long time or who has just come a long distance to meet you, have pity on his physical condition. He may have had travel delays and problems; he may have had little sleep but a lot of stress. Don't make him go to a noisy, crowded cocktail party where he'll have to stand up and inhale smoke. Don't take him to a restaurant—no matter how great its reputation—where the two of you will have to stand waiting a long time, perhaps drinking at the bar, before your table is ready. Don't take an obviously exhausted person to a noisy restaurant, particularly a place with loud music, where it is difficult to think much less talk.

If your out-of-town guest is young, full of energy, and obviously not tired, he or she may be greatly pleased by an invitation to dine in a place featuring music and lots of action. Ask your visitor on the telephone before he arrives to name his preference in restaurants. Ask him in advance what kind of food he particularly likes, and choose the place accordingly.

Beware of being overly creative. A lawyer friend of mine quite innocently put one of his visiting clients through a torturous evening in a small Japanese restaurant where diners either kneel or sit on the floor. The guest, who suffered badly from arthritis but was not about to admit it, went through the meal in agony. His host had hardly picked a winner for his guest's first night in town!

When someone passes through town, it's an opportunity to put your city's best culinary foot forward. However, never exceed your budget unnecessarily. No business deal was ever consummated solely because someone took someone else to lunch at the town's most expensive restaurant. (After all, major deals have been forged over food like pizza in places like the parking lot!)

If your company has put you on a modest entertaining budget, you can always invite a business acquaintance passing through town to "come and have a drink at home" with you (*see also* Inviting Someone Home to Dinner). If you are busy for dinner, explain that and provide a good suggestion for a restaurant he might enjoy—on his own, of course.

Never be too proud to suggest to a business colleague that you go to a modest restaurant. When times are tough, expensive lunches are anachronistic. But the quality of food and service should still be taken into account. There are lots of modest restaurants proffering good food and friendly service. Don't treat a colleague to a noticeably inferior restaurant experience.

The Care of an Out-of-Town VIP Visitor

(*See also* Being Courteous to Visiting Foreigners in Your City, in Chapter 5.)

A visiting guest of honor, particularly one from another country, deserves very special treatment. An official or high-ranking individual, the head of a company, a visiting lecturer of great distinction—all come under the category of "VIP visitor."

Here are some things to remember:

- He (or she) should be met at the airport by someone of sufficiently high rank, such as a company vice-president. He will require help with his baggage and he usually arrives with many questions to answer.
- There should be welcoming flowers or a plant in the hotel room, liquor or wine of his choice (researched before his arrival), soda water, an ice-bucket full of ice, and some soft drinks. There might be a basket of fresh fruit (with a plate, fruit fork, and fruit knife); perhaps also a small box of chocolates to satisfy the cravings of a sweet tooth.
- A personal note of welcome from the CEO or the highest ranking company person he will see during his visit should be awaiting him.
- The guest should be provided with a complete schedule of events for his stay. If he has a health problem (like a heart condition), his schedule should *not* be overtaxing. If he has come from another country, he will be very tired and probably jet-lagged; his schedule should be *very* easy the first day.
- If he does not know your city, provide him with a short history or a guidebook containing the important facts about the area.
- He should be asked if there is anyone he has met previously whom he would like to see during his stay.
- Comfortable transportation should be provided at all times for him.
- He should be provided with an adept interpreter if his command of English is inadequate.
- He should be given a *carefully annotated guest list* for every meeting and every business/social event, so that he will be well-briefed on the cast of characters. Giving him a mere list of names is totally useless. His list should explain who the people are, what their businesses are, why they are important. Interesting information on their spouses should be included, too.
- When the VIP is escorted to each meeting and social event, he should be carefully introduced. If a reception is given in his honor, he should stand in a receiving line with his host.
- Whenever wine is served at a meal, the guest of honor should be given a

toast by the host of that meal. (*See also* Practical Entertainment for Hosts and Guests, Toasting, toward the end of this chapter.)

When You're Handling a Celebrity

When a real star has been booked for the corporate function's entertainment, he needs to be treated with consideration, or that person may be too exhausted to perform well. There are some things you (and everyone else) should refrain from doing when handling a celebrity:

· Don't talk his ear off.
· Don't take him to your home to show him off to your family and friends.
· Don't ask him for favors other than perhaps to send you a signed photograph for your children when he has returned home.

If he is trying to eat a meal and people keep interrupting him for autographs, ask the celebrity if he would mind signing a few autographs *after* he finishes eating. Then protect him and let him finish his meal in peace.

Arrange for the photographers from the press to have a photo session with him, get their pictures, and leave. If you make life comfortable for him, he will remember you and your company always—with affection.

Where You Entertain

A Dinner Party or a Weekend Lunch Party at Home

If you are senior enough in your company (or rich enough on your own!) to entertain at home, and if you have a beautiful place in which to entertain, use it as the preferred place to entertain. There is so little entertainment at home today that you can make a tremendous impression giving a party there.
Some advice:

· There should be comfortable sitting and eating space for every guest.
· If your house is difficult to reach, send everyone a clear map with instructions along with your invitation.
· If you live near a major city where some people rely on public transportation, send a car to meet them at the train or bus station.
· If your home is out in the country, feed people a meal, not just cocktails; if having a dinner, schedule it on the weekend at a reasonably early hour, to permit people to reach their own homes at a decent hour after the party.
· Serve your guests cocktails for forty-five minutes to an hour before serving dinner. A short cocktail hour, plus the serving of hors d'oeuvres helps control excessive drinking.

- You should have sufficient *trained* help to make the service flow smoothly.
- If your party is very large, it's a good idea to have car parkers help the guests with their cars.
- Be prepared after a big weekend evening party, to bed down any guest who has had too much to drink to drive.

The Organization of a Business Dinner at Home

The Designated Staff Person

- Supervises design, production, and mailing of invitations; helps compile guest list
- If the female spouse does not wish to participate in the planning, oversees the flowers and all coordinating activities with the caterer
- If there are menu cards, places them at each guest's place; puts the place cards in their proper places at the tables
- Checks in guests as they arrive and shows them where to check their coats
- Calls to check on absent or tardy guests; handles all incoming telephone calls during the party
- Coordinates the entertainers, if there are any, showing them where to dress, giving them refreshments, etc.
- Pays everyone at the conclusion of the party

The Caterer

- Hires the necessary staff; prepares the food; prepares the bar (liquor may be provided by host or caterer); brings rental equipment for anything lacking in the house
- Brings ice
- Sets up coatcheck facilities; employs and supervises car parkers
- Serves the meal after cocktails; serves after-dinner drinks
- Cleans up everything pertaining to party, including putting furniture back to where it was before the party

The Spouse

- Assists in compilation of guest list if the couple has mutual business-social friends
- May be in charge of flowers and may also wish to supervise the catering staff in all its activities. (On rare occasions, male spouses have undertaken this chore, and very successfully, too!)

The Spouse's Cohosting Duties at Home

- Helps introduce guests to each other, if they do not know each other. (This may require constantly glancing at the guest list, transferred to a card held in one's hand, but it's an important help to the executive host.)
- Keeps an eye on the service of the meal (or on the service of drinks at a cocktail party) to make sure that everyone is properly served
- At lunch or dinner, helps the host move the guests from the cocktail area into the dining room or dining area, and helps seat the guests in their proper places
- Rises when it's time to move out of the dining room, as a signal to the guests to follow; supervises the service of coffee and after-dinner drinks to the guests

Cohost When There Is No Spouse on Home Turf

An executive host who does not have a spouse may rely on another executive close in rank to himself or herself to cohost a large gathering. There is an important nuance here. An executive may certainly have an executive of the opposite sex act as cohost of his party any place except his or her home. In other words, in a male executive's house, a woman who is not his wife would not be his cohost (it is too symbolic a traditional role for the wife *in the home*). In turn, it is not appropriate for a female executive to have a male as a cohost when she is doing business entertaining in her home. A cohost of the same sex does not pose the problem. This subtle rule also applies to the executive's secretary.

The Imaginative Place for Your Party

When your company party is held in a really unusual place, the creative touch usually makes people remember it for years to come as an exciting event. America is presently a treasure trove of places with historic and nostalgic value, many of them restored and renovated, so that in return for a corporate donation, a social function or a meeting may be held there. Entrepreneurs in some cities have published listings of unusual places for party giving. One of these is Tenth House Enterprises, Box 810, Gracie Station, New York, NY 10028, which annually publishes a book about New York called *Places: A Directory of Public Places for Public Functions.* Such publications give many details, including the size of the facility, and tell you how to book it.

The following are nontraditional types of places in which corporate parties have been staged in the last few years:

In a circus tent
Among the fountains of an urban plaza
On an old Indian trail in the mountains
In a squash court
On a boat pier
In an empty pool
In a museum
On the opera stage
On a coal barge
In the botanical gardens

In an airplane hangar
On an ocean liner's deck
In an old mill
In a dance studio
In a movie theater
On a TV sound stage
In a barn
In a public library
On a football field

Caterers seem to be able to tackle any project these days, no matter how difficult it may be logistically. One night I watched a cold marble office building lobby transformed into a cozy sheik's tent. A crystal chandelier hung from the top of the tent, and we sat on Oriental rugs that covered the marble floors, eating a wonderful feast that we plucked from the center bowls with our fingers. Belly dancers performed around us to the exotic music of Egyptian musicians.

I once watched a sportswear manufacturer show his new spring line on aerialists who performed to the live music of a British rock group . . . in a circus tent. I've attended an "Alice in Wonderland" fantasy given by an insurance company, which completely transformed an old roller rink into a magic place. And I have danced in an old warehouse transformed for the evening by a computer software company into a masked ball in Venice (the only thing missing were the canals!).

If your company wishes to be creative with its special event, don't choose a way-out place unless you know you can successfully cope with the logistics. Ask yourself some important questions:

- Does the place, when transformed, conform to our corporate image? By holding the event in this place, will we achieve the hoped-for corporate objectives?
- Will our budget stretch to cover the costs?
- Can we comply with the fire laws?
- Will the climate be a plus or negative factor at this time of year?
- Can the available caterers handle this complicated a project?
- Will our guests be able to reach the party location easily? Is there parking? Is there public transportation available? Are taxis cruising in the area?
- Will our guests be comfortable during the party, from the point of view of temperature, seating, and room in which to move around?
- What kind of restroom facilities are available?
- Is there enough lead time to arrange everything properly?
- Have we enough staff assigned to supervise the overall operation?

When a company party is held in an unusual place, one that is not accustomed to events like the one you have planned, as hosts you must work harder to assure the comfort of your guests.

The Executive Dining Room

Management of a company blessed with an executive dining room (or several) is always unanimous in considering this combination of a service and a perk well worth the administrative costs involved. The executive dining room is the place where the business elite of an organization gathers for lunch—and sometimes for breakfast—to discuss business at hand and to arrange deals with colleagues on the outside.

It is a place for business entertainment in its most classic sense. It is an ideal place in which to discuss the most sensitive of subjects, such as mergers and acquisitions. The host enjoys a psychological advantage, because he can woo his guests in a perfect trysting environment, his own home turf.

Many executive dining rooms have large round or rectangular communal tables at which an executive lunching alone can find an empty place and some amicable conversation with fellow executives. It provides an excellent opportunity for new executives to get to know the "old hands" and pick up a considerable amount of office gossip.

An executive dining room should be attractive, well-managed, and well-appointed, with a good chef or cook; otherwise it is better not to have one. The dining room is a highly visible symbol of the company's image—either first- or second-rate.

It's impressive when the meals served are of the standard that Miss Charlotte served for so many years at the Dean Witter Reynolds New York headquarters. I remember during my days as a director of that company how we looked forward to the break in long hours of meetings in the boardroom to indulge at table in her sinfully rich concoctions. I remember other executive dining rooms where crystal goblets were etched with the corporate logo, the logo was embroidered on the white damask napkins, and the china service was custom-made, with the logo hand-painted in gold in the center of the plates and cups. I remember the beautiful flowers at the Chase Manhattan Bank and the wonderful omelets made by Rudy Stanish at Goldman Sachs.

Nothing quite compares with Malcolm Forbes' style of executive dining room entertaining, however. He has at least three that I am aware of: a dining room in the landmark house attached to the Forbes Magazine building, where the table is set with hand-painted Venetian gold goblets and exquisite Dresden figurines; a red brick wine cellar made into a dining room, with sterling silver stag-head mugs hanging from the heavy ceiling beams (each engraved with the name of a prominent business leader who has lunched in the cellar); plus a large motor yacht with a smartly dressed crew, the scene of great business parties, where such notables as HRH Prince Charles have been entertained.

A corporate dining room can become a valuable public relations tool in the community. Some companies allow civic groups to have access to their dining rooms during non-business hours. The First National Bank of Chicago, for example, allows major charity groups to hold dinners and receptions on the premises, often at the bank's expense, sometimes for a nominal fee, which helps the charity organizers sell tickets to opening night performances of Chicago's performing arts groups.

Your Behavior in the Executive Dining Room

In most companies, a person must achieve a certain level in the executive suite before he or she is permitted the use of the executive dining room. Good manners are important, whether an executive is lunching in his own dining room or in someone else's. Here are some points to remember:

- Don't take a second drink before lunch, even if it is urged upon you. Even if you are not a heavy drinker, if you take a second one at lunch, you are sending a strong signal that you might be.
- When you approach the dining table from the area in which you had cocktails, as a guest you should stand back from the table and wait to be waved to a seat or until someone says, "Sit down, everyone." If you are the host, instruct each person where to sit, remembering, of course, your protocol: The guest from the outside sits on your right. (For more information on proper seating, *see* Seating a Large Formal Meal, in the next section of this chapter.)
- Don't order more courses than the others; it slows up the meal, and the others will sit anxiously thumb-twiddling while you eat. One of the purposes of eating in the executive dining room is to consume a meal that is served nicely but quickly.
- Keep your voice down. As a newcomer or as a guest, you are conspicuous; you are on show. Act in a nonboisterous fashion; executive dining rooms are usually quiet and peaceful.
- If no one is smoking at your table, don't ask if you may smoke. Take it for granted that you may not. (*See also* Party Smoking Manners for the Host and Guest, in the last section of this chapter.)
- If you want to make a big hit with your own company chef, or with that of another company's dining room, tell the waiter before you leave to pass your compliments to the chef for a splendid meal. (This is the kind of gesture that makes people proud of their jobs.)

Entertaining in a Private Club

A club with attractive dining room facilities, excellent food, and well-appointed private rooms for parties is the perfect place to hold many different types of business-social functions. It is the closest thing to giving a party in a beautiful home.

Most people are very complimented when a business colleague asks them to lunch at a club. (It is for this reason that many companies pay for their executives' memberships.) The best way to entertain many executives is to invite them for a game of golf, tennis, squash, or racket or paddle tennis at a club, followed by drinks and a meal. Other executives would most appreciate being invited to lunch or a dinner party at an exclusive eating club like Washington's historic F Street Club, where probably every President of the United States has dined since its founding. Business people enjoy dining at the famous Duquesne Club in Pittsburgh and the Metropolitan Club in New York, which now admits women members. An invitation to the all-male bastion of the Pacific Union Club in San Francisco is considered a treat by executives (women are allowed for dinner), and lunching at the Metropolitan Club in Washington means you have a good chance of seeing powerful members of the government.

If you want publicity for your party and wish the press to be present, stay away from private clubs. There press coverage is discouraged, to put it mildly.

Female executives invited to a business meal in a men's club and compelled to use a special entrance or elevator usually resent it. (I know I do.) When women are in a club for a business purpose, they should not be discriminated against in this fashion. (Many women feel, as I do, that men have the right to their private clubs but that business meetings should be held in a place other than a club that insists on treating women as inferiors.)

If you are having a large party in a club, you deal with the banquet manager exactly as you do with a hotel banquet manager. You sign a contract after making your menu and beverage selections. Each club has its own rules as to how far ahead you must guarantee the number of guests and what cancellation fee you must pay if your party is cancelled.

The club manager will arrange for your flowers for the party unless you wish to supply your own. (If the club is to supply them, be sure they are included in the estimated cost of the party that you are quoted.) For a seated lunch or dinner, if you send over your place cards (and menu cards if you're providing them) and a seating chart in advance, the maître d'hôtel will arrange everything for you on the tables.

Even though the club will add a 15 to 20 percent gratuity (as well as any tax) to your bill, you might wish to tip some of the staff separately. Some clubs forbid all tipping; if it is permitted, it should be done very privately, which isn't all that difficult to do. If your club does not allow tipping, you can always increase your yearly contribution to the employees' Christmas fund (a pool of money contributed by members on a voluntary basis and split up among all the staff).

When You Are Someone's Guest in a Club

You may want to give a business function in a friend's club. Each club has its own rules regarding the kind of affair they allow a nonmember to hold there. In every case the nonmember must be sponsored by a member and the member must be present at the function. Clubs today are in a very difficult position in respect to their tax-exempt status and are being challenged on their rights to this exemption. Therefore, some clubs discourage any use by people other than members, even though they need the kind of profit they would make on the nonmember's party.

If an executive is permitted to give an affair in a private club on a friend's membership, he should remember that he has a serious responsibility in regard to his own and his guests' behavior. Nothing should be allowed to happen that would bring disapproval or censure upon the club member because of badly behaved guests at the sponsored host's party.

If the friend of an executive who uses the club for a business party wishes to tip the staff over and above the gratuities charge, he should make out a check to that club's employees' Christmas fund.

When you have been invited to a colleague's club for a drink or a meal, wait for your host in the proper waiting area. Never wander about unescorted, no matter how curious you may be to see the premises. There are certain areas that are off-limits to everyone but members; one must respect the rules.

What You Serve

Food: Symbol of a Company's Hospitality

Food is a costly part of the entertaining budget. A company function that is overly opulent and wasteful of food, particularly during poor economic times, reflects very badly on the hosts; so does the serving of insufficient amounts of food or uncreative food that makes the company look cheap. I can speak from experience, having been served apple pie for breakfast, and having been given caviar at an emergency fund-raising meeting for a city's homeless. Companies often do not understand the relationship between food, hospitality, and suitability.

Chefs in restaurants, hotels, catering establishments, and executive dining rooms should welcome the suggestion of new, delicious recipes to try. If

they are successful in making a new dish, it usually is added to their permanent repertoire; a party planner should never be afraid to give a chef a recipe
for his corporate party. (A caveat here: The chef should first test the recipe
and the party planner should taste the results of the experiment before the dish
is put on his corporate party menu.)

There are times when creativity can get out of hand in our present coura-
geously gourmet society. It is still a good idea to give people what they like to
eat, rather than subject them to a menu of new and exotic foods at your party.
(In other words, save the snakemeat canapes and the blanquette of hare for
your personal parties!)

Menus

The company party planner (i.e., director of special events, meeting manager, or whoever is in charge of menus for company functions) should keep the
following guidelines in view:

- Always keep the budget in mind when deciding on the menu, and never
  go over budget.
- Choose what is fresh and in season. The food will cost less and taste a lot
  better than out-of-season selections.
- Select a menu appropriate for when it is served. That means, don't serve
  a light fruit salad on a cold winter's night, and don't serve a hot, filling
  beef stew for a hot summer's day lunch. In other words, use common
  sense!
- Make your menu balanced and nutritious. Stay away from an all-fried or
  all-starch menu. Don't over-sauce the dishes. People are health and diet
  conscious. Two courses are enough for lunch, and three for dinner (four
  for a very special dinner).
- List the vineyard and vintage (if any) of each wine that you serve. Generally a white wine is served with the fish course, and red with the meat or
  fowl. For special occasions, champagne is served with dessert, to enable
  special toasts to be given. If you can't serve a good champagne, don't
  serve any at all.

Sample Menus for Sit-Down Meals

BREAKFAST

Selection of fruit juices, to be passed by the waiter:
orange, apple, grapefruit, or tomato

A plate with melon slices and a wedge of lemon

Fluffy omelet

Basket of breads, muffins, and crackers
Butter and margarine

Choice of coffee, decaff, and tea.

LUNCH

Broiled chicken
Brown herbed rice
Spinach and mushroom salad

Lemon ice
Coffee or tea

DINNER

Hearts of palm and artichokes

Broiled veal chop
Fresh broccoli and carrots in butter

Hot Apple Brown Betty with vanilla ice cream
or
Fresh pear and Bel Paese cheese
Coffee or decaff

NOTE: Do not serve salad as a separate course between the main course and the dessert course unless you are serving a green salad with cheese and crackers. Normally the salad should be served on a separate plate with the main course.

For a large crowd, it's a good idea to have a cold first course already served at each place when the guests come into the dining room. This saves a lot of time and service work.

Sample Menus for Buffet Meals

BREAKFAST

Omelets (if chef can make them to order)
Scrambled eggs
Sausage and bacon
Baked fruit
Orange, apple, or grapefruit juice
Grits (down-South style)
Pancakes and syrup
Muffins, biscuits, and toast
Coffee, decaff, or tea

BRUNCH

Sandwiches of chopped fried bacon and
marinated tomato slices with mayonnaise
Rice croquettes

Cold asparagus vinaigrette
Chicken salad in baked spinach ring
Tossed green salad
Small hot orange sticky buns
Iced canteloupe filled with honeydew melon balls
Coffee, decaff, or tea

DINNER

Cold roasted meats
Vegetable "Pasta Primavera"
Shrimp salad
Tomatoes with basil and mozzarella
Chinese lemon chicken
Beef Burgundy
Green salad
Baked fruit
Chocolate mousse
Coffee, decaff coffee

Menu Cards

When the host goes to the effort of giving his guests menu cards, the atmosphere of the meal immediately becomes special. A menu card is just one of those little extras that lends distinction. When the guests sign the back of a menu card for a foreign visitor, it becomes a very special souvenir of his trip.

Menus are hand-written, typed, or printed on heavy stock paper. They may be any size (but generally are no bigger than 5″ × 7″). Traditionally they are of white or ecru stock, but they may be of any color paper if color is part of the decor. The nicest graphic look for menu cards and place cards is that of the host company's logo embossed in its own colors on both the menu and place card, as the illustration shows. They should follow the design of the invitation and other party graphics.

A menu card may be placed on the table in any one of several ways: lying between one person's napkin and his neighbor's outside spoon on the left, lying on top of the napkin, propped against a wineglass, lying on the table above the dinner plate (see the illustration of the Formal Dinner Place Setting, page 293).

Ideally, each guest has his own menu; however, it is also proper to place a menu between two guests' places, to be shared by them.

When hotels and restaurants provide the menu, they tend to list superfluous information—everything, including things like radishes, nuts, and crackers. A menu text should be simple; all that is necessary is the appetizer and/or soup, the entree and its sauce (if any), and the dessert and wines. If there will be entertainment of any kind during the meal, it should be included in the

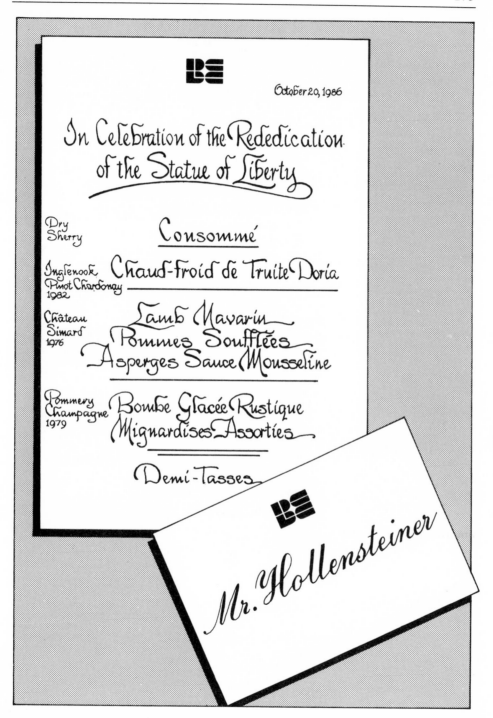

MENU AND PLACE CARD

lower right-hand portion of the menu card or on the back (in a double-fold menu, the entertainment should be indicated on the left inside page and the food listed on the right inside page).

The wines are listed on the left-hand side of the food menu, each one opposite the food course with which it is to be served, or the wines may be listed in the lower left corner.

In the following menu, for example (of a lunch for a retiring executive), only one wine is served, so it is placed in the lower left corner of the menu card.

February 9, 1987

Lunch

In honor of George Lane
For his fifty years of service with
Lancor

Watercress soup

———

English Grill
Green beans in butter
Broiled tomatoes
Mixed green salad

———

Cranberry sherbet
Vodka sauce
Demitasses

Schramsberg Grand Reserve
1978

The Service of Wine

There are some differences between the service of wine in a restaurant and in home entertaining. One thing that is important to remember is that today we are no longer the purists we used to be in following the traditional French separation of drinking reds with certain kinds of food and whites with others. Some people prefer white wine on every occasion; others find it too acidic and prefer only red wine. The considerate host therefore usually provides his guests with both.

Wine at Home

There is no ritual of "wine tasting" at a dinner party at home. The host is supposed to have opened and tasted any bottle of red wine in the kitchen to allow it to breathe at least a half hour before serving it. White wine does not have to be opened in order to breathe before it is served. It should be kept well chilled until served.

If You Are Serving a White and a Red Wine
with a Business Dinner at Home

If you are following tradition, you would serve white wine in a white wineglass with the fish course and red in a red wineglass with the meat or fowl course. In this case the waiter (or waitress) serves the white wine *as soon as* the guests are seated at table, even before food has arrived, serving counterclockwise beginning with the person on the host's right. When the entree is served, the waiter again passes counterclockwise around the table, this time pouring the red wine. It is perfectly all right for a guest at this point to say to the waiter, "I would prefer some more white wine, please." It is the host's responsibility to arrange for more white than red wine prior to the party if he feels his guests will be drinking more of it than red, including during the cocktail hour. An illustration showing the proper glasses for each wine appears on page 293.

If there are no waiters serving your home party, place a bottle of red and a bottle of white on the table (using coasters for each, to help protect the tablecloth). The host, cohost, or hostess serves the guests their preferences, and refills their guests' glasses (without the guest having to ask). A host may call down to the other end of the table and ask one of his or her guests to take care of the wine at that end of the table—"Jeff, would you please be our wine steward down at your end?" Jeff, in accepting the assignment, should keep those glasses filled. A guest who is greedy and wants to fill his own glass more often than the others displays bad manners if he ignores Jeff and grabs the bottle to pour himself a glass.

If a dinner party at home consists of several small tables instead of a large one, one person at each table should take it upon himself to serve the wine. However, a guest may serve himself if he wishes once the first glass has been poured.

Decanters of red and white wine look very decorative on the table and in today's society are appropriate to use at any kind of party, formal or informal. The decanter has another useful purpose. If you're not exactly proud of the wine you are serving, the decanter renders it anonymous.

Wine in a Restaurant or Hotel Dining Room

In a very fine restaurant, a sommelier (wine steward) handles the wine service, although this person is a disappearing breed in many cities. Often the captain or even the waiter is trained to handle the wine service with almost the same *eclat* as a sommelier. A good bottle of red wine is uncorked; the cork is then handed to the host, who pinches it in his fingers (to test for moisture) and then sniffs it to make sure it is not dried out. After nodding approval to the wine steward, the latter proceeds to pour a small amount of wine in the host's glass. The host first sniffs the wine's bouquet (not conspicuously, but quietly), then takes a sip, pauses a second, and nods approval once again to the wine steward or waiter. The wine is then poured into each guest's glass—no more than half full. The host's glass should be the last one filled. Another reason for pouring some wine first into the host's glass is to catch any bits of loose cork that might have lodged in the neck of the bottle when the cork is pulled—the cork bits should be in the host's glass, not a guest's. If there is an obvious bit of cork, the good wine server will give the host a fresh glass before pouring half a glass full.

A host also tastes the white wine he has ordered before serving it to the guest, but he does not sniff the wine for its bouquet, because most white wines do not have the bouquet of the reds.

A young manager from out of town, unskilled at hosting and unknowledgeable about such matters as wine, gave a dinner for his customers at a fine New York restaurant. When the wine steward handed him the cork, he looked at it in perplexity for several seconds, then made a decision, as all good managers do. He bit off a piece of the end and ate it!

If you are hosting a lunch or dinner in a restaurant and know nothing about wine, give the wine list to a guest you know to be a connoisseur. The wine steward or waiter should be instructed, when the wine is brought to the table, to offer the first sip for inspection to the guest who ordered it, not to you. (If you are hosting more than six people, you should select the wines yourself.)

If you happen to be the guest ordering the wine for your host, go easy on his or her expense account. If you're already in an expensive restaurant, you logically will conclude that your host knows what he is in for, so you do not have to order the cheapest thing on the wine list. On the other hand, you don't want to send him back to the comptroller of his company with an outrageous wine bill on his expense sheets. Order in the lower middle range of prices.

If you are hosting a meal, never be embarrassed at ordering a modest wine—including the house wine in a carafe, particularly at lunch. (Ordering the house wine is less appreciated at an evening meal, but usually you can find a modestly priced bottle of wine on the list.)

I saw a young person order a carafe of house wine for his lunch group one day. When it came he insisted the waiter pour a small amount in his glass for him to sip and approve before it was served to the others. (He was suffering from a case of misplaced pretension!) When you're drinking the house wine, don't sniff it, don't discuss its pedigree or lack of one; just drink it and enjoy it without editorial comments.

If you have any doubts about what you're doing, don't return a bottle as unfit to consume. If a wine has definitely turned, of course it should be sent back for another one at no cost to you. A wine that has turned has a sour or vinegary, overly tart taste; it is cloudy and burns the throat. If you think your wine has turned, ask your wine steward or waiter to taste it. If they keep saying it is fine but you know it is not fine, hold your ground.

In deciding whether to order red or white wine when the waiter comes to take your order, you might ask your guests which they prefer. If most of the group is drinking red wine, to accompany their meat course, but one guest is having fish and might prefer white, the host should offer that person a glass of white wine. The host should offer him another glass of white when the glass is empty. If half the group prefers white and half red, the host should order a bottle of each kind and then reorder whichever is consumed the fastest.

If you drink white wine, and your host orders a magnificent bottle of red (such as Château Haut Brion), this is not the moment to order white for yourself. Sharing a bottle of really great wine should be treated as a very special experience. Drink a very small amount of the red (let the others have the larger amount in their glasses). If your host has ordered an exceptional wine like that, your asking for a glass of white wine is a killjoy act—and an unsophisticated one at that.

If you are learning about wines, you may certainly carry to the restaurant something as informative as Hugh Johnson's *Pocket Encyclopedia of Wine* (Simon and Schuster, 1984) to check your vintages. Also recommended is Barbara Ensrud's *Pocket Guide to Wine* (Perigee, 1982) and, of course, *Grossman's Guide to Wines, Beers and Spirits* (Charles Scribner's Sons, 1983) is very helpful.

The main thing to remember about wines is that, as the host, you make sure your guests' glasses are filled before yours!

Entertaining in a Big Way

"Managing" the Large Social Event
(*See also* Chapter 5, Meetings, Conferences, and Seminars)

The largest part of business entertaining in this country is simple in nature and is carried out by the executive host, perhaps with the assistance of a secretary or staff assistant and, in the case of a party at home, with the help of the host's spouse. A large business-social function, on the other hand, requires the planning abilities and constant attention of someone either on staff, or someone in a consulting capacity to management. This inside staff executive or outside consultant must maintain an effective three-way coordination among senior management, the manager of the facility where the event is to be held, and himself. A cocktail party for two hundred people or a dinner party for a hundred is the kind of event that requires a professional touch.

The Inside Staff Person

The kinds of people who run the parties on management's team are commonly called meeting planners, directors of special events, or (as in some banks) protocol officers. These staff people direct the operations and oversee everything that goes into assuring a successful party.

Responsibilities of the Party Manager

- *The guest list*
  Compiles guest list and gets it approved
- *Invitations*
  Oversees design, production, and mailing of invitations
  Compiles RSVPs
  Prepares final guest list for staff use at party
- *Coordination with hotel, restaurant, or club banquet manager or with caterer*
  Selects menus and beverages
  Makes decisions on decor of the party location (flowers, linen colors, etc.)
  Makes sure that entertainment is properly backstopped by hotel (electrical and sound system requirements, etc.)
- *Entertainment*
  Signs contracts with musicians, entertainers, and performers

Oversees their travel, rehearsal time, etc.
- *Protocol*
Organizes check-in desk and table card numbers, or seating charts
Oversees placement of place cards
Organizes receiving line and introductions to hosts and honored guests
Coordinates program, engages master of ceremonies, and determines dais seating

Training a Staff Person to Handle Entertainment Functions

When a small to medium-sized company (too small to have a meeting manager on staff) begins to engage in a fair amount of entertaining as part of its business plan, it is wise to train an executive who has good social skills to handle this function along with his or her other responsibilities. This should be a person of taste who knows how to organize, is perceptive, and handles people well (traits essential for almost any management function!). This special events coordinator should be able to withstand severe pressure, cope with emergencies, and be both creative and efficient. He or she should plow through the entertaining section of my *Amy Vanderbilt Complete Book of Etiquette* (Doubleday, 1978), as well as a good book on decorating with flowers (like Ronaldo Maia's *Entertaining with Flowers,* Harry N. Abrams, 1978) and some good books on entertaining (like Martha Stewart's *Entertaining,* Crown, 1982).

Beside reading up on entertainment, this executive should:

- Ask to spend a couple of days with the caterer ordinarily used by his company for large parties, to observe at first hand the scope of the preparations for someone's very large party
- Observe some other large corporation's functions at close hand. This can be arranged if his CEO knows someone in senior management at another corporation, and explains that the staff person is in training and would like to watch events unfold there during preparations for a major event.
- Take some special events people or party consultants to lunch to pump them for helpful information

Outside Consultants Retained to Manage Large Functions

The special events and party business has grown to such proportions in the business world that a whole new spectrum of professional consultants has developed within the last decade, particularly within large cities. Among these are special events firms, party consultants, and caterers who are also party designers.

Special Events Firms

These specialize in fund-raising events for political groups and nonprofit institutions; they also stage company parties.

They may be retained by companies and by individuals. They can be located by word of mouth or by watching for newspaper reports on successful events. (In the latter case, call the secretary of the party host to find out the name of the firm that handled it.)

Party Consultants

Among these might be:

• A leading hostess in town
• An interior designer known for his or her taste and flair
• A florist with an ability to design the entire party, not just floral decorations
• A department store display director who moonlights doing parties

Working with a Caterer

We live in a catered world, whether we know it or not. We are repeatedly fed by caterers who have prepared and served the food at anything from lunch in a boardroom to dinner in the lobby of a movie theater. We rely on caterers to provide our lunches on corporate jets, to feed us at corporate-sponsored clambakes, or to wine and dine us in splendor at the opening of a new corporate headquarters. Caterers supply us with everything from cocktail parties in the office building courtyard to breakfasts at physical fitness meetings.

Some caterers are very sophisticated party designers. Some are very simple Mom-and-Pop operations. You should know your caterer—and know his limitations as well as his outstanding creative abilities—before you retain him for your business entertaining functions.

Finding the caterer. The best way to find a good caterer is through word of mouth references. Perhaps you recently attended an impressive party. Ask the waiters what caterer they represent. (In New York, waiters at catered parties usually keep business cards that they whip out of their pockets at any suggestion of interest on a guest's part.) After you have obtained several caterers' names, call two or three of them, ask them for references, and then check on those references.

Coordinating with your caterer. If you and the caterer have worked together before, you may be able to work out the arrangements for the party by telephone. Otherwise, a representative of the catering establishment will call on you. The place, date, size and type of party, budget, and ideas for decor should be discussed at this very first meeting, so that the estimate drawn up will be realistic. When a caterer presents his estimate, you might try calling a couple of others to compare the total cost, in order to find something less expensive. Generally you will find the estimates quite comparable. (A caterer will be less expensive on one budget item but more expensive on another.) Once you've made your decision, put your trust in your caterer; promise him further business if he does a great job for you. If he performs well and keeps his eye on costs, you will probably have great success in your association with him.

It's standard procedure for a caterer to request an advance deposit from the host corporation amounting to anywhere from 15 to 50 percent of the total charges for the party. Some caterers request final payment before the party begins; some require the total payment to be made at the conclusion of the party, before leaving the premises.

If a company cancels its party within two weeks of the date, many caterers will charge for the profit they would have cleared on the party (i.e., the difference between the total price contracted for and their actual party expenses).

Before doing business with a caterer, the corporation's party planner should study the fine print of the contract for his event. If a large function is to be held out of doors, for example, it might be wise for a company to buy weather insurance, so that if the event has to be canceled, the insurance company will pay the caterer's cancellation fees.

Once you have every detail finalized, leave the follow-through to your caterer. The responsibility is his. Many a job has been delayed, impeded, even sabotaged because the person who hired the caterer wouldn't let him or her do the job. Incessant nagging and corporate staff following the catering staff around with suggestions and general interference in the production of the party will handicap any caterer, no matter how good he is. Think out in advance all instructions you would like your caterer to follow, write them down, give him the list, and he will follow through.

I once retained Donald Bruce-White for an all-day party inaugurating the new Baker Furniture showrooms in New York. He and I spent a great deal of time planning (nit-picking, Donald would say) and negotiating before the event. Once the function began late in the morning, I stayed out of it, because the Bruce-White organization had to produce three totally different kinds of parties within a time slot of eight hours. There were several thousand guests attending this open house, which began with a morning brunch and entertainment and then progressed to a three o'clock tea party with another kind of entertainment and, of course, different food served. Finally, at five thirty, a full-fledged cocktail party, with a new group of entertainers, greeted the arriving guests. (The waiters told me afterward that they noticed several guests who came in the morning and stayed on through until eight o'clock!) The Bruce-White organization moved through the day like a well-trained army on maneuvers, in spite of the fact that there often were a thousand people in the showroom at one time.

Urge the banquet manager or caterer to take pains with the presentation of the food. And remember that food presentation is not only visual. When a plate for a hot dish is presented piping hot and that for a cold dish icy cold, the food on those plates tastes twice as good. Corporations that spend hundreds of thousands of dollars on their social functions should insist on a beautiful and tasteful presentation.

Caterers are leading the way these days in food presentation, often vying to display the most original ideas. Glorious Foods, in New York, makes the food on its buffet tables look like a Ghirlandaio Renaissance painting. They roll seedless grapes in a mixture of Roquefort and cream cheeses, then roll the grapes in crushed pistachio nuts and arrange them on a platter in large clusters, like exotic grapes fresh from the vine. Los Angeles caterer Tony O'Meara fills a child's toy sailboat with crudités and "floats" it on a sea blue cloth against a tropical island background of fruits, vegetables, ferns, and dried plants. Gaper's, in Chicago, serves mouth-watering fresh raspberries in baskets made from woven strips of pastry. Braun's, in Washington, puts a bird's nest made of tomato vermicelli on a buffet table and fills it with marinated quail eggs decorated with tiny flowers. Ridgewell's, in Washington, serves an English trifle for dessert in a small clay flower pot, complete with a decoration of small green leaves and a toy trowel for the guests to use as a spoon. New York's Donald Bruce-White tucks tiny sugared violets into the caramelized egg-white of his floating island (Oeufs à la Neige).

The party planner in one corporation invites the chef of his executive dining room to look at the food presentation every time the company hosts a large function that is catered, so that the chef can get new ideas about the decoration of platters. Food tastes better when it is presented in an appealing manner.

Understanding the Importance of the Meal Service

One of the most important aspects of the job of a meeting planner, party consultant, or director of special events is to oversee the quality of service of the food at company functions. How the waiters or waitresses look—their uniforms spotlessly clean and well-pressed, their hands and nails clean, their hairstyles neat—is terribly important in creating the proper atmosphere for a lunch or dinner. A waiter's attitude—his cheerfulness and willingness to answer questions and to make an extra trip to the kitchen, if necessary—can really make a good party.

I know one meeting planner in charge of all entertaining for her company who gives all the serving help a pep talk before the meal, and when it's over, she gives them a "Well done!" speech. As a result, for her, *they really try* to make it a successful event. She has told them that in her opinion they are the most important key to the entire evening. Her success in motivating them is unquestionable. She makes them proud of the job they are doing.

Some staffs are not well motivated by the meeting planner or supervisor of the restaurant, hotel dining room, or catering establishment. They are barked at to do things fast, to get going at any cost (and when as a result they "get going," soup often ends up on someone's jacket or dress). Some waiters are so pressured that they grab your fork from your hand in their eagerness to clear off a course. That kind of service gives everyone indigestion. It is the duty of the person supervising the party to keep an eye out for negative details such as this and to correct them by speaking to the head waiter.

Another important aspect of the service of a meal is the way the food is apportioned onto the plates. There should never be a wasteful amount—too much looks unappetizing. An overly skimpy portion is bad, too—it leaves the guest wondering why his host chose to stint on the food. The party planner should make sure that just the right amount of food is placed on each plate and that it looks attractive, perhaps with something small used to garnish the plate.

Money is saved on the number of waiters needed when the food is served onto plates in the kitchen, and then a plate is put before each guest. However, it is far more gracious, if the waiters are skilled enough, to have the waiter serve each guest from a large platter (always serving from the left, of course). In this case the waiter holds a large serving spoon and fork pincerlike in one hand, while he holds the platter from beneath with the other hand. He lifts each guest's portion of food off the platter and places it neatly, even decoratively with the garnish, onto the guest's warm (or chilled) plate. A typical serving platter might contain something like (per person) two slices of beef, one potato puff, one grilled tomato, a stack of five small asparagus covered with a strip of red pimento, and one large stuffed mushroom.

Sauces should be served separately.

The Service of Coffee and Liqueurs After Dinner
(For cigars, *see* Cigar Manners, near the end of this chapter)

In formal entertaining, coffee should be served *after* dessert (not during the meal) in demitasse cups. Many restaurants do not have demitasse cups, in which case their regular cups will be fine.

Guests should be offered a choice of milk and sugar or nonsugar sweetener. Guests should be offered a choice of coffee or a decaffeinated brewed coffee.

Liqueurs are not served at lunch, unless it is a formal diplomatic affair. In the evening, liqueurs should be passed on a tray with their own special glasses, following the service of after-dessert coffee. There should be at least two choices offered, perhaps something in the cognac (brandy) field and something in the sweet class, like an orange or a cream liqueur. (In a restaurant, one may order from a wide choice of liqueurs.)

For a dinner party at home, coffee and liqueurs may be served at the table or in the living room, library, or terrace, to which all the guests move after leaving the table. Most American women do not at all like the old European tradition of separating the sexes after dinner. Therefore, a wise business host does not leave the men at the table and banish the women elsewhere for their coffee and liqueurs.

Thanking for a Job Well Done

At the conclusion of a very successful party, the party planner should thank the head of the catering staff and his associates for their efforts. It is nice to tip the head waiter $20 and the waiters $10 extra, but it is not obligatory.

Perhaps the most important thanks the head of the catering group can receive is a letter signed by the CEO, congratulating the firm for a job well done. This kind of letter is an invaluable business reference to obtain future business from other companies.

Organizing a Large Social Function: A Checklist

The logistics of organizing a large business-social function are so complex that a checklist is necessary for the person in charge of the event.

It's a good idea to use a more or less standardized format for your checklist rather than to work up the checklist for each event in a haphazard fashion. That will ease planning the logistics of the event. You will have an organizational framework within which to work. You will be less likely to overlook an important last-minute detail. In addition, you will find each checklist becomes a valuable reference that is easily consulted when preparing for a subsequent event.

The one illustrated here is for the planning of a black-tie dinner dance held inside a new industrial plant to be officially opened the next day. Dinner in the plant for a very distinguished group of guests is followed by dancing in a tent constructed for the occasion in the parking lot.

The elements of this particular event—which we will describe in detail—are organized in a notebook as follows:

Who, What, Where, When, and Why

LARGE IMPORTANT DINNER

(date)_____

Address: Phone #:   Mgr. Name:

Time:
Type of affair:
Host:
Cohost:
Purpose:
Desired number of guests:

Guest List Information

Division responsible:
Person in charge of compilation for division:
Telephone ext:
Total invitations sent:
Date final list ok'd:
Name of officer who ok'd:

Party Budget

It is very important to have an approved management figure for the budget and an accurate list of costs as they are incurred, so that there will not be a variance between the two totals.

The following is the kind of budget checklist that would be made for the dinner dance given in the new industrial plant:

Event_____ Date of Event_____ Place_____
Total of management-approved budget: $_____
Established by: __(name of division officer and title)__
Facility rental: __(not applicable in this case)__
Caterer's budget breakdown: (a hotel or restaurant budget would differ, of course)
    Personnel hired (waiters, valet parkers, coatroom attendants, restroom attendants, kitchen staff, etc.) _____
    Food _____
    Liquor and beverages _____
    Rental of equipment (linens, china, crystal, flatware, serving platters, coatracks, tables, chairs, carpeting if necessary, etc.) _____

    Tax, gratuities, and extra tips to key personnel _____ TOTAL: _____
Tent construction (including carpeting, flooring, lighting) TOTAL: _____
Florist's budget breakdown:
    Floral arrangements_____
    Centerpieces for tables_____
    Rented trees and plants_____ TOTAL: _____
Music and entertainment, including lighting and sound costs (before, during or after dinner) _____
Stationery costs: (invitations, place cards, menu cards, programs) _____
Extra security: _____
Limousine service: (for honor guests) _____
Photographer: _____
Contingency fund: _____
    GRAND TOTAL: _____

The Invitation

INVITATIONS

Number to be ordered:_____

DESIGN

    Designer's name:_____

    Name of firm:_____

    Address of firm:_____

    Phone number:_____

    Date design submitted:_____

    Date design approved:_____ Who approved:_____

    Date finished artwork to be delivered:_____

PRINTING

    Printer's name:_____

    Name of firm:_____

    Address:_____

    Tel. no.:_____

    Date job delivered to printer:_____

    Date finished proof OK'd:_____ Who approved:_____

    Date finished job to be delivered from printer:_____

MAILING

    Supervisor of addressing, stuffing, stamping & mailing:_____

    If mailing house to handle: Name:_____ Address:_____

        Contact_____ Tel. no.:_____

    Date material delivered to mailing house:_____

    Date invitations mailed:_____

NOTE: You may also want to provide space for the actual invitation copy for quick reference, together with an indication of who is to supply that and whose approval may further be required. (*See also* Chapter 9, Invitations and Their Replies, for advice on invitation wording and format.)

Alphabetized Guest List Pages

A–Z LIST OF INVITED GUESTS
FOR: (date) _____

CU—Customer
S —Staff member
CV—Civically prominent
O —Official with rank
CE —Celebrity
FR—Friend of company
      (banker, lawyer, etc.)

A —Accept
*R —Regret

	As of (date)	Total No. Acceptances
	_____	_____
	_____	_____
	_____	_____
	_____	_____
	_____	_____

NAME	TITLE	ADDRESS	PHONE	CATE-GORY	ACCEPT/ REGRET	DATE RECV'D

*SECOND-CUT OF GUESTS   DATE INVITED:

_____

_____

_____

*If there are many regrets and there is time, the person in charge of the guest list should hand-deliver invitations to the "second cut" of guests to assure a full representation at the dinner.

Caterer's Responsibilities

CATERER'S CHECKLIST

Name_____ Address_____ Contact_____ Tel No._____

Food to be served	Liquor, wines, nonalcoholic drinks to be served

Cocktail _____   _____   _____
Hour   _____   _____   _____
   _____   _____   _____
   _____   _____   _____
   _____   _____   _____

Dinner _____
   _____
   _____
   _____
   _____
   _____

After _____   _____   _____
Dinner _____   _____   _____
(in the _____   _____   _____
tent) _____   _____   _____

Help hired:
   No. in kitchen_____ No. of waiters & waitresses_____
   Coat-checkers_____ Valet parkers_____
   Restroom attendants_____

Restrooms
   Suitable for guests?_____ Need guest soaps, guest
   towels?_____ Are portable facilities necessary?_____

Extra security
   Necessary?_____ Will caterer provide?_____
   No. needed_____ Name of outside company handling_____
   Contact_____ Tel.:_____

Florist

As with all decorations, the flowers and greenery should be selected with a thought to what will be happening in or around the area in which they are to be placed. You do not want to discover belatedly that they interfere with some of the interaction between people at the function. For example, always advise the florist to provide table arrangements guests can easily see across. (I learned this during the Kennedy administration in the White House, when we abandoned the traditional towering flower arrangements on the tables that had successfully prevented any guest from seeing anyone across the table.)

FLORIST

Name_____Address_____Tel. No._____

Flowers and Greenery for:
    Cocktail area _____

    _____

    _____

Dining area
    Table centerpieces: No. needed_____ Scheme_____
    Head table arrangement?_____
    Rented trees and plants to disguise the area?

    _____ _____ _____
    _____ _____ _____

Tent
    Tent poles decorated?_____
    Greenery around bandstand?_____
    Small arrangements needed on the little tables?_____
        If so, how many?_____

Room Setups

ROOM SETUPS
(to be drawn for each party)

Cocktail Area

(Show position of bars, small tables, chairs, and musical trio and microphones, if pertinent.)

Dining Area

(Show placement, shape, and size of all dining tables. Number each table.)

Tent Area

(Show dance floor, where band is positioned, where bar tables are, and placement of tables and chairs—cafe style—for guests)

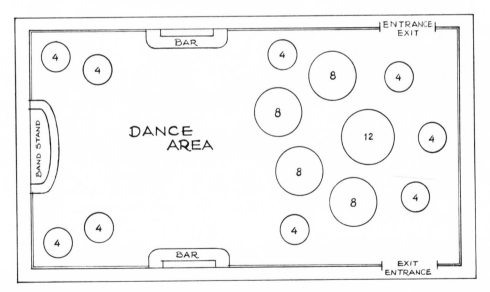

Room setup for tent with dancing after dinner (small tables only are needed, since people will be dancing)

Protocol Checklist

PROTOCOL CHECKLIST

Staff needed to check in at door_____

No. of tables needed_____

Table cards?_____ In stock_____ To order_____

    No. needed_____ Person in charge_____

Seating charts to be made?_____ Blown up to what size?_____

    By whom?_____

Place cards: No. needed_____ In stock or to be ordered_____

    Names to be: Handwritten_____ Typed_____ Done in

    calligraphy_____ Person responsible_____

Menu cards: No. needed_____ Handwritten_____

    Typed_____ Calligraphy and offset_____

    Person responsible_____

Person in charge of seating_____ Tel. ext._____

Receiving Line: Where?_____ Names (in order of standing in line)

               _____

               _____

               _____

Will there be an introducer?_____ Name_____ Ext.:_____

Names of staff "party workers" _____ _____

    and extensions _____ _____

                  _____ _____

No. of copies of guest list required_____

The more courses, the more flatware is needed. One eats from the outside in. First the soup spoon; the next course is fish, so the fish fork and knife are used; the next course is lamb, so the dinner fork and knife are used.

On both the lunch and dinner it is easy for everyone to place the dessert implements at the top of the plate. Notice that there is one wineglass shown for lunch; for dinner there is a sherry glass for the consommé on the outside right; then, moving inward, a white wineglass for the white wine for the fish course; then a (larger) red wineglass for the lamb; and finally a champagne glass (tall and slender) for the dessert champagne. The large glass closest to the dessert implements is for water.

FORMAL DINNER PLACE SETTING

LUNCH PLACE SETTING

ARRANGING A BUFFET TABLE PROPERLY
A buffet should be attractively arranged, with fruit or flower centerpieces, and with different shapes of serving pieces. The plates, eating implements and napkins should be placed together.

Tent Rental

THE TENT
(for after dinner)

Name of tent company_____ Address_____ Contact_____ Tel. No._____

Shape_____ Colors_____ Dimensions_____
Color of indoor-outdoor carpeting_____
Dimensions of dance floor_____
Heaters needed?_____
Date to be constructed_____
Date to be dismantled_____

Entertainment Arrangements

PROGRAM AND ENTERTAINMENT

Printed programs provided on tables?_____ Person responsible_____
     No. to order_____

Master of ceremonies:_____

Tel. No._____

Names of speakers: _____   Tel. No._____

                              _____   Tel. No._____

                              _____   Tel. No._____

Entertainers: _____   Agent's Name & Tel.:_____

                              _____   Agent's Name & Tel.:_____

                              _____   Agent's Name & Tel.:_____

Music organizations: _____   Contact & Tel.:_____

                              _____   Contact & Tel.:_____

                              _____   Contact & Tel.:_____

Invocation_____ Name of clergy_____Tel.:_____

Hour program should begin_____ End_____

List sequence of events in the program below:

    1.

    2.

    3.

    4.

    5.

    6.

Name of company constructing bandstand:_____ Tel. No._____

Sound and lighting equipment needed_____

Company supplying_____ Tel. No._____

Sound system in dining room_____ In tent_____

Mikes needed in dining room_____ In tent_____

Lecterns needed in dining room_____ In tent_____

Professional lighting required_____

Advice on Cutting the Budget

If you overshoot your budget, it will have to be cut. There are several ways of doing that, and there are several ways *not* to do it.

Ways to Cut	*Ways Not to Cut*
Cut the number of guests invited.	Don't cut all the young people off a guest list that is top-heavy with older, "big brass." The latter like to have some young attractive faces around to add zip to the party.
Delete total luxuries like caviar, and cut the number of courses in the meal. You might omit the fish course and leave the soup; you might cut the salad-and-cheese separate course, and just add a small salad to the main course.	Don't cut the quality of the food you serve. It's better to serve only two courses but to have them *delicious*.
If you have a white and a red wine on the menu, serve only one wine. If you have champagne on the menu with dessert, cut it.	Don't have really cheap, poor quality wine served. It's better to give your guests only water.
Cut out the entertainment, if you must, or reduce the number of musicians or number of acts performing.	Don't replace a fine performer with one you've never heard of who comes "cheap." It's better to have *no* entertainment than *poor* entertainment.
Cut down on the number of flowers in the centerpieces and substitute greenery instead. If you were planning on something very exotic and expensive as a floral scheme, change it to something simple but still beautiful.	Don't replace fresh flowers and greenery with plastic or any kind of fake stuff. It's better to have nothing at all on the tables.
If you are extensively over budget, delete the tent with its dance floor. Arrange for dancing in the area where dinner was served—indoors.	Don't replace live music with taped music for a formal dance. It is better not to have dancing.

Compiling a Guest List

The preparation of an effective, well-honed guest list is, of course, a most important prerequisite of successful entertaining. Many observers feel that corporate guest lists are sometimes carelessly organized, full of more "freeloaders" than people of distinction, who should be preferred.

Probably the most important guest lists in existence are those at the White House for the President and the First Lady's parties. When I headed Mrs. John F. Kennedy's staff at the White House, we organized potential guests into separate categories according to their professions and interests. For example, we had separate lists of senior government and administration leaders; politicians; the most important national (and international) figures in the arts, education, and science; foreign diplomats; the leaders of the nonprofit sector; the chief executive officers of the major corporations; sports figures and stars of the entertainment industry; local Washington society figures, and the like.

It was a simple matter to produce a distinguished and well-balanced guest list by taking the names from all those different lists. We mixed young and old. The mixture was important because celebrities from one field enjoy meeting the celebrities from other fields. The same theory holds when you're compiling a guest list for your company, even if you do not have celebrities on hand. The computer geniuses of this world need the exposure of sitting next to concert pianists and baseball stars and vice-versa. The average person tires of seeing the same small group of people socially year in and year out. Fresh new faces are the greatest insurance there is for a successful party.

Each company, large or small, should maintain its own computerized lists of potential guests. In a small to mid-sized company, the lists would probably be best maintained in the CEO's office; in a large corporation, they would be maintained in the office of the person who handles corporate entertaining (the meeting manager, special events director, etc.).

These lists might be broken down into these categories:

- *Business "musts"*—leading customers and clients; potential customers; senior executives in the company's bank, law firm, ad agency, public relations company, and accounting firm; vendors, etc. All senior executives should take the responsibility of feeding into the master list the names of top priority suggestions, whenever the occasion arises.
- *Officials*—the governor of the state, mayor of the city, the member(s) of Congress from the state and district, etc.
- *"Lustre-adders"*—local writers, artists, scientists; presidents of the local universities; hospital and museum directors; musicians, entertainers, sports heroes, etc.
- *Press.* If you are giving an important function, you probably want coverage by the local press, and that should be arranged by your in-house public relations staff or your public relations agency. Many times, however, you will be giving a business-social function that does not warrant press coverage. This is the perfect opportunity to invite distinguished journalists in your town (newspaper, television, radio, and magazine) to

attend your function (to be accompanied by their spouses, if it is an evening affair where spouses will be present). This builds goodwill with those journalists, and most business guests are flattered to talk to leading members of the Fourth Estate.

If you're a small company with no public relations capabilities and you are holding a social affair which will be attended by people of renown in your city, invite your favorite television newscaster or the metropolitan editor of your newspaper to attend in the capacity of a distinguished citizen guest, not as a reporter. The journalists may be too busy to come, but if you continue to extend invitations to the media in your town, some of the recipients will attend, and your contacts in the media will grow in an important way.

• *Staff guests.* The members of the staff who attend company functions should be chosen with care—because of their seniority, because the reason for the affair falls within their area of company responsibility, or because they are talented "party workers."

A good staff "party worker"—an extrovert who is at ease anytime anywhere and can be relied upon to step forward and do something if there is an awkward situation—is always a plus. (Every company should be lucky enough to have one or two of these on staff.)

Keeping Guest Lists Up to Date

Guest lists need constant reassessing. The names of those who no longer have reason to be invited should be removed and the names of others who should be invited to something during the year should be substituted. Someone should be charged with feeding corrections into the list, including when a person changes his or her title, business address, marital status, or name.

The best kind of record shows not only the person's correct name, title, business address, and spouse's name, but also the occasions on which that person or couple has been invited, and whether the invitation was accepted or regretted. If it is not possible to store this information in a computer, then a 3" × 5" alphabetical card file should be kept. The following might be an example of an entry kept current:

```
LEGUAY, Dr. and Mrs. Roger (Colette)
    Director of Research, VICNODAX INC.
    Address:                Tel. No.
    Invited:
        Lunch      4/4/83     Dr. Attended
        Dinner     12/3/83    Dr. & Mrs. regretted
        Cocktails  6/17/84    Dr. & Mrs. attended
```

It is also advisable to mark divorces and names of new spouses when remarriage has occurred.

Remember, when you have a guest from another city as your guest of honor at a social event, it is not only gracious but also good business for everyone if you send him a well-typed, annotated list of guests who will be attending your function. The guest of honor will be able to study the list and will then react much more intelligently to the people he meets. The list should mention the title and any significant facts about both husbands and wives on the list—anything from "They have nine children!" to "He was chairman of this corporation when he was only twenty-four."

Having Entertainment When You Entertain

It's very complimentary to the guests—and certainly to the guest of honor, if there is one—for a host to provide good entertainment at a business-social function. It obviously marks a very special event. For example, entertainment might be appropriate for the party the company is hosting on one of the nights at a three-day, all-industry meeting; when the company's top producers for the year are being honored at a dinner party; when it's a special company anniversary; or when the company hosts a supper following the last game of the World Series in which the hometown team has played (and either won or lost).

"Good entertainment" means something appropriate for that particular group of guests on that particular occasion. "Good entertainment" means a performance by some experienced performer or by fresh new local talent in a well-produced segment of the proper length. Guests usually appreciate the fact that their host has gone to a great deal of trouble, and sometimes expense, to provide this entertainment. It creates a special atmosphere at a party, and gives everybody a lift.

Entertainment at a small corporate dinner is not necessary; the guests are usually absorbed in their own conversations. To thrust entertainers in their midst makes everyone self-conscious and artificially attentive. However, when a cocktail party grows in size to thirty or more guests, the sound of a pianist playing a Cole Porter medley in the background is very pleasant indeed. When a dinner party list grows to thirty or more, a short period of after-dinner music is usually very relaxing and nice.

The Person in Charge of the Entertainment

The meeting planner, the director of special events, or the on-staff person in charge of entertaining might find it useful to retain the services of an outside entertainment consultant who is familiar with the available talent and has experience dealing with performing artists and their contracts. (The artists are either reached directly or, as is usually preferable, through their agents.)

Entertainment consultants keep themselves abreast of the entire field of performers, from rock to opera and from jugglers to ballet dancers. They know when a football star is also secretly studying to be a concert baritone (he might be invited to make some remarks and then surprise everyone with an aria); they know when a famous star is too drug-abused to be able to perform anymore. They know how to achieve programs of quality and style within a definite budget, as well as how to handle a temperamental artist and what to do in case of last-minute cancellation by the artist.

An entertainment consultant can find bagpipers in kilts for a plant opening, or a professional roller-skating ballet for a company employee party in the parking lot. He can find an acappella choir to sing carols in the office lobby at Christmas or arrange for an ice-cream vendor who sings opera to be part of the company anniversary celebration.

A good entertainment consultant is found by word of mouth. Get recommendations from meeting planners who have used them.

Sometimes you do not have to go to a professional to find professional talent. Sometimes there is excellent local talent—for example, in the local university's departments of music, dance, or theater. It is a double plus when a company gives public exposure (and a small fee, too) to the good regional talent available.

When booking the various entertainers and musical groups for your company's social function, refer to the Checklist for Handling Speakers or Entertainers, in Chapter 6.

Background Music

When a company provides its guests with the pleasure of background music—during the cocktail hour before dinner, for example—one should always keep in mind that the guests want and need ample opportunity to be able to talk to each other without straining to make themselves heard. The sound of music should be controlled at a moderate volume, so that the guests' eardrums remain intact. Some companies make the mistake of placing the musicians too close to the guests or else turn up the volume so loud that the party sounds like a frantic disco rather than a company reception. When this happens, the guests become exhausted and frustrated, trying to make themselves heard over "the noise."

Good background music is soothing and low in volume. It does not have to be "antique music," as young people sometimes call music from before 1970, but it should not be loud or dissonant. It's polite of party guests to clap when a nearby jazz combo finishes its set or a nearby chamber music quartet finishes a piece. It means a lot to the musicians to know that at least some people are listening to them and appreciating their music. A thoughtful person makes a point of passing close to the musicians at some point and telling them that they're "really good, a pleasure to listen to . . ."

A Program After Dinner

A musical program after dinner should never last more than half an hour. People are tired and usually longing for bed once they have consumed a large meal at a business function. A short concert delights them; a long concert exhausts them. When you have musicians (or anyone, for that matter) performing after dinner, you should provide your guests with a small program explaining who the performer is and what he or she will do. Those program notes may be the launch of a new career.

Chairmen of testimonial dinners sometime make the dreadful mistake of scheduling speech after speech after speech after dinner, then add two or more acts by performers. The President of the United States sets a good example. The toast-speeches at White House state dinners are confined to the two heads of the two countries; each lasts from ten to fifteen minutes. The program of music, theater, or dancing following the meal never lasts longer than thirty minutes, sometimes less.

Caution on Comedians

Comedians are often superb performers, but you should see their act before booking them for your company. Some comedians use material that is tasteless and full of sexual innuendoes, which may be fine for Las Vegas but not at your company function. A comedian can alienate rather than entertain an audience.

A really clever comedian, however, someone who doesn't rely on dirty jokes for laughs, can assure a successful party and thoroughly entertain the guests, particularly if he has been given information on your company and can work in some gentle teasing.

PROTOCOL MATTERS IN LARGE FORMAL DINNERS—DOING THINGS PROPERLY

The way in which things are "supposed to be done" in entertaining is not just someone's fantasy. It is a time-honored set of traditions that have evolved as a result of trial and error over centuries of trying to find the most efficient and honorable way of receiving kings and queens, diplomats and world leaders.

You may not receive any kings, queens, or world leaders in your executive dining room or in your home, but everyone who achieves a certain level in the business world either should know what to do himself or herself or *should know how to tell someone else what is proper.* Much of corporate America—at all levels—is hopelessly inadequate when it comes to understanding the intricacies of organizing events and handling people of rank properly.

It takes a lot of work. The bigger the function, the more work, obviously, but the basic rules of organization remain the same, regardless of the size of the project. Ignoring protocol only leads to a sloppy, disorganized function, with unhappy guests. That might be called a waste of money!

Role of the Cohost and the Party Helper at a Large Event

The cohost of a business function may be a peer or a subordinate; for a party with spouses, the cohost is the host's spouse. In the case of a very large party, with many round tables, there should be a company host, and perhaps a company cohost, at each table, to make sure that the guests are introduced, properly fed, properly informed about the proceedings (and incidentally about the host company), and that everyone has a good time.

Fellow executives who are personable and gregarious make good cohosts. So do distinguished friends of the company or firm, such as the firm's lawyer, head accountant, head of the ad agency servicing the company, head of the company's public relations firm, etc. A company host or cohost at a large function has a very important role to play in making things work smoothly at his or her table.

Staff people who help out at parties, and who are good at it, can make the difference between success and failure of an event. Usually bright young executives make the best party aides. When they are present at a business function, they are not there to enjoy themselves, but to make that function a success. They are there to help introduce, to bring wallflowers into the group, to mix up conversational groups where people look unhappy and stuck. They are there to make sure that Mr. Big meets Ms. Big who is visiting from another city, because big shots like to meet each other. They are there to introduce the lesser lights in the organization to Mr. Big and Ms. Big, because it would mean so much to the former to have a word with the celebrities.

With practice, staff people become very good at helping out. Does the widow of the former chairman have a ride home? Has the head of the Japanese trade delegation lost his glasses? Has a member of the press buttonholed the company president, who looks trapped and miserable? The party workers are supposed to have eyes on all sides of their heads and jump to assist whenever and wherever they can. (When they become CEOs themselves, they can let someone else do the dirty work!)

Introducing Guests Before a Function

When There Is No Receiving Line

When there are fewer than sixty guests, a receiving line doesn't make sense, but one or two staff members should see to it that every person who arrives is introduced to the host(s) of the affair. This is particularly important if the host does not know all of his guests personally.

The host should stay near the door of the room so that he is available to meet all his guests. It is a common tendency for a host to glimpse a good customer or close friend and go off in a corner for a lengthy conversation. This can ruin the party mood very quickly. At a party for fifty, for example, everyone in the room is aware of where the host is and to whom he is speaking and for how long. All of the guests should have more or less equal time, even if the host would much rather be off in a corner with an important person.

A staff person should remain at the door and make sure that each person entering the room is brought to the host. Once the guest has been introduced, the host or the staff person should call over a waiter or else direct the guest to the bar. The staff person should also introduce each newcomer to one or two people, so that the newcomer will be able to join a conversational group and not be left alone as a stranger, not knowing anyone and feeling like a typical wallflower.

The Receiving Line

A receiving line is a tremendous aid at a business-social function with more than sixty guests. If many of the guests do not personally know their host(s) or each other, a receiving line and badges will help identify people to each other and make conversation easier. Nothing is drearier than being wedged into a large room crowded with scores of unrecognizable faces and wondering who they all are. Guests who have no idea of who or where the hosts are soon begin not to care. The party is then cold, impersonal, and certainly off to a bad start.

- *The proper location must be found* for the receiving line, so that the traffic flow will not be obstructed and so that the majority of the other guests will be able to view the receiving line as the party progresses. (There is a natural curiosity about who is arriving; receiving-line watching is a corporate sport for some people.) The line should be formed inside the party area, near the entrance but not near a crowded passageway or a staircase that blocks the door. It should not be close to the food service and bar, which would cause an instant traffic jam.

- *The length of time the receiving line should stay in formation* depends upon the size of the party. For a cocktail party for five hundred of a two-hour duration, the hosts should stay in line for over an hour, so that almost every guest will have had the opportunity to shake hands with them. If the great majority of the guests have arrived within a short space of time, the line can break up and the hosts can circulate around the room.

- *The composition of the line is, of course, very important.* It should be as short as possible. For a strictly business party, spouses should not stand in line. However, if the guest of honor from another city or country is accompanied by his spouse, the corporate host's spouse should also stand in line with the two visitors.

- *If a female executive is part of the official receiving line,* the spouses of male executives who are also in that receiving line should not expect to stand with their husbands. The female executive is there for a business, not a social reason.

- *If several corporate hosts' names were on the invitation,* it is preferable that they not all stand in the line together. It makes the process too long. The hosts should spell each other in groups of three or four, so that guests can pass by quickly. A party with a long, cumbersome receiving line quickly becomes a tiresome logjam, with guests impatient because they don't like waiting that long.

- *When a staff assistant sees the line bogged down,* he or she should step in at a certain point to break it up. This may mean a warning to the senior host: "The line is now out to the street. Do you think we might speed things up a bit?"

  If the party helper keeps a sense of humor and apologizes about pushing people quickly through the line, he won't be resented. He's only doing a job that has to be done, and everyone will benefit in the long run.

- *Drinking in a receiving line should be done very circumspectly if at all.* If you're standing in a receiving line, waiting to greet your guests, you should refrain from drinking in too obvious a manner. You might have a drink placed on a table behind you and swing around every so often to take a sip; you shouldn't hold a drink in your hand as the guests come by to shake your other hand.

  Guests shouldn't hold a drink, either, as they go through the line. If, however, the line is interminably long, a guest may either leave it, go get a drink, and then come back later into the line, holding his drink. However, by the time he reaches his hosts, he should have dispensed with the glass on a nearby table or on a passing waiter's tray.

The Very Important Role of the Introducer

In the case of a large party, it's a great help to have a company person serve as an "introducer." This man or woman, stationed at the beginning of the receiving line, should be well rehearsed in all the names and titles on the guest list and should be able to introduce each guest properly and clearly to the first person standing in line. A host should not have to guess at his guests' names. When guests introduce themselves, often they do a poor job of it—they mumble their names, with the result that the host still doesn't know who they are. An introducer who voices the name and title of the person with a clear enunciation is a tremendous asset for the party and its host.

The introducer should greet each guest with a friendly smile and a handshake and then guide him toward the front of the line (if the guest is not already patiently waiting at the front of the line). The guest should supply (without having to be asked) his name and company name, which the introducer then repeats in a clear, well-enunciated manner to the first person in the receiving line: "Mr. Caldwell, may I present Janet McKenzie, our media buyer at the Spence Agency?" The introducer then turns to the woman guest: "Miss McKenzie, this is Mr. Alexander Caldwell, our chairman." Mr. Caldwell and Ms. McKenzie then shake hands while the introducer returns to his station at the receiving line to bring another person forward. Mr. Caldwell, in the meantime, should turn to the person on his right in the line and introduce Ms. McKenzie to that person: "Charlie, this is Janet McKenzie, who does the media buying for our ad agency." Charlie would then shake her hand and give her his full name, followed by some little expression of welcome: "I'm really glad to meet you." Ms. McKenzie then passes on to the next person in line, putting out her hand to shake that person's hand, and this time she gives her own name and company: "Janet McKenzie, the Spence Agency." She gives her name and company name to each person on down the line, and each person in the receiving line in turn gives back his or her name as the handshake is consummated.

It's very flattering to be properly introduced at a corporate function. Perhaps it is so flattering because it happens so seldom!

Seating a Large Formal Meal

Seating is a sensitive and logistically important aspect of good entertaining, whether one is giving a private dinner at home or a lunch for four hundred in a hotel. Seating at U.S. business-sponsored events is often inefficient, haphazard, and incorrect from a protocol point of view. I myself have had a hand in a few major seating gaffes. When I was a social secretary in the American embassy in Paris, I sat a top foreign government official next to his wife's lover, thus embarrassing everyone concerned, including the host, the American ambassador. At a White House dinner during the John F. Kennedy administration, I put the French ambassador to Washington in a seat that (according to him) was beneath his proper rank, so he stalked out of the White House in the middle of the *Consommé Printannier.*

Senior management often does not understand what a difficult job it is to seat a large function, particularly when guests drop on and off the guest list right up to the last minute. For example, when the guest of honor at an official dinner has to cancel at the last minute, the entire table has to be reseated. (That happened to me at the White House, too, when a top U.S. senator decided to come to dinner after all, without notifying us. I had to reseat about fifty of the top-ranking guests as everyone walked into the State Dining Room to take their places.) When you are seating a business group in your executive dining room, in a restaurant, or in your home, you should know how to rank your guests and seat them accordingly (we will explain this). You should know when something is threatening to go wrong at a function that your office sponsors, and you should know how to make it right.

Place Cards

Elsa Maxwell, the late internationally famous party-giver, once stated that "the most certain route to chaos at a dinner party is not having place cards telling everyone where to go."

Place cards, which may be hand-written, done in calligraphy (the nicest, of course), or even typed, should be used when ten or more people will be your guests at a seated meal.

A place card, either flat or folded, sits on top of the napkin, on the tablecloth, propped against a glass, or placed above the plate at the place setting.

For a dinner at home, the host and his or her spouse do not have place cards. (They are supposed to know where they sit!)

The proper social form in writing a place card is to use the guest's title and family name only, such as:

> Ms. Jenkins
> Mr. Hurd
> Dr. Guttenberg
> Judge Duke

Separate place cards are provided for husband and wife, as they will be sitting apart. If there are two people with the same name, you would naturally use both their given and family names:

> Mr. David Smith
> Mr. Richard Smith

If you are hosting a business meal at which people do not know each other, you may waive the etiquette rules pertaining to how you write a place card and write both the given and family names on the cards. This will help each guest's neighbor learn exactly who this person is.

The nicest place cards used in business are those embossed with the company's symbol or logo on the top (and the nicest menus are those that match). See the illustration of menu and place card on page 273.

Where Spouses of Hosts Sit

When spouses are present and one table is used, the host husband and wife sit *opposite* each other. If more than one table is used and spouses are present, husbands and wives sit at *separate* tables. The illustration showing spouses sitting opposite each other also shows how the most important male and female guests are seated, according to their importance.

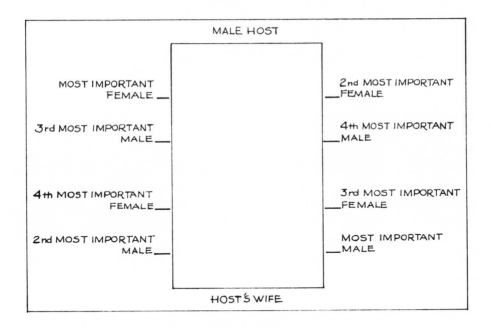

In certain size groups, the male and female cohosts cannot sit opposite each other. In groups of eight, and successive multiples of four, spouses do not sit opposite one another if there are an equal number of male and female guests, in order to preserve the seating balance that alternates male/female/male/female, etc. The female spouse of an executive would sit "down" one seat instead of opposite her husband, if there are eight at table, and if there are four men and four women guests. (This is assuming use of only one table for the meal.)

Host

Female Guest	Female Guest
Male Guest	Male Guest
Female Guest	*Hostess*

Male Guest

Learning How to Rank Your Guest List
(*See also* Chapter 10, Proper Forms of Address)

At a business lunch or dinner where spouses are not present, guests should be ranked *in order of their importance* and seated accordingly, without reference to their gender. If there is only one woman at the table, she does not sit on the host's right unless she is the number one ranked guest present. It isn't that chivalry is dead, but rather that things are becoming logical in the workplace.

Executive Host

Guest #1	Guest #2
Guest #5	Guest #6
Guest #4	Guest #3

Cohost

Seating people properly has a logic to it. Someone of official rank (government official, military officer, etc.) deserves to be seated in the place of honor. You should also be aware of the nuances of seating people who are *not* official but who for one reason or another should be given the seat on the right of the host or a seat close to the host. For example, you would give a seat of honor to:

- A foreign guest
- Someone who is visiting you
- Someone who is elderly
- A person who has had a distinguished career
- Someone who formerly held an appointed or elected office or military rank
- Someone who is celebrating his birthday, an anniversary, a promotion, etc.

These are other points to consider:

- Seating for nonranked guests should alternate whenever possible (man-woman, man-woman, etc.), but often there is a shortage of one sex, in which case men have to sit next to men or women next to women.

- Husbands and wives should never sit next to each other (except, of course, at a table for four).
- Dates may or may not be seated next to each other.
- Husbands and wives should sit at different tables if there is more than one table.
- At a large function, seat a younger person on one side of an elderly person (which will please the older person), but give the younger person someone nearer his own age on his other side (so that he won't feel intimidated).
- If there is a guest from a foreign country in which one of your colleagues has done a great deal of business, seat them together.
- If there are guests who do not know each other but who share passionate interests (such as music, civil rights, whatever), seat them together.
- Seat a painfully shy guest next to a very talkative one, so that one can talk and the other can listen.
- If a wife outranks her husband in position or title, she should be given a better seat than he.

Who Outranks Whom

If you are handling the seating and are uncertain as to who outranks whom among city officials, call the mayor's office. In the case of a state official, call the state capitol and ask the operator who handles such matters. (Sometimes it's the governor's office; sometimes it is another department.)

As for Congress, anyone dealing with elected representatives and senators to the United States Congress should purchase an up-to-date *Congressional Directory* (Government Printing Office, Washington, D.C. 20401; telephone: 202/783-3238). Senators outrank congressmen; if you have several senators or several congressmen to seat, rank them by seniority (i.e., length of consecutive service) unless they hold a major position, such as House Minority Leader.

Ambassadors from foreign countries are also ranked according to length of service, but in their present post only. If you have any questions in general on this subject, the Ceremonial Section of the Office of Protocol of the Department of State in Washington, D.C., is very helpful (202/632-8999).

For military protocol, precedence is determined by an officer's rank. (If you have a group all of the same rank, the one who has held the rank the longest takes precedence, and you can only find that out by calling all their offices!)

There are two books that will help you understand protocol and how to seat ranked guests. One is my own *Amy Vanderbilt Complete Book of Etiquette* (Doubleday, 1978); the other is *Protocol,* by McCaffrey and Innis (Prentice-Hall, 1977).

The "Table Plan" for Each Table

The staff person working on a large lunch or dinner is faced with matching a long list of names to a series of tables, some of which may be in different shapes and have different seating capacities.

- The first step is to make two alphabetical lists of your guests, one for the men and one for the women. (It helps in doing the seating if you write or type the men's names on one color of paper, and the women's names on the other.)
- With scissors, cut out each name into a little tab (2½″ × ½″, for example). Place them in alphabetical order, so that names can be easily located when you want them.

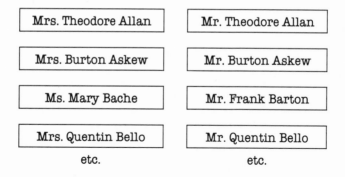

- Take a large piece of paper to represent each table for the function. Number each table and draw its shape on the paper (round, oval, rectangle, or, very rarely, square). Put small lines around the outside of each table, representing where the seats are at that table.
- Now take each name and attach it to a seat, via cellutape, seating first, of course, the host, cohosts (if there are any), guest of honor and spouse, second most important person and spouse, third most important person and spouse, etc. Using cellutape as shown in the illustration permits you to keep changing the placement of the guests until you have the right formula. (For a large function, the seating takes *hours*.)

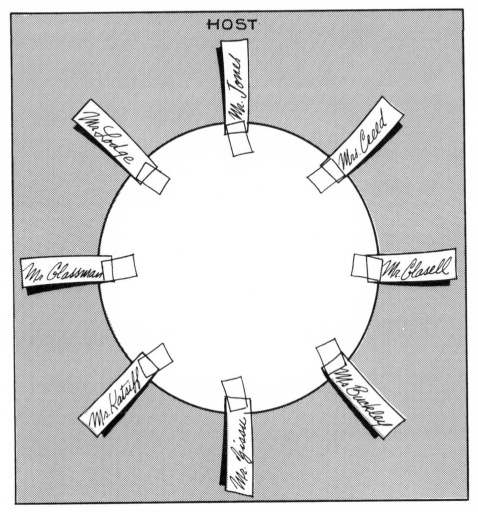

PRELIMINARY SEATING PLAN

The Door List

The door list, kept at the check-in desk for a large event, is an alphabetized list of each guest's name, with his or her table number indicated. Each staff member working the party should have a door list, to help the guests find their tables inside the room.

It's a good idea not to run off duplicate copies of the door list until the very last minute, for the simple reason that the guest list keeps changing right up to the last minute. That means that the seating and the table assignments keep changing, too.

How to Politely Inform the Guests Where They Sit

Guests arriving for a big party should check in at the front door, and be shown where to sit by one of two procedures:

- *A table plan showing all of the numbered tables and where each person is seated.* A staff member at the check-in desk points to the guest's name on the chart and advises him of his table number. These table plan charts are often blown up to a large size, so that the names are easily legible. They can be put on easels, like flip-charts, for easier viewing by arriving guests.

No matter how complicated directors of special events may consider their business parties to be, the problems of organizing and seating a White House function are far worse! The seating plan reproduced here for a dinner given during the Kennedy administration is typical of those prepared by the Social Office in the White House. There is a rectangular head table for eighteen, and ten additional tables seating ten each. The name of the host at each table is underlined (all United States government officials or their wives).

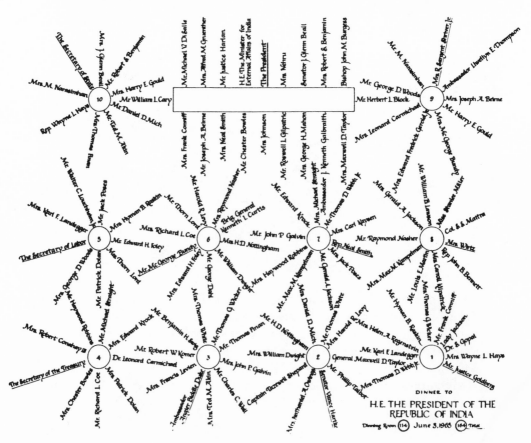

DINNER TO
H.E. THE PRESIDENT OF THE
REPUBLIC OF INDIA
Dining Room ⑴⑷ June 3, 1963 ⑴⑹⑷ Total

A company can follow the same procedure in recording its table plans for important dinners. The White House does all lettering in calligraphy; business people should settle for typewriter lettering, since very few corporations have a calligrapher on their staff. (The White House has a team of them.) If you are having a large dinner like the one shown in the White House illustration, you would also draw a floor plan (in your organizer's notebook only) for the dancing area in a tent. You would have small tables for people to use when they wish to sit for a while, such as in the tent illustration earlier in this chapter (*see* Room Setups).

- *Table cards, which are given to each guest as they arrive.* The table cards (approximately 3½″ × 1½″) are placed alphabetically on a table near the front door. As each guest arrives, he or she is handed a table card upon furnishing his or her name. The little white card has the guest's name on the front and the table number on the back. (It can also be a double fold, with the table number on the inside fold.) Each guest pockets this card, to refer to later when entering the dining area. The guest finds the table with the same number on the stanchion as on his card. There he has only to look for his place card at that table.

A Guest May Not Change the Seating

Occasionally one sees a person arrive at the table ahead of the others who does not like the way the seating has been arranged. This person then proceeds to change the cards around to make his or her seat more advantageous.

This kind of behavior can only be labeled despicable. The corporate hosts have their own reasons for seating their guests as they see fit at a seated meal, and the guests have no right to change the decisions that have been made.

Open Seating

In open seating there are neither table numbers nor place cards. As people enter the room, they are urged to fill up the tables as they go. This system is necessary for a party that is too big to seat (such as lunch for a thousand) or for a party in which the definite acceptances and regrets are not known.

It is important for the staff party workers to make sure that each table is filled completely before a new one is started. In this way, any empty tables can be removed, after everyone is seated. If people fill up only a part of each table, it is difficult to serve, it looks terrible, and people have an awkward time talking across empty chairs to their neighbors.

Another system that works if you have more or less equal numbers of men and women is to have people draw table numbers from bowls (one for men, one for women).

When strangers find themselves at a table, they should seat themselves man-woman-man-woman as much as possible, rather than having the women all sitting together and the men also clustered in a group like birds on a telephone pole.

Staging a Formal Dinner Event
with Guest Speaker(s)

When a company produces a large, complicated event, one of the most important things to remember is that the graphics should be unified. In other words, if the corporate colors of royal blue and white will be used in the decoration of the party area, it makes sense to use the same corporate colors for all of the graphics—for the invitations, the badges, the admission tickets, the menu cards, the place cards, the programs, etc.

Admission Tickets

If you expect a large number of guests, you may need to provide tickets of admission for the event, for reasons of order *and* security (particularly if you have an important official or celebrity as your guest). These tickets should be numbered and sent by return mail to the guests when the RSVP cards, marked with their acceptances, are returned by the guests. A list of those who have accepted, with their ticket numbers opposite their names, must be kept at the door, both to avoid admitting crashers and to be able to assist the inevitable few guests who arrive without their tickets of admission.

The admission ticket should be printed with the corporate logo and the following:

- Name of event
- Date
- Address
- Time
- Necessary information, such as "Guests must be seated in the Auditorium by 8 P.M." or "This ticket not transferable" or "Parking in _____"
- Indication of rain date, if that is necessary
- The ticket number

The Printed Program

The program printed for a prestigious event should repeat the design theme of the invitation, of course. A program for an official luncheon or dinner might contain the following:

- The outside cover, of heavy stock embossed with the corporate logo and the name of the event, would state in whose honor the event is held, and the place and date of the event.

- Printed on the inside left cover would be the menu, including the wine(s) to be consumed.
- On the first page (right) inside the cover, the program of events would be printed, including the name of the clergyman giving the invocation, the name of the person presiding (master of ceremonies), the dignitaries who will make the toasts (if the guest of honor is, for example, a head of state or an important foreign official), the names of anyone giving a speech, and also any entertainment to take place.
- On the back side of the program page there might be a short, well-written history of the host company and the reasons for this special celebration.
- On the inside back cover or in an insert, the "Seating List" might be given, showing who is sitting on the dais, and listing all other guests alphabetically, with their table numbers by their names.

The program makes a wonderful souvenir to carry away from the event. It makes the guest feel special and it gives great dignity to the occasion.

Opening Procedures

When a large corporation hosts a lunch or dinner on an important civic occasion—a national holiday, a major anniversary, a "Welcome home" ceremony for returning heroes, etc.—it may be appropriate to pull out all the patriotic stops, complete with bands, flag, and the national anthem.

The order of procedure at a banquet once all the guests and dais guests are seated is the following:

- The posting of the colors (if that is to take place). Everyone rises.
- The Pledge of Allegiance (rarely done anymore)
- The singing of the "Star Spangled Banner" (which may now be sung in A-flat, much easier to sing than in B-flat, the key in which the national anthem was written)
- The clergyman's invocation

The Invocation

When there is an invocation, the master of ceremonies for the event should prompt the audience: "Please rise and remain standing for the invocation, to be delivered by Reverend John Madison Barr, pastor of the Church of St. John." No one should talk, eat, or drink at this moment, but remain silent, with head bowed. If the ceremony is out of doors and any men present happen to be wearing hats, they should remove them during the invocation.

Even if a clergyman considers it an honor to his ministry to be asked to deliver the invocation, the corporate host may wish to send him a small, unsolicited check immediately following the event, enclosed in a letter of thanks for coming. The host might write something like "This small check is only a symbol of the esteem in which our company holds your ministry." An individual might send the clergyman a check for $25 for the invocation, while a major corporation executive might send a check for anything from $200 to $500.

The National Anthem

When the "Star Spangled Banner" is played, everyone should remain standing at attention (and most properly of all, with the right hand over the heart). Military personnel stand at salute. It helps, if the national anthem will be sung, to provide background music for support, such as a piano. Otherwise, the singing of it can sound more like a funeral dirge than a patriotic song—unless you are lucky enough to have someone like Beverly Sills standing at your microphone!

Displaying the Flag

If you are going to display a group of flags at a meeting, banquet, or any event sponsored by your company, remember that the flag of the United

SPEAKER'S LECTERN

American   State   Organization's
flag   flag   flag

States of America is always accorded the place of honor, positioned on its own right. The flag should be on the speaker's right, the audience's left; the other flags (state, corporate, etc.) should be positioned to the left of the speaker.

When a group of domestic flags are on display, the United States flag should be in the center, on some kind of a platform, raised above the others or to its own right. When flags of other countries are displayed, all flags should be of the same size, on separate poles of the same height, and displayed in a straight line. The United States flag should always be to its own right (the audience's left) as in the illustration here.

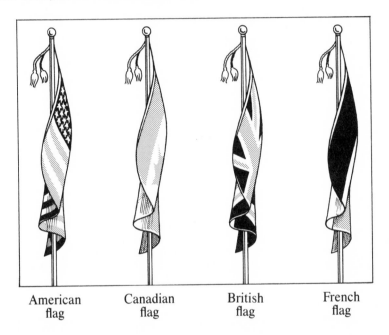

| American flag | Canadian flag | British flag | French flag |

When displaying the flag against a wall, vertically or horizontally, the flag's union (stars) should be at the top, to the flag's own right and the observer's left.

The flag should never be used to cover the lectern or to drape a platform. For that it is proper to use bunting of red, white, and blue stripes, with a blue stripe on top. (For detailed information on flag etiquette, contact the National Flag Foundation, Flag Plaza, Pittsburgh, PA 15219; 412/261-1776.)

The Dais

It is a distinct honor to be invited to sit on the dais. Such an invitation means you are either a person of great distinction or you are involved in a top level capacity with the purpose of the function.

Spouses of those invited to sit on the dais are not included, except for the spouse of the main speaker, who may be invited to join the dais.

It is important that you communicate to anyone being asked to sit on the dais at a fund-raising benefit whether or not the invitee is supposed to pay for his or her dinner or lunch ticket. (The answer usually is yes, except for the speakers.) In your letter of invitation to a dais guest, indicate either, "We are enclosing a complimentary dinner ticket for your use" or "You may purchase your benefit ticket by filling out the enclosed card and mailing your check to. . . ."

Organizing the Dais Group

Dais guests should be invited to convene in a special room (usually close to the ballroom or the area where the function is to be held) half an hour before the dais guests are supposed to march in formation into the ballroom. Company staff members should be present to greet them, show them where to check their coats, introduce them to the company hosts and guest of honor, make sure they are served drinks, brief them on the scenario for the affair, and make sure they are in their proper place in line before marching into the ballroom.

On rare occasions, there is a very large dais of from twenty to fifty people. In this case the dais is built in rows, like a bleacher, usually on the ballroom stage.

When organizing a dais of this size, you would be wise to line up rows of chairs in the "dais convening room," to duplicate exactly the rising platforms in the ballroom. (The important guests will be placed on the lower levels of the ascending platforms.) Each chair should have a name tag. The dais guests should be lined up in the proper order in the convening room and, just before going into the ballroom, should sit in their assigned chairs so that they are ready to march to the dais in proper order. Unless this is perfectly organized, dais guests will wander forlornly back and forth trying to find their places. That is very undignified and does not reflect credit on the sponsoring hosts.

When everything in the ballroom is ready, the maître d'hôtel will signal the company official in charge of the dais group that it is time to assemble in proper order and to enter the ballroom. The maître d'hôtel then goes to the microphone in the ballroom and announces, "Ladies and gentlemen, the honored guests!"

The musicians should then begin to play something military and brisk, suitable for marching, so the dais guests enter at a quick pace to mount the steps to the stage and the dais platforms. The guests should applaud enthusiastically as the dais guests appear; there should be some staff members planted in the audience to applaud on cue, thus prompting the entire ballroom to begin applauding.

The music that heralds the dais guests is really important, whether it's a piano arpeggio, an accordion flourish, a roll of the drums, or even a trumpet flourish. (Dais guests who walk limply to their places at a large function without a musical introduction always look to me like a funeral procession!)

The Seating on the Dais

The most uncomfortable seat on a dais is the end one on either side. The person on each end is left without anyone to talk to during a great part of the meal. This problem can be solved simply by putting guests close to each other *in pairs.* In addition, no one should be seated behind the lectern, for he or she would be totally obscured from the audience. The guest of honor should sit on the right of the host; the second ranking guest should sit on the right of the second ranking corporate executive. At Company X's civic dinner, the dais might look like this:

DAIS TABLE SEATING

Substitutions on the Dais

Never send a substitute for yourself on the dais. If a dais guest cannot attend the function at the last moment, he must have someone notify his dinner hosts, regardless of how busy he may be. It is the height of rudeness not to let the hosts know, because this means there will be an empty seat on the dais, which will look like a front tooth missing in someone's smile.

It is not proper for a dais guest who cannot attend the function at the last minute to take upon himself the selection of a substitute to attend in his place. This is a decision for the host company to make—either to find a substitute or to remove his place from the dais.

Alternatives to the Dais

It is not all that interesting to sit on the dais once you've done it once or twice. In fact, it can be extremely boring to sit facing everyone under their constant gaze. There are alternatives. One alternative is to seat the honored guests and celebrities around the room, one at each table. (This can be done at large functions with many round tables.) The presence of a "star guest" pleases everyone at that particular table. The "star guest," of course, is seated to the right of the company host of that table. Another alternative is to seat the master of ceremonies and the honored guests together at a large round table on a raised platform in the center of the room. In this way, everyone's view of the VIPs is excellent.

When using either of these alternatives, the master of ceremonies or dinner chairman—whatever you wish to call him—should introduce each honored guest individually (speaking through a microphone). As each person is introduced, a spotlight beam should fall on him, making him visible to everyone in the room. He should stand when his name is read and remain standing while the master of ceremonies talks about him. The audience should applaud at the conclusion of the announcement of all the names.

The Role of the Master of Ceremonies

A master of ceremonies is necessary if the dinner includes a program of speakers as well as entertainment. Someone has to introduce the stars of the event, make statements that might seem too self-serving for the host to make, and keep things moving along in a lively manner for performers and audience alike. It is an honor to be asked to be the master of ceremonies at a function. It means that you have a sense of humor, know how to project your voice, and can handle audiences. It means that you have the gift of being able to "think fast on your feet," so that you react quickly in an emergency. (An "emergency" arises when the lead entertaining act has not arrived, when the main speaker falls ill and has to be taken home, or when the air-conditioning ceases to function and the microphones don't work!)

The master of ceremonies (who may be male or female) should be a fairly high-ranking executive or a person of distinction—and someone who knows enough to hold his alcohol consumption to a minimum on the day and evening of the event. The M.C.'s role includes the following:

- He introduces himself to the audience, even if he thinks everyone knows who he is. He reminds the audience why they are present on this occasion.
- He makes brief introductions. Since he has requested good biographical information on everyone in advance, his well-prepared introductions sparkle with clarity and wit.

- He puts the audience at ease. He handles everything with a light touch. Even a subject like cancer research does not have to be treated in a funereal manner. A good M.C. can always find a way to make people smile every so often and to keep their attention drawn to the podium. Also, the guest speaker usually makes a much better speech if he has been relaxed by an amusing, flattering introduction given by the M.C.
- He acts as timekeeper for the speaker(s). The M.C. should slip a note to the speaker, asking him to finish quickly, if he has been droning on for too long. If the speaker has had too much to drink, the M.C. might have to cajole him to leave the podium, rather than have the audience continue to suffer through an embarrassing presentation.
- He fills in inadvertant brief gaps in the program. The M.C. should know how to ad-lib when stalling for time. For example, I remember a lunch when the M.C. announced a special performance, but when the drums rolled, the performers failed to appear. The M.C. quieted the audience's laughter and asked them to get out pencils and paper. Then he proceeded to give them his grandmother's "Spaghetti alla Carbonara" recipe, which he knew by heart. Three minutes later, before he was finished, the act signaled from the wings that they were now ready to go on stage. "Well, they're ready now." He said to the laughing audience. "Do you want the rest of the recipe first?" The audience, by now in a really good mood, roared back, "Yes, yes!" so he finished the recipe. None of us will ever forget that M.C.
- The perfect M.C. makes the audience feel they have profited from attending the function, and that they have also had a good time.

DIFFERENT KINDS OF PARTIES

This section deals with some of the different kinds of business parties given today—from the prosaic cocktail party to the two-day forum culminating in a private concert. Good food and drink as well as quality and creativity in planning are keys to the success of these events.

Entertaining Involving Cocktails

The cocktail party, cocktail-buffet, or reception provides a way for a large number of people to be entertained in a short amount of time, usually for the least amount of money. However, in a city like New York the least amount of money has become a considerable amount. In 1975, for example, one could have entertained at a cocktail party in a first-class hotel or restaurant for about $18 per person. Now the minimum charge (including the food, cocktails, tax, and gratuities) may be anywhere from $35 to $75 per person. A cocktail party therefore can involve a considerable investment of money and requires as much work as any other kind of entertaining.

The Different Kinds of Parties Involving Cocktails and Hors d'Oeuvres

People often confuse the terms *cocktails, cocktail buffet,* and *reception.* This chart should help explain the difference between the terms. (Menus typical for these parties follow.)

	Cocktails or Cocktail Party	Cocktail-Buffet	Reception
Type of Event	Informal invitations are sent. People mostly stand up and circulate through the rooms. This may be an impromptu spur-of-the-moment party or a way to entertain a couple of hundred customers. It is the most common type of entertaining of a large group.	A more formal occasion. There should be a place to sit down to eat for the guests after they fill their plates at the buffet. Often some small tables and chairs are set up at random. This is a special event, not just a gathering of people. It could be an opening night party of an association meeting, a party to honor someone, or a chance to commemorate something.	The most formal. Usually for a distinguished guest of honor or for a special event, such as a party before or after a museum opening or a performing arts event, or for an anniversary.
Hours	For 1½ to 2 hours, held usually in the evening, starting anywhere after 5 P.M. and ending by 8:30 P.M.	For a 2- or 3-hour duration, usually between 6 and 9 P.M.	Usually from 6 to 8 P.M. or, if after an event, from 10:30 to midnight.
Dress	Business dress	Business dress (Women can be very dressy)	Very dressy, business attire, often black tie
Food and Drink	Cocktails, wine, soft drinks; hot and cold hors d'oeuvres	Same as cocktail party, but there is a buffet table with more food and one or two hot dishes included. Guests may make dinner out of this buffet.	*Before dinner:* elaborate cocktail party food. *After event:* late supper menu. Champagne a must at this type of party.

Sample Menus

Cocktail party

Nibbling food (nuts, popcorn, cheese straws)
Small chicken sandwiches
Small egg salad sandwiches
Cheeses and crackers
Stuffed eggs
Peanut butter and bacon on toasted rounds
Small sausages (hot) on toothpicks
Hot cheese puffs
Crudites (raw vegetables) with dip
Broiled pieces of bacon covered in brown sugar
Endive with pâté on the tip
Hot stuffed mushrooms
Water chestnuts wrapped in bacon
Greek grape leaf and phyllo dough hors d'oeuvres

Elaborate:

Fresh crabmeat, crab claws
Fresh lobster bits
Fresh oysters and clams
Beefsteak Tartare
Hot charcoal-broiled swordfish with crackers
Pâté de foie gras with crackers
Caviar
Fresh shrimp

NOTE: For the average cocktail party, a choice of three hot and three cold hors d'oeuvres is sufficient.

Cocktail-Buffet

Oysters on half shell
Platter of assorted pâtés with crackers
Small pieces of smoked pheasant in aspic

Veal stroganoff served with rice
Cold poached salmon with green sauce and
small buttered brown bread slices
Hot "Pasta Primavera" (contains fresh vegetables)
Mixed green salad

Selection of desserts (brought out after everyone has almost finished eating):
Pears poached in wine (sour cream sauce on the side)
Angel food cake with vanilla ice cream
and fresh peach sauce
Mousse au chocolat

NOTE: Both red and white wine would be served with this buffet. Demitasses would be passed by waiters, or coffee would be left on the buffet (self-service) in a heated container.

Reception

Before dinner: See menu for elaborate cocktail party.

After event (for a simple 10 o'clock reception):

Champagne (white wine if the budget won't allow)
Nonalcoholic beverages
Open bar (optional)

Small sandwiches

Cookies and small cakes (for the champagne drinkers)

Cheese and crackers

For more elaborate 11 o'clock reception:

Champagne
Nonalcoholic beverages
Open bar

Made-to-order omelets
Caviar
One-inch squares of filet mignon tidbits on toothpicks

Lobster Newburgh or Crabmeat Maryland with rice

Mixed green salad

Small chocolate cakes, fruit tarts, etc.

NOTE: You must provide plates, napkins, forks, and spoons for this kind of service. People will be too tired at this hour to stand, so there must be cloth-covered tables as well as chairs set around the food service area.

What Makes a Good Cocktail Party?

An enjoyable and successful cocktail party is one in which:

- Invitations went out far enough in advance so that the guests were able to arrange their schedules to attend.
- The guest list was carefully prepared, so that an interesting mix of guests is on hand, including new faces.
- The room is not overcrowded, nor too hot and smoky.
- There is a receiving line if hosts and guests don't know each other.
- There is a sufficient number of trained company people helping host the party—introducing people around, bringing them up to meet the host, seeing that the guests both have people to talk to and drinks and food, etc.
- There is a sufficient number of bars, so that people don't have to fight to obtain their drinks.
- There are some small tables and chairs to allow people who are tired to sit down.
- The music is good and kept low enough to allow for easy conversation. A party at which people have to shout to be heard is very counterproductive.

NOTE: the bar should be shut down one half hour after the concluding hour given on the invitations. In other words, if the invitation read "from 5 to 7 P.M.," the bar should be closed down at 7:30.

Cocktail Party Checklist

The easiest place to host a cocktail party, cocktail-buffet, or reception is in a public place like a hotel, as the work is done for you by the establishment's banquet services department.

The nicest party, of course, is the one you give in your home. If yours is large enough, comfortable, and convenient to get to, your guests will enjoy themselves in a relaxed way. The extra work you have to go through in organizing your home and the party food is worth it; the anticipation of success makes it seem worthwhile.

Whether you are dealing with a caterer and renting equipment to use for the party in your home or whether you are dealing with a hotel's banqueting department, there are many details that must be checked out beforehand:

Basic Equipment

- Bar tables and cloths to cover them, with a simple floral centerpiece for each table

- The right kind of bar glasses (don't use plastic unless you absolutely have to—such as if you are in a garden, on the beach, or on a boat)
- Small tables (these usually need cloths) and chairs for those who want to sit down if there isn't enough available seating space
- Coatracks with hangers (and someone to guard the coats and other possessions checked)
- A container for umbrellas, if it's raining
- Large and small trays for passing drinks and hors d'oeuvres
- Nice cocktail napkins. Cloth napkins are the nicest to use in your own home. Otherwise, purchase pretty paper ones from a party store. You might have them printed up with a special message if your party has a special theme or guest of honor.
- Colorful toothpicks to use for the hors d'oeuvres requiring them
- Ice, crushed or in cubes, delivered in large multigallon containers or paper sacks. Be sure to place the sacks in containers to catch the water that seeps through the bags when the ice melts.

The Bartender Will Need

- Bar knife and small cutting board
- Angostura bitters
- Lemon squeezer and strainer
- Precut lemon and lime wedges or lemon peel "zests"
- Sugar bowl with spoon
- Cherries, olives, and cocktail onions
- Pitcher with long-handled stirring spoon
- Large water pitcher
- Cocktail shaker
- Measuring spoons
- 1½-ounce jigger
- Bar towels

Drink Makings for the Well-Stocked Bar

This list comprises the most popular before-dinner drinks, although there are many more on the market than listed here:

- A selection of nonalcoholic drinks, including a fruit juice and two kinds of soda (including one that is caffeine- and sugar-free)
- Salt-free soda water, tonic water, and ginger ale for mixers or for people who do not want alcohol
- Tomato juice for Bloody Marys
- Vodka

- Gin
- Scotch
- Blended whiskey (or Irish whiskey)
- Bourbon
- Rum (dark or light)
- Wine (both white and red)
- Beer (particularly if you are going to have young guests)
- Sherry (sweet or dry)
- A sweet aperitif (Dubonnet, red Cinzano, etc.)
- Campari
- Dry vermouth (as an aperitif or to use to make martinis)

If your budget limitations prevent you from having a fully stocked bar, you can offer a minimum of drink choices, such as the following:

- Soda and diet soda
- Soda water and tonic water
- Vodka or gin
- Scotch or Bourbon
- White wine
- Dry vermouth
- Beer (both "full" and "light")

Helping Control Costs at Your Party

The considerable expense of serving liquor can be kept to a minimum if the party planner is both careful and thorough. He or she should instruct the bartender "to control his free hand" while pouring from the bottles. There are about twenty-two drinks in a litre bottle of liquor. Bartenders should be requested to pour all drinks with a 1½-ounce jigger so that they will neither exaggerate the amount of liquor in each glass nor cheat on the amount.

Make sure the head bartender knows the exact hour at which the bar is to be shut off at the conclusion of your party; otherwise stragglers will keep running up your party cost, both for liquor and for overtime for the bartender.

If you're having a dinner party in a hotel, allocate from forty-five minutes to an hour for the cocktail hour before taking your guests in to dinner. The restaurant, hotel, or club management should be given firm orders before the event in order to hold to your schedule.

The most economical way to work with a hotel is to keep count of the bottles actually used and to pay by the bottle. Return the unopened bottles to the hotel's inventory. Bringing in your own liquor does not help keep costs down, since the hotel will charge you an expensive corkage fee (for handling the glasses, providing the ice, mixers, and water, and for opening the bottle).

The "unlimited consumption plan" is one whereby the establishment charges the corporate host a flat fee per guest, no matter how much or how little that guest consumes. For example, if the drinks cost $5 and you are figuring approximately three per person at your cocktail party, the price charges per guest for the liquor would be $15 plus gratuity.

A corporate host should always order more than enough liquor and wine, because it is embarrassing to run out. The liquor should be good quality, too. To save money a company should cut down on the number of parties it gives or the number of guests invited, rather than on the quality of its offerings.

When a company hosts its own people on occasions such as sales meetings, a cash bar is a good idea before dinner. This cuts down on company expense and also on the company executives' drinking. However, when customers are present, the drinks should be on the house.

What to Do If There Is No Standing Room for Cocktails Before Dinner in a Restaurant

Naturally, the easiest and most ideal circumstances under which to entertain a large group in a restaurant (twenty guests or more) is a private room, with a large enough area in which guests can meet each other and circulate during the service of cocktails. Sometimes the restaurant does not have such an area; guests must go right to the dinner table and sit there; thus their conversational partners are only those close by.

If this is the case, it's a good idea to invite your dinner guests to your home first (or to one of the other guest's homes near the restaurant) for drinks. In this way the guests can mix and talk to each other, even if they won't be able to circulate in the restaurant.

If a friend who is attending the dinner party lends you his home for your cocktail gathering, be sure to supply all of the liquor, mixers, ice, hors d'oeuvres, and any serving help needed. The owner of the home should be spared any preparation or cleaning chores or any extra expense in connection with your party.

The next day be sure to send this person a thank-you note and a gift (or flowers).

The Cocktail Party Guest's Manners

Basic manners come into play at even as impersonal an affair as a giant cocktail party of several hundred people. Just because you are invited to attend a big bash does not mean that you should be any more relaxed about your responsibilities as a guest.

• A cocktail party invitation with an RSVP deserves an immediate reply.

- Don't bring a guest without calling first to ask your host's office if it is all right to do so. *Give the name of your guest.*
- Don't monopolize the host or celebrity guests; others want the opportunity to talk to them, too. At a cocktail party one should *circulate.*
- When someone comes up to your conversation group, introduce him or her around, even if you can't remember names.
- Don't arrive at the very end of the party and expect an enthusiastic greeting from your hosts.
- Hold your iced drink in a cocktail napkin; when you shake someone's hand, give him a dry hand, not a cold, wet one.
- Don't "pig out" on the food. It's nice to let some other guests get close to the buffet or to the delicacies being passed!
- If you're standing and smoking, find an ashtray; don't just let your ashes fall on the carpet.
- Don't drink too much. Know your limit and drink accordingly.
- If you accepted the cocktail invitation and at the last minute did not go, without notifying anyone, call your host's office the next day to apologize and to explain why you couldn't make it.
- Write a short thank-you note to your host for his party. It is a nice thing to do, and it will make a *big* impression on him.

A Business Tea Party—Why Not?

It's nice to surprise people once in a while. People always remember a party that is different. A change of routine, an altered format, and a different party hour add a pleasant touch of the unusual to a social occasion. A tea party is one such different event. (Europeans, notably the British, have known this for centuries.)

The place where a tea party is held should be warm and attractive. The tea hour conjures up visions of a fireplace, a library, or a view onto a garden. A particularly pretty public room in a hotel or in a restored historic building is also appropriate for a gathering at the tea hour—around four o'clock in the afternoon (and lasting until five or five thirty at the latest). After this hour, people expect cocktails.

There is something about taking a break in the late afternoon that is healthy and enjoyable. It is a tension reliever; a cup of tea really refreshes the spirit. I have organized corporate tea parties from coast to coast, and each one was a success—because of the novelty of it and because it was a moment of relaxation in the guests' super-charged schedules. After tea, one can return to work, if necessary (whereas it is very difficult to return to work after a function in which alcohol is served).

A tea party need take only an hour (or even forty-five minutes) out of one's schedule. If there are remarks to be made by the business host (such as at a press conference attended by others), the exact time of the remarks should be marked on the invitation (*see* Chapter 9, Invitations and Their Replies).

One way of serving tea is to set large silver tea (and coffee) urns on a large table that has been covered with a pretty cloth. Each guest approaches the table, picks up a cup, and is served individually. He serves himself from the food on the platters, and he also picks up his own tea food plate, napkin, spoon, and dessert fork. He then goes to sit down at one of the small cloth-covered tables scattered around, or he wanders around talking to various people, sipping his tea and eating the goodies while standing up.

The second way of serving tea is to have each guest served while seated at a small table. Waiters or waitresses bring each guest tea and pass the food. Each guest has a napkin and flatware awaiting him at his place at the table, as well as a teacup and saucer. There might be a bud vase in the center of each little table, with a blossom or two. A footed compote dish crammed with a variety of cookies and petits fours and perhaps a small dish of chocolates would also be placed on each table.

A tea menu might look something like this:

Tea
Coffee
Sparkling water
Small crustless bread sandwiches (egg salad, mushroom pâté, cream cheese and watercress, etc.)
Warm scones, biscuits, or muffins with butter and different jams and honey
Warm cheese straws
Hot cinnamon toast
Fresh strawberries and cream
Small cups of sherbet
Small cookies and cakes

A tea party should look very special. The silver should be gleaming. The napkins should be linen, not paper. The china should be pretty. The service of tea is a ritual, and the waiters or waitresses should be properly trained in it. An invitation "to have a proper cup of tea," as the English would say, is an intriguing idea to business people.

Entertaining to Introduce a New Product

Some of the best parties in corporate America are held to launch a new line or to introduce a new product. The party is of utmost importance, because:

- It draws the buyers and exposes them to the new products.
- It gives the products press exposure.
- It creates goodwill all around.
- It gives the salesmen an opportunity to establish a good personal relationship with their customers.

One of the most famous traditions in new product entertaining was the annual Milliken Breakfast, hosted by Deering Milliken, a major textile company, at the Waldorf in New York. While enjoying a sumptuous breakfast, buyers and press watched an original, professionally staged musical comedy, performed by a star cast. The script and lyrics were based on Milliken's new market offerings. To the buyers of fabrics, hosiery, and domestics, an invitation to the Milliken Breakfast was as coveted as an invitation from the White House. Nothing comparable to it has been presented since.

The great masters at new product launches are, of course, the Detroit automobile manufacturers. I will never forget my firm's involvement with the planning and implementation of the introduction of Chrysler's new Fifth Avenue model at a twenty-four-hour celebration in New York City. Since the car celebrated a special avenue in Manhattan, Saks Fifth Avenue's windows were full of clothes dedicated to it; the Museum of the City of New York gave us slides of Fifth Avenue from its earliest days, which we flashed around the Plaza Hotel ballroom on screens during a VIP-studded lunch. Bringing the car into the hotel (by taking down the front door) and up into the Plaza mezzanine was a logistical *coup* in itself. The car was "revealed" on a curtained stage, complete with multimedia audiovisual effects directed by Jim Sant'Andrea. It reminded me of the wonderful Radio City Music Hall stage shows. (Nothing is too good for Detroit.) The final celebration for the new model car occurred at nine o'clock that night when New Yorkers were treated to a thirty-five-minute display of fireworks set off over Central Park. George Plimpton provided commentary simultaneously on the radio and over loudspeakers to the crowds, describing the international fireworks and the symphonic music that accompanied them. It took two ad agencies, my PR firm, and what seemed like all of Chrysler's brass to orchestrate this giant twenty-four-hour party.

And New York will never forget the party Cartier gave to celebrate the reissuing of the first wristwatch ever made, the Santos watch, invented by Paris jeweler Louis Cartier early in this century for his aviator friend Santos. Ralph Destino, president of the American Cartier company, invited a couple thousand notables to a black-tie evening at the National Guard Armory at 66th Street and Park Avenue. The place was transformed into a combination airplane museum and discotheque! Antique planes that were still in flying condition were either displayed on the floor or suspended like historic mobiles from the high ceiling. Aviators, dressed in the flying garb worn at the turn of the century and during World War I, stood by their planes to answer questions.

The guests were served dinner at elaborately decorated tables. Then Destino presented some awards to some famous celebrities, and the guests watched a vintage film showing Santos early in the 1900s in France in some of his daring aerial escapades. The program was climaxed by a laser beam show high over the audience's heads, the first time most guests had ever witnessed such an event. Dancing afterward to a rock band in an area of the Armory (turned into a disco) was almost an anticlimax. No other wristwatch ever enjoyed such a tribute.

Perhaps the biggest continual spenders on product-launching parties, other than the manufacturers of automobiles, are the cosmetics and fragrance companies. When a major product is to be introduced, there is usually a major party given in New York and covered in breathless detail by the gossip columnists. Then Los Angeles or Chicago has its own kind of party, with the designer or personality for whom the fragrance is named in attendance as a drawing card. These are followed by "mini parties" given by stores all over the country to introduce the product locally, with expenses often shared by the company and the store.

New Yorkers are still talking about the "decadent" party Yves St. Laurent gave several years ago to launch his Opium perfume, marketed in this country by Squibb. The party was held on a luxurious Chinese junk moored in New York harbor; there were lavish fireworks and an enormous entourage of French celebrities was flown over to impress the normally blasé New Yorkers. When Lancôme launched its new fragrance Magie Noire, the company took over an immense disco for an evening for a lavish, glamorous black and gold dinner dance for several hundred people. When Max Factor introduced Tai and Rosita Missoni's new perfume Missoni, they took over the Engelhard Courtyard of the Metropolitan Museum of Art to use as their party space. Five hundred people milled around the beautifully landscaped courtyard, admiring its giant Tiffany stained glass window and watching a fashion show of colorful Missoni knits in the museum setting. This is typical of what is happening in imaginative party spaces all over the country. Museums, opera houses, libraries, and other nonprofit institutions are lending their facilities to corporations for entertainment purposes—in return for a nice donation, which for some locations is as low as $500 and in other places, like major institutions in New York, as high as $50,000.

The Chryslers, the Cartiers, the Missonis, the textile giants are not the average manufacturer. However, by examining what the giants do in their product launches, a small company can be inspired to try innovative ideas, adapting those for a budget that is within their capabilities. It might be a question of giving a party in a local historic house, having a small fireworks display at the conclusion of a cocktail party, or featuring a local entertainer who works the company's product names into his or her performance. Price is not the final criterion. *It is something done well that spells success.*

The Company Entertains Its Employees

A company or firm of any size can raise staff morale with a well-organized party for the employees. Some companies have one during the Christmas season, but it does not have to be a holiday party. Some companies give their annual party:

- On Valentine's Day
- Before the Fourth of July holiday (with family picnics)
- At Easter (with an egg hunt for the children)
- On St. Patrick's Day (if the firm is Irish)
- On Columbus Day (if the firm is Italian)
- On Founder's Day (the day the company officially opened)
- On the Feast of Santa Lucia (if the firm is Swedish)

If desired, the party may be tied into a fitting national holiday or ethnic or historical theme.

The best kinds of employee parties are those:

- To which the families are invited
- Held in an accessible spot, not too difficult to reach by company bus or by public transportation
- Including games, competitions, sports (with prizes for those who win, prizes for those who almost win, and a prize for "the slowest" or "the worst"—taking care to ensure that the person who receives a "worst" prize takes his participation in a joking way and is not offended)
- Recorded by a photographer (whose prints can subsequently be ordered)
- Featuring soft drinks, really good food, and plenty of it
- Attended by the *top brass.* (This is no time for a senior manager to stay home.)

The Office Christmas Party

The company holiday party has undergone radical changes in the last decade. Too many corporations have witnessed what overconsumption of alcohol can mean—embarrassing episodes or, worse, serious automobile accidents on the way home. There are options:

- If alcohol is served, the company pays for taxis home for the employees.
- The company buys a block of seats for its employees and families to a

performance of a play, opera, concert, dance recital, or even a movie preview complete with popcorn.

· Employees receive a half-day vacation, instead of a party.

· Employees are informed how much the party would have cost the company; a committee of employees then selects a local charity to receive the money instead, and the employees do the presenting of the check.

· Employees invite underprivileged or handicapped children to a party at company headquarters, instead of having a party for themselves.

Some companies throw a big party for the employees at the end of a very successful year, to show how much they value the employees' part in that success. Jerry Sanders III, the flamboyant head of Advanced Micro Devices, in Sunnyvale, California, invited 8000 employees and guests to a Christmas party in 1983 in San Francisco, spending almost $750,000 in the process. *Fortune* magazine referred to it as a "Gigabuck Bash" (*giga* means billion), because the host was using the party to motivate his employees to reach for $900 million in sales for the forthcoming year. For the AMD employees, it was an event they would never forget.

A Party Given for the Arts

A corporation often has the power to help a local writer, artist, or performer's career in a major sense by honoring that person with some kind of reception.

If a friend of the company or one of its own executives publishes a book, someone in management can give a cocktail party for bookstore owners, press, prominent citizens, and local librarians. If the company is helping a young local artist, it can host a cocktail party preview of that artist's show in the gallery or museum where the work is on display. The company might also put that artist's work on exhibit in its own lobby or somewhere else on the corporate premises.

The company might host a party following a musician's concert in their hometown; guests would be served a glass of wine and meet the performer. Again, the press would be invited (to help the musician but also to help the company image), and the affair would be a social event, a musical event, and a good public relations effort all in one.

A company might mount an exhibition in its offices of the work of the artist who executed the paintings illustrating that year's annual report. The originals of the artwork in the report would, of course, be included with other works by the artist—an excellent public relations idea.

The company's invitation to any such event should relate to the works being honored. For example, for a book party, the book jacket might be used for the invitation. An invitation to a party "in honor of the architects and designers of our new building" might incorporate reproductions of the original drawings or renderings of their work.

A Company Entertains Foreign Guests, Customers, and Employees Together: A Case Study

A small company can learn much from the successful, well-planned efforts of a giant corporation such as the Chase Manhattan Bank. The key prerequisites of planning and coordination were certainly visible in 1980 when Chase Manhattan held a "Forum on China's Economy" that was attended by the largest group of important Chinese officials ever to visit an American nongovernment organization and by the chief executive officers of many major American corporations. The forum and coordinate entertainment culminated on the second day with an important cultural event—a concert performed just for the bank's guests and employees at Avery Fisher Hall in New York's Lincoln Center.

Invitations to the Chinese and the American CEOs were issued four months before the June date. The bank's special events department had to plan simultaneously for:

- Opening dinner for the forum participants at the Rockefeller country estate near Tarrytown, New York
- All-day forum meetings the next day, including lunch and a reception at Chase Manhattan's headquarters in the Wall Street area
- The events at Avery Fisher Hall that evening:
    Cocktails and dinner for forum participants
    Cocktails for the other guests in the Grand Tier lobby before the concert
    Champagne served in the lower lobbies to everyone following the concert

The preparations included the design, production, and mailing of thousands of invitations to the Chinese (theirs were delivered in one group to the head of the delegation), the American CEOs, the bank's employees, and the bank's customers. All of the envelopes were hand-addressed in script. Menus for the meals, programs for the concert, and briefing sheets for the forum participants were printed in both English and Chinese. For several days before the event, the Chase Manhattan office lobby bustled with florists, caterers, security men, interpreters, and bilingual stenographers hired just for this event. One office at Chase was assigned the seating of the dinners on both nights and the forum lunch.

The familiar dark blue Chase Manhattan logo appeared on each invitation and on every printed piece relating to the events of both days. Those who were invited to participate in the forum received a simple RSVP card to fill in and return. The attention to detail was readily apparent. Invitees were even asked if they wanted their nickname on their badge! The RSVP card here reproduces the Chase format that worked so well.

(Company Logo)

FORUM ON CHINA'S ECONOMY
June 5–6, 1980

☐ I will participate in the Forum.   ☐ I cannot join you for the Forum.
I will be accompanied by:
(Name) _____
(Title) _____
Our plans for attendance at the Forum will include:

	Myself	My Colleague
Working Session, 5 June	☐	☐
Working Session, 6 June	☐	☐
Luncheon, 5 June	☐	☐
Luncheon, 6 June	☐	☐

I/we will be staying at _____
I/we plan to arrive in New York on _____ at _____ A.M./P.M.
Signed _____
_____
Your Name (typed or printed)
Your nickname, if desired, for name badge _____

NOTE: For immediate confirmation of your place at the Forum, please call the office of Vice President and Division Executive, People's Republic of China Division, at (000) 000-0000, before mailing this form.

The opening dinner was hosted by the David Rockefellers at their family estate, Pocantico Hills. Included in the formal invitation was an RSVP card with a self-addressed, stamped return envelope. When the bank received an acceptance, a card was mailed back stating how pleased the Rockefellers were that the person or couple in question would be able to attend. A map for those who planned to drive to Tarrytown and instructions on how to reach the estate by chartered bus also were included in this mailing.

Three hundred thirty-five distinguished Americans and Chinese dined that night under a yellow and white tent. The tablecloths and flowers were yellow and white. A program with the menu and a list of the Chinese official party and the American guests sat at each place. A group of "Strolling Strings" violin players serenaded the guests, walking among the tables. By the end of dinner, the Chinese and Americans had relaxed and become very comfortable with each other.

The forum meeting the next day began with coffee at 8:30 A.M. There was a coffee and tea break at 10:05 followed by lunch at 12:15. The forum adjourned at 3:00 P.M. During the meeting itself, participants sat on comfortable chairs, two each at narrow tables. Interpreters, secretaries, and telephone operators were available to help the participants with any urgent business that had to be transacted on the side during the day.

That evening "Chase Night at the Philharmonic" took place in Avery Fisher Hall at Lincoln Center. It was the culmination of a full year's work for the executive staff. William Toran, marketing vice-president, had his hands full with the seating of 2700 people. There were twice as many requests for seats as there were places available. Toran appointed one person in each department of the bank to be responsible for that department's customers. Cocktails were served before the concert to all of the concert guests; the VIPs in the meantime were served cocktails and dinner in the Metropolitan Opera Club at Lincoln Center, a handsome room with a black and silver Art Deco design. The tables were covered in pink cloths; the flowers were pale pink peonies in Chinese teak containers. Each guest found a place card and a menu at his place. The beauty of the setting helped impress the Chinese even more.

The guests who attended the concert had each received an invitation with a stamped return envelope. (The invitation text appears on page 338.)

The actual program for the concert, found on every seat in the hall, was printed both in English and Chinese. The bank's chairman and president gave a message of greeting and engaged in some public relations editorializing:

> We take great pride in our support of the New York Philharmonic and other activities of Lincoln Center for the Performing Arts. Chase is also privileged to have provided support throughout our long history to many of New York's other cultural institutions which serve to enrich the quality of life for residents and visitors.

A month after the concert every guest received a record album in the mail from the bank. On the cover was a color photograph of Avery Fisher Hall at night, the building magically reflected in the rain in the great plaza; the title was *A Commemorative Album of Chase Night at the Philharmonic.* The Beethoven concert program was printed on the other side, surmounted by the Chase logo floating like a halo over Beethoven's head. This was just another

The Chase Manhattan Bank
requests the pleasure of your company
at a private concert

Chase Night
at the Philharmonic

Eugene Ormandy,
Guest Conductor

The New York Philharmonic Orchestra

Andre Watts,
Piano Soloist

Thursday, June 5, 1980
at 8 p.m.
Avery Fisher Hall
Lincoln Center for the Performing Arts
Broadway at 65th Street

R.S.V.P. card enclosed   *Business Attire*

graceful and professional touch reminiscent of the way in which the entire operation had been handled.

How a Small Company Can Copy a Large Company's Ideas

A president of a medium-sized company might hear about the Chase Manhattan Bank and the Rockefeller style of entertaining and wonder how that could possibly apply to his own way of producing special events. Everything is relative; the Chase formula can be adapted on a limited scale to a much more simple and less costly affair, provided there is access to a local performing arts group and provided a concert hall or theater is available. (Sometimes even the company's auditorium is very suitable for a concert.)

The president might invite his foreign guests to a seminar that he stages on the company premises. He could entertain them for dinner that night at home or in a restaurant and follow dinner with a concert by a local group of musicians, to which he could invite all of his employees and customers as well as his foreign guests.

Generally people from other countries greatly enjoy an evening of the performing arts, and to know that such an evening was organized especially for them is the height of flattery.

PRACTICAL ENTERTAINMENT PROTOCOL FOR HOSTS AND GUESTS

Your Manners and Responsibilities as a Host or a Guest

Your manners on view in public strongly affect your company's image as well as your own. You should be aware of the nuances of behavior whether you are acting as a host or as a guest. Even a seemingly insignificant act, such as the way you order from the waiter, can become a strong negative in others' opinion of your executive potential and presence. A company president told me that he took one of his aspiring young executives to lunch one day—the first time he had lunched with him alone—for the purpose of telling him he was to be sent to Paris to run the small branch office there. It was a plum of a job. The president ruefully reported afterward that "by the time this young man had crumbled his roll over half the tablecloth, left his butter knife *on* the tablecloth, dipped his napkin in his water glass in order to wipe his mouth, and said 'Gimme' three times to the waiter while ordering his food, I knew this guy was not going to represent us in Paris!"

You should be sensitive to the kind of relationship you have with another individual and extend your invitations accordingly. Common sense should dictate the kind of invitation you give someone. In other words, the invitation should match your relationship with that person, as well as the goal you have in extending it, which might be as simple as getting to know that person better. The nuances of your role as host include these:

- An invitation to dinner at home would be extended to a good business friend; spouses would be included, of course. This is a very personal kind of invitation.
- You wouldn't invite someone you have just met home for dinner. A dinner party at home is one thing; an invitation to an informal meal, one-on-one at home, is quite another.
- Quite logically, if you're trying to repay someone or get business out of them, you would invite him to the nicest restaurant you can afford.

- A female executive would invite a married male executive to lunch, but not to dinner, without his spouse. An evening invitation by someone of one sex extended to a married person of the other sex and excluding the spouses is improper; even though it may be an innocent idea, it looks suspicious.
- A young executive who's new in the company wouldn't invite a senior manager to lunch. It looks pushy and like he's apple-polishing.
- If a colleague and spouse invite you and your spouse to a very modest restaurant, don't reciprocate with an invitation to a very expensive one. It might embarrass the other couple. Reciprocate in kind.
- If you offer cocktails to someone who has taken you to lunch or dinner in a first-class restaurant, you have not repaid your obligation. You should reciprocate in kind.

Restaurant Manners

Ask a restaurant owner what he considers the rudest form of customer behavior, and he will probably cite the business people who call to make firm reservations and then are "no-shows" without calling. The owner must as a result contend with empty tables and a substantial loss of revenue.

One should always cancel any dining reservation that will not be fulfilled as early as possible. If your party is going to change from one of eight people to one of five people, call the restaurant to let them know. It may very well mean they can book another table that would otherwise remain empty.

Protocol for Hosts and Guests in Restaurant Dining

From the Host's Point of View	*From the Guest's Point of View*
Who Pays	
Make it clear beforehand that *you* are paying the bill. As host, you set the date and time, make the arrangements, and pick up the bill.	If you clearly have been invited, don't argue when the check comes. You can always do the inviting and paying the next time.
Timing of the Invitation	
For non-urgent business lunch, extend the invitation at least three days beforehand, but preferably a week beforehand. A last-minute invitation sounds as though lunching with the person you have invited does not have much of a priority in your life.	Don't keep your host dangling with your response. Don't say, "I'll have to let you know," and then keep him waiting for longer than twenty-four hours. If possible, call him back with your answer the same day.

Canceling or Changing the Date

Don't change the date of your lunch unless it is absolutely necessary. If you cancel, make sure it's for a good reason, and arrange another date within a couple of days. If you must cancel, call yourself; don't have your secretary do it.

Don't cancel out of an invitation you have accepted for any reason other than a most important, urgent one. If you must cancel, call yourself; don't have your secretary do it.

Confirming

Call your guest or his secretary the morning of the lunch or dinner (or the evening before the breakfast meeting) to confirm the date, time, and place. This is to avoid any error concerning the details.

If your host hasn't called to confirm, you would be wise to call your host's office the evening before a breakfast, or the morning of a lunch or dinner, to check on the details again.

Arriving on Time

Be on time. In fact, arrive a few minutes early, so that you will be there to greet your guests (and not be greeted by them).

Be on time. It's embarrassing for anyone to have to sit alone waiting for you in a public place. Even ten minutes late is very rude in these circumstances. If you are unavoidably held up, call or have your secretary call the restaurant to inform your host of your tardiness. If you are very late, join your host and his other guests in the course they are eating. Don't order the previous courses, too, for you will slow up everyone interminably and irritate them all.

If You're the First to Arrive

If you go to your table to await your guest, don't eat bread or order a drink before he or she arrives. The table should be pristine, with napkin folded, when your guest joins you.

If you're awaiting your host at the table, don't eat or order a drink until he arrives. The table should look untouched

How Long Do You Wait for Your Luncheon Partner?

Call the office of the overdue person after fifteen minutes. If the office does not know where he is or why he is late, order yourself a drink and wait until forty minutes have gone by. Then either order lunch or call the waiter, explain your predicament, and leave if you wish, but give him a $5 to $10 tip, for you have tied up his table as a nonpaying customer for an entire lunch setting.

Taking Your Seat

If you approach your table with your guests in tow, make sure they are seated before you sit down.

If there are three or more people, don't first grab any chair and sit down. Wait until your host gestures you toward a specific seat.

Ordering

When the waiter comes for your order, have your guests' selections taken before your own. Mention the good food this restaurant is noted for. Urge them to have a first course. If they're wondering about ordering something that might be considered too expensive (like fresh oysters), if your budget will allow it, urge them to have the fresh oysters, clams, smoked salmon or any other extravagantly priced first course. If one of your guests has ordered an expensive course but no one else has, you should join him in that course. Otherwise he may feel uncomfortable.

If you are in a large group and no one else has ordered a first course, don't be the only guest to order it (particularly if your host hasn't urged you to). Perhaps everyone is too busy to take the time to have a first course. Never order one of the most expensive things on the menu unless your host has urged you to or has said something like, "I don't know about all of you, but when it comes my turn to order, I'm going to have the oysters."

When to Begin Eating and Drinking

At any meal, the host should wait until all of his guests are served before partaking of a cocktail, a sip of wine, or a bite of food.

At a larger gathering the host should urge everyone to begin eating immediately upon being served in order to preserve the quality of the cuisine.

At a small gathering, the guest of honor (seated to the right of the host) should begin eating first, once everyone is served.

At a larger gathering, if the first course is hot, the guest of honor should begin eating as soon as he is served, whether or not the host remembers to tell him to begin. If the first course is cold, he should use his judgment. If the service is slow, he may start eating before all are served.

Complaining and Criticizing

If the food is a disaster and the service terrible, don't lament this to your guests or make a scene with the waiter. Just say once to your guests, "The restaurant is not in good form tonight, I'm

Never complain about *anything*. If you have been given a chipped glass, drink out of the other side of it. If the waiter forgets your order, mention it casually to your host. Don't criticize the food. If sorry." Don't belabor the point, or your guests will become upset on your behalf, and the entire meal will be an embarrassment instead of a pleasure. Complain to the management out of earshot of your guests and write a strong, carefully worded letter the next day to the owner, stating exactly what was wrong. (*See also* Complaint Letters, Chapter 3.)

a bug crawls out of your salad, dispense with it without making anyone aware of the incident. If you are missing something like a fork, mention it casually to your host. Let *him* deal with the waiter. The guest is not supposed to call the waiter to the table.

The Unwritten Rules of Restaurant Behavior

- Be careful to conform to the dress code, if there is one. If people are not allowed to wear jeans, and if men are required to wear jackets and ties, don't try to force the management into making an exception in your case. One should dress appropriately according to the restaurant, some of which have high prices and a formal atmosphere that the clientele happens to like.
- *The host should have his restaurant seating thought out ahead of time,* so that things are done properly and there isn't an awkward confusing time with people standing in the aisles, obstructing the waiters, while the host makes up his mind where people will sit.

  If there is a bad seat at the table, such as in the path of the kitchen's swinging door or in the center of a terrible draft, the host automatically should occupy it, so as not to penalize a guest.

  If there are armchairs and side chairs, the host should give his guests the armchairs.

  A host should always give the banquette to his guests. If a couple is entertaining another couple, for example, the host and his or her spouse should take the outside chairs and put the guest couple next to each other on the banquette (rather than seat both women on the banquette, with both men in the outside chairs). The best seats *always* go to the guests.

  The male host should sit across from the female guest, and the female host across from the male guest. It makes for better conversation.

  A handicapped person or someone with a weight problem should be given the outside seats, simply because it is easier to get in and out of them.
- When spouses are present, the executives should remember not to talk business exclusively during the meal, thus boring the other half of the group. A person who is incapable of talking about anything but business gives the others a case of heartburn. (*See* The Art of Conversation, Chapter 3.)

- Boisterousness and raucous laughter may mean you are having a good time, but they constitute selfish behavior that intrudes on other paying customers around you.
- Table-hopping is considered obnoxious by most of the restaurant's clientele and most certainly by all of the restaurant's waiters, whose service is obstructed. This kind of behavior shows the person feels a need to be conspicuous; it is a sign of a basic inferiority complex, rather than popularity.
- A person who talks constantly on the telephone in those restaurants that bring the telephone to one's table may think he looks like a big shot, but the real impression made on others is exactly the opposite. (Most powerful executives inobtrusively use the public telephones in restaurants.)
- Combing, smoothing, or even touching the hair in a restaurant is, of course, improper.
- If there is an *overly slow eater,* for the sake of the other guests who may be anxious about the hour, the host should say, "I hope you don't mind if I have the waiter bring the next course. There are some people at this table who have a tight schedule today." When the slow eater receives this signal, he should either step up his pace or skip a course, so that he will be finishing at the same time as the others.
- One of the most insulting things you can do to your host and to the restaurant is to *ask for catsup when the main dish is a piece of high quality meat or fowl,* cooked with an exquisite sauce by a real gourmet chef.
- If you have to get up at the table to go to the telephone, excuse yourself, fold your napkin neatly, and leave it in your chair. Do *not* throw it on the table while you're gone. Push your chair back into the table before you leave.
- *A woman should never leave her handbag on the table.* For one thing, it looks terrible; for another, it is very unsanitary.
- Don't leave a briefcase on the table—or a lot of files.
- *A thoughtful host preorders the dinner for a group of ten or more.* Otherwise ordering the dinner becomes a logistical nightmare, with everyone ordering different things and eating different courses. Both guests and staff become impatient with the delays.

There is an increase in the number of people who don't eat meat. Because of this, the host who has preordered dinner should ask at the beginning of the meal, once everyone has taken his seat at the table, "Is there anyone present who doesn't eat meat?" If there is, then the host should summon the waiter and ask for a substitute vegetarian platter.

Tips on Tipping

Tipping is an integral part of the entertainment and service industries. Many people feel that poor service in a restaurant requires no reward whatsoever, and logically they are right. But I believe you should tip anyway, since the tip is often an important part of that employee's salary.

If you tip after having insolent, indifferent, or inefficient service, you can always resolve never to return. The best way to handle this is to write a polite letter to management detailing exactly why the service or food was unacceptable. The management of that place needs to hear that, so you are doing everyone a service by bringing it to their attention. (*See* Complaint Letters, page 109.) On the other hand, if the service you received was really exceptional, it's a nice gesture to write management a note of appreciation in addition to leaving a tip.

Here are two formulas for tipping, one in a modest, one in an expensive restaurant:

Modest Restaurant	*Expensive Restaurant*
Give the waiter 15 percent of total bill. There is no captain or maître d'hôtel to worry about, just your waiter and the owner.	Give 20 percent of the total bill; break down this sum into 75 percent for the waiter, and 25 percent for the captain of your table (the one who supervises the waiter and busboy assigned to your table and attends to any complicated service, such as fileting a fish or flaming a dish at your table).
There is no wine steward to worry about. Your waiter pours your wine.	Give the sommelier (wine steward) a tip of from $3 to $5 per bottle, or in a very posh restaurant, 15 percent of the cost of the wine.
There is no attendant to worry about.	Tip ladies' room attendant $1 per woman guest using the facilities.
Tip coatroom attendant fifty cents to seventy-five cents per coat.	Tip coatroom attendant $1 per coat.
There is no doorman.	Tip doorman $1 for summoning your car or getting you a taxi.
Tip garage attendant from fifty cents to $1.	Tip garage attendant $1 or $2 for bringing your car to the front.

Invitation Diplomacy

Not Attending After Accepting/Sending a Substitute Guest

It is a sad fact of life that people today will accept something as important as a dinner invitation and then decide not to go at the last minute, without notifying anyone. Often such a person thinks that the dinner to which he has been invited is a large buffet affair and that therefore his absence will not be noted. Often he is wrong; it may well be a seated affair, and if he is high-ranking himself, he will have been placed between two other high-ranking people who now will have to share an empty chair between them. His host will notice that empty chair, too, as though it had a spotlight upon it.

When you commit to a party, you should go, unless you notify your hosts immediately.

It is equally rude, if you decide not to attend a business function, to send a substitute without notifying your hosts. You may have had a very special seat at the dinner reserved for you, and if you send a junior executive simply to fill up the table, you may be committing a gross error. There are functions at which it is perfectly all right to send junior people (who like to have a reason to get dressed in evening clothes and go out to a free dinner), but you should know what you're doing before dispatching a substitute.

If at the last minute you cannot attend a dinner you had accepted, call your host's office, transmit your apologies to the host, and ask "if it would help matters" if you sent someone from your office in your place. Give your host the opportunity to digest his or her disappointment at your last-minute cancellation and then to decide whether there is someone in his or her company who should fill your place at the table. (The host probably would rather fill in with one of his own people than with a low echelon person from your office.)

When You Have Not Been Invited

No one's business career has been ruined by failing to be invited to a party. However, many careers have been ruined by overanxious people trying to get themselves invited to a particular party. A person who pushes his way into obtaining an invitation may be momentarily successful in reaching his goal, but in the long run his actions are usually self-destructive.

Investigate if you think it was only a clerical error that kept you from receiving an invitation. Ask a friend who was invited to inquire casually of the secretary of the host if your name was on the guest list. If it was not, don't try to put it there. Nothing makes a worse impression than an executive "operating" to get himself invited to a function where his presence is not a priority.

Inviting the Boss and Being the Boss's Guest

It is pretentious of a junior person to invite the boss and his or her spouse to dinner—unless the junior person knows them well.

You put your boss on the spot by asking him to dinner "anytime—you name the date, any night." It's the wrong thing to do. If you have known your boss all your life, of course, and you have been to his house for dinner, you have a right to ask him to dinner. However, the fewer who know about it, the better. You should not discuss it around the office (nor should the boss's secretary), because it will make your peers jealous.

If you have invited your boss and his spouse to a meal and both are much older than you and your spouse, you might invite another couple nearer their age, along with your own friends (outside the office). They will enjoy the younger group, but having one other couple of their own vintage will make an even better bonding of the group.

If you have worked in your job for a year or more, and if you don't know your boss socially, you may certainly invite him and his spouse to a cocktail party you and your spouse are hosting. Your boss can easily regret your invitation; if he and his wife accept, it is not as personal a commitment on their part as the acceptance of a dinner invitation would be.

Sometimes a junior executive and his or her spouse are repeatedly on the receiving end of the boss's invitations to dinner parties. If you are singled out like this, it means that you give a lot in social situations and help make the party work. Again, it's not wise to talk about these invitations around the office.

You need not feel you must invite back your boss and spouse each time you are invited there for cocktails or dinner. You are not expected to return the invitation, because you have been helping them entertain—you have been rendering them a service.

Even if you have been "working" each time at the boss's party, you should still send a thank-you note soon afterward. It's the polite thing to do.

Does the Executive or His Wife Do the Inviting?

In arranging an evening dinner date between couples, there is often great confusion over whether the wife of one executive should call the wife of the other, or whether one should extend the invitation to the other executive and ask him or her to pass it on to his or her spouse. It is particularly confusing if a female executive is issuing the invitation. Should she call her colleague's wife, whom she may not know, or should her colleague transmit the invitation to his wife?

Some thoughts on the subject:

- If you do not know your colleague's wife, it is easier to invite the executive to lunch during the week and forget about getting spouses together. However, if you have met the executive's spouse, it may be helpful to your career if you ask the two of them as a couple to dinner.
- Always invite the spouse if you are extending an invitation for an evening or weekend engagement.
- If your spouse will be with you and the executive you invite for dinner is single, ask if he would like to bring a guest along. (The word *guest* sounds a lot better than *date*.) Don't try to arrange a date for him if he is single (this applies equally to a single woman); it is far better to have an evening with a comfortable threesome than an uptight foursome!
- If the person you are inviting for dinner is from out of town and you have important business to discuss, it would still be very rude of you not to include the visitor's spouse, even if your own spouse will not be with you. She (or he) should not be left to languish in a hotel room while you and the visiting executive enjoy a business dinner.
- A female executive and male client or associate, both of whom are married, invite gossip and criticism if they are seen in public dining alone together in their hometown. They should do their business at lunchtime instead. If they are both in *another* city on business, their dinner date is quite another matter. Dining while on the road should not invite malicious gossip.

An Invitation to a Single Person Does Not Automatically Imply "Bring a Date"

An executive should bring a date to a party only if he has been asked by his hosts to do so, or if he has requested to do so and the request has been granted.

If the invitation you receive has your name on it and the additional words "and guest," you may certainly bring along someone, but you should let your host's office know the name of that someone. It is really rude to show up with a date unless it has been cleared beforehand by your hosts. You may have been invited by your hosts as a badly needed single man or single woman.

Some single people think it is perfectly all right to show up at a cocktail party with a date (or even with members of their family). If the place where the party is being given is small, the host may have had to pare down his or her guest list carefully. Your showing up with someone who was not invited can cause hostility in your beleaguered host's mind.

In other words, never take anything for granted. *Ask* beforehand. Your host or your host's secretary will probably be very frank with you about whether or not it is all right to bring along someone.

Important: If the invitation is to a *meal,* don't even ask to bring a guest.

When a Married Executive Takes a Date to a Company Function

One of the quickest ways in which a married executive can lose a fine reputation and attract negative attention is to appear at a company function with someone other than his spouse as a date. It doesn't matter whether the party is a retirement get-together for "good old Jerry" or a black-tie supper following the opening of the opera; the other company spouses feel uncomfortable, and an atmosphere of hostility builds in defense of the missing spouse.

No matter how free-thinking our society may have become in certain quarters, American business is basically conservative. The heads of institutions and businesses are expected to comport themselves in public with dignity—and flaunting a lover is undignified behavior.

The executive and his or her lover have many other options to be together, removed from the spotlight of the corporate world. An executive having trouble with his or her marriage should either show up without a date at a corporate function or not show up at all. (*See also* When Mates Come Along, in Chapter 6.)

When Your Guests Won't Go Home

Some people just don't know when to go home. They may have had too much to drink, or they may be lonely and feel comfortable in a convivial group for the first time in a long time. Whatever the reason, they should not penalize their hosts. Guests who won't go home should be gently prodded to go home, even if it's a Saturday night. Most people must spend precious free time in activity rather than sleep the next day.

It's simple to handle departures if the party is in a restaurant. The host calls for the check and settles it away from the guests. His actions mean he obviously is calling it a night. Usually the guests begin to stir when the host returns and says something like, "Well, I guess it's time to let these good people clear off the table and finish for the night."

At home it is more awkward. As a host you may feel you can't push an exit button for your guests, but you may certainly take the initiative in gently and graciously ushering them out of your home.

If you have an official guest of honor, someone like an elected official or a foreign dignitary, that person is supposed to know his protocol and be the first guest to leave. At an eight o'clock dinner in Washington and most other cities, eleven o'clock is a good hour (during the week) for the official guest of honor to depart, giving the signal for the others to follow almost immediately after.

If you have no official guest of honor, or if you have one that does not know his protocol, you, the host, can rise from your chair and in a very cheery manner, proclaim, "It's late. I'm sure everyone wants to be able to get through tomorrow. Let's all get some rest!"

If you, the host, do urge your guests out the door at an early hour, it helps if you have prewarned all of them that it will be an early evening because you have so much to do afterward. If you warn them in advance, and if you get them going with great cheer, they will likely be very grateful to you for getting them home at a decent hour.

Toasting

Toasting is an art. Some people are born hams; they make good toasters. Others are nervous wrecks when they know they have to make a toast. (They shouldn't *have to*.)

If you are a good toaster, you should do it often, because it flatters the person or people you are toasting—your host(s) or the guest(s) of honor.

A good toast is an essential part of a really successful business meal when a special guest is present, whether that guest is the mayor or someone with whom your corporation wants to do business. Here are some things to remember:

- A toast should be light and short. Three minutes is maximum; one minute is often better.
- *Timing is everything.*
    People should have wine or champagne in their glasses.
    Waiters shouldn't be noisily clattering around—the toaster should wait until things have quieted down in the room.
    The best time is usually after dessert has been served, when the wineglasses have been refilled, or when the champagne has just been poured.
    The toast should not be made too late—when people are already starting to get up from the table.
- Protocol must be observed. If the host plans on giving a toast, he or she will not welcome a junior executive popping up in the middle of the meat course and prematurely toasting either the hosts or the guest of honor. The host should have the prerogative of making the first toast.
- If it looks as though no one is going to give a toast, toward the end of the dessert, the executive who wants to toast the host or guest of honor or

both should whisper to the host, "Would you mind if I raised a toast?" Most hosts will say, "Yes, please do."

- If you're desirous of getting on your feet but you've had several drinks, restrain yourself. People who are tipsy make very unfortunate, sloppy toasts.
- Never give an off-color toast. A story that is great when related in the locker room may be offensive in mixed company at a dinner table.
- Never belittle the host or guest of honor. A toast is never a time for putting someone down, even if you can be terribly funny while you're doing it. A toast should build someone up, not make fun of him.
- If you're the guest of honor, you should respond at once to a flattering toast from your host or anyone else. You should thank your hosts, and say something pleasant:

> "Thank you, George, for those warm words of welcome. And, Grace, you have given us an absolutely superb dinner tonight. It's nice to come home to Cincinnati. I had almost forgotten that this is where really great food, fine conversation, and wonderful friends combine at table. I thank you all for being around this table tonight to welcome me home. And, George and Grace, I raise a toast to you for helping make Cincinnati the great city that it is!"

If you can be amusing, so much the better.

- If you are making a toast, you should rise at your place. Generally, the other guests do not have to rise when they raise their glasses, because it is clumsy and difficult to do so. If the person being honored and toasted is someone like an official from a foreign company, a general, judge, ambassador, or a very elderly distinguished person, then all the guests should rise at table to toast him.
- A toast is not a time to make a political statement or any other kind of serious statement. Some people are so excited to be holding an audience captive that they start expounding on everything from foreign affairs to the latest city scandal. A toast should be light, warm, and short. It is no time for philosophizing.
- If you are having lunch or dinner as guests of someone in a restaurant, it is nice if you raise your glass informally to your host, remaining seated as you do so:

> "Jan, I think we owe you a toast for having organized this delightful lunch. You've given us a wonderful time, a delicious meal, and we are all grateful!"

- If someone raises a toast and you have no wine left in your glass, raise your glass as a gesture and pretend to drink. If you never had a wineglass, raise your water glass.

· When the host or guest of honor has been toasted, raise your glass and look that person in the eye and nod your head in a sort of bow before sipping. If two people were toasted, raise your glass and look at first one and then the other before you take a sip.

· It's nice also to turn to each of your dinner partners separately, raising your glass and nodding, then sipping, at the conclusion of the *first* toast of the evening.

Canceling a Party

Sometimes a party has to be canceled. The host may be ill, the weather may make travel extremely hazardous, it may be a time of national mourning when it would be bad taste to entertain, the guest of honor may suddenly be called away, the company may have suffered serious financial losses and feel it unwise to commit to such a major expense, etc.

A cancellation clause is inevitably built into all contracts with outside suppliers for the event, including the food and beverage service and the entertainment. (The consumer protection laws governing cancellation differ from city to city.) Usually no penalty is due for the hotel, restaurant, or caterer if you inform them of the cancellation several months prior to the event. However, if the caterer or banquet manager has your party booked for a certain night and is unable to schedule another party into that slot, you must pay a certain percentage of the total amount contracted for (and sometimes all of the amount). Carefully read any contract with a hotel, caterer, or restaurant owner before signing it. The matter of cancellation penalties will be spelled out. Once you sign the contract, you should be prepared to pay them.

As for the musicians and entertainers you may have contracted for, local union rules help determine the number of days within which one can cancel without penalty. Some regulations require only forty-eight hours' notice, some five days, some even more. A company that books the entertainers for its corporate party through a production company (such as Ray Bloch Productions in New York) may get a better deal for the company host in cancellation clauses than if the company books the entertainers directly—unless, of course, there is a proficient meeting planner on staff who knows how to negotiate entertainers' contracts to advantage.

Sometimes it is the entertainer who will want to get out of his or her contract in order to accept a lucrative television commercial or movie deal. The entertainment contract should lay requirements on the entertainer, too, requiring 120 days notice before canceling out on the company party.

One of the nicest stories I ever heard about canceling a party concerned a corporation that had planned an expensive dinner for over a hundred prominent guests. On the morning of the dinner, the chairman of the board died of a heart attack. The president, out of respect for the deceased, called off the dinner. Since all of the food had either been prepared or was in the process of being prepared, the caterer was ordered to complete its preparation. That night the food and the formally clad waiters were sent to a large home for the elderly, where the residents probably ate the greatest feast of their lives. The local newspaper printed two lead editorials the next morning, one eulogizing the late chairman of the board and the other praising the company for its touching gesture toward the elderly in a very difficult moment.

Alcohol: To Serve or Not to Serve

People who are invited to a business meal outside the office usually expect to be offered something to drink—a cocktail before and perhaps wine with the meal.

For those numerous executives who are against alcohol on religious grounds, perhaps an event arranged for the breakfast, lunch, or teatime hours is the most suitable, because alcohol does not have to be served at those times.

Every host is entitled to decree that there will be no liquor or wines served, but even if he does not drink himself, it is gracious of him to offer a glass of wine or sherry before the meal or some wine with the meal.

Remember when entertaining Arabs and other Moslems in your home, that although they may not drink in their own countries, in this country they sometimes do. Ask them, "What would you like to drink?" and wait for an answer. Don't assume they want only soda. (I shall always remember the attractive Arab who confided to me that the "only soda" he ever liked was a "chocolate ice cream soda, with rum to flavor it.")

Fortunately, in spite of the rise of cases of alcoholism in this country, especially among women and young people, our understanding of this disease is growing, too, and so are the laws controlling the consumption of alcohol.

When entertaining, a corporate host wants to insure his guests' enjoyment, but he does not want to endanger their physical welfare. Getting everyone "smashed" should never be a corporate goal in entertaining; it has never been the sign of a successful party, only of a miserable one.

On the subject of drinking, it is wise to remember the following:

- *It's the company's duty to keep the allotted time for drinking at a minimum.* A cocktail party really does not have to be longer than an hour and a half. Always arrange to cut off the bar thirty minutes after the hour the party was scheduled to end.
- *If a guest has obviously overindulged in alcohol and is driving a car,* it's

the host's responsibility to have that person taken home by another means.

- *If a man or woman becomes the unwelcome object of an inebriated executive's sexual advances,* the latter should be fended off good-naturedly; help should be obtained from someone at the party if the offender becomes too hard to handle.

- *If a guest is obstreperous at a company function, regardless of his high position, he should be removed from the gathering.* Someone from the company should be assigned to accompany that person home. A loud, abusive person at a party ruins the enjoyment of every single person present.

- *Invite a guest with a drinking problem to functions where liquor is not served.* This is a time to be creative. An important client with a drinking problem should be entertained with events like afternoon baseball games or tennis tournament finals, where everyone is drinking only soft drinks. Invite him to morning coffee after viewing an exhibit or a new installation together. Take him to a mid-afternoon screening of a movie, where popcorn and sodas are served. Invite him to tea at four in the afternoon.

Entertaining a Recovering Alcoholic

Care should be taken in selecting the menu of recipes when a recovering alcoholic will be among your guests. Wines and liqueurs that burn off in the cooking process are harmless; wines and liqueurs poured at random over food might seriously upset the rehabilitation of the recovering alcoholic.

Examples of harmful things to do are pouring Kirsch over fresh raspberries or dousing a Crème Brûlée dessert with brandy. The correct way to handle the serving of a sauce containing alcohol is to pass it separately and to make sure that everyone knows it has alcohol in it. Don't pour vodka over fruit sherbet, for example. Pass the vodka separately in a small decanter and tell your guests what it is. The recovering alcoholic will not touch it. If it's already been splashed over his dessert, he might innocently consume it (which could result in a terrible setback in his fight against alcoholism).

When an associate returns from long difficult weeks spent in a recovering alcoholics program, he or she does not want to be treated differently from anyone else, nor made to feel conspicuous. However, when a recovering alcoholic wants to talk about his problem on a one-to-one basis, it's the time to listen with full attention. (A party is usually not the place for such a conversation.)

Too many times a host will greet a recovering alcoholic at the door of his or her home during a party and say something thoughtless like this: "You're not allowed to drink now, are you? What kind of soda do you want?"

The conversation should go like this instead: "What would you like to drink?" When you bring the soda or fruit juice or whatever it is (sometimes coffee) to this guest, it should be served in one of your prettiest glasses.

If an alcoholic says at your party, "I'd like a gin and tonic," give it to him without comment. It is, after all, the alcoholic's personal business to indicate what he or she wants.

The place setting of a recovering alcoholic guest should be the same as everyone else's at the table, including wineglasses. Do not turn his wineglass upside down (nor should any guest, for that matter, turn his own glass upside down when he comes to the table). When the wine is being poured, the universal sign of not wanting any served is to put the fingertips on the rim of the glass—a gesture that signifies either "None, thank you" or "No more, thank you." A recovering alcoholic may also allow his glass to be filled with wine and then not touch it through the entire meal (a true show of the strength of his willpower).

When toasting time occurs at a dinner party, the recovering alcoholic will take his water glass and toast along with the others or, if he's superstitious about toasting with water, as some people are, he might raise his arm in a gesture of holding a glass—a kind of salute.

One of the best toasts I ever heard was made by a recovering alcoholic at a dinner honoring the retiring chairman of the board of his company. He gave a brilliant four-minute speech that had everyone on their feet laughing and crying at the same time. No one noticed he was holding only a glass of water in his hand—that was irrelevant.

Party Smoking Manners
for the Host and Guests

There are those who will not permit any smoking in their home. It is their prerogative. They are certainly free to establish such a ban, but their smoking guests may consider it totally antisocial. It is unkind to confront a heavy smoker in your home with the fact that he will have to suffer through a smoke-free evening. He might have preferred not to have come at all, if he had known of your policy. Therefore, warn your guests when you invite them: "By the way, I thought I'd better tell you. We don't smoke in our house. I hope you don't mind." If the person is a real nicotine addict, he would rather do anything than spend an evening in your home not smoking. So give him the option of regretting your invitation.

There are those who don't like smoking but who permit their guests to do it. A host is no longer obliged to have cigarettes to offer guests all over his home. He no longer has to put them on his dining room table, although for smokers he should have ashtrays, to use after dessert when everyone is sitting at table. Some hosts ask their smoking guests to wait until after dinner, when they are sent into a special room or ushered out of doors in good weather, to smoke in communal warmth.

Smoking Manners for the Guest

If there are no ashtrays in evidence in your host's home, you should ask permission to smoke before lighting a cigarette. You will probably be given an ashtray, or if your host is a dedicated non-smoker, you will be asked to go outside to smoke. ("Outside" might put you in a garden, on a lawn, in an apartment corridor, or on a New York apartment fire escape!) Don't smell up your host's bathroom by locking yourself into it with your cigarette. It will smell of smoke for days, exceedingly unpleasant for the other people. Even if your host is relaxed about smoking, *don't light up at the table until after everyone has finished or almost finished dessert.*

Wherever you smoke at a party, be careful of your ashes littering, and watch your smoke. Blow it away from people's faces. If you are sitting in an air-conditioning draft, be careful where your smoke is streaming; it might require your shifting your position in your seat to be able to control the stream.

I have yet to see anyone turn down a very polite, apologetic person sitting next to him who asks, "Would you mind *very* much if I smoke?" That courtesy is important for a smoker to remember when seated at dinner in a public place, like a hotel or restaurant.

Unless a restaurant table is in a segregated "No Smoking" area, people sitting at that table feel they have a constitutional right to smoke at the end of the meal if they want to. Just as it is reprehensible for someone in a social situation to blow smoke in non-smokers' faces, it is also wrong for a non-smoker in a social situation to make a scene about someone's smoking. The non-smoker who loses his temper can ruin the lunch or the dinner very quickly for the host—and for the other guests.

I am reproducing here the dialogue between two men who sat next to me at a lunch for security analysts and press in a New York restaurant the other day.

> Guest to man who has just lit a cigarette: "For God's sake, put that thing out!"
> Smoker, stunned at this outburst: "You have no right to order *me* around."
> Non-smoker, in an exceedingly nasty tone: "I bloody well do. I don't have to sit here and inhale something that kills people!"
> Smoker: "My cigarette smoke is hardly going to kill you."
> Non-smoker: "It certainly is. Put it out!"
> Smoker: "I will not. If you hate it so much, why don't you leave?"

Non-smoker: "I sure will." He gets up, throws his napkin down on his chair in disgust, and with flaming red cheeks, turns to his host and says, "Sorry, I must leave." He departs.

If the non-smoker had turned to the smoker and said in an earnest, polite, and apologetic tone that smoke disturbed him greatly, and would the smoker "mind terribly waiting to smoke until later?" the smoker most likely would have said, "Of course, I'm very sorry," and a confrontation that embarrassed the host and the rest of us who were present would not have occurred.

Cigar Manners

The primary rule of cigar etiquette is that *a guest should not even attempt to smoke a cigar in someone's home or in a restaurant unless his host either offers him a cigar or urges him to smoke his own.*

No one should smoke a cigar while people are eating, because the strong odor of the smoke makes many feel ill when it mixes with the odors of food.

In a restaurant:

- A cigar should not be lit until after everyone at the table has finished eating.
- A cigar should not be lit until after everyone at the nearby tables has finished eating (and all are sipping coffee or drinking).
- A cigar should not be lit unless the host has given the signal and unless the permission has been asked and granted of the diner's neighbors at the table.
- A host should not light up his own cigar without offering one to his male guests.

At home:

- A guest in the home of non-smokers should not even try to smoke a cigar; it would be considered totally offensive.
- If a host is offering cigars to his guest, he should offer them at the end of the meal and suggest that the cigar smokers retire (for the duration of their cigar) to another area—another room or an open area like the patio. Anyone who wishes to join them—and their smoke—would, of course, be at liberty to do so. After their cigar, they would rejoin the rest of the group.
- When cigars are being passed, either in a restaurant or in a home, a woman whose husband or friend is a cigar smoker and who is absent from that social function may certainly take a cigar for him. She can explain that she is not a closet cigar smoker but has taken one for her husband.

The considerate host keeps windows open around cigar smokers, and the considerate cigar smoker blows his smoke in any direction other than someone else's face.

A word about butts: A cigar smoker should personally take care of disposing of his cigar butt and not leave it around in an ashtray. A cigar butt is probably the worst kind of visual pollution!

The Use of Drugs at a Party

Illegal drugs are evil. Using them is also a federal offense. As a host, you have the right and the duty to stop drug use; as a guest, you have the right to leave the scene. There is no *drug etiquette.*

If you are a guest, just make an excuse, whether it's suddenly not feeling well or having an important deadline to meet before tomorrow morning, and depart. Don't deliver a lecture. The party will go downhill from here on; you do not have to witness that and be bored stiff by the behavior of people who are not in charge of themselves.

As a host, when one of your guests starts to use or distribute drugs at your party, it is your responsibility to tell that person either to stop it at once or to leave. Again, refrain from lecturing on the subject of drug abuse. Just say in your own words that you don't want marijuana smoked at your party or "We don't use cocaine in this house. If you feel you have to have it, please leave."

It is important that you be counted as someone who stands up to the tragic trend that takes hold of people at parties when their defenses are down. Drug addiction often begins around someone else's coffee table. It is doubly ironic to see social use of controlled substances that can maim, cause brain damage, and kill human beings tied to the social lives of people in business and the professions.

In time potential drug abusers might begin to notice that it is only the losers who take drugs, that the really attractive, bright people—the leaders—do not take drugs. Then it won't be the smart thing to do anymore.

9

Invitations
and Their Replies

A business invitation should not only make the recipient look forward to attending a function, it should also reflect the image of the sender in a very good light. What constitutes good taste in the design of an invitation is relative, of course, because what is effective for a cosmetics manufacturer may not be effective for a bank, and vice versa.

The overall appearance of the invitation is obviously important. Its size, colors, graphic design—even its texture—must all work together to achieve the desired effect. Most importantly, an invitation should communicate perfectly the nature of the event. It should also be mailed sufficiently far in advance, preferably four weeks. (A reminder card sent two weeks before is an added attendance aid.)

Invitation etiquette is the responsibility of both the host and the recipient. How an executive responds to an invitation is as important and says as much about him as the quality of the invitation he or his company sends out.

It is sad that there are so many invitations passing through the mails today that are sloppy, inaccurate, and badly phrased. Today's top managers seem to be unaware of the errors or the lack of good communication in their expensive invitations. It is important for the person in charge to know the right way to invite people on behalf of his company so that he can judge whether an invitation to be sent out by his company is correct or not.

359

"Save the Date" Cards

It makes sense, if you are hosting a large, important function that out-of-town business colleagues and customers will be attending, to let them know the date well ahead of time. This enables them to schedule your company's affair in their agendas and keeps them from accepting a conflicting engagement.

A "Save the Date" announcement, sent to your entire guest list, is usually printed on a card with matching envelope. (More informally and less expensively, the message may be printed on one side of a postcard.)

Ideally, the designer of the invitation also designs the "Save the Date" announcement, in a format and color scheme identical to the invitation to follow. The text of two sample "Save the Date" cards follow:

A dinner in honor of
The Governor of the State of Ohio
will be given by
The President and Board of Trustees
of Kenyon College
in Gambier
on Friday, October seventh
Details will follow

Please hold the date of
Saturday, July fifteenth,
for a dinner in honor of
Justin Squires
in Pittsburgh
(Invitations to be mailed later)
/s/ Anthony McGee
CHEMCORO INC.

The Invitation and Its Parts

In the sample given here you see the ten elements that go into an effective, properly worded invitation.

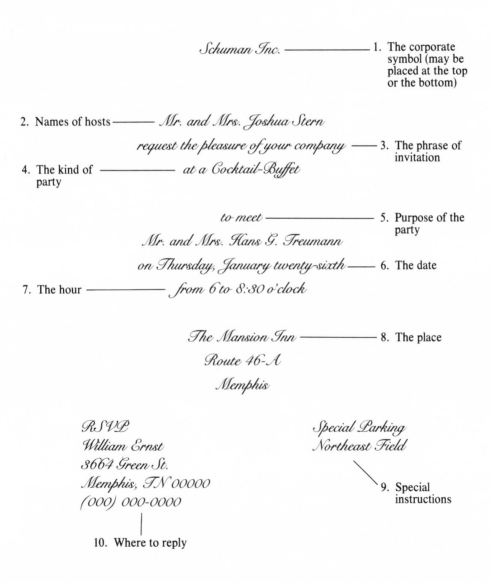

Schuman Inc. —————— 1. The corporate symbol (may be placed at the top or the bottom)

2. Names of hosts ——— *Mr. and Mrs. Joshua Stern*

request the pleasure of your company —— 3. The phrase of invitation

4. The kind of ——————— *at a Cocktail-Buffet*
   party

to meet —————————— 5. Purpose of the party

Mr. and Mrs. Hans G. Treumann

on Thursday, January twenty-sixth ——— 6. The date

7. The hour ——————— *from 6 to 8:30 o'clock*

The Mansion Inn ————— 8. The place

Route 46-A

Memphis

RSVP   *Special Parking*
William Ernst   *Northeast Field*
3664 Green St.
Memphis, TN 00000
(000) 000-0000   9. Special instructions

10. Where to reply

The Company Name, Symbol, or Logo as It Appears on Invitations

- When the company name is part of the logo on the invitation, or if it is included in the RSVP address *on* the invitation itself, it does not have to be repeated in the body of the text. For example, if "Managers Inc." is part of the logo, the host's name on the invitation would read: "Alicia Freer, Chairman," not "Alicia Freer, Chairman, Managers Inc."
- The company's address, ZIP code, and telephone number should be included somewhere on the invitation or RSVP—usually as part of the RSVP information.

Hosts' Names and How to List Them

Many invitations cross our desks today with only the name of the corporation as the host. The effect is cold and impersonal. One always wonders, "Isn't there anyone within that organization who is hosting the event?" In other words, a corporation doesn't host a party; *a person or people within the organization* do.

- Give the host's name and company title on the invitation:

> SMITHTEL
> Henry Greco, Chairman
> cordially invites you to, etc.

- On occasion, a group of people will be named as the hosts:

> The Board of Directors
> of the SMITHTEL CORPORATION
> requests the pleasure of your company
> etc.

- When there are two hosts, their names and company titles may be placed horizontally or vertically in order of their rank.

> SMITHTEL
> Henry Greco, Chairman   James William, President
> request the pleasure of your company
> etc.

> SMITHTEL
> Henry Greco, Chairman
> James Williams, President
> cordially invite you to
> etc.

• The names of three hosts may appear vertically listed or in a triangular form, as shown here. (When one of the hosts has a title, as in the case of the doctor, all hosts must be given a title.)

Mr. Robert A. Lee   Ms. Suzanne D. Ford
Chairman, Major Foods   Chairman, Allied Foods

Dr. Hanning Rosenhaupt
Chairman, Department of Nutrition
Ellingford University

cordially invite you to a seminar, etc.

NOTE: In this example, the two corporate hosts who are paying for the party are listed first; the nonprofit sector representative (Dr. Rosenhaupt) is listed as a host for the sake of public relations, since his name lends authority.

• When there are a number of hosts of more or less the same rank, they are listed alphabetically. Note the sample invitation given on page 364. (The hosts' names appear following that of the guest of honor.)

Spouses as Hosts of a Business Event

• When an executive and spouse are jointly hosting an event, it is important to include the executive's company title, as in the following:

Mr. John Allison, President of ACORN Inc.
and Mrs. Allison

Mr. Bennett Barton, Chairman of SURETY Inc.
and Mrs. Barton

Ms. Jacqueline Dearman, Vice-President of ERCO
and Mr. George Dearman
request the pleasure of your company, etc.

• When a couple hosts a party for the wife's business associates and she works under her own name, she would be wise to put her name first on

(Logo of)

The Alliance for
Italo-American Trade

In Honor of H. E. Dott. Giuseppe Maroni
Minister of Foreign Trade for the
Republic of Italy
Giovanni Amarillo, The Buitoni Company
Teodoro Bosco, The Fante Group
Maria Cadoro, Cadoro Jewelry
Tomasso Dantini, Dantina Tessuti Importers
Pietro Pasquale, Fiat/New York

request the pleasure of your company
at cocktails
Tuesday, March 23rd
6 to 8 p.m.
The Rainbow Room
Rockefeller Center
New York City

RSVP
Mrs. Corloni
Società Azzurra
234 Park Avenue
New York, NY 00000
(212) 000-0000

the invitation, so that her business associate guests will understand that it is indeed her party. For example:

Anne Smith

and John Brown

request the pleasure of your company

at cocktails

in honor of Timothy Breward

and the publication of his new book

Anne Smith Designs

Thursday, June 21st

etc.

- If the wife of the executive host has an important official position and will play an active cohosting role, protocol decrees that her name should come before his on an invitation, for example:

    The Honorable Louise C. Mills and Mr. John Mills, etc.

    However, when John Mills gives a party that is really for his business only and his wife will attend, but not in a working capacity, the invitations should read:

    Mr. John Mills and the Honorable Louise Mills, etc.

- If a married couple, both doctors, hosts a party for a medical group, they could be listed either as "The Doctors Reed" or as "Dr. Harold C. Reed and Dr. Anne G. Reed."

The Phrase Used for Inviting

The phrase that does the actual inviting may be worded in several ways. The most common are listed below. (I prefer the first two.)

- "request(s) the pleasure of your company at"
- "cordially invite(s) you to"
- "request(s) your presence at"
- "invite(s) you to"
- "request(s) the honor (or honour) of your presence" (used only for the most formal of occasions, such as when you are hosting the mayor or governor or a foreign dignitary)

The Type of Party

The type of function being held goes on the line below the phrase used for inviting. (The preposition used will depend on the phrasing of the preceding line.) For example:

- "at dinner" (used with "request the pleasure of your company")
- "to dinner" (less formal, used with "invite you to . . .")
- "at lunch"
- "to lunch" (less formal)
- "to a reception"
- "to a breakfast"
- "to dinner and dancing afterward"
- "to tea and a press announcement"

Guest of Honor and Purpose of Party

The reason for the party and the guest of honor's name would go below the kind of party line. For example:

- "in honor of" (or more formally, "in honour of")
- "to meet so-and-so"
- "to mark the fiftieth anniversary of"
- "to celebrate the opening of"
- "on the occasion of"
- "to inaugurate"
- "to launch"
- "to introduce the new line"
- "in celebration of"

The name of the guest of honor may be communicated in any of several ways:

- By writing the name, underlined, in the upper left hand corner of the invitation
- By writing it in the middle of the invitation text:

at dinner
in honor of Anne Sert, Ph.D.
Winner of the Nobel Prize for Science

(See also the illustration of the formal dinner invitation. p. 373.)
- By writing the honoree's name and some information on his or her background on a separate insert for the invitation

The Date

The date of the party appears on the next line of the invitation:

- "on Wednesday, the tenth of June" *(formal)*
- "on Wednesday, June tenth" *(less formal)*
- "on Wednesday, June 10th" *(least formal)*

Never abbreviate the day of the week (e.g., "Wed."), no matter how informal the invitation may be.

The year is usually omitted, unless it is important, such as in an invitation marking a special anniversary. For example:

to lunch
to mark the 100th anniversary of *Owens Mills*
founded September 1, 1887

Monday, September 1, 1987
at one o'clock

The Hour

The time goes on the line below the date:

- "at seven-thirty o'clock" *(formal)*
- "at 7:30 o'clock" *(less formal)*
- "at 7:30 P.M." *(least formal)*

In case of a cocktail party or a reception, specify the hours during which guests may arrive:

for cocktails
5:30 to 7:30 P.M.

If someone is giving a speech or a presentation, the exact time should be noted on the bottom part of the invitation to a cocktail party or reception, to enable the guests to arrive in time for the presentation:

at cocktails

Six o'clock to eight o'clock

The Charles Hotel

at Harvard Square

Cambridge, Massachusetts

6:30 P.M.	Remarks by His Honor the Mayor
6:45 P.M.	Caroling by the Junior Club Choir

The Address

The address where the affair is to be held should appear on the line below the hour. If the location is a well-known hotel in a small city, it is not necessary to include the street address, only the town. In a large city, the street address of the hotel, the city, and the name of the banquet room should be included.

Special Instructions

Special instructions to inform or to assist the guests should be placed in the bottom right- and/or left-hand parts of the invitation or printed on a separate insert. For example:

- To impede gate-crashing, to discourage guests from inviting other people without permission, and to discourage sending an unwanted substitute:

  "Please present this invitation at the door"
  "Invitation not transferable"
  "Only those on the door list will be admitted"
  "Because of space limitations, we will be unable to accommodate guests of invited guests"
  "This invitation admits one only"
  "This invitation admits two"
  "This invitation is for your personal use only"

- To communicate the special arrangements that have been made for parking:

  "Parking provided in Garage XYZ for guests"
  "Valet Parking"

- To assist with transportation to and from the event:

  "Map enclosed"
  "Plane, train, and bus schedules enclosed"
  "Chartered buses will leave from the Plaza Hotel every ten minutes between 4:30 p.m. and 5:30 p.m."
  "Limousine pick-up service has been arranged at all commercial airports"
  "Taxis will be provided for the return trip"

- To communicate weather arrangements:

  "Rain date: June 26th"
  "In case of inclement weather, call 000-000-0000, Ext. 000"
  "In case of rain, the picnic will be held in the Auditorium"

- To communicate clothing requirements (*see* Chapter 4, Dressing for Business):

> "Black tie" (if guests are to wear evening clothes)
>
> "Business attire" (men in suits and ties, women in dresses), which usually is not necessary to include
>
> "Beach attire" (in case the company's party is by a pool or on the beach)
>
> "Tennis and golf" (to signal that guests should bring the proper clothing for those activities)
>
> "Jackets and ties required for men in the Club Dining Room"
>
> "Dress warmly" (a warning that the affair will be held outside and it might be chilly)
>
> "Boat shoes" (if the party will be held on a boat)

The Design of the Invitation

The design of an invitation is not something to be entrusted to an amateur. It should be handled by a professional. There may be someone on the art department staff who is qualified to work out the design; the project may be assigned to the company's advertising agency or to a free-lance graphics designer; or the company's printer may have a graphics designer on staff (but be careful—printers don't always have good staff designers).

Management's Input

Before the design and production of an invitation can proceed, management must make certain decisions, including the following:

- What is the date, time, place, and nature of the function?
- How much money should be designated for invitations in the budget for this function?
- What are the company's objectives in the function, so that the invitation will properly reflect those?
- How should the text read?
- Who should be on the guest list?
- How many invitations should be ordered?
- When are they needed, in order to have them addressed and mailed in sufficient time?

The Role of the Company Person in Charge of the Function

The meeting planner, party consultant, or whoever is running the function takes the answers to the questions put to management and then, together with the designer of the invitations and the printer, implements those decisions. (*See also* Managing the Large Social Event, in Chapter 8.)

The Designer's Role

In accordance with management's wishes, the designer assumes responsibility for the following:

- The overall design
- Selection of colors for both stock and lettering
- Selection of weight and texture of stock
- Implementation of management's decision on whether the invitations will be printed, thermographed, or engraved
- Choice of typeface(s)
- Coordination of the sizes of the various elements of the invitation mailing (invitation, envelope, RSVP card and envelope, possibly a map, possibly an information sheet, etc.), keeping in mind the weight of the overall package, so as not to incur extra postage costs that can be avoided
- Coordination on the timing for production and delivery, including the date by which the text and concept must be given to the designer, the date on which the designer's rough is returned, the date of management approval of corrected rough, the date final artwork is to be reviewed, the date finished artwork is to be delivered to printer

Different Invitations, Different Events

Each day hundreds of thousands of company invitations pass through the United States mails—for seminars, concerts, baseball games, parties in zoos or botanical gardens, celebrity auctions, opera performances, jogging races, formal dinners, square dances, movie previews, wine tastings, and hard-hat tours of buildings under construction.

The invitations sent out by your company should match its style. A firm dealing in junky merchandise may very well send out a cheap, "chintzy" kind of invitation, but a company that cares about how people feel about it selects the design of the invitation with great care and thought about image.

Engraved Fill-in Invitations

When companies entertain in a formal manner on a continuing basis, it is wise (and makes economic sense) to keep in stock for management's use engraved invitations with blank spaces to fill in by hand in black ink. It is very expensive to engrave invitations each time there is a company event; by using the fill-in kind that are always available, one avoids the headaches and expense of ordering new invitations each time.

Fill-in invitation cards can be engraved with or without the logo embossed at the top center, but only the chairman or the president of the organization would have personalized fill-in invitation cards with name and company title engraved under the logo. For the other executives, there would be a blank space for them to write in their names and titles when hosting an event.

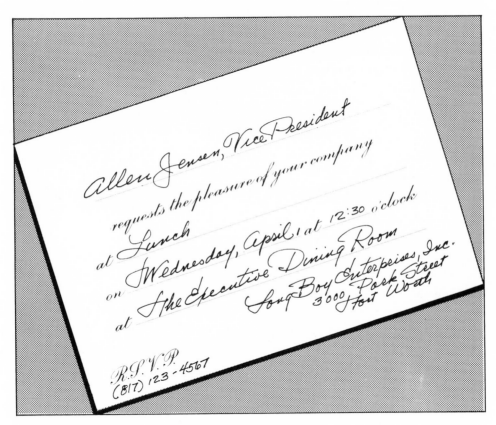

FILL-IN INVITATION

If a senior officer and his or her spouse entertain frequently at home on behalf of the company, their stock of engraved fill-in invitations would look like this:

Logo

Mr. and Mrs. Henry Vaughan

request the pleasure of your company

at

on

at

1030 Fifth Avenue
New York City

R.S.V.P.
Address of the office
Tel. No. of Vaughan's secretary

It is also a very nice touch to supply *executives who entertain in the company executive dining room* with fill-in invitations of this nature:

Logo

[space for host(s) name(s)]

request(s) the pleasure of your company
at lunch
on
at   o'clock

The Executive Dining Room
135 State Street
Denver, Colorado

RSVP   *Parking Facilities on*
000-0000   *Level B*
Ext.

The Classic Formal Invitation

The classic invitation is one that is printed or engraved in black on a white or ecru card or double-fold invitation (just like a wedding invitation). The typeface is usually traditional. This kind is used by conservative businesses, particularly those that handle people's money, and by companies and nonprofit organizations in the fields of health, education, and religion. The invitation is meant to inspire confidence and to denote integrity.

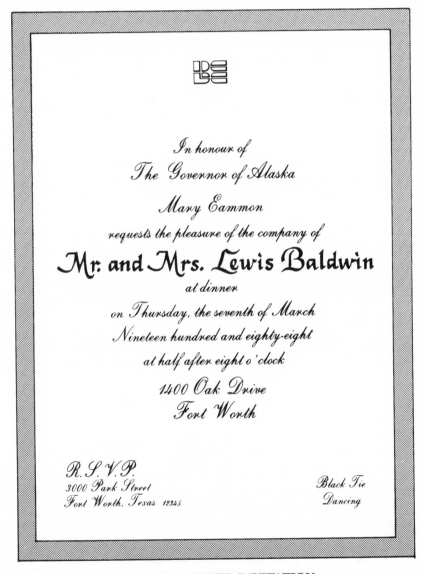

In honour of
The Governor of Alaska
Mary Eammon
requests the pleasure of the company of

Mr. and Mrs. Lewis Baldwin

at dinner
on Thursday, the seventh of March
Nineteen hundred and eighty-eight
at half after eight o'clock
1400 Oak Drive
Fort Worth

R. S. V. P.
3000 Park Street
Fort Worth, Texas 12345

Black Tie
Dancing

FORMAL DINNER INVITATION

The invitation does not always have to be boringly black-on-white. The designer can generate some excitement by doing any of the following:

- Changing the color scheme of both the stock and the lettering—for example, using dark brown lettering on tan stock, navy on pale blue stock, dark red on gray stock
- Putting a narrow border in color on the invitations
- Having the envelopes tissue-lined in a color that coordinates with the invitation colors

The Fashion Look

The invitation with a fashion look is used by people in the design business; the cosmetics, fragrance, and fashion industries; retailing; home furnishings, etc. For businesses that need a fashion image in their dealings with the public, there is a wide choice of materials and colors from which the creative designer can choose—rough-textured papers; metallic mylars; dark, shiny coated chrome stocks; etc. I once received an invitation to the launch of a bath products line that was painted on a French toile de Jouy printed fabric. An invitation from China Seas to a showing of new batiks was actually printed on batik. The invitation to the launch of a new Missoni fragrance at the Metropolitan Museum of Art was a photograph of a Missoni fabric—a purple and pink flame-stitch pattern—with silver lettering and silver gray envelopes. I opened the famous Red Door on a white Elizabeth Arden invitation and found behind it a parade of wonderful black silhouettes of mannequins wearing the new season's fashions.

The Unusual Invitation

I have seen invitations that were mirrors, architectural drawings, and pop-ups. There is no dearth of ideas in the business world today for invitations that are memorable. For example:

- The invitation you have to blow up in balloon form in order to know to what you've been invited
- The invitation that comes in a jig-saw puzzle form, requiring you to put the puzzle together in order to read what the party is all about
- The invitation in a surprising shape. I have seen invitations in the shapes of a gorilla, a computer terminal, an ice-cream cone, and a grand piano. Naturally, the shapes were all related to the businesses of the hosts.
- The invitation meant for everyone, such as inviting everyone in town to the opening of a new mall through a newspaper ad or by having a skywriter write the invitation in the sky at noontime.

One of the best invitations I ever received was for a "Very Large Press Party That Will Not Take Place." The host, Roger Horchow of the Horchow Catalog in Dallas, sent a press release about the company's new catalog in a very handsomely wrapped gift box, delivered by messenger to the recipients' offices. The box also contained a plastic champagne goblet, a split of good champagne, small sandwiches and cakes, a bag of confetti, a noisemaker, and a party hat.

Invitation Design for a Formal Reception

An invitation to a formal affair should be printed or engraved (preferably engraved) in black on white or ecru stock. The guests' names are filled in by hand, as shown in the following:

Oxforth Logo

Mr. and Mrs. Gerald Lee Fox
request the pleasure of
Mr. and Mrs. Green's (this is handwritten)
company at a reception
in honour of
The Honorable Malcolm Bainbridge
Secretary of Commerce
on the occasion of the inauguration of
The World's Commerce Fair
Sunday, April tenth
at nine p.m.

St. Regis Roof
Hotel St. Regis-Sheraton

R.S.V.P.   *Black Tie*
Office of the President
Oxforth Inc.
1400 Broadway
New York, N.Y. 00000
000-000-0000

For an Event Requiring Two Invitations

It is not unusual for an event to be celebrated with a ceremony held more or less in public and then to follow that with a luncheon or dinner for a selected number of guests. In that case, two invitations are called for—one for the ceremony and one for the luncheon or dinner. There may well be two guest lists. Members of the community invited just to the more open ceremony will receive only the invitation to that. Colleagues and dignitaries invited to both functions will receive two invitations.

#1   George N. Marcos, Chairman
       and the Management of ISM Inc.
       cordially invite you to the
       opening ceremonies of
       INTERNATIONAL MALL INC.
       on Saturday, May 3rd
       at 11 A.M.
       Junction 47, Exit 17 North
       Riverdale, Idaho
       Program:
       11:15—Riverdale High School
                Band Concert

       11:30—Address by the Honorable
                So-and-So, Governor of
                Idaho

#2   *In honor of Governor So-and-So*
       Mr. and Mrs. George N. Marcos
       request the pleasure of your company
       at lunch immediately following the ceremonies

       Mountain-Top Inn
       Junction #47, Riverdale
       RSVP card enclosed

NOTE: The second invitation to lunch with its RSVP card and envelope tucked inside are clipped to the front of the larger opening ceremonies invitation.

For a Product Launch

Ada O'Connor, President
Herley's Imports
cordially invites you to
a dinner
in honor of **Drury Scotch**
Herley's newest import
Monday, November 17th
at 8 o'clock
The Charles Hotel
Cambridge, Massachusetts

RSVP Card Enclosed   *Black Tie or Kilts*

Invitation to a Breakfast

Many people are not interested in attending a breakfast. Pains should be taken to make the invitation as appealing as possible, in order to combat a possibly negative reaction to being entertained at breakfast.

I once received a breakfast invitation in the shape of an egg, with the text printed on the back. There was nothing on the front to destroy the graphic beauty of that egg. (The hosts received an overwhelming response; almost everyone came.) Another invitation promised the guests: "We'll get you going with the aroma of rich hot coffee, sizzling bacon, and warm brioches with three kinds of honey. . . ." (I was ready for that meal the minute I read the invitation.)

Manufacturers and importers often host breakfasts at trade shows and dealer meetings, because early in the morning is the best time to present the new lines.

Appleyard Cutlery Inc.
(Logo)

Manny and Marie Appleyard
invite you to a hearty feast

"Breakfast in Goteborg"

to view the new Swedish cutlery lines
Monday, January 25th
7 a.m. to 9 a.m.
etc.

A Surprise Party for a Retiree

LOGO

Mary Lee Chin
President of WATCHWORKS
hopes you will join the many friends
of *Richard Renwick*
at a surprise party luncheon
on the occasion of his retirement
12 noon
Pearl's Restaurant
345 First Street
San Francisco

RSVP Card Enclosed   Please, No Gifts

Celebrating a Merger and Communicating a New Combined Logo

When two companies are merged, it is appropriate to provide each equal billing in the invitation to join in celebration of the merger. Naturally, the new corporate name under which they will henceforth be operating should also be prominently given.

Ralph Morley of
Antics
(the former logo)

Marian Smiley of
Bumblebee
(the former logo)

We hope you will join us

for cocktails

to celebrate the merger of our two companies

into

Bumbleantics

Thursday, November 1st

5 to 7 P.M.

The Green Room

Northern Hotel

Seattle

RSVP
Smith & Ozmik Public Relations
1201 Main Street
Seattle, WA zip

There will be a brief
presentation at 6 p.m.

An Invitation to a Boat Party

For a business party on board ship, you might let the designer of the invitation carry out a nautical theme. The text would be something like the following:

Ralph Jordan
President of GRENVILLE

invites you to

A Floating Lunch

on Wednesday, July 15th
at noon
aboard "The Blue Rigger"
Chicago Yacht Club at Belmont Harbor

Boat sails promptly at 12:30 p.m.
Returns to harbor at 3 p.m.

RSVP Card Enclosed

NOTE: This kind of invitation might also include special instructions on recommended attire, taking into account the degree of formality to be observed and/or a need to dress warmly. If the event's going through is at all contingent on the weather, it is advisable to indicate that.

Benefit Invitations
(*See* The Charity Benefit with Corporate Sponsorship, in Chapter 12)

An Informal Supper for Customers Before a Ball Game

Company

(Trademark)

Jane Menchoff, Chairman

Barbara Poulet, President

invite their customers

and their families

to an old-fashioned picnic

before the Lions-Antelopes game

Friday, June 20th

6 p.m.

210 South Street Parking Lot

Boulder

RSVP Card Enclosed   *Rain-date: Friday, June 27th*

Parking available at lot   *Tickets to the game will be*

adjacent to Minico's   *distributed at the picnic*

Restaurant

Getting the Invitation into the Mail

Having the invitation designed and produced is one thing; most people don't realize how much additional trouble and expense is involved in moving the finished invitation from the hands of the printer into the hands of the recipient.

The company person in charge of the event should:

· Establish a firm schedule for the date when the printer's proof is to be ready to be checked for accuracy

- Determine the date the finished invitations will be delivered to the place where they will be addressed, stuffed, sealed, stamped, and mailed
- Decide on how the envelopes will be addressed (by hand, typed, etc.)
- Decide on how they will be stamped (and which stamp will be used)
- Confirm in advance the date on which the invitations will actually be mailed

If there are no in-house capabilities to do the job properly, these operations should be carried out by a good mailing house.

Stuffing

The person in charge of the event should supply the mailing house with a sample invitation properly assembled, with all components in proper sequence (the most important item on top), so that the mailing house can copy it exactly. When you open an invitation, you should be able to pull out the invitation right side up, with the most important elements on top and the least important on the bottom (or the lesser elements in such a sequence inside a large double fold invitation).

If a paper clip is necessary to hold the parts together, have the designer select the clip. A detail even this little can reinforce, or damage, the integrity of the entire design.

Addressing the Envelopes

Envelopes for a business invitation should be:

- Neatly typed
- Hand-written in black ink by someone with beautiful handwriting, when it's for a very special occasion
- Written by a competent calligrapher for your most important events— provided you can locate one, provided he or she can finish them in time, and provided you can afford these expensive services

An important invitation should *never* be addressed by computer or pressure-sensitive labels.

Remember to put the company's return address on the upper left-hand corner of the *front* of the envelope. (The post office is responsible for returning something undeliverable only when the sender's address is on the front of the envelope.)

Protocol Points in Addressing the Envelopes
(*See* Chapter 10, Proper Forms of Address)

Postage

A host who wants his invitations to look special never sends them through the office postage meter machine, but instead has them hand-stamped (and with care). The stamps should be specifically selected at the post office, in order to find the most appropriate ones. For example, if your business is sports-related, you might choose stamps depicting an athlete; if your company makes airplane parts, you would choose a commemorative stamp with an aeronautical theme; if your party is going to be a summer outdoor affair, you might choose a stamp of a beautiful flower; if your company is known for its modern art collection, the stamp would appropriately be a subject by a renowned contemporary artist, etc. Pick a stamp that is related to your business, to the time of year of the party, or simply to something or someone you admire.

How Far in Advance Should Invitations Be Mailed?

The more advance warning you give your invited guests, the more attention they will give your invitation, and as a result, your function will be given priority over anyone else's.

Here are some guidelines:

- For an important seminar or conference requiring executives to come from other cities: *six months to eight months*
- For an important dinner—a prestigious affair—again, with out-of-town guests: *four to six months*
- Luncheon: *three to five weeks*
- Tea party: *two to three weeks*
- Breakfast for large group: *two to four weeks*
- Cocktail party: *two to four weeks*
- Evening reception (before or after another event): *four weeks*

Calling for a Response to an Invitation: The RSVP

(*See also* Invitation Diplomacy in the Practical Entertainment
Protocol section of Chapter 8)

American business is hopelessly remiss in its manners when it comes to responding to invitations. Whether it's because executives are just lazy or because they were never taught the importance of replying to an invitation, there is a lamentable casualness in this country that borders on rudeness when it comes to responding to an invitation. When people do not respond, the host does not know how much food and drink to order, and the result usually is substantial waste and unnecessary expense in providing for many more than those who attend.

We do not have to RSVP to a party for which we are asked to pay money in some form—buying benefit tickets, attending an auction, etc. We should certainly respond to other RSVP invitations, however, *and within a week's time.* There are many ways of responding, and several ways of asking for a response, including the following:

The RSVP on the Invitation

If there is no RSVP card enclosed with the invitation, information regarding the reply should be placed in the lower left-hand corner of the invitation. The maximum information that might be included in the RSVP is as follows:

> R.S.V.P.
> Mrs. Gertrude Ranney
> Office of the President
> REMCAR Inc.
> 1411 13th Street
> Syracuse, New York 00000
> (000) 000-0000

In most cases only the following is necessary (but only if whoever answers at that number is authorized to record regrets and acceptances):

> R.S.V.P.
> 1411 13th Street
> Syracuse, New York 00000
> (000) 000-0000

The Favor of a Reply Is Requested by a Certain Date

Another means of extracting an answer is by adding a plea phrase to the invitation: "The favor of a reply is requested by such-and-such a date" (often ten days before the event). This addition is made in the hope that it will propel the recipient of the invitation into action. It sometimes works.

"Regrets Only"

Still another way of soliciting a reply, in this case a negative reply, is to place "Regrets only" in the lower left corner of the invitation, which should be followed by a telephone number. I personally feel that "Regrets only" signifies a huge impersonal bash, and it makes me immediately decide *not* to attend. But more and more companies are using it as a device to estimate the number of guests attending. Unfortunately, many recipients of the invitation who do not expect to attend do not bother to telephone their regrets anyway. Therefore, in my opinion, the phrase serves no great purpose.

An RSVP Card in the Invitation Solicits a Response

It's common practice today in business to make it easy for one's prospective guests to respond to an invitation. An RSVP card, simple to fill in, with a matching envelope (addressed to the person at the company who will be handling the RSVPs) is included in the invitation.

An RSVP card should be no smaller than $3\frac{1}{2}'' \times 5''$; otherwise the post office will not guarantee its delivery. It should be of the same design (stock, color, typeface) as the invitation itself. If the invitations are engraved, a company does not have to go to the additional expense of having the RSVP cards and envelopes engraved. They may be printed.

I am also of the opinion that the envelope for the RSVP card does *not* have to be stamped by the host company. (The invited guest ought to be able to cough up the money for a postage stamp on the return RSVP envelope!)

Bringing a Date

A single person should never ask to bring a guest to a seated meal unless specifically asked to do so. The RSVP card usually gives the clue as to whether or not one should bring a guest to a cocktail party or a buffet. If the card has a line for "Guest," a single person should fill in the guest's complete name and business affiliation (if there is one) in the space provided. The fact that there is a space for a guest's name is *not* a command that a single invitee come with a date.

LOGO

M/M _____

Name of Guest _____

Accept _____   *Regret* _____   *Tel. No.* _____

Lunch, February 1st at 1 p.m.

Bancroft Hotel

4th and D Streets

Tacoma, Washington

The Guest RSVPs to the Host

You have not properly responded to an RSVP if you accidentally run into your host somewhere and tell him, "I'll be there." You must call his office or send him a written reply.

There are several ways in which a guest may respond to the host's invitation:

- *By returning the RSVP card* properly filled out (the easiest way, of course)
- *By telephoning the host's office* to leave the response. Sometimes the problem of time makes telephoning a response expedient; sometimes a telephoned reply is requested on the invitation.
- *By sending a typed or hand-written formal reply* to the host, on good notepaper (the nicest, most polite way, but, alas, disappearing)
- *By sending a Mailgram*
  An example of a Mailgram acceptance sent by the guest to the host when time is short:

  > Morgan Tilson accepts with pleasure Evangeline Jenkins' kind invitation to the Market Breakfast on Sunday, January 3rd, at the Biltmore Hotel.

- By sending a personal letter in reply.
  If a guest must regret an invitation extended by a good personal friend, the most polite thing he can do is to write a letter explaining why he cannot attend, expressing his sincere regret:

  > Dear Vangie:
  >   Unfortunately I'll be on the West Coast the day of your market breakfast. I'm triply sad about it—first, because I know your market introduction will be a significant one in our industry and I would like to see it before the big launch; second, because I know the party will be a big success, because it always is; and third, because I always enjoy seeing *you*.
  >   I will be with you in spirit. Good luck with the new products!

The Secretary Replies for her Boss

If an executive is away on an extended trip, his secretary should handle his RSVPs. If the boss knows a certain person well, the secretary should do more than simply check the "Accept" or "Regret" part of the RSVP card. She should accompany the RSVP card with a short note:

> Dear Ms. Jenkins:
>   Mr. Tilson is in the Far East but will return the day before your market breakfast at the Biltmore. I am certain he will wish to attend, so I am taking

the liberty of accepting on his behalf, and I know he would want me to convey his best wishes to you for a successful market.

/s/ Gemma Howard
Executive Secretary

Responding to a Wedding Invitation

If the secretary regrets a wedding invitation for her boss and spouse because they are away on a long trip and she knows the parents of the bride, she might include her own personal note inside the formal response:

Dear Mr. and Mrs. Johnson:
    I know how terribly disappointed Mr. McCann and Ms. Truesdale will be to miss your daughter's wedding. I'm sure it will be a very wonderful occasion for all your family, and I would like to extend my own best wishes to the bride and groom.

A Formal Reply to an Invitation

Whether she is typing or hand-writing it, an executive secretary should know how to set up a formal reply in the third person to an invitation sent to her boss and his or her spouse. It should be centered on the page.

A Formal Acceptance

The secretary would use a piece of good personal stationery (either plain or with the name or monogram of her boss engraved) to accept for her boss and spouse (who in this case have two names):

Mr. William D. McCann and Ms. Anne Truesdale
accept with pleasure
Mr. and Mrs. Johnson's
kind invitation for
Saturday, the third of December.

A Formal Regret

Mr. William D. McCann and Ms. Anne Truesdale
sincerely regret that
due to their absence from the country
they are unable to accept
Mr. and Mrs. Johnson's
kind invitation for
Saturday, the third of December.

Reminders for Invitations

A Reminder Card

A reminder card is sent for any one of three reasons:

1. There has not been enough time to mail the invitations for an event, so invitations were extended by telephone. As those who have accepted have no official record of the time, date, and place of the party, it is wise, if time allows, to send them a reminder card. The reminder is useful, even if it arrives only a day before the party.
2. When a company issues its invitations for a major event many months before the date, those who accept often lose or even forget their invitations. It is good planning to send an informal card to arrive ten days to two weeks before the event to provide once again all the necessary details pertaining to the event.
3. When a company has issued its invitations a month to six weeks before an event and must change the locale of the party, the sending of an informal reminder card noting a change of place is an easy way to communicate this change.

The following is a sample text for a reminder card that is printed or engraved and sent to those who have accepted an invitation by telephone:

Aparicom Inc.

1314 Sixth Avenue

Jacksonville, Florida 00000

Caroline Espinosa   Today's Date
President

To Remind

Lunch In Honor Of

The United States Davis Cup Team

Monday, November 2nd

12 o'clock

The Seacrest Inn

40th and Western Avenue

(North Parkway Entrance)

(000) 000-0000

NOTE: *"To Remind"* may also be placed in the upper left-hand corner of the reminder card.

The following illustration shows an engraved fill-in reminder card available at fine stationers and kept in stock for use by executives (and/or their spouses) when they give parties for which there is no time to prepare proper printed or engraved reminder cards:

Other Forms of Reminders

- *An executive can always have his secretary call the guest list* to remind them of the upcoming event. This is done only if the event is extremely important and if there is any doubt that the details of the event might be hazy in guests' minds.
- *A Mailgram may be sent.* It's an expensive way to send a reminder, but useful in last minute emergencies:

> TO REMIND: LUNCH IN HONOR OF AMBASSADOR GERTRUDE CHENEY
> WEDNESDAY, SEPTEMBER 25TH, ONE P.M., HUNTINGTON HOTEL,
> SAN FRANCISCO
>
>   DAVID WAINWRIGHT, VP RESCO

- *A letter may serve as a reminder:*

> Dear Andy:
> This is just to remind you of the lunch in honor of Ambassador Gertrude Cheney on Wednesday, September 25th, at 1 P.M. at the Huntington. We look forward to having you with us. . . .

Changing the Date of the Event

If for any reason the date of the party has to be changed after the invitations have already been issued and acceptances received, local residents should be informed by telephone and out-of-towners by Mailgram. The company host should furnish a reason for the date being changed.

A Mailgram message would read as follows:

> REGRET TO INFORM YOU THAT DUE TO UNEXPECTED SCHEDULING CONFLICT IT WILL BE NECESSARY TO CHANGE DATE OF DINNER HONORING BRUCE ROCKWELL FROM NOVEMBER 23 TO NOVEMBER 28 AT 7 P.M. RED LION HOTEL KANSAS CITY. BUSINESS DRESS. HOPE THIS DOES NOT INCONVENIENCE YOU AND THAT YOU WILL BE ABLE TO ACCEPT. PLEASE NOTIFY MY OFFICE (000) 000-0000 EXT 000.
>
>   NORMAN MASON, CHAIRMAN PANTCO

In sending out the second set of invitations, the host should include those who had been asked the first time but who had declined. The Mailgram to those who had regretted first time around would read as follows:

> DUE TO BUSINESS SCHEDULING CONFLICTS WE ARE CHANGING DATE OF DINNER HONORING BRUCE ROCKWELL FROM NOVEMBER 23 TO NOVEMBER 28 AT 7 P.M. RED LION HOTEL KANSAS CITY. BUSINESS DRESS. SINCE YOU RE-GRETTED PREVIOUS DATE WE HOPE YOU WILL BE ABLE TO ACCEPT FOR THE NEW DATE NOVEMBER 28TH. PLEASE NOTIFY MY OFFICE (000) 000-0000 EXT 000.
>
>   NORMAN MASON, CHAIRMAN PANTCO

Canceling an Event

When a company-hosted event must be canceled:

- If time is of the essence, each guest should be reached by telephone (if not the guest, his or her secretary or a member of the family). The staff person should write down the date, time, and name of the person who took the message for each guest.
- If guests are unreachable by telephone, a Mailgram should be sent.
- If there is a great deal of lead time, the company host should write a personal letter to each guest.
- If there is a great deal of lead time but the guest list is extremely large, a printed card should be prepared and mailed to each guest, explaining the circumstances.

Always give a reason for the cancellation (and the truth is always best):

- "Because Mr. Mason is ill" (give the nature of his illness)
- Because of a major change in business plans (e.g., "We are going to delay the introduction of the new shampoo line until three other new products we have been testing can be introduced at the same time.")
- Because the host has unexpectedly been called away on urgent business ("Mr. Mason has been called suddenly to oversee an important development in our European group of companies, and he may be abroad for several weeks.")

A social-business event canceled several weeks before it is to take place permits the host to send a printed or engraved card to all of the guests:

> *Norman Mason*
>
> *Chairman of Pantco*
>
> *sincerely regrets*
>
> *that due to the death of Mr. Bruce G. Rockwell's wife*
>
> *the dinner in his honor*
>
> *November 23rd*
>
> *will not take place*

The Well-Organized Invitation: A Case Study

David Rockefeller traditionally gave a party each year for insurance executives when he was chairman of Chase Manhattan Bank. One year the invitation was issued in the form of a very colorful mini press kit. The press kit cover was a bright kelly green, with the Chase Manhattan logo blind-embossed on the front; the envelope was beige, marked with "Office of the Chairman." The various informational inserts were printed in dark green on lemon yellow or gold paper. The message from the host on one of the sheets read:

> It is always a pleasure to have friends in the insurance industry join my Chase colleagues and me for a day of sports and relaxation at Pocantico Hills. We will have our regular golf and tennis tournaments, and if you plan to participate, please bring your own equipment. If not, you may swim, bowl, play squash or croquet or simply relax.
>
> We will begin promptly at 9:00 A.M. with the first tee-offs and tennis sets. Coffee will be available at 8:30, luncheon at noontime, and adjournment is planned for 4:30 to permit an early return home.
>
> I look forward to hearing that you can be with us. More information and travel directions will be sent to you if you plan to attend.
>
> /s/ David Rockefeller

The RSVP card was designed so that the recipient could check off activities in which he wanted to participate, such as golf (handicaps were requested) and tennis.

The invitation was impressive in its design. (There were six parts tucked into the mailing envelope: the green "press kit cover"; the invitation itself; a card with a graphic design reflecting a golf and tennis theme; the RSVP card with return envelope; and the message from Mr. Rockefeller.) It communicated a wonderful day ahead for all concerned.

The President of a Small Company Has a Country Outing, Too

The president of a small company can design just as eye-catching an invitation for a country party as the Chase Manhattan Bank. He can invite guests to his country club for organized activities and lunch.

The invitation might include sketches of the various sports in which guests can participate. The RSVP card can request information that will enable the club's staff to match players and golf partners, according to their skills:

RSVP

(Logo of host company)

Quohog Country Club—Sunday, July 20th

M/M _____

Accept _____   Regret _____

Telephone number_____

His golf handicap _____   Her golf handicap _____

    His tennis game: Her tennis game:

Excellent _____ Mediocre _____   Excellent _____ Mediocre _____

      Forget it _____   Forget it _____

10

Proper Forms of Address

People care more than perhaps you realize how they are written to, spoken to, introduced, and listed on programs and committee rosters. Whether an outside person is overly sensitive on the subject or whether your office is overly casual about this subject, someone should care enough to do something about it. A CEO should give priority to an examination of how his or her organization uses or abuses titles and forms of address for people on the outside. To address others properly is not only a question of courtesy, but also of a well-polished company image, continued good business relationships, and profitability.

Whether corresponding with an ambassador, a colonel, a priest, or a cabinet officer, the communication should be addressed correctly. Half the battle is knowing where to go to obtain the proper information. Most of the time it means picking up the telephone, perhaps even calling long distance, to reach the office of the person to ask the secretary how that person should be addressed. The cost of the long distance call is well worth the good impression made by your letter when it reaches the recipient correctly addressed.

The charts contained in this chapter are a compilation of information gained from books including my own, *The Amy Vanderbilt Complete Book of Etiquette* (Doubleday, 1978); *Protocol,* by Mary Jane McCaffree and Pauline Innis (Prentice-Hall Inc., 1977); *The Social List of Washington, D.C.* (Jean Shaw Murray, 1985); and Debrett's *Etiquette and Modern Manners* (Tigerlily

394

Ltd., London, 1981); as well as from conversations with the Social Office in the White House and the Protocol Office of the Department of State. (For related information, *see also* the section Protocol Matters in Large Formal Dinners, in Chapter 8 of this book.)

Titles Before Names

Omitting a Title in Writing

It is frankly inexcusable to address any piece of mail to "Richard Jones" without writing "Mr. Richard Jones." When mail comes without a person's title, the recipient has a right to feel that the sender just doesn't care.

It takes very little time and effort to put a person's title in front of his name, whether it's Mr., Mrs., Miss, Ms., or a professional title.

The use of Ms.

Ms. is in such common use that there is very little discussion anymore on the subject. A woman may call herself what she pleases in her personal life, but in the workplace she should become accustomed to being written to as "Ms. Mary Jones" rather than "Mrs. Mary Jones" or "Mrs. Howard Jones" (if that is her husband's name). When she is in the workplace, she is herself, not her husband's wife or her ex-husband's wife.

But again, if she objects to being called "Ms. Jones" (and the objections usually come from the older, not the younger generation), mark in your Rolodex and files that one should write to her as "Mrs. Mary Jones." Keep the peace.

Using a Professional Title or Affiliation After the Surname

If someone writes you with the initials of a professional title or organization after his name, you should always address communications to him in the exact same manner. When you use a professional title, you do not also use *Mr., Mrs., Miss,* or *Ms.* For example:

- Horace Goddard, M.D. (*not* Dr. Horace Goddard or Dr. Horace Goddard, M.D.)
- Mary O'Reilly, R.S.C.J. (*not* Sister Mary O'Reilly, R.S.C.J.)
- Esther Hernandez, R.N. (*not* Ms. Esther Hernandez, R.N.)
- Nicholas Nardini, Ph.D. (*not* Dr. Nicholas Nardini, Ph.D.)

A person who lists his professional organization membership after his name should be addressed in the same manner. For example:

- Jeffrey Boomer, F.A.S.I.S. (a Fellow of the American Society of Interior Designers)
- Margaret Chan, A.I.A. (a member of the American Institute of Architects)

Esq. *and* J.D. *for Lawyers*

The English frequently use *Esquire,* when writing to one another on business or government matters. In this country *Esq.* in the abbreviated form is used as a matter of choice after the surname of a lawyer, male or female. It is written: "John Jones, Esq.", not "Mr. John Jones, Esq." (Some people think it's stuffy for a lawyer to use *Esq.* after his name.)

Esq. is never used when writing a social invitation to a couple, one or both of whom might be lawyers. *J.D.* (Doctor of Jurisprudence) is used optionally after the surname of someone who has such a degree: "Maria Scott, J.D."

Jr. *and* Sr.; 2nd, 3rd, *and* 4th

When a man uses *Jr.* after his surname, it signifies that he has the exact same name as his father. If the two men live in the same city, the father will usually use *Sr.* after his surname, so that there is as little confusion as possible with identical names.

When the father dies, the son usually retains *Jr.* for a few years, then drops it because there is no longer a need to make a distinction between him and his father.

When a man who is a Junior gives his son the exact same name, that son becomes "the 3rd" or "III."

A child named after his uncle or grandfather becomes the "2nd." For example:

Two brothers:	*George Allan* has a son who becomes: *George Allan, Jr.* He in turn has a son whom he names: *George Allan III* (or 3rd)	*Christopher Allan* has a son and names him after his uncle George, i.e., Christopher's brother: *George Allan II* (or 2nd)

Addressing Executives as "Sir" or "Ma'am"

Generations of young people in both the social and business worlds have been taught to address their elders as "sir" or "ma'am," rather than to use the elder's name. Today, except for its use in the South and Southwest (and except for the use of *sir* when addressing people who hold a very high office), these terms are no longer used.

We say, "Good morning, Mr. Jones" instead of "Good morning, sir."

We say, "Yes, Miss Black" or "I certainly will, Ms. Smith" instead of "Yes, ma'am."

Many Southerners still use *sir* and *ma'am,* a holdover from their tradition of beautiful manners. However, when Southerners come to other parts of the country on business, they would be wise to refrain from the "sir" and "ma'am" habit, simply because that often embarrasses people who consider it a remnant of a bygone era of servitude.

Addressing Letters and Envelopes to Nonofficial People

Business Letters

- If you don't use a position title:

Mr. David Jones
Surety Realty Co.
2000 Peachtree Road, N.W.
Atlanta, GA 00000

- If you do use a position title:

Mr. David Jones
President, Surety Realty Co.
Street address
City, state, 00000

- When a professional title goes after a name:

David Jones, M.D.
Office address
City, State, 00000

David Jones, Ph.D.
Address
City, State, 00000

David Jones, Esq.
Address
City, State, 00000

- When a title goes before the name:

President David Jones
Wentworth College
Address
City, State, 00000

Invitation Envelopes

- To man and wife:

  Mr. and Mrs. David Jones
  Home address

- When his wife has kept her own name:

  Mr. David Jones
     and Ms. Elizabeth Boyd
  Home address

- When she has a title and he does not:

  Mr. David Jones
     and Dr. Elizabeth Jones
  Home address

- When both are doctors:

  The Doctors Gillespie   *or*   Dr. Ralph Gillespie
  Home Address   and Dr. Angela Gillespie
                                             Home address

NOTE: When the spouse's name goes on the line below, indent three spaces.

Introducing People Commensurate
to Their Station in Life
(*See* The Art of Introducing People in Chapter 1)

Addressing Foreign
Business People Properly
(*See also* Chapter 5, International Business Manners)

A great deal of international business is transacted either by letter, telephone, or face to face, involving interaction between people in business and government. American business people should therefore learn the protocol of each country with which business is conducted. Most of the protocol tenets governing how to address, speak to, and introduce a person of rank are rooted in centuries of custom. When we Americans do not give this subject any priority (and we are the most casual people of all), we can offend the sensitivity of our foreign friends. We may not care about how *we* are introduced or seated at the lunch table, but people of other countries usually do, particularly when they have worked long and hard to reach a high point in their careers.

Foreign Professional Titles

In certain countries, particularly Italy and Germany but also to some degree in Scandinavia and the Low Countries, executives are very proud of the titles preceding their names that either show their education or their profession.

In Italy, anyone who gets a degree immediately becomes "Dottore" (a woman becomes "Dottoressa") and an abbreviated form goes in front of his name for the rest of his life. He wants to be written to as "Egr. Dott. Giacomo Verde," and he wants to be introduced as "Dottore Verde." If he is an architect, then he will abandon "Dottore" for the professional title "Architetto Verde," which abbreviates to "Arch. Verde." If he is a lawyer, he is addressed as "Avvocato Giacomo Verde" (shortened to "Avv. Giacomo Verde"). Americans doing business with the Italians should take heed of these titles; they are important.

In Germany and other countries to the north, the bosses are often called by their position titles rather than by their names. "Herr Direktor" is a very prestigious title for senior management. A doctor is known as "Herr Doktor," an engineer as "Herr Ingenieur," etc.

An American business person should pick up these title signals when doing business abroad. Doing so shows the difference between a person who is aware and thoughtful and one who is neither.

Military Rank

The Army, Air Force, and Marine Corps have the following commissioned officers according to rank:

- General
- Lieutenant General
- Major General
- Brigadier General
- Colonel
- Lieutenant Colonel
- Major
- Captain
- First Lieutenant
- Second Lieutenant

The Navy and Coast Guard have the following:

- Admiral
- Vice Admiral
- Rear Admiral

- Captain
- Commander
- Lieutenant Commander
- Lieutenant
- Lieutenant, junior grade
- Ensign

NOTE: All officers in the Navy and Coast Guard are addressed as "Mr." up through the rank of lieutenant commander. A woman officer is addressed "Ms." or "Miss," never "Mrs."

A captain in the Navy or Coast Guard has a higher rank than a captain in the Army, Air Force, or Marine Corps.

A warrant officer's rank lies between that of a commissioned and a non-commissioned officer.

How to Address a Military Man or Woman

Examples of Military Rank	*Making Introductions/ Addressing Envelopes*	*Letter Salutation*	*When Speaking To*	*Place Card*
First lieutenant	First Lieutenant Richard Dix, USMC *or, socially:* First Lieutenant and Mrs. Richard Dix	Dear Lieutenant Dix:	Lieutenant Dix, *or,* Lieutenant	Lieutenant Dix
Captain in the Navy	Captain Joseph Piteo, USN *or, socially:* Captain and Mrs. Joseph Piteo	Dear Captain Piteo:	Captain Piteo, *or* Captain	Captain Piteo
Lieutenant colonel	Lieutenant Colonel Frank Haig, USMC *or, socially:* Lieutenant Colonel and Mrs. Frank Haig	Dear Colonel Haig:	Colonel Haig, *or,* Colonel	Colonel Haig
Chief warrant officer	Chief Warrant Officer Jane Turner *or, socially:* Chief Warrant Officer Jane Turner and Mr. Anthony Turner	Dear Chief Warrant Officer Turner: *or, informally:* Dear Ms. Turner:	Chief Warrant Officer Turner *or, informally:* Ms. Turner	Ms. Turner
Noncommissioned officers in Army, Air Force, and Marine Corps	Master Sergeant Tony Tatum *or, socially:* Master Sergeant and Mrs. Tony Tatum	Dear Sergeant Tatum:	Sergeant Tatum	Mr. Tatum

(Follow same form for any rating, including Sergeant Major, Sergeant First Class, Platoon Sergeant, Corporal, Specialist (classes 4 to 9), Private First Class, etc.)

Examples of Military Rank	Making Introductions/ Addressing Envelopes	Letter Salutation	When Speaking To	Place Card
Enlisted person in Navy	SN Robert Peltz Address of his command *or, socially:* Seaman and Mrs. Robert Peltz	Dear Seaman Peltz:	Seaman Peltz	Seaman Peltz
Retired officer in Army or Air Force	Major Robert Orr, USAF Retired Address *or, socially:* Major and Mrs. Robert Orr	Dear Major Orr:	Major Orr	Major Orr
Retired officer in Navy or Coast Guard*	Rear Admiral Spencer Davis, USN Retired Address *or, socially:* Rear Admiral and Mrs. Spencer Davis	Dear Admiral Davis:	Admiral Davis	Admiral Davis
Cadet at West Point (same for Air Force Academy, with address change)	Cadet Mark Boland, U.S. Army Company __, Corps of Cadets United States Military Academy West Point, NY 10996	Dear Mr. Boland: *or,* Dear Cadet Boland:	Mr. Boland	Mr. Boland
Midshipman at U.S. Naval Academy; Cadet at U.S. Coast Guard Academy	Midshipman Joan Doan U.S. Naval Academy *or* Cadet Stephen Cole United States Coast Guard Academy	Dear Ms. (*or* Miss) Doan: Dear Mr. Cole:	Ms. *or* Miss Doan Mr. Cole	Ms. Doan

*Only Navy and Coast Guard officers with rank of commander and above retain their titles after retirement; officers in the Reserve do not.)

NOTE: Try to put the name of husband and wife on one line on the invitation envelope. For example:

Captain and Mrs. Robert Smith
(address beneath)

If the names are too long for your envelope, indent the spouse's name three spaces on the second line. For example:

Captain
   and Mrs. Jerome Alexander Gallipuccio
(address beneath)

The limitations of space in this and the following charts do not permit us to give the address lines in preferred form.

Religious Officials

In closing a letter to a very high religious official, use "Respectfully yours" or use "Sincerely" or "Sincerely yours."

Protestant Clergy

Official	Making Introductions/ Addressing Envelopes	Letter Salutation	Speaking To/ Place Card
Clergyman with Doctor's degree	The Reverend Dr. Amos E. Long *or, socially:* The Reverend Dr. Amos E. Long and Mrs. Long	Dear Dr. Long:	Dr. Long
Clergywoman without Doctor's degree	The Reverend Anne Smith *or, socially:* The Reverend Anne Smith and Mr. Peter Smith	Dear Ms. or Miss Smith:	Ms. or Miss Smith
Presiding Bishop of the Episcopal Church in the United States	The Right Reverend James Gard, Presiding Bishop *or, socially:* The Right Reverend James Gard and Mrs. Gard	Dear Bishop Gard:	Bishop Gard
Bishop of the Episcopal Church	The Right Reverend David Webb Bishop of Washington *or, socially:* The Right Reverend David Webb and Mrs. Webb	Dear Bishop Webb:	Bishop Webb
Methodist Bishop	The Reverend Michael Forest Methodist Bishop *or, socially:* The Reverend Michael Forest and Mrs. Forest	Dear Bishop Forest:	Bishop Forest
Dean	The Very Reverend Angus Dunn *or,* The Very Reverend Angus Dunn Dean of St. John's *or, socially* The Very Reverend Angus Dunn and Mrs. Dunn	Dear Dean Dunn:	Dean Dunn
Archdeacon	The Venerable Stewart G. Dodd Archdeacon of Boston *or, socially:* The Venerable Stewart G. Dodd and Mrs. Dodd	Dear Archdeacon Dodd:	Archdeacon Dodd
Canon	The Reverend Randolph Tate Canon of St. Andrew's *or, socially:* The Reverend Randolph Tate and Mrs. Tate	Dear Canon Tate:	Canon Tate

Notes on Protestant clergy:
- Clergy with degrees optionally use the initials of their degrees after their names. For example: The Right Reverend James Gard, or The Right Reverend James Gard, D.D., LL.D.
- A member of the Episcopal clergy who is not in a religious order may call himself "Father." In writing him, you do not use his Christian name, but rather his surname: "The Reverend Father Stimson."

- A Protestant minister who retires remains "The Reverend So-and-so." If he or she resigns, that person normally becomes "Mr." or "Ms."

Mormon Clergy

Official	Making Introductions/ Addressing Envelopes	Letter Salutation	Speaking To/ Place Card
Mormon Bishop	Mr. Timothy Blake Church of Jesus Christ of Latter-day Saints *or, socially:* Mr. and Mrs. Timothy Blake	Dear Mr. Blake:	Mr. Blake

Roman Catholic Hierarchy

Official	Making Introductions/ Addressing Envelopes	Letter Salutation	Speaking To/ Place Card
The Pope	His Holiness, the Pope *or* His Holiness, Pope Augustus III	Your Holiness:	*Speaking to:* Your Holiness
The Apostolic Delegate in Washington (the Pope's representative)	His Excellency The Most Reverend Bishop of (City) The Apostolic Delegate Address	Your Excellency	Your Excellency/ His Excellency the Apostolic Delegate
Cardinal	His Eminence, Joseph Cardinal Sheehan Archbishop of St. Louis	Your Eminence: *or,* Dear Cardinal Sheehan:	Your Eminence/ Cardinal Sheehan
Bishop and Archbishop	The Most Reverend Paul Murphy, Bishop (Archbishop) of Chicago	Your Excellency: *or,* Dear Bishop Murphy:	Excellency/ Bishop Murphy
Monsignor	The Right Reverend Julius Cuneo	Dear Monsignor Cuneo:	Monsignor Cuneo
Priest	The Reverend Father James Orr Church rectory address	Dear Father Orr:	Father Orr
Brother	Brother David Maxwell	Dear Brother David: *or,* Dear Brother Maxwell:	Brother David *or* Brother Maxwell
Nun	Joan Reynolds, R.S.C.J. *or,* Sister Mary Annunciata	Dear Sister:	Sister Reynolds *or* Sister Mary Annunciata

Eastern Orthodox Communion

Official	Making Introductions/ Addressing Envelopes	Salutation	Speaking To
Patriarch	His Holiness, the Ecumenical Patriarch of Constantinople	Your Holiness:	Your Holiness
Bishop and priest	Same as Roman Catholic Church		
Archimandrite	The Very Reverend Gregory Costos	Reverend Sir:	Father Costos

Jewish Faith

Official	Making Introductions/ Addressing Envelopes	Letter Salutation	Speaking To	Place Card
Rabbi	Rabbi Melvin Schwartz Address *or, socially:* Rabbi and Mrs. Melvin Schwartz	Dear Rabbi Schwartz:	Rabbi *or* Rabbi Schwartz	Rabbi Schwartz
Cantor	Cantor Samuel Stein Address *or, socially:* Cantor and Mrs. Samuel Stein	Dear Cantor Stein:	Cantor Stein	Cantor Stein

Military Chaplains

Making Introductions/ Addressing Envelopes	Letter Salutation	Speaking To	Place Card
Major John Martin, Chaplain Address	Dear Major Martin: *or,* Dear Chaplain: *or, for a Catholic chaplain:* Dear Father Martin: *or, for a Jewish Chaplain,* Dear Rabbi Martin:	Chaplain *or* Major Martin	Major Martin *or, for Catholic,* Father Martin *or, for Jewish,* Rabbi Martin

United States Officials

Any executive who deals with government officials should have a copy of the latest United States official ranking in his or her office, in order to know how to address them properly and how to seat them at a meal. Each President of the United States makes a few changes to suit him in the precedence of the officials he addresses or sees. The chart that follows shows the latest changes made by President Reagan in March of 1985:

The Official Ranking for United States Officials

The President of the United States
The Vice President of the United States
The Speaker of the House of Representatives
The Chief Justice of the United States
Former Presidents of the United States
The Secretary of State
The Secretary General of the United Nations
Ambassadors of foreign powers
Widows of former Presidents of the United States
Associate Justices of the Supreme Court of the United States

The Cabinet
    The Secretary of the Treasury
    The Secretary of Defense
    The Attorney General
    The Secretary of the Interior
    The Secretary of Agriculture
    The Secretary of Commerce
    The Secretary of Labor
    The Secretary of Health and Human Services
    The Secretary of Housing and Urban Development
    The Secretary of Transportation
    The Secretary of Energy
    The Secretary of Education
The Chief of Staff for the President
Director, Office of Management and Budget
Director of Central Intelligence
The United States Representative to the United Nations
Special Representative for Trade Negotiations
The Senate (Senators are ranked with each other according to length of continuous service)
Governors of States
Former Vice Presidents of the United States
The House of Representatives (ranked according to their state's date of admission to the Union)
Assistants to the President
Chargés d'Affaires of foreign powers
The Under Secretaries and Deputy Secretaries of the Executive Departments
Administrator, Agency for International Development
Director, U.S. Arms Control and Disarmament Agency
Secretaries of the Army, Navy, and Air Force
Chairman, Board of Governors of the Federal Reserve System
Chairman, Council on Environmental Quality
Chairman, Joint Chiefs of Staff
Chiefs of Staff of the Army, Navy, and Air Force (ranked according to date of appointment)
Commandant of the Marine Corps
(5-star) Generals of the Army and Fleet Admirals
The Secretary General, Organization of American States
Representatives to the Organization of American States
Director, United States Information Agency
Administrator, General Services Administration
Administrator, National Aeronautics and Space Administration
Chairman, Civil Service Commission
Director, Defense Research and Engineering
Director of ACTION

Administrator, Environmental Protection Agency
Deputy Under Secretary of State
Commandant of the Coast Guard
Assistant Secretaries of the Executive Departments
Chief of Protocol
Members of the Council of Economic Advisers
Active or Designate U.S. Ambassadors and Ministers (career rank, when in the United States; when they are in their foreign country posts, they are given much higher rank)
The Mayor of the District of Columbia
Under Secretaries of the Army, Navy, and Air Force
(4-star) Generals and Admirals
Assistant Secretaries of the Army, Navy, and Air Force
(3-star) Lieutenant Generals and Vice Admirals
Former U.S. Ambassadors and Ministers to Foreign Countries
Ministers of Foreign Powers (serving in embassies, not accredited)
Deputy Assistant Secretaries of the Executive Departments
Deputy Chief of Protocol
Counselors of embassies or legations of foreign powers
(2-star) Major Generals and Rear Admirals
(1-star) Brigadier Generals and Commodores
Assistant Chiefs of Protocol

Addressing Government Officials: A Sampling

Personage	Introduction and Addressing Envelopes	Letter Salutation	Speaking To	Place Card
The President	The President The White House Address (Abroad he is introduced as "The President of the United States of America.")	Dear Mr. President:	Mr. President	The President
The First Lady	Mrs. Madison (She is the only official woman always addressed out of respect as "Mrs. Madison," without a given name.) *A social invitation would be addressed to:* The President and Mrs. Madison	Dear Mrs. Madison:	Mrs. Madison	Mrs. Madison
The Vice President	The Vice President The White House Address *A social invitation would be addressed to:* The Vice President and Mrs. Adams	Dear Mr. Vice President:	Mr. Vice President	The Vice President

Personage	Introduction and Addressing Envelopes	Letter Salutation	Speaking To	Place Card
Vice President's Wife	Mrs. John Adams Address	Dear Mrs. Adams:	Mrs. Adams	Mrs. Adams
Speaker of the House	The Honorable Michael Duncan Speaker of the House *or, socially:* The Speaker of the House and Mrs. Duncan	Dear Mr. Speaker:	Mr. Speaker	The Speaker of the House
Chief Justice	The Chief Justice The Supreme Court Address *or, socially:* The Chief Justice and Mrs. Warner	Dear Mr. Chief Justice:	Mr. Chief Justice	The Chief Justice
Associate Justice	Justice Zissu The Supreme Court *or, socially:* Justice Zissu and Mrs. Zissu	Dear Justice: *or* Dear Justice Zissu	Justice *or* Justice Zissu	Justice Zissu
Cabinet Member	The Honorable Desmond Palmer Secretary of Labor Address *or, socially:* The Secretary of Labor and Mrs. Palmer	Dear Mr. Secretary	Mr. Secretary *or* Secretary Palmer	The Secretary of Labor
Under Secretary of Labor	The Honorable Otto Norgren Under Secretary of Labor *or, socially:* The Undersecretary of Labor and Mrs. Norgren	Dear Mr. Under Secretary:	Mr. Under Secretary (*subsequently* Sir)	The Under Secretary of Labor
Attorney General	The Honorable Edward R. Warden Attorney General of the United States *or, socially:* The Attorney General and Mrs. Warden	Dear Mr. Attorney General:	Mr. Attorney General (*subsequently* Sir)	The Attorney General
Director of Central Intelligence	The Honorable Agnes L. Schmidt Director of Central Intelligence Address *or socially:* The Director of Central Intelligence and Mr. Helmut Schmidt	Dear Director:	Madam Director	The Director of Central Intelligence
U.S. Senator	The Honorable Frederick H. Lee United States Senate Address *or, socially:* Senator and Mrs. Frederick H. Lee	Dear Senator Lee:	Senator *or* Senator Lee	Senator Lee

Personage	Introduction and Addressing Envelopes	Letter Salutation	Speaking To	Place Card
U.S. Representative	The Honorable Sarah Thune House of Representatives Address *or, socially:* The Honorable Sarah Thune and Mr. Christopher Thune	Dear Ms. Thune:	Ms. Thune	The Honorable Sarah Thune *or* Ms. Thune
American Ambassador Abroad	The Honorable David R. Luce American Embassy Address *or, socially:* The Honorable David R. Luce and Mrs. Luce	Dear Ambassador Luce: *or* Dear Mr. Ambassador:	Ambassador Luce	Ambassador Luce
Governor	The Honorable Francis L. Fine Governor of Florida Address *or, socially:* Governor and Mrs. Francis L. Fine	Dear Governor: *or* Dear Governor Fine:	Governor *or* Governor Fine	The Governor of Florida
State Senator	The Honorable Jorge Morales *or, socially:* State Senator Jorge Morales and Mrs. Morales	Dear Senator Morales	Senator Morales	The Honorable Jorge Morales
Mayor	The Honorable Stanley Breck, Jr. Mayor of Providence *or, socially:* Mayor and Mrs. Stanley Breck, Jr.	Dear Mr. Mayor: *or* Dear Mayor Breck:	Mayor Breck	The Mayor of Providence
Judge	The Honorable Robert Quinlan Judge, Appellate Division Supreme Court of the State of New York *or, socially:* Judge and Mrs. Robert Quinlan	Dear Judge Quinlan:	Judge Quinlan	Judge Quinlan

"The Honorable"—A Title of Respect in America

"The Honorable" in front of a person's name is a title held for life by a person who holds or has held high office at the federal, state, or city levels. However, there is a nuance that must be remembered: A person who is addressed by others as "The Honorable" should not put the title on his own business cards, his own personal letterhead, or on the invitations he extends. If, for example, an ex-official is now a partner in a law firm, on the firm's stationery his name would be listed with the other partners with "The Honorable" before it, but if it is his stationery alone, his name should not bear that honorific. In other words, it is a distinction bestowed by someone else on a person, not by the person on himself.

How to Address an Envelope Using "The Honorable"

	To a Woman	To a Man
Use three lines for the title	The Honorable Julia Rosen Treasurer of the State of Maine Address	The Honorable George Voutas United States Senate Address

Indent three spaces for spouse's name when addressing invitation	The Honorable Julia Rosen
	    and Mr. Geoffrey Rosen
	Address
		The Honorable George Voutas
		    and Mrs. Voutas
		Address

When someone is no longer in office, "the Honorable" is still used (name and title on one line)	The Honorable Julia Rosen Address	The Honorable George Voutas Address
Addressing invitation to couple when official is no longer in office	Mr. Geoffrey Rosen and the Honorable Julia Rosen Address (The wife's name goes after her husband's when she is no longer in office.)	The Honorable and Mrs. George Voutas Address (When a person is no longer in office, it is permissible to use the abbreviation "The Hon.", as in: The Hon. and Mrs. George Voutas

NOTE: When a woman who has held a high official position remarries and changes her name, she still retains the right to "The Honorable" (or informally "The Hon.") before her given name.

The following are among those who carry "The Honorable" title:

The President and the Vice President
Cabinet members, Deputy Secretaries, Under Secretaries, and Assistant Secretaries
Presidential assistants
American career and appointed ambassadors
American representatives (including alternates and deputies) to international organizations
The Chief Justice of the Supreme Court, Associate Justices, judges of other courts
All members of Congress
The Secretary of the Senate; the Clerk of the House
The Sergeants at Arms of the Senate and House
Librarian of Congress
Comptroller General (General Accounting Office)
Heads, assistant heads, and commissioners of U.S. government agencies
Governor and lieutenant governor of a state
Secretary of State, Chief Justice, and Attorney General of a state
State Treasurer, Comptroller, or Auditor

State Senator, Representative, Assemblyman, or Delegate
Mayor
Members of the City Council, Commissioners, etc.

Addressing Officials in Conversation and in Writing

The Use of "My Dear So-and-So" as a Salutation in a Letter

To write an important person as "My dear Mr. So-and-so" or "My dear Ambassador So-and-so" in a letter salutation is an old tradition. However, in modern times it seems archaic, like dancing a minuet or leaving your calling cards on a silver tray on someone's hall table. In other words, you can skip the "My dear" in any salutation; use the recipient's name (Dear Mr. Agyropoulos:) or the recipient's position (Dear Mr. Attorney General:).

Addressing Officials by Their Titles in Conversation

It is customary to address a very important official by his title and not by his name. (I am grateful for this custom, since I habitually forget names, yet always remember titles.) For example:

"Mr. President" (or "Madam President") when speaking to him (or her)
"Mr. Secretary" or "Madam Secretary," for a cabinet position
"Mr. Under Secretary" or "Madam Under Secretary"
"Mr. Ambassador" or "Madam Ambassador"
"Mr. Mayor" or "Madam Mayor"

Note that we say "Governor" when talking to a governor, not "Mr. Governor." We say "Mr. Ambassador," not "Mr. Special Representative to the United Nations." The only definitive statement we can make concerning American protocol is that there is no rule without an exception.

- A person of rank should either have his place card written according to his position (e.g., "The Secretary of Labor" or "The Ambassador of Great Britain") or his place card should contain his title and surname ("Judge Atkins"; "Major Jones"; "Dr. Clark"). See the charts given earlier in this chapter for the correct forms of address.
- If you are in doubt as to someone's title, or as to whether or not you should put "The Honorable" or the guest's position on the card, use "The Honorable." With the exception of medical doctors, judges, and the military, you can always flatter a person who holds or has held an official job by putting on the place card "The Honorable David Atwater" or "The

Honorable Susan Walters." It's a safety valve—like calling a woman from another country "Madam" when you can't remember her name.

· It's important to remember that a U.S. Senator's and a U.S. Representative's place cards are not done identically. For the Senator use "Senator Lawson," but if the person is a Representative, his card should read "Mr. Lawson" or alternatively—and I like this much better—"The Honorable William Lawson."

Addressing Women in Particular

The wife of an official goes by her husband's name in official life—i.e., *Mrs. Theodore Wells* (rather than Mrs. Elise Wells) in the United States; *Signora Antonio Carici* in Italy; *Madame Henri Blanche* in France, Belgium, and the French part of Switzerland (as well as French-speaking African countries); *Frau Hans Kauffman* in Germany, Austria, and the German part of Switzerland; *Señora Miguel Flores* in Spain and Spanish-speaking Latin America.

In the United States, women who work under their own names are addressed by their own names, but rarely does that work for the American woman who accompanies her official husband abroad. She should not try to use her own name when she is with her husband on a trip involved with his work, not hers. It creates protocol problems for the officials of a host country that does not have many, if any, women in top positions.

Of course, if it is the woman official who is the senior ranked person and her husband is accompanying *her* on her mission, she would use her own title and name, not his.

Use "Madame" When Addressing a Woman from a Foreign Country

We call women in this country "Mrs.", "Miss," or "Ms.", followed by a surname. When we meet a woman from another country, we often have trouble catching a complicated name, and we don't know whether to call her "Miss" or "Mrs." The solution is to call her simply "Madame." French is the language of diplomacy throughout the world, and "Madame" is almost as catchall as "Ms." in the American idiom.

Use "Madame" for a woman who is out of her teens or if you know for a fact that she is married. It makes life very simple. You don't have to say "Madame Abdourahmane" when you're talking with her. Just "Madame" will do.

Addressing the Spouses of Officially Ranked People

	Introducing/ Addressing an Envelope	Letter Salutations	Speaking To	Place Card
When an official's wife uses her husband's name	The Secretary of Commerce and Mrs. Roe	Dear Mrs. Roe	Mrs. Roe	Mrs. Roe
When an official's wife goes by her own name	The Secretary of Commerce Mr. Ralph Baldwin and Ms. Marian Smith	Dear Ms. Smith	Ms. Smith	Ms. Smith
Spouse of high-ranking woman	Senator Ann Green and Mr. David Green	Dear Mr. Green	Mr. Green	Mr. Green
When both husband and wife have rank*	The Honorable David Green and The Honorable Ann Green	Dear Senator Green	Senator Green	Senator Green
	Commander Jerome Tate and Lieutenant Tate	Dear Lieutenant Tate	Lieutenant Tate	Lieutenant Tate

*If the wife outranks her husband, her name properly comes first.

Official Business
with People from Abroad

"His Excellency" or "Her Excellency" for Foreign Officials

Americans use "The Honorable" as a title in front of a person's given name and surname to note the importance of the person's present or former position. For the heads of state, ambassadors, cabinet officers, etc., of other countries (as well as for high-ranking members of the clergy), it is proper to use "His Excellency" (or "Her Excellency") before the given name and surname. For example, an envelope is addressed:

His Excellency   or   His Excellency
Giovanni Nanni   The Bishop of Cleveland
Ambassador of the Republic of Italy

We would introduce the dignitary to an assemblage in the same manner. In most cases, we address the envelope in the way we formally introduce the person. (Note, however, that the Commonwealth nations do not use "His Excellency," but rather "The Right Honorable.")

What is confusing is that what we properly call a foreign official in the United States may not be the way he is properly addressed in his own country. For example, we address a foreign ambassador to this country as "His Excellency" on the envelope and letter address as well as in an introduction, but we call him "Mr. Ambassador" to his face. In many foreign countries, he is called "Your Excellency" to his face. The nuances are subtle but important. It is important to learn how to address foreign officials in this country. If you have business abroad, you should also learn the protocol in whatever country or countries you are doing business.

The United Nations

Unlike the diplomatic corps accredited to Washington, D.C., the United Nations diplomats change in rank and precedence on a rotating basis (which means that length of service in the job or importance of the country has little to do with who outranks whom). If you are having a dinner party with more than one United Nations ambassador in attendance, call the United Nations Protocol Office (212/754-7170) to find out how to seat your dinner as of that moment.

Official	Introducing and Addressing Envelope	Letter Salutation	Speaking To	Place Card
The Secretary General	Her Excellency Françoise d'Estain Secretary General of the United Nations	Dear Madame Secretary General:	Madame Secretary General (Madame d'Estain, subsequently)	The Secretary General of the United Nations
A foreign UN ambassador	His Excellency Koto Matsumada Ambassador of Japan Permanent Mission of Japan to the United Nations	Dear Mr. Ambassador:	Mr. Ambassador (Sir, subsequently)	Ambassador Matsumada
The United States representative to the United Nations	The Honorable Henry Gregory United States Representative to the United Nations	Dear Mr. Ambassador:	Mr. Ambassador (Sir, subsequently)	Ambassador Gregory

Invitations to UN ambassadors and their spouses are addressed to their residences as follows:

His Excellency Koto Matsumada or Her Excellency Françoise d'Estain
and Madame Matsumada and Monsieur Eric d'Estain

The British: Our Friends with Many Titles

Since we do so much business with Great Britain, it is important for those having a great deal of contact with the country to understand its layers of leadership: the Crown, the government, and the peers of the realm.

Protocol for the Royal Family is carefully prescribed, and even though philosophically we Americans do not adhere to the principles of a monarchy, we should respect our British friends' admiration for it. It is impossible to please the British in their own country and to please British business people visiting here if we are completely unknowledgeable about their country's history or the Crown.

Some pretty silly, petty storms have ranged in past years over such questions as whether or not an American ambassador's wife should make a formal curtsey in greeting the Queen. When the Queen is in the United States an American woman's slight bow, made while shaking hands with Her Majesty, would appropriately replace a curtsey. However, in the presence of the Queen in England, I believe one should do as the British do. If all the British women curtsey to the Queen, why should the wife of the American ambassador be any different? Or for that matter, an American business woman in England on a business trip who is fortunate enough to meet her?

It is quite logical that Americans are not as formal as the British are with their own officials and the peerage. The following charts on English officials and the titled peerage represent what is proper for an American business person to do when speaking to, introducing, or writing to them.

Members of the British Commonwealth outside of England are not as formal as the English; certainly the Canadians are informal by comparison.

The Royal Family

- One does not write directly to a member of the Royal Family, but to "The Private Secretary to . . ." One writes, for example, to the secretary of the following:

Her Majesty the Queen

His Royal Highness, Prince Philip,
   The Duke of Edinburgh

Her Majesty Queen Elizabeth, the Queen Mother

His Royal Highness, The Prince Charles
   Prince of Wales

His Royal Highness, The Prince Edward

Her Royal Highness, The Princess Anne
   Mrs. Mark Phillips

Her Royal Highness, The Princess of Wales

His Royal Highness, The Prince Andrew

Her Royal Highness, The Princess Margaret
   Countess of Snowden

- Introductions are made and place cards are written exactly as the titles above.
- Except for the Queen and the Queen Mother (both of whom are addressed as "Your Majesty"), all family members are addressed as "Your Royal Highness," and all are subsequently addressed as "Sir" or "Ma'am."
- If you are presented to a member of the Royal Family, you do not speak first. You wait for the royal personage to speak first. Your conversation will be limited at best. For example, at Wimbledon the Queen might praise the American players' performances, to which you would reply, "Thank you for those kind words, Your Majesty."

The British Government

Official	Introducing and Addressing Envelope	Letter Salutation	Speaking To	Place Card
The Prime Minister	The Rt. Hon. Mary Smith, P.C., M.P. The Prime Minister (P.C. means Privy Councillor; M.P. means Member of Parliament) *or, socially:* The Prime Minister and Mr. Ivan Smith	Dear Prime Minister:	Madam Prime Minister	The Prime Minister
The Home Secretary (Equivalent of our Secretary of State):	The Rt. Hon. Ronald Coates, P.C., M.P. Home Secretary *or, socially:* The Rt. Hon. Ronald and Mrs. Coates	Dear Mr. Coates: *or, if titled:* Dear Sir Ronald: *or* Dear Lord Coates:	Mr. Coates *or, if he is titled, it might be:* Sir Ronald *or* Lord Coates	The Home Secretary

(Other cabinet posts would be addressed in a similar manner.)

Official	Introducing and Addressing Envelope	Letter Salutation	Speaking To	Place Card
A British Ambassador to the United States	His Excellency David Leeds Ambassador of Great Britain *or, if he is titled, it might be:* His Excellency Sir David Leeds et cetera	Dear Ambassador Leeds: *or, if titled:* Dear Sir David:	Mr. Ambassador or Sir David	The Ambassador of Great Britain

NOTE: The British would close a letter to one of their officials with "Yours faithfully," which an American may use in a letter to a British official; "Sincerely" or "Sincerely yours" is also proper.

Many British officials and peers have initials after their surnames, standing for orders, honors, and knighthoods. You should always write to such a person in the same manner he writes his name to you—with or without the initials. For example, a titled knight might be addressed as: Sir George Creighton, G.C.M.G.

The Peerage

Peer	Introducing; also Addressing Envelope	Letter Salutation	Speaking To	Place Card
A nonroyal duke	The Duke of Oakford *or* The Duke and Duchess of Oakford	Dear Duke: Dear Duchess	Duke Duchess	The Duke of Oakford The Duchess of Oakford
	(The English often address a duke and duchess as "Your Grace" and speak of them as "His Grace the Duke of . . ." but Americans are not expected to follow this procedure.)			
Duke's eldest son and daughter-in-law	The Marquess of Chester *or, socially:* The Marquess and Marchioness of Chester	Dear Lord Chester: Dear Lady Chester:	Lord Chester Lady Chester	Lord Chester Lady Chester
Marquess's eldest son; Earl's wife, a countess	The Earl of Meads *or, socially:* The Earl and Countess of Meads	Dear Lord Meads: Dear Lady Meads:	Lord Meads Lady Meads	Lord Meads Lady Meads
Viscount, eldest son of an earl	Viscount Brentwood *or, socially:* Viscount and Viscountess Brentwood	Dear Viscount Brentwood: Dear Lady Brentwood:	Lord Brentwood Lady Brentwood	Viscount Brentwood Viscountess Brentwood
Baron Baroness	The Lord Lyndhurst *or, socially:* Lord and Lady Lyndhurst	Dear Lord Lyndhurst: Dear Lady Lyndhurst:	Lord Lyndhurst Lady Lyndhurst	Lord Lyndhurst Lady Lyndhurst
Baronet	Sir Albert Northrop, Bt. *or, socially:* Sir Albert and Lady Northrop	Dear Sir Albert: Dear Lady Northrop:	Sir Albert Northrop Lady Northrop	Sir Albert Northrop Lady Northrop

Canadian Officials

	Introducing and Address on Envelope	Letter Salutation	Speaking To	Place Card
Governor General	His Excellency Eric C. Johnson *or, socially:* Their Excellencies Governor General and Mrs. Johnson	Dear Governor General	Governor General	The Governor General of Canada
Lieutenant Governor of Canada	His Honour The Honourable Gerald L. Dowd Lieutenant Governor *or, socially:* Lieutenant Governor and Mrs. Dowd	Dear Lieutenant Governor:	Lieutenant Governor Dowd	The Lieutenant Governor of Canada

Official	Introducing and Addressing Envelope	Letter Salutation	Speaking To	Place Card
Prime Minister of Canada	The Right Honourable Andrew C. Fitch, P.C., M.P. Prime Minister of Canada *or, socially:* The Prime Minister and Mrs. Fitch	Dear Mr. Prime Minister:	Prime Minister Fitch	The Prime Minister of Canada
Premier of a province of Canada	The Honourable Carolyn Cadré Premier of the Province of Quebec *or, socially:* The Honourable Carolyn Cadré and Mr. Jacques Cadré	Dear Madame Premier:	Premier Code	The Premier of Quebec
Member of Senate	The Honourable Laura Flynn The Senate, Ottawa *or, socially:* The Honourable Laura Flynn and Mr. Lesley Flynn	Dear Senator Flynn:	Senator	The Honourable Laura Flynn
Member of House of Commons	Samuel Morris, Esq., M.P. House of Commons *or, socially:* Mr. and Mrs. Samuel Morris	Dear Mr. Morris:	Mr. Morris	Samuel Morris, Esq., M.P.
Mayor of a city or town	His Worship Mayor Kenneth Woods City Hall *or, socially:* His Worship Mayor Kenneth Woods and Mrs. Woods	Dear Mr. Mayor:	Mr. Mayor	The Mayor of Toronto
Chief Justice	The Right Honourable Roger C. Bolton, Chief Justice of Canada *or, socially:* The Right Honourable Roger C. Bolton and Mrs. Bolton	Dear Mr. Chief Justice:	Chief Justice Bolton	The Chief Justice of Canada

NOTE: Since people in Great Britain and the Commonwealth spell it *Honourable,* with the *u,* it is a nice touch to address them with their own spelling.

Writing to Officials of Foreign Republics

When you write to officials of a foreign republic, follow the style given in this chart for the country of France:

Official	Introducing; also Name on Envelope	Letter Salutation	Speaking To	Place Card
President of the Republic	His Excellency Henri Vaudoyer President of the Republic of France Address *or, socially:* The President of France and Madame Vaudoyer	Dear Mr. President:	Mr. President	The President of the Republic of France
Prime Minister of the Republic of France	His Excellency Jean de l'Abeille Prime Minister of the Republic of France *or, socially:* The Prime Minister of France and Madame de l'Abeille	Dear Mr. Prime Minister:	Mr. Prime Minister	The Prime Minister of the Republic of France
Minister of Foreign Affairs of the Republic of France	Her Excellency Jeanne d'Arcy Minister of Foreign Affairs *or, socially:* The Minister of Foreign Affairs and Monsieur Pierre d'Arcy	Dear Madame Minister:	Madame Minister	The Minister of Foreign Affairs of the Republic of France

Western European Titles

The king or queen of any foreign country is addressed as "Your Majesty," and referred to as "His Majesty" or "Her Majesty" respectively.

The prince consort to the queen is referred to as "His Royal Highness" and is addressed as "Your Royal Highness."

When royal titles still exist in a country that is not a monarchy, even though these titles are meaningless, they are still treated with respect by the people in that country. Western Europe has a long history and a love of tradition, and therefore people who have inherited defunct but legitimate titles may use the royal crest on their stationery, engraved on their silver flatware, etc.

In order of rank, the titles are these:

- Prince and princess. (You call them by their title and surname, not their given names, when introducing them; in conversation call them "Prince" and "Princess.")
- Duke and duchess. (You call them by their title and surname, not their given name, when introducing them; in conversation, call them "Duke" or "Duchess.")

- Marquess and marchioness (*marquis* and *marquise* in France, *marchese* and *marchesa* in Italy, *marques* and *marquesa* in Spain)
- Viscount and vicountess
- Count and countess
- Baron and baroness

You would write an invitation to them in this manner: "Count and Countess Philippe de Beaumont." If one of the couple is titled and the other is not, use the title for the one who holds it: "Signor Emmanuele Capriccio and Contessa Eleanora Capriccio."

Many Western Europeans do not use their titles when doing business in the United States, but when you write to them in their country and when you are visiting in their country, you should use their titles.

11

The Receptionist, the Administrative Assistant/Executive Secretary, and the Company Image

There are important positions in the corporate world that do not receive enough attention—and often not enough compensation—but they all play a vital role in good company image. The people in these positions are the first persons you encounter when you walk into a company's office.

The Receptionist

The reception a visitor receives inside your office is as important to the corporate image as the state of the bricks and mortar of the building.

The person who greets the public on behalf of the company should be a smiling, well-dressed man or woman (perhaps in uniform), comfortably seated and presiding over a neat desk. If the ashtray is filled with cigarette butts and he is reading newspapers while slumped in his chair, a visitor may conclude that this company cares little about the impression made on visitors and probably cares very little about the quality of its goods and services.

It is the duty of the company's personnel officers to make tough demands when screening applicants for this important assignment, to set strict rules, and to be very clear about the do's and don'ts of this job. If the applicant feels Personnel is being too restrictive of his or her rights, then the applicant should look for another job.

A receptionist's job is too important to be accorded a very low salary. The salary should be adequate, and only conscientious and capable people should be hired for the job, with a promise of promotion within a year if they do a good job and learn the company's business.

Since many more women than men fill the job of receptionist, I have used the female pronoun for simplification in the following set of behavior guides for the position:

- She dresses conservatively. She wears pants only if her figure is perfect and her pants are very well cut.
- Her makeup and hairstyle are neat, well-done, and conservative; she does not fuss with her face or her hair once she is on the job.
- She wears little jewelry, and what she does wear is noiseless and inobtrusive.
- She does not eat, chew gum, smoke, or drink at her desk.
- She does not read newspapers at her desk, since they are so messy. She reads either magazines or a book hidden on her lap—and only when there is no activity in the area over which she is presiding.
- She keeps her hands and fingernails presentable.
- Her desk is neat, with everything in its proper place.
- She smiles when she greets each visitor and her demeanor shows she is glad to see each one. Her voice is cheerful when she uses the telephone to announce the visitor.
- She transmits orders and directions to the visitor in a very clear manner, so that she can be easily understood.
- She does not take personal calls of any length while on the job; she never continues a conversation she is having when a visitor approaches her desk, unless it is an important one. When she is on the telephone, she does not turn her back to the visitor, as though trying to shut him out.
- She makes sure that the reception area is clean at all times and equipped with good company reading materials, including company product catalogs, annual reports, etc.
- If a visitor is kept waiting longer than usual, she herself calls to see what is happening and then reports to the visitor.

- She treats executives, visitors, and employees with equal courtesy as they enter and leave her area.
- She calls everyone by his or her last name, so that her reception area has an air of dignity.
- She fastidiously keeps the company directory up to date, with accurate names, numbers, and locations of all personnel.
- She knows senior management—their titles, what they do, and how they fit into the hierarchy—so she can intelligently answer any question asked by a visitor.
- She makes sure her area has everything it needs, including a guest telephone, sufficient closet space, an umbrella stand, etc., as well as the proper sign-in book, if signing in is company policy for security's sake.
- If the receptionist is responsible for fire and bomb evacuation drills, she takes this duty very seriously and informs herself of every single detail.

The receptionist should have a signal to press in an emergency as well as a number she can call to give a code signal meaning "Come help. There's a suspicious-looking individual here."

The well-mannered executive understands what an important role a good receptionist plays in the organization and treats her with respect. He remembers the promise made to her to move her up within the company if she gives a stellar performance.

The Executive Secretary or Administrative Assistant

The personal traits of a highly qualified secretary or administrative assistant were described in *Fortune* magazine (March 12, 1979) as:

A metabolism that seems to improve under pressure
A natural instinct for creating order out of chaos
An appetite for the toughest chores and the ability to complete them without supervision
A clamlike facility for keeping secrets
A sure-handedness in dealing with even the most difficult people, which may include her/his own boss.

Many people feel that the secretarial profession is in a sad state in this country for two reasons: Secretaries and administrative assistants who are competent and professional are not always properly recognized or compensated; conversely, recent business school graduates, often ill-equipped in typing and spelling skills, may lack professionalism in their bearing. My remarks about secretaries in this chapter will *not* touch on the latter group.

Experienced executive secretaries are indispensable, since they help senior management in all areas of their work. They are not just close to the seat of power; they are part of it. Yet, while they may help polish the image of their bosses, they are rarely recognized for the important role they play.

There are two types of excellent secretaries. The first, while attached to her boss and company, has no desire to climb the corporate ladder. Her main objective is to serve her boss, to receive adequate compensation and suitable retirement benefits, to be respected within the organization, and to be an admired role model in her profession. This person is someone who has made a conscious career decision to be a secretary the rest of her working life.

The second type of good secretary has strong managerial ambitions and uses her immediate position as a basic training ground to learn what she can about her company. Her goal is to attain a senior secretarial position, followed by an assistant manager's slot. If she fulfills her obligations and responsibilities to her boss, he should unselfishly recommend her for a promotion.

The effective manager respects either type of good secretary. And if his secretary performs for him, he should help her achieve her goals.

The really capable secretary

- Is discreet. She does not talk about her boss's business, private life, or financial affairs. She never relays office gossip inside or outside the company.
- Handles the telephone with great tact, calming and satisfying everyone from the boss's mother-in-law to his board of directors.
- Is meticulous about keeping files up to date—her boss's calendar, his address book, her Rolodex, the Christmas card list, etc.
- Takes the initiative—to apologize for her boss when she knows he will be late to his lunch; to bring matters he has overlooked to his attention; to write letters that can be handled in a routine fashion for his signature, such as thank-you notes.
- Keeps her boss informed about what is happening within the organization—who is performing well, whose nose is out of joint, etc. She keeps her lines of communication open at all times.
- Understands priorities—which call should be made first, which letter should be written first, which person should be admitted first.
- Understands the importance of family pressures and helps to coordinate family-related matters.
- Keeps her boss's expense account and other records up-to-date.
- Keeps her boss on schedule—knows how and when to rescue him from an overlong appointment or telephone call.
- Makes certain that individuals in the company who need to know her boss's schedule or plans are apprised of them.

The Keeper of Office Manners

(*See also* Executive Telephone Manners, page 83)

A secretary with beautiful manners greatly enhances her organization. She actually sets the tone for her office—and other offices, too. If she handles the telephone and the relationships between her boss and his world inside and outside the company with consideration and tact, she elevates the entire company image.

The really proficient secretaries I know have an envelope addressed to the boss's host waiting on his desk on his return from a function or a meal to which he was invited. The boss automatically jots a short note of thanks to his host, and it goes out in the mail that very day—something that enormously impresses a host (particularly since he or she will hear from only approximately 5 percent of the guests).

The good secretary handles people so gracefully when she tells them no that she makes them feel as good as if it had been yes. That requires the diplomacy and tact of an international statesman.

Changing Her Title to Upgrade Her Job

Technological advancements and changes in the business world have not obliterated the secretary's position; they have, instead, freed her from many tiresome, routine tasks and enabled her to assume responsibilities of a more diversified nature. An efficient executive secretary should be considered part of the management team. As she advances in stature, she may want to have her title changed to raise her status within the organization. Here are some options:

> Executive Assistant
> Personal Assistant to . . .
> Administrative Assistant
> Staff Assistant
> Staff Coordinator
> Executive Office Manager
> Executive Staff Assistant
> Executive Coordinator

A secretary who is upgraded in position should have her salary adjusted accordingly and receive increased benefits.

How a Manager Refers to His or Her Secretary

A relatively formal relationship between an executive and his secretary denotes a sense of respect and dignity. In this relaxed world of ours, people tend to be on a first name basis much too quickly.

There are many corporations where the senior officers and their secretaries are on a "Mr." and a "Miss" or "Mrs." basis. As one executive told me, "It goes with the beautiful furniture and the all-wool carpeting." He smiled when he said it, but what he meant was that the rather formal overall image created by the company was unified; everyone felt it and was proud of it.

There is no excuse for a manager who refers to his secretary, whatever her age or physical characteristics, as "my girl." United Technologies placed an ad in major newspapers several years ago—an editorial on this subject that was applauded by secretaries all over the country.

Let's Get Rid of "The Girl"

Wouldn't 1979 be a great year to take one giant step forward for womankind and get rid of "the girl"? Your attorney says, "If I'm not here just leave it with the girl." The purchasing agent says, "Drop off your bid with the girl." A manager says, "My girl will get back to your girl." *What* girl? Do they mean Miss Rose? Do they mean Ms. Torres? Do they mean Mrs. McCullough? Do they mean Joy Jackson? "The girl" is certainly a woman when she's out of her teens. Like you, she has a name. Use it.

A senior secretary—any secretary—should be properly introduced by her boss to visitors whom she does not know. He should not say, "This is Sally, my secretary," but "This is Miss Jones (or Sally Jones), my secretary," or whatever title she uses.

An executive who asks his secretary to run a personal errand should not force the issue if she appears reluctant. If she does agree, it should be on her personal time, not the company's, and she should be compensated for it right from her boss's pocket. And for every executive who might say, "You have extra time, I see, Miss Brown. Would you mind going to Marshall Field's to pick up some athletic socks for me?" there should be one who will say, "I see you have some extra time, Miss Brown. Would you like to learn more about our new computer reporting division? I'll call Stimson and tell him to expect you for a tour. *I'll* answer the phone while you are gone."

A Word About "Going for Coffee"

The "going for the boss's coffee syndrome" has been blown out of all proportion. When I was a secretary, I provided my bosses with coffee or anything else they might want (and incidentally, anything I myself wanted at the same time). Look upon this as running an errand or performing a function in which one shares. It is not as much an act of servitude as some secretaries think. This whole syndrome of "I'm not a go-fer" sprang from the growth of the women's movement in the late sixties.

In my opinion, a secretary should use her precious energy to improve her position with the company in a constructive manner, not waste it fighting requests to serve coffee or tea. However, the boss should go fetch the coffee for everyone on the office staff from time to time, too, just to show that he or she shares responsibility for the comfort as well as the work of the staff.

Looking at Her in a New Light

After a period of two or three years' service, an executive should analyze and evaluate his secretary's performance to decide whether her abilities are compatible with a managerial position.

If your secretary cares enough to advance her position within the company and you feel she is qualified to do so, *help her attain this goal.* Give her managerial responsibilities when it is logical to do so. Take the time to explain your philosophy on certain business transactions, the major decisions you make, and what risks you take and why you take them. If she is ambitious and smart, she will automatically absorb what you tell her.

If she has a constructive business idea, provide her with guidelines on how she can best present it to the company. Let her see how frustratingly slow the period can be from the inception of an idea to its fruition—or abandonment.

How to Help Your Secretary or Administrative Assistant with Constructive Advice

If your secretary is not working out, you should let her go and find one who will. This job is too important in any executive's life to permit a negative situation to continue. Give her two or three warnings first; be fair and constructive. If you do let her go, give her your time when you give her the news. Sit her down and tell her exactly what she has done wrong *and right* in working for you, so that she can learn from the experience, build on her strengths, and perhaps not make the same mistakes again.

Get right to the point: "Antoinette, your job in this office is not working out, and we have discussed this before on two or three occasions. I'm going to have to let you go. I know this is very tough for you to hear, and I don't like having to say it. I have enjoyed knowing you and working with you, but it hasn't been a success for the following reasons. . . ." Then list them, let her interrupt and defend herself, but go down the list you have written, so she does not miss any of the negative points of her job performance.

End the discussion saying you are sure that Personnel will help her seek another job, and that you wish her well in her future life.

If your secretary *is* working out well, and if she has ambition to do better in her job and in her career, help her with constructive criticism. This does not mean that you are "on her back" all the time, harping on every detail. It does mean, however, that if she has an unpleasant voice, you find a good voice teacher and even help pay for her lessons if the company won't pay. If she does not know how to dress well, put her in the hands of a fashion consultant in a department store. If her experience has been extremely limited, encourage her to go to museums and lectures to learn, to read good books, to take adult extension courses at night. (Offer to pay for part of the tuition.) Whether she needs to change her hairstyle or change her deodorant, give it to her straight:

> "Mary, this is difficult to say and difficult for you to hear. The only way for me to handle it is to come right out without beating around the bush. I think you should check your deodorant. There, I've said it."

> "Susan, I respect your professionalism so much, I think I ought to pass on to you the fact that several people in this company have remarked that the rather flamboyant color of your hair is not in keeping with the image I'm sure you would like to project. I hope I'm not out of line by suggesting that you tone down the color. People should notice what a wonderful secretary you are—not the color of your hair."

Don't expect Personnel to do your dirty work for you if your secretary has a personal problem like the ones above. The only one who can handle it gracefully is you, her boss, and she'll take it from you if you give her the praise she deserves for her work as well as the criticism she needs for her problems.

In a Social Situation, Treat Your Secretary as an Equal

A professional executive secretary who excels at her job resents being treated by a boss of many years as someone who is not on the same social level as he is. A certain amount of deference must exist in the workplace, but out of it, in a social situation where both have been invited as guests, he should allow her to be a guest. He should not keep making demands on her, asking her to make this and that call, to get this and that for him. The secretary should certainly not attend a party to which she has not been invited, but when she has been invited, the boss should respect her presence as a guest.

I have noticed that when the boss and the secretary are invited to the same party, it works best if the secretary circulates at the opposite end of the room from her boss. If she stays by his elbow, out of shyness, she embarrasses everyone. She should develop her own social skills, quite apart from being his right arm, and learn to be a good conversationalist on subjects *other than the office.* One secretary I knew well was finally let go by her boss just because of her lack of social tact. They traveled on the corporate jet all over the world, and she was always invited to the big lunches held in most countries in his honor. She used to lean across the table, out of sheer nervousness, and in a loud voice bring up a subject absolutely no one else could contribute to: "Mr. B., wasn't that funny about Albert Hilte in the telex message this morning?" Mr. B. would smile and wince, realizing no one else could appreciate that question.

However, for every secretary who is totally inept at carrying on a good social conversation, I know ten more who are very good at it (in fact, many are better at it than their bosses). One sure way for a secretary to make a good impression is to be able to talk with enthusiasm, accuracy, and intelligence about the company for which she works and its goods or services.

A Tribute to an Executive Secretary

An executive secretary who remains with her boss for many years becomes an extension of that person, and often a member of that person's family.

I have heard many executives pay loving tributes to their secretaries through the years, but the most touching one of all was the tribute paid by Professor Arthur Schlesinger, Jr., a former special assistant to President John F. Kennedy, at the funeral of his long-time secretary Gretchen Stewart.

> I first met Gretchen Stewart some twenty-two years ago—in February 1962, when I arrived in President Kennedy's White House, took my oath as special assistant to the President and was assigned an office and a secretary in the East Wing. Through a great stroke of luck, about which I never ceased to marvel in later years, the courteous young woman who greeted me in my new office turned out to be Gretchen.
>
> She had begun her White House career in the Truman presidency a dozen or so years before and had continued her service through the Eisenhower years. A true professional, she regarded the ardent young newcomers of the New Frontier with welcoming tolerance. At first, I thought how nice it was to have such a pleasant and knowledgeable aide. Soon I discovered that, beyond this, Gretchen was a most uncommon person— uncommon not only in her charm but in her quiet integrity, in her compassion and in her wisdom.
>
> There began an association that lasted for nearly a quarter of a century. After President Kennedy's death, she helped me when I wrote A Thousand Days. When I left Washington for a few months for the Institute for Advanced Study in Princeton, she went to work for Senator McGovern; but when I later moved on to the City University of New York, she decided to throw over Washington and abandon government for academic life. Through all these years in Washington and New York, Gretchen eased and ordered my life, saved me from excess and error, acted as my protector and my conscience, stayed far too long hours and worked far too hard—and did it all with an exacting sense of standards and of responsibility, with incomparable tact and efficiency and with inexhaustible sweetness of temper.

Anyone who understands modern organization knows the great power of secretaries and the great importance of the secretarial network—women who may often know each other only by the voice on the telephone but nonetheless have a companionship forged in common undertaking and shaped by urgency and crisis. In Washington and in New York, Gretchen was a greatly trusted and admired figure. Everyone who dealt with my office was treated with impeccable courtesy, even when they did not deserve it. My friends counted unquestioningly on her judgment and discretion. My wife and children were devoted to her. It would be hard to count the number of people I have encountered since her illness began who have asked about her, sent their affections to her, and told of their sorrow over her troubles.

She endured illness with extraordinary gallantry and courage. She never complained, insisted on continuing to work too long and too hard, and discharged all her tasks with rare dedication and total fidelity. I can never adequately express my debt to her.

I must add that through all these years in the alien corn of Washington and New York, her heart remained in Kansas. Nothing gave her greater pleasure than her annual trips home. Nothing attracted her more than the thought of a Kansas retirement where she would at last be free to pursue her genealogical studies. When she could work no longer, her one desire was to go back to Kansas and rejoin her family. . . . She leaves a vacancy in all our lives. She died as she lived—a truly good woman.

12

Good Relations with the Nonprofit Sector

This chapter deals with what is obviously one of the most important aspects of the human side of business: the social responsibility that is a crucial part of corporate character.

The highly developed sense of responsibility to one's fellow man is often what the public most admires in a company. It is evident when the company manufactures products that are safe, of good quality, and fairly priced. It is evident when services are performed for and products are given to the community without charge. It means the company acts to protect, not damage our environment. It means the company is a fair and concerned employer.

When a company has a good sense of corporate responsibility, it contributes to the limits of its abilities to the institutions that:

- Educate our leaders
- Care for the sick and the needy
- Carry on research that will benefit all mankind
- Provide cultural enrichment for the general public

A corporate citizen's actions for the common good are not sheer altruism, they are also good business. People like to buy goods and services from a company with a reputation for social responsibility.

Not all businesses are doing what they could. For example, many businesses have a long way to go before reaching the maximum 5 percent charity deductions allowable on their pretax incomes. There have been all too few companies like Dayton Hudson, which for four decades has contributed 5 percent of its pretax profits and helped make the entire business community of its hometown, Minneapolis, aware of its public service responsibilities.

In spite of those who feel management has no right to spend the shareholders' money on matters not directly concerning the company, and in spite of others who claim that the business sector must be tough with the recipients of corporate donations and demand strict accountability, most companies who do their part in the nonprofit sector today feel their actions have helped not only their image but their profits. That there is a positive relationship between the company's work environment and community environment is also evident in what companies themselves look for when expanding or moving. Cities have discovered that when they stress the quality of their educational system, their health services, and their flourishing cultural environment, they can more easily attract new business. Without the support of individuals who have made money in business, and without the support of business itself, there would not be much "quality" anything in our communities today.

A Company Needs a Policy on Corporate Support

The hands seem to be stretched out from every corner. Lobbying is intense, and a company faced with many requests for donations needs a policy to refer to and a framework in which to give its money. Executives can become slightly paranoid—colleagues from other companies stop them on the golf course to request contributions for their pet causes; wives are hounded by other wives for corporate donations; there's pressure for financial support from the children's schools. Everyone seems to be running a fund drive or having a benefit. The cry of need comes from all sides. The public library is in a dismal state; the local animal shelter might have to close; the hearing-disabled center needs a new roof; the ballet troupe will have to disband without an immediate money transfusion; the chairman's son's Boy Scout troop has an exciting community project to fund.

What are the options for ensuring an orderly, manageable response?

· A large corporation may solve its donation problem by establishing a foundation to handle all funding requests. In this way the company executives can resist pressures to exert personally any influence they might otherwise bring to bear: "It's entirely in *their* hands."
· A middle-sized company may retain the services of a professional consultant to develop a plan for its corporate support policies, which includes what kind of letter to send in answer to requests for donations.

- Entrepreneurs and small businesses may establish a modest, general fund that enables the company each year to purchase benefit tickets and take ads in benefit journals.
- A company's options for giving include these:

    The same charity is benefited each year, and others learn not to ask. For example, if a company has committed itself to helping keep alive its local public television station, other charities learn not to ask that company for support. In talking to people on the telephone and in answering letters asking for donations the company says, "We feel we can be most effective in the nonprofit sector by focusing our support efforts on an organization that affects this whole community—our local public television station."

    The same general field is benefited each year, but each time a different organization within the field receives the money.

    A designated beneficiary receives a contribution for five successive years; then the company initiates a new five-year cycle with another institution.

How a Company Can Provide Support

There are numerous options to choose among when it comes to what the company specifically does to show support in the community service area. It can

- Pay the fees and expenses for a year or two of an established professional fund-raising organization to help an institution with its major fund drive. (Check out a prospective fund-raising organization with its other clients; if it holds membership in the American Association of Fund-Raising Counsel at 25 West 43rd Street, New York, NY 10036, that is an excellent recommendation in itself.)
- Give money outright as a contribution or as a matching grant
- Support benefits by purchasing tickets
- Pay for company ads in the programs or journal of the charity's benefit
- Pay all the expenses of a benefit, thus becoming "the corporate sponsor"
- Place institutional ads on a charity's behalf in the news media. (*See* Institutional Advertising to Support the Nonprofit Sector, later in this chapter)
- Contribute company products to an organization
- Organize programs for the public in health fields, such as getting donors to give blood, having people check for early cancer, or having them check their blood pressure regularly

- Lend company premises for special meetings of nonprofit organizations
- Lend executives to serve as trainers and advisers; give free legal, accounting, and public relations advice
- Encourage its employees to become volunteers, either working in the institutions or helping with fund-raising
- Make a generous donation to a charity and note that on the back of the company holiday greeting card
- Sponsor performing arts events; make art exhibitions possible in museums
- Tour performing artists and art exhibits to other parts of the country
- Contribute to faculty enrichment of colleges and universities
- Give grants for research
- Endow chairs and pay for lecturers in the educational field
- Assist in civic events, providing manpower and funds
- Enable hospitals to purchase needed new equipment
- Lend computer capabilities to organizations that cannot afford to have their own
- Host a "corporate dinner" to benefit a charity, for which fellow executives from other companies buy tickets. During this event, usually held in a hotel, a designated CEO honoree is extolled to the skies for his civic endeavors. This kind of dinner can be a real money maker. When James Robinson of American Express was honored by Phoenix House, a New York-based drug rehabilitation organization, in April of 1983, the charity netted $400,000 from the dinner (aided and abetted in no small way, of course, by the presence of First Lady Nancy Reagan).

The Charity Benefit with Corporate Sponsorship

One of the most popular fund-raising techniques (and one of the biggest sources of revenue for the hotel industry, incidentally) is the charity benefit, primarily social in nature, but dependent in most cases on corporate funding to meet the basic expenses. This party may be held in any of a number of places—on the institution's premises, in a mansion or on a historic property, or (and this is most common) in a hotel ballroom. A board of socially prominent women usually runs the event; if there is a "Men's Committee," its purpose is to sell tickets in the corporate sector. Tickets sell from $100 to $1000 per person. A great deal of very hard committee work goes on behind the scenes, and a great deal of money is spent to make the party look, sound, and taste distinguished. One or more corporate sponsors are needed to pay for the basic expenses, which allows the benefit committee to turn over to the charity a check for the difference between the total revenues and any additional expenses, if any. In New York, as of this writing, a dinner dance for 350 guests in a well-known hotel might cost anywhere from $50,000 to $75,000 (more for a *very* splashy benefit). If tickets cost $300 per person, and if a corporation picks up the expenses for the evening, the charity could easily clear $105,000. The resulting public relations benefit of the event for both the beneficiary and the sponsor is another strong plus when it comes time for the annual fund-raising appeal.

The Expenses of a Charity Benefit

The expenses would include:

- The design, printing, and postage for eye-catching invitations
- The services of someone to hand-address and stuff the invitations
- The services of a professional social secretary to handle the RSVPs, the mailing of tickets (if this is necessary), and the supervision of the check-in desk at the door of the party
- The banquet costs of the hotel, including liquor, wines, coat-checking facilities, gratuities, and tax
- The flowers and decoration of the ballroom
- The entertainment (together with the sound system and lighting related to it)
- The printing of the ball program or journal
- The cost of retaining a professional publicity agency to handle the media and promote the event—an unnecessary expense if the benefit committee volunteers know how to handle publicity
- The cost of extra security guards, parking valets, etc.

The Income Derived from a Charity Benefit

This would include:

- The corporate sponsors' donations
- The proceeds from the sale of the tickets
- The proceeds from the sale of higher priced "Patrons Tickets"
- The profit from the sale of ads in the program journal distributed free to each guest
- The sale of raffle tickets for donated goods and services

Benefit Invitations Donated by the Sponsor

If a company is paying for a nonprofit institution's benefit invitations, it naturally should assure that the invitations are in keeping with the company's image—it should have final approval of the invitation dummy before that goes to the printer.

An invitation should:

- Be well designed and not cheap looking
- Communicate clearly the charity being benefited
- Contain all the important logistical information in proper sequence (the who, what, where, etc.)
- Contain an efficient RSVP card and return envelope to use for ordering benefit tickets or for mailing in a contribution
- Give appropriate credit to the sponsoring company

The following are sample invitations extended for different types of community events:

A Cultural Evening, Not a Benefit,
to Which Guests Are Invited by the Corporation

Mr. David L. Reed

President of Maiden Products, Inc.

and Mrs. Reed

and

The Honorable Wolfgang Schwartzenberg

Consul General of Austria

request the pleasure of your company

at a special performance of

The Viennese Opera Company in Concert

Entirely underwritten by Maiden Products, Inc.

on Thursday, December second

at eight o'clock

San Diego Opera House

300 Market Street

R S V P Card Enclosed   *Black Tie*
Tickets will be issued   *A reception will be held*
in order of receipt of   *on stage following the*
request.   *concert.*

We regret that this invitation is not transferable.

A Fund-Raiser Conceived of and Hosted by a Corporation

This hypothetical fund-raiser is a Saturday breakfast staged in the lobby of the corporate headquarters building, during which the closing ceremonies of the Summer Olympics are to be watched on television monitors placed throughout the lobby. The invitation reads as follows:

(Dalton Logo)

James Q. Sneed, President
and the employees of
The Dalton Corporation
hope you will join them at a breakfast
to benefit the **Utah Youth Clubs' Athletic Program**
on the occasion of the closing ceremonies
of the Summer Olympics
Saturday, August 20th
9 A.M. to 12 noon
Promenade and Lobby of the Dalton Tower
14 Regent Street
Salt Lake City

RSVP Card Enclosed

Catering and food service
courtesy of
the employees of Dalton

Program:
9 A.M. Telecast of the Closing
    Olympic Ceremonies
10 A.M. Address by Governor
    So-and-So
11 A.M. Performance by the
    Mormon Choir
11:30 A.M. Performance by the
    UYCAP Pentathlon Team

The RSVP card provided here has the Dalton president's name and address on the return envelope:

(Dalton Logo)

Thank you for your support of The Utah Youth Clubs programs

Breakfast and Olympics Wrapup
Saturday, August 22nd
9 A.M. to 12 noon
Dalton Tower

Number of reservations @ $100 _____
Names of your guests: _____　　　　_____
　　　　　　　　　　　 _____　　　　_____

Enclosed is my check for $_____
I regret I am unable to attend, but I wish to make a contribution.
Enclosed is my check for $_____
Name _____
Address _____Tel: _____
　　　　　　　Make checks payable to UYCAP
　　　　　　　Contributions are tax deductible

A Case History of a Firm Policy on Corporate Sponsorship: Philip Morris Sponsors Art

When George Weissman headed Philip Morris, he decided that the corporate donations policy was to be primarily one of a commitment to art. The support system he established in the field of art was one of the most comprehensive since the days of the Medici in Renaissance Florence. Philip Morris activities in the last decade have included:

- Funding the installation of a branch of the Whitney Museum of American Art in the company's new headquarters building in New York
- Placement of original works of art throughout company offices and plants, thereby helping to support artists and giving pleasure to the employees
- Sponsorship of numerous major art exhibits that have toured museums throughout America, with a major institutional advertising campaign in newspapers and magazines to promote the art in those exhibits
- Granting matching funds for all employee contributions to art organizations

- Encouraging the sponsorship of art by other corporations through provision of expert planning assistance. (To Philip Morris the sponsorship of art is not patronage, but "a business and a human necessity.")
- The donation of 30 percent of the corporation's total contributions to art

When a company becomes known for support in a particular field, that is evidence a policy on giving is in effect; it becomes easier to turn down other requests. Another advantage to being a specialist in one field of giving is that the company executives handling the funds become very knowledgeable about what is going on in that field. There is less opportunity for exaggeration or deceit on the part of the organization requesting aid.

A Small Company Can Also Support the World of Art

The head of a small company may feel like David contemplating Goliath when he compares himself to a company of Philip Morris's size. Relatively speaking, however, a small company can still become a formidable patron of art, increasing its impact, of course, as the business grows. Some feasible ideas:

- *Hang attractive art on the office walls,* perhaps in the form of good quality framed posters or prints, or perhaps works of art on loan from the local museum's inventory of rentable art. It is important that a committee of the employees, perhaps in conjunction with a decorator, be allowed to make the art selections that will dominate their office environment. Once the art is hung, the employees should be furnished with information on the various artists. Works of art make the employee's surroundings a better place; the employee becomes more knowledgeable about art in the process, and the art world prospers with the purchase of or the rental fees for the art.
- *Pay for part or all of the membership fees of the employees to the local museum,* thus encouraging more of them to use the museum's resources and to develop an interest in art.
- *Urge the employees to attend all of the major exhibits;* make it easy for them to go, even if it means helping with transportation or giving them a half hour extra time off. Make them proud of their local museums.
- *Make small contributions to the museum exhibitions,* thereby tying the company more closely to that institution.
- Organize a small library of art history books somewhere in the office, for the enjoyment and education of executives and employees alike.

Communicating a Corporation's Generosity

These are some of the ways in which a company communicates to the public its community service:

- In an institutional ad in the newspaper (*see* below)
- In the annual report
- In the program of a performance in the performing arts
- In the catalog of an exhibition it sponsors
- In the press releases of both the company and the institution
- In a brochure published for press, stockholders, employees, VIPs, customers, and clients
- In a tag-line of a sponsored public service television or radio spot: "This performance was made possible by a grant from _____."

Institutional Advertising to Support the Nonprofit Sector

A newspaper or magazine ad is very expensive, and when used to promote a nonprofit venture, many executives, not to mention the stockholders, wonder if it is worth it to them. No immediate profit-related results can be measured. No one can prove that any products were sold or that the value of the stock rose in response to an institutional ad's appearance. However, this kind of advertising can be a powerful communicator of a bright and shiny corporate image, as well as a reflection of a company's good citizenship.

An institutional ad powerfully promotes a museum, library, botanical garden, opera company, symphony, dance company, or theatrical group when it furnishes the dates and times of special shows, exhibits, and performances. Pfizer, the pharmaceutical company, promotes the arts and medical research (as well as itself) in public service spots on television when they advertise Byron Janis playing a piano recital and talking about the Arthritis Foundation.

Corporate Support and the Employees

The company that teaches its employees the importance of contributing both time and money to the nonprofit sector is the best citizen of any community. It is not enough for a company to give money to needy institutions. It's equally important to instill in every executive and employee a sense of appreciation for and willingness to help local institutions.

There is also an urgent necessity for corporations to help fight the hedonistic spirit prevailing today in the workplace—to inspire mid-managers to give the same amount of time they expend working on their bodies to working on cultural and intellectual pursuits. These are some of the ways in which a company prompts involvement on the part of its own people:

- *The company organizes volunteer programs* through which employees serve in the field of their choice, perhaps working as nurse aides in a hospital, working with young people in sports activities, reading to the blind, serving as museum and library volunteers, helping schools with remedial reading programs, or visiting the elderly. Some companies give time off for part of this volunteer work; in any case the individual employee's contributions are recognized and applauded by management, whether through an article in the company newsletter ("The Volunteer of the Month"), or through a verbal citation by the CEO at a meeting of employees.

- *The company pays half or in full for membership dues* to local cultural or educational institutions. This familiarizes employees with what is available to them locally; the program enriches their lives and makes them happier individuals.

- *The company matches donations* to nonprofit organizations up to a limit—either by half or in full.

- The company provides a "ticket fund" for local performances in the performing arts for the employees' enjoyment. Pairs of tickets are made available on a rotating basis; employees often become enthusiastic supporters of the arts. Their lives are enriched, and the performers are given an audience.

- *The company sponsors special educational programs to help employees understand and appreciate their local institutions.* Employees may be bused to universities and museums for special lectures after work. Group tours of museum exhibits are conducted with a museum guide provided. Once the employees become involved in these activities, they tend to pursue further interest without any help from the company.

- A great way to promote more volunteerism among company employees is to salute them in an institutional newspaper ad. Ashland Petroleum Company, for example, took a full page ad honoring a Buffalo refinery worker who had mastered the technique of CPR (cardiopulmonary resuscitation). The text made the company, the workers, his family and friends, and the city of Buffalo feel proud—a lot of goodwill for a small amount of cash:

> . . . His job is demanding. And yet he spends his spare time protecting lives in his community, and teaching his neighbors how to save lives as well.

Service on the Board of a Nonprofit Institution

It is an honor to be asked to serve on the board of a nonprofit institution. Such a call to service should not be taken lightly, but unfortunately some senior executives do react that way. They lend their names to several prestigious organizations and mistakenly think this gesture is sufficient, as long as they purchase a couple of company tables at the annual benefit.

A nonprofit institution naturally wants famous names on its board, but it also *needs* their active help. There is no excuse for executives consistently missing board meetings. A solution is for the top-ranking executive to give his name to the board but to have a younger executive represent him at every meeting, keep him well informed, and develop expertise in planning and problem solving for the institution in question. A young executive who serves as a junior member on the board of a nonprofit institution eventually matures into a senior executive thoroughly conversant with the institution's work and better able to advance it.

There should be less hypocrisy in board membership, more actual company brain power expended at all levels of management, and more effective contributions made by business to the nonprofit sector.

Corporate Good Manners Toward Nonprofit Institutions

Good manners should govern the way in which a corporation relates to any nonprofit institution it assists. The company should, for example:

- Make its donation in a philanthropic (derived from two Greek roots meaning "love of mankind") rather than totally self-serving manner. The company should refrain from repeating, "But what are *we* going to get out of it?" Nor should it expect an attitude of obsequious gratitude on the part of the institution benefited.
- Assign a well-mannered executive, senior enough in rank to serve as an effective company representative for the CEO. One of this person's responsibilities should be to keep the CEO advised of all activities involving the company and the nonprofit institution; another, to gain the maximum possible cooperation of his company in helping the institution.
- Treat the head of the institution with respect, not with a patronizing attitude.
- Make sure that all company tickets purchased for the institution's charity benefit are used. Empty places at any event are a strong negative. The tickets should be used by appropriately dressed company representatives or by important customers.
- Expect no more than four to six free tickets to benefits it sponsors. The purpose of the benefit is to raise money, and even though the corporate donation may be generous, the charity's purpose for staging the benefit is to *sell* tickets, not to give them away free.
- Not use a benefit as a forum for self-promotion. If the CEO makes some remarks to the assembled guests at the benefit, he should not use the

occasion to give a long speech (three minutes is *plenty*), nor should he use his time to broadcast a commercial for company products or services. He should quickly thank the benefit committee, praise the charity, reaffirm his company's commitment to it, and sit down.

· Avoid interfering with the day-to-day activities of the institution. When a company sponsors a concert, for example, a company representative should not try to change the musical program. If the company is one of the sponsors of a new hospital wing, it should not try to interfere with the architect's plans (unless, of course, a serious error has been detected). The company should offer its expertise to the organization it is helping, but then let the organization's staff handle things on its own. There should be an atmosphere of trust in the working relationship between donor and recipient.

An Institution's Good Manners Toward a Sponsoring Corporation

The nonprofit institution should demonstrate its own good manners toward the benefactor by remembering to:

· Keep the company informed of its activities when the information would be of obvious interest to the company
· Show appreciation for a gift regardless of its size
· Wait a suitable length of time before asking for another gift (six months to a year, depending on the size of the last gift)
· Assign either the executive director or the assistant director to attend institution-company meetings
· Credit the major corporate sponsor on all appropriate publications, press releases, etc. The sponsor of a benefit, for example, should be acknowledged in the invitations, press releases, program, and from the floor when the benefit chairman makes his or her remarks.
· Say "thank you" in creative ways. One CEO, reminiscing about his long and distinguished career, said the most memorable nonprofit experience in his life came as a result of his company donating a special hospital wing for children. Several months after it was opened, the president of the hospital presented him with a large scrapbook, its pages filled with letters, drawings, and poems made by the children patients in that hospital. It was a "gift of their gratitude." The CEO circulated it throughout his organization and printed excerpts from it in the company newsletter. (The corporation has been a firm supporter of the hospital ever since.)
· Record a major donation in a manner to be visible to the public, such as placing a plaque on the wall or carving an inscription in the stone facade of a building to which a company was a major contributor

- Thank the sponsoring corporation from the stage for a corporate-sponsored performance. I remember one moving evening when the entire cast of a Shakespearean drama assembled at the foot of the stage at the end of the play to shout "Thanks, Company X!", smiling and blowing kisses over the footlights at the executives in the front row. (In the newspaper the next day, a front page photograph showed this scene; everyone agreed it was company money well spent!)
- Host a social event (not opulent) for the major donors. Appropriate *short* speeches of thanks should be made to the companies involved.
- Give the donor or donor company a small memento of a major gift like a building—perhaps a framed architect's rendering in color of the new building, accompanied by a suitable inscription from the institution to the company
- Arrange a series of guided "familiarization tours" of a donated facility for the employees of the donor company, so that they will understand and appreciate their company's role in the project

13

When an Executive Retires

One day a letter from the CEO of Allegheny Castings Inc. is posted on all employee bulletin boards:

> George Marchand Sudler, Senior Vice-President of this company, will retire as of March 4, 1987. It should not be necessary to remind you that one of the reasons this company is highly successful is because Mr. Sudler joined Allegheny Castings forty years ago this month. He has helped shape the policy of this company and has actively contributed to its growth during his entire career.
>
> We are going to miss him, and I personally am going to miss him more than I can express. I hope you will join me in giving George Sudler a royal send-off on March 2nd at 5 P.M. in the company cafeteria.

What the Company Can Do

Retirement comes to all of us one day, even if we're not as high up in the hierarchy as George Sudler, who merits a party organized by the CEO. If you ask a retiree what the most important thing in his life is at this stage, he might reply, "A comfortable pension and group health insurance coverage." What he may also need, however, particularly after long service with one company, is to maintain an association with the overall corporate family. He also needs to feel useful to society. A compassionate corporation prepares executives and employees for retirement during the last year of work; it may even provide training for retirement and programs that will enhance the retirees' lives. This may be an expensive undertaking, but it is also indicative of a caring, concerned company that appreciates an employee's long, devoted service. Then too, the good deeds of retired volunteers in the community are perfect reflections of the company's own good citizenship.

Some Company-Sponsored Retirement Activities

- The company may organize retired executives into consulting groups that provide professional advice for other small companies (Textron does this).
- The company may channel retirees into badly needed volunteer positions in hospitals, nursing homes, and schools (Honeywell, Inc. does this).
- The company may recruit retirees to join with professional staff members in visiting or telephoning elderly or ailing retirees (Levi Strauss does this).
- Certain companies encourage executives (soon to retire) to spend a day a week in community work at the beginning of their last year of work; by the final quarter of the year, they are working only one day a week and four days as a volunteer.
- Very few programs are as inspiring as the former Bell System's "Telephone Pioneers of America," many of whom are retirees. These skilled people use their retirement hours to help not only their local communities but mankind in general. The engineers use their retirement time to invent things that help people with problems—for example, making it possible for blind children to ride bikes and blind teenagers to play soccer and helping autistic children learn how to communicate by placing two-way radios in teddy bears, so the child thinks the teddy bear is talking to him. There are many other examples of good old-fashioned human compassion in this program.
- Many companies urge the retiree to seek further education; some companies, like IBM and Pitney Bowes, contribute financially to courses, both for the retiree and his or her spouse.
- Some companies make available the lifelong use of the company store or provide the opportunity to purchase the company's products at a discount.
- The company may invite the retiree annually to the Christmas party, as well as send him a birthday and/or holiday greeting card.
- The company may pay for his membership in the American Association of Retired Persons.

The Retiree Mails an Announcement of His Retirement

The individual who is retiring may wish to communicate this fact by sending a card to his business associates. A list of names and addresses should be compiled from his address file or Christmas card list.

Ann Keagy, formerly an executive at Parsons School of Design, for example, sent a 4½″ × 5½″ white card with matching envelope to hundreds of business friends she had made over the years. Her message was printed in black script with a facsimile signature:

> At the end of this month I will be leaving Parsons School of Design after 35 years as Chairman of the Fashion Design Department.
>
> In the interest of time I take this means to say a warm "thank you" to you as one of the many wonderful people I have come to know and work with. I trust our paths will cross from time to time.
>
> /s/ Ann
>
> Mrs. J. Rodman Keagy
> (Her address was given here)

The announcement was nicely phrased. It supplied her friends with her address and prompted them to promise to keep in touch.

If the retiree will be working as a consultant in his field, that fact should be included in the text of the card. In this case, both home and office telephone numbers would be included.

The Company Gives a Retirement Party

Some companies have a policy discouraging in-house celebrations for any occasion, whether it be a birthday, wedding, or retirement. Other companies have a fund that allows an employee to take three or four close colleagues to lunch before his retirement. Some companies provide a festive treat like a decorated cake with the retiring employee's name written on the frosting. This is then presented in the company cafeteria or in the office on one of the last days of that person's employment. One company records the employee's last day, including the party, on videotape. The cassette is later given to him as a present.

A senior executive's retirement is often noted at a private party held in another executive's home or in a club or restaurant. This may be a cocktail party, lunch, or dinner. At the climax of the occasion, there are usually toasts (as well as a "roasting" of the executive, done with affectionate good humor). A gift is usually presented, too. (*See* For Special People and Special Occasions, in Chapter 16, The Art of Business Gift Giving.) If possible, the retiree's family should be present.

Many executives actually dislike being the guest of honor at a farewell gathering, and in this case, the person's wishes should be taken into consideration. The corporate gift can always be presented by a member of senior management without elaborate fanfare.

It's nice to surprise the retiring CEO with a mass meeting of employees at corporate headquarters or at the factory complex. One CEO was touched when an unannounced meeting was held in his honor. He was presented with two framed front pages of the local newspaper—one dated on the day he began work at the company, forty years earlier, and one printed on his official retirement day, the day of the meeting. The paper's actual headline had been deleted and a substitute headline printed: COMPANY X TOTALLY DESPONDENT AS FAVORITE BOSS RETIRES.

The Retirement Speech

When a member of top management retires, at some point he or she may have to give a "good-bye" speech. It's nice if it is laced with humor and kept short. It also should show gratitude toward the people who have really been the key to the retiring executive's success and happiness—like his executive secretary and his spouse. The speech can later be printed in the company newsletter.

John Elliott, Jr., the outgoing chairman of the Ogilvy & Mather ad agency, made his retirement speech at the annual staff meeting in New York before some 1500 employees. Although he had played a major role in making the agency the great company it had become, he spoke more about other peoples' success than his own, and the trade publication *ADWEEK* reported that everyone in the audience realized that day that "strength of leadership is not directly proportionate to size of ego."

The Junior Executive's Attitude
Toward the Retiring Executive

Some young people, without really realizing it, act in a patronizing fashion toward the older executive who is nearing or at retirement age. Because this is often such a difficult period for retiring executives, the way in which younger executives treat them is very important. Retiring executives should not merely be shrugged off as "being on their way out." They should not be treated as though they don't count any more. Sometimes a panting eagerness is displayed by younger people impatient to move up in the hierarchy within an organization, and that eagerness may be shown openly around the older executives. (The junior executives should keep reminding themselves that it will not take long before they are in the same position.)

The intelligent younger executive, instead of dismissing a senior member of management who is about to retire, gets to know him. The imminent retiree has more time for visits and chats. The younger person, in seeking him out for his advice and his general sense of the state of the business, does him honor. But the younger person is also acquiring a tremendous amount of invaluable information he can use for the rest of his life. This is another case where being thoughtful and polite is the same as being very, very smart.

The Tactful Retiree

A retiree should be sensitive to the number of times he returns to his old office. The temptation to keep showing up will be great, but he must learn to let go and to turn his energies toward other interests and different people.

The retiree should not criticize the efforts of his successor in public, regardless of how much he disagrees with the new style or regardless of the comparative success or failure of his successor's efforts.

14

When an Executive
Dies

When an executive dies while in the
employ of the company, there may be an urgent need for the company to act in
the role of an extended family for the surviving spouse. This is often the case
when there are no other immediate family members or when the other family
members are scattered far and wide.

What the company does to help the survivors of the executives, quite
apart from disbursing the pension or benefits accrued, is up to the discretion of
management. Certainly a company that plays a compassionate role during the
highly emotional, stressful time after a death is admired by everyone in the
community, as well as by everyone within the company.

The Company Takes Action When a Senior-Level
Executive Dies

What a Company Should Do at the Home of the Deceased

- *A colleague from the executive's division should go at once to the hospital or to the home of the deceased to be with the family* until no longer
  needed.
- *The company executive in charge should survey the situation and offer to
  help* in specific areas where he may be needed in the absence of a family
  member capable of organizing these matters. For example:

Small children may need attention, in which case he should arrange for it.

There may be no one to answer telephones, in which case he should arrange to have someone (intelligent) answer all calls.

Arrangements should be made to provide food for the bereaved family.

- He should see to it that the deceased's lawyer is notified.
- The company executive should offer to have a company person *notify all family members* wherever they may be.
- If there is no family member in charge, the company executive should *offer to serve as the liaison on all funeral arrangements,* including dealing with the funeral home, the cemetery, the selection of the casket, etc.
- He should make sure that *all arriving family members from other cities:*

     Have the proper information about the date and hour of the funeral

     Have accommodations

     Have transportation if they need it
- He should make certain there is *someone responsible at home to make an accurate list* of all telephone calls, Mailgrams, letters, flowers, gifts of food, etc., so that those persons can be thanked later.
- He should offer to *help the family place the paid public notice of death* in the newspapers (by helping devise the proper wording and calling it into that section of the local newspaper).
- *Executives and employees of the company should pay a call, if they wish to, on the family during the hours they are receiving at the funeral home.* Except for the executive in charge of helping the family, only a very intimate colleague from the office would make a call on the family at home. (*See also* Special Observances for Families of Deceased Jewish Executives or Employees, below.) Those who go to the funeral home should sign the book with their formal names (not "Al Jones," but "Mr. Albert Jones").

     The family certainly does not have to acknowledge by letter or card the visit of everyone at the funeral home, their attendance at the funeral, or their telephone calls. But an acknowledgment should be sent to those who sent Mailgrams, flowers, gifts of food, mass cards, letters, or sympathy cards.

What the Company Should Do at the Office

- *Notify all employees in that office* and, in the case of a high-level manager, you may close the office on the day of the funeral service, out of respect.

- *Instruct the telephone operators what to say when people call from the outside,* such as press, business colleagues, etc. All calls should be directed to one particular office, but the operator should react to any emotional comments from callers by saying something like, "Yes, we are all very shocked by the news of Mr. McLean's death. One minute please, and I'll pass you to the office that is handling calls regarding Mr. McLean."
- *Notify all of the decedent's business associates in other towns,* by telephone or by Mailgram. Also notify the board of directors. A Mailgram may be sent to the least important names on the list:

Regret to inform you that beloved Chairman of Texocon Fredrik McLean died very unexpectedly of pneumonia complications morning of January 11 in Our Lady's Hospital, Des Moines. Funeral arrangements pending but funeral not before January 14. Details furnished when finalized. Widow Virginia McLean is at their home, 1400 Plainview Avenue, Des Moines 00000. No calls to the home, please. Three surviving teenaged children: Louise, Nana, and Anthony.

> Gerald Hunt
> Senior Vice-President
> (000) 000-0000

- *Place an ad-notice in the business section of the next edition of the local newspapers.* This ad, usually no smaller than an eighth of a page, may have its text set within a black border. It would read something like this:

With profound sorrow we announce the death of our friend and our beloved Chairman and Chief Executive Officer, Fredrik Jon McLean January 11, 1986.

> The executives and employees of Texocon, Inc.

It is optional to include in this kind of notice that "Out of respect for his memory our offices will be closed on Friday, January 14th."

- *Help write the late executive's obituary,* get it approved by the family, and appoint someone within the company to disseminate it. This should be done immediately (*see* below).

The Obituary

In a small town, if a person is well known, his obituary will appear almost automatically. In a large city, it's almost as difficult to get someone's obituary published as it is to get someone's engagement published. In a large city, only a very prominent person's obituary makes it.

The company should keep on file an updated biography and a recent black and white head shot of each senior executive. If a death occurs on a weekend when offices are closed, the executive's secretary or the duty officer should know how to locate a copy of the biography and photograph.

If the photograph sent to the newspapers with the obituary is more than two years old, it should be dated on the back. Be sure to include the name and telephone number of the person to contact for verification of the material.

The following list is a guideline for information that should be kept current on all senior executives:

- Name
- Address
- Place of birth
- Education, including degrees and honorary degrees
- Military service, if any
- Current title and important past career information
- Corporate directorship; nonprofit board memberships
- Any major awards received
- Titles and publishers of books, plays, films, etc.

When death occurs, the person in charge of distributing the obituary to the media should add these facts to the deceased's biography:

- Date, place, and cause of death
- Names and relationships of immediate survivors (spouse, children, parents, brothers and sisters)
- Details, if applicable, concerning funeral home hours, the funeral, or memorial services. If interment is private, it should be so stated. (Some newspapers do not want this information, some do.)
- Name and telephone number of person to contact for further information

The person assigned by the company to disseminate the obituary (usually the public relations officer) should send a copy by hand to the local and suburban newspapers, as well as to the AP and UPI local bureaus. A copy should also go to the alumni class secretary of the late executive's schools and any boards on which he served at the time of his death.

In the case of a death of a prominent executive in the New York area, one would call the Metropolitan Desk of the *New York Times,* which might assign a reporter to the story. (*The Wall Street Journal* does not publish obituaries.) Most newspapers maintain a running file on prominent people in their area, so that when death occurs, ideally only a short updating of the bio is necessary. A local reporter usually makes every effort to place an obituary story in the next edition of his paper. However, if no one is available to answer his calls for information, a woefully short, inadequate story is apt to appear.

When the fictitious Fredrik McLean died, his obituary would have been written by the company person in charge in conjunction with a knowledgeable family member. The result might look like this:

Fredrik Jon McLean, Chairman and Chief Executive Officer of Texocon Inc., died suddenly of complications from pneumonia on January 11, 1986, at Our Lady's Hospital, Des Moines, at the age of 61. A lifelong resident of this city, he graduated from Deerfield Academy in Massachusetts in 1939 and from Kenyon College in Ohio in 1943. He served with the 9th Armored Division in World War II, attaining the rank of Major, and was awarded the Purple Heart and the Bronze Star for valor at the Remagen Bridge in Germany. In 1950, his book on that battle, *Remagen Bridge Revisited,* was published by Rawson Associates.

Mr. McLean began his career with the Norpin Company in Dallas. He joined Texocon in 1960. In 1978 he became President and four years later was made Chairman and Chief Executive Officer. At the time of his death he served on the boards of General Electric, Warner Communications, the First National Bank of Des Moines, Our Lady's Hospital, the International Institute of Education, and the World Wildlife Society. He was a trustee of Kenyon College.

Mr. McLean is survived by his wife, the former Marian Sheehy, two daughters, Louise and Nana, and a son, Anthony. Other survivors include a brother, Ludwig, and a sister, Dorothy McLean Bridwell, both of New York.

What the Company Should Do for the Funeral Service

- *Flowers may be sent from the company to the funeral home, to the church, or to the grave site,* according to the family's wishes. The accompanying card would be white, with the following kind of message handwritten in black: "With the deepest sympathy from everyone at Texocon."

  The envelope for the card would be addressed simply to: "The Funeral of Mr. Fredrik Jon McLean," followed by the address of the place to which the flowers should be sent.

  If in doubt, one should inquire of whoever is handling calls at the family's house to ask whether it is appropriate to send flowers. For example, flowers are never sent to an Orthodox Jewish funeral. At a Catholic service only the family's spray and perhaps one altar bouquet are permitted.

  Flowers sent to the funeral home are usually transferred to the cemetery for the interment.
- *The company should make it easy for any executive or employee to attend the funeral* of a senior executive.
- *If the executive's funeral is in another city, an executive of the same rank*

or higher than the deceased should be sent to represent the company at
the services.

• *Those who attend the services should dress in somber, dark clothes.* (A
man should wear a jacket and tie—his darkest suit, in fact—and a woman
should wear a dress or suit of a quiet color.)

Ushers and Pallbearers

Occasionally male friends and business associates of the deceased are
asked by the family of a distinguished man or woman to serve as ushers and
honorary pallbearers at a large church funeral service.

The ushers help seat people as at weddings, using a seating plan designat-
ing the areas in which certain people should sit (the family in the front pews on
the right, for example, the pallbearers in the front pews on the left, people of
official rank directly behind them, etc.). The ushers are often younger friends
of the deceased, young executives from his or her company, or perhaps
nephews, nieces, or godchildren. Traditionally they are men, but there is no
reason to deny either sex from serving as usher or pallbearer.

In Christian funerals, from four to ten honorary *pallbearers* escort the
casket in or out of the church, preceding it in a procession of two by two. If
the casket is already in place at the altar, the pallbearers march in just before
the service begins and sit in the front pews at the left, opposite the family.
These honorary pallbearers do not handle the casket (the funeral home has
experts who do that). Rather they are present to symbolize the distinction a
great person has achieved in his or her life. Honorary pallbearers are people
like heads of companies, presidents of museums, distinguished doctors, lawyers, educators, etc.

In the "old days," pallbearers wore cutaways, and the ushers wore morning suits, but today either usher or pallbearer dresses in a dark suit and white
shirt with either a black or a very conservative tie.

When there are no honorary pallbearers, the ushers march up two by two
and sit in the front pews on the left just before the service begins. When there
are pallbearers, the ushers, after finishing their ushering duties, sit in the back
of the church.

It is a distinct honor to be asked by the family of the deceased to be an
usher or honorary pallbearer. It is an honor one does not refuse unless there is
a terribly good reason.

The Eulogy

The family may ask a close colleague of the deceased executive to deliver
the main eulogy at the funeral or memorial service. A well-prepared, compas-

sionate eulogy should mention members of the immediate family, and should be:

- Brief (no longer than seven minutes)
- Respectful
- Delivered well, in a strong, articulate manner
- Affectionate, touched with humor and good anecdotes
- Descriptive of the positive legacies left by the deceased

The executive who delivers the eulogy should express his personal feelings for his late colleague and explain why that person was so beloved and appreciated by his associates. The following excerpt is from the eulogy delivered in May 1983 by David Bathurst (then president of Christie's in New York and now chairman of Christie's United Kingdom) at the memorial service for Jane Cohler, who had been vice-president for public relations and communications. After talking about the loss they all felt and Ms. Cohler's many contributions to Christie's, Mr. Bathurst finished on an eloquent note of tribute:

> "More important, in my view than that, were her qualities as a joyous human being and the effect her character had on those around her. She gave Christie's unsparingly of her time and involvement and she gave us, her colleagues, the full range of her love for life. Then came her own major crisis, and her dignity grew with her adversity. She was respected and loved within the family of Christie's and, added to that, she has now earned our deep admiration."

What the Company Does After the Funeral

The Company Holds Its Own Memorial Service

When the funeral of a particularly popular executive is held in another city, the company may honor him later at its own local memorial service for all company employees. Since the occasion is more meaningful when family members are present, the date and time of the service should be at the family's convenience.

The service does not have to be long or elaborate. I know of one that was held at a factory complex where the CEO gave a three-minute eulogy following the minister's opening prayers. He capsulized the late executive's career in an affectionate, amusing manner. Others who spoke for a few minutes each were a factory foreman who had worked under the executive for twenty-eight years, his secretary, and his longtime driver, a Greek immigrant whose children he had sent through college. The service ended with a woman factory worker singing a favorite hymn. This short ceremony (twenty minutes) united the employees in a salute to a man they truly admired and respected and was worth far more than the money lost in company time.

A Mass Card: A Gesture to a Catholic Family

If the executive who dies is a devout Catholic, it would be very appropriate for colleagues to send his or her family a mass card in lieu of flowers. The donor obtains a mass card from a priest in any parish, who then notes on the card the date and hour of the mass to be said for the deceased. The card and an envelope are then given to the donor, who either gives it or mails it to the family. Nuns in convents also have "novena cards," assuring the family of so many series of prayers said for the deceased in their convent.

Although no one is obligated to make a donation for a mass card or novena card, most people do (from $5 to $25, in cash or by check). They hand the donation in an envelope to the priest or nun. This kind of gesture is in lieu of flowers sent to the funeral.

When a special mass arranged by a friend is to be said in memory of the deceased executive, it is particularly nice if a member of the family can be present at that mass.

Special Observances for Families of Deceased Jewish Executives or Employees

When a Jewish executive or employee dies, an appropriate corporate gesture is to send a basket of fruit to the family of the deceased or to make a donation to a charitable organization (preferably one that relates to the interests of the deceased).

Company employees who were close to the deceased should pay a condolence call to the home where the family is "sitting shivah" (observing the seven-day period of mourning during which families honor their departed loved ones). On such visits, it is traditional to bring gifts of food, as mourners are not permitted to do any work during this period. One should bring kosher food (or fruit) if the family is known to observe the dietary laws or if one does not know the religious practices of the family.

A note of condolence is always appropriate, particularly from a close business associate who is unable to pay a condolence call.

A Donation Made to a Nonprofit Institution "In Memory of"

Sometimes the family will include in the death announcement published in the newspaper the instructions "In lieu of flowers, donations may be sent to the American Cancer Society," meaning that those who would have sent flowers to the funeral should instead send an equivalent check to the American Cancer Society, if they wish.

Or colleagues of the late executive may band together and decide on a charity to which they can make a donation in memory of their friend. In the case of the late Fredrik Jon McLean, for example, his colleagues, knowing of his love for his alma mater, might send a check to Kenyon College in his name. This would set off a flurry of acknowledgments, according to the rules of etiquette. For example:

- The donor group would send the check to the president of Kenyon.
- The president of Kenyon would write them a grateful letter of acknowledgment.
- The president of Kenyon would write to the McLean family, informing them of the gift.
- A McLean family member would write to one of the donors, thanking him or her and the whole group on behalf of the family.

This may seem like a lot of letter-writing, but it is a nice, efficient way of handling the matter and communicating the gesture properly.

Setting Up a Memorial

Occasionally a special memorial is established in the name of a beloved executive by family, personal friends, and business colleagues. Senior management would make a corporate contribution to a memorial for their executive, and the employees could make contributions if they wished to. (They should not be solicited, however.) When employees initiate a memorial project for one of their colleagues, it is customary for management to contribute as well. A list of names of those who contributed to the memorial should be sent to the family.

A memorial should be in keeping with the philosophy and interests of the person for whom it is named. The funds collected might be used to pay for the education of children of the deceased who are not yet old enough for college, for scientific research in the field of the illness that killed the executive, to buy new books for the local library, or to purchase badly needed equipment for the hospital where he died.

No one in the office, executive or employee, should feel compelled to contribute to any kind of memorial fund. It should be done quietly and anonymously.

Keeping in Touch with the Spouse

Even if the family of the deceased requests that no flowers be sent to the funeral, that does not mean flowers wouldn't be appropriate at a later date. For example, a CEO might send them to an executive's widow a couple of weeks after the funeral, with a note asking her how she's "coming along" and expressing concern for her. This kind of gesture is very important—to remind the survivor that her extended family has not forgotten her.

The colleagues of the late executive should take turns calling the widow once or twice a month to ask if there's anything she needs. Obviously, the same protocol obtains if it is a woman executive who has died. Her husband is then the recipient of concern.

Published Tributes to the Late Executive

A Tribute in the Company Newsletter or Magazine

An important executive deserves a special tribute in the company's house organ when he dies. The following is an example of a warm, affectionate tribute from an editor boss to his late reporter. Geoffrey Precourt (former editor of *ADWEEK,* an advertising trade magazine) wrote in the January 11, 1982, issue on the subject of his young national editor, Alan Frank, who died the week before:

Alan Frank: In Appreciation

Alan Frank, our colleague, died last week after a long illness.

Even though it's been months since he first entered the hospital, it's still difficult to imagine the ADWEEK offices without him . . . especially at deadline. He was a volcano of energy, browbeating recalcitrant sources, pounding his typewriter, exulting in his countless "scoops." He served his readers well.

Few people are as fascinated with the advertising industry as Al was. He knew the right people at agencies throughout the country and he surely knew how to employ those contacts to produce news. No one did it better.

He never stopped asking questions. He never stopped probing. There was a story behind every personnel change, a confounding tale behind every account switch. Al kept pushing ahead until he had all the answers.

It was not the easiest way to make friends. Yet, scores of people in the advertising business will miss Al and his manner. His style generated respect. And that respect begat friendship. People knew that he cared.

He cared about advertising, he cared about ADWEEK. He also cared about his family. Last summer, Barbara and Alan doubled the size of their household with twins: Joseph Cortlandt Frank and Lucas Alan Frank. Just before Christmas, Alan let us know, "At five months, the little bruisers are tipping the scales at 18–18½ pounds each, have grown to approximately 26½ inches tall and already seem anxious to walk."

In that same note, Al offered some gentle banter: "Regrettably, I have no hot tips to pass along because Aberdeen [Al and Barbara's home in New Jersey] is not what you would call the advertising mecca of the world." He signed the holiday message, "From someone who's been there."

Al may well have spent some time beating the bushes in suburban New Jersey for news on advertising. It was in his blood. He *had* been there. At 30, he had a lifetime of contacts and knowledge. He was a tough, strong, cocky reporter; a tough, strong, cocky, kind man.

That, presumably, is the way he wanted to be remembered.

A Tribute in the Annual Report

The annual report is another way in which the death of an important executive should be noted. Levi Strauss & Company did this in 1979 with style in the opening text of the annual report:

> For Levi Strauss & Co., 1979 was a year of high achievement and deep sadness. . . . The sadness began early in December with the passing of two former executives who over some 50 years established the human values and standards of business excellence which underlie the company's success. They were Walter A. Hass, Sr., honorary chairman of the board, and Daniel E. Koshland, honorary chairman of the executive committee. . . .

The report continues with the business messages to the shareholders, followed by a full-page tribute to Walter Hass and Daniel Koshland, including a summary of both men's past efforts to promote the welfare of minority groups at a time when such involvements were relatively unknown in the U.S. business scene.

While this kind of tribute may be addressed to an individual, it is just as revealing of the company itself.

Noted in the Minutes of the Directors' Meeting

After the death of a senior member of management or a member of the board of directors, it is appropriate for someone to read a tribute to the deceased into the minutes of the meeting. This statement may be typed or lettered in calligraphy and framed and sent to the next of kin. It is a testimonial to remind future generations of the distinction and achievement of this person when he or she was alive.

When an Executive Dies at a Post Abroad

The body of an employee who dies "en poste" in another country is usually brought back to this country for burial. If the family agrees, the company should first arrange a simple memorial service in the city where death occurred.

The American consulate should assist in arrangements to transport the body to the United States. The corporation should pay for the memorial service abroad, the disposition of the employee's foreign home and the return of his personal effects to the United States, and the cost of transporting the body and family home.

It is thoughtful for senior management to invite the surviving family members to lunch in the executive dining room upon their return to this country, as a small gesture that the company shares in their sorrow.

When an executive dies abroad, corporate headquarters should send an updated obituary and photograph to the newspapers in the city where the executive died, as well as to the local newspapers where the corporation has its headquarters.

Condolence Letters

It is very gracious for colleagues of an executive who dies to write to his or her spouse or family, and by colleagues, I mean anyone from the receptionist to the CEO. A good condolence letter conveys not only feelings of sadness and praise of the deceased, but also the offer of a helping hand to those left behind. A well-written condolence letter is treasured, is usually passed around, and is often passed down through future generations.

Sending flowers to the funeral or attending the funeral is no substitute for a condolence letter. The letter—or short note—should be sent regardless of any other gestures you make.

A condolence letter should be written by hand in black ink on good personal notepaper (but using office stationery is better than not writing the letter at all). If your handwriting is totally illegible (like mine), type your letter.

Condolence Letter from an Executive to the Mother of an Unmarried Colleague

Let the bereaved know:

Dear Mrs. Jenkins:

We heard of Ritch's death only yesterday and were shocked to learn that someone so young, physically fit, full of energy, and blessed with the love of life could be struck down so tragically by a heart attack.

That you know what a terrible loss it is . . .

I know what this loss means to you and your children. When one of my brothers died at Ritch's age, the family felt as though our own family structure had disintegrated—forever. Fortunately, life does go on for the survivors, while the family grows closer into itself. You'll realize that Ritch's spirit will help sustain all of you in your sorrow.

. . . but things will get better.

Mention your relationship with the deceased and praise him.

Ritch was a favorite of every person in this company with whom he came in contact. My staff and I welcomed his periodic visits to my division. He had a warm, mischievous smile, a wry sense of

Say how much he will be missed.

Offer your assistance to the family.

humor, and a genuine interest in other people that was a great asset to his career. I personally will miss him both as a friend and as a business colleague.

Please let me know if there is anything I can do for you; it would give me great pleasure to be of service, and if you come to our city, I hope you will let me know, so I can take you to lunch in our company dining room, where Ritch and I often lunched.

You and your family are in our thoughts and prayers.

Sincerely yours,

Condolence Letter from an Employee to an Executive's Family

Dear Mrs. McLean:

My deepest sympathy goes to you and to each member of your family in this time of terrible sorrow. I admired your husband more than I could ever express. As head of the Mail Room, I saw him quite often. He had a habit of sticking his head in the door on his way to the Board Room, asking with a smile, "And how's everything going today in the nerve center of this organization?"

There has never been a chief executive officer who showed more concern for his employees, not just the senior officers. He made us all feel part of the team. He knew many of our names (including mine), and we looked up to him as a leader and as a gentleman.

Everyone in the Mail Room joins me in sending you our prayers and heartfelt condolences. Mr. McLean will *always* be missed in this company.

Sincerely,"

Condolence Letter to National of a Foreign Country Whose Leader Has Died

When a head of state or any beloved leader dies in a country where your company does business, the death should be noted and acted upon.

Send a telex message to your offices and plants in that country, expressing the sympathy of your senior management as well as all of your company's local employees. If you are writing a business letter to a colleague in that country during the following weeks, be sure to enclose a short hand-written note saying "how saddened we all are for your country during these difficult days. . . ." When a foreign leader or a crowned monarch dies, the people in that country usually feel the loss for a long period of time.

It is courteous for a business executive to call on the foreign country's embassy or consulate in his city. The diplomatic representatives usually place a ceremonial book in the reception area of the office. Diplomats, friends, and business associates of that country pass by to sign the book as a mark of respect and mourning. The book is eventually sent to the officials of the foreign country so they may know who paid tribute to their leader.

On a Personal Note: A Condolence Letter from a Former Senior Executive to the Family of Another Senior Executive

When my father, H. Malcolm Baldrige, recently died at the age of ninety, my brothers, Mac and Bob, and I received many wonderful condolence letters. Not many of them came from my father's peers, because very few were still alive, but one of the most cherished ones we received came from Alton Hyatt, a Yale classmate of the class of 1918. (If you learn how to write a good letter of condolence, you have no idea of how many pairs of eyes will eventually read it.)

Dear Children of Malcolm Baldrige,

As secretary of the Class of 1918, I write to you expressing sincere sympathy upon the death of your dad. There are only about 30 of us left who would be able to join in expressing the sentiments of this letter, but I am certain that the entire original class of 400-plus would have wanted to be included if they were still with us.

It is a well-known fact amongst us all that Mac was a truly outstanding member of our class. He was not only a great athlete in both football and wrestling, but he also had a great personality, backed up perfectly by an impressive stature and a stentorian voice. His public services throughout his life were of the highest quality, and I never heard a word spoken against him.

Many were the good times we all had together, and it was always a pleasure to see him at our annual class of 1918 lunches at Mory's in New Haven.

With great admiration for our outstanding classmate,

/s/ Alton R. Hyatt

Acknowledging Expressions of Sympathy

The Family Acknowledges Friends' and Colleagues' Gestures

When a prominent person like the hypothetical Fredrik McLean dies, there is an inevitable flow of mail (sometimes hundreds of letters and Mailgrams) and telephone calls, flowers, and donations made in the memory of the deceased. It becomes difficult to send a personal note to every person who extends his or her sympathy. An engraved or printed card may be sent to everyone, acknowledging the individual's gesture of sympathy in a general manner, such as the following message, engraved or printed on a black-bordered white card:

The Family of the late Fredrik Jon McLean gratefully acknowledges your expression of sympathy. We shall always remember your kindness.

It is much more gracious, of course, if a member of the family personalizes the card by writing a sentence or two by hand, with a signature beneath, on the card. A sentence or two will suffice, mentioning the specific act of sympathy of the recipient:

Thank you for coming to the funeral. Fred always spoke of you with affection.

Thank you for coming to the funeral home. We feel we know you, because Fred has often mentioned you.

Your flowers were particularly beautiful, and your card was very kind.

We are very touched by your generous donation to Kenyon College. You know how much Fred loved his college. Thank you from us all.

If the executive who dies was not a well-known person, the acknowledgment list would not be long, and therefore it would not be necessary to order sympathy acknowledgment cards. A family member should write a short note to acknowledge each person's expression of sympathy (within three months maximum):

. . . You were so nice to bring us that wonderful basket of fruit. The whole family enjoyed it.

We are all doing pretty well, considering our terrible loss. Having friends like you helps sustain us. Thank you, Richard.

The Family Acknowledges the Company's Gestures

When a company takes an active role in helping the family of the deceased, someone from that family should write to the head of the company, thanking everyone on the family's behalf. In Fredrik McLean's case, his widow should write to the executive who is temporarily in charge of the company:

. . . You cannot imagine how grateful our entire family is to the company for the many kind and wonderful things done for us. From the first minute you brought me the news of Fred's death, through the sad, confusing days that followed while we planned and executed the funeral, I don't know how we would have coped without you. Every thoughtful gesture meant so much to us, including the fact that you taped the children's eulogy of their father at the services, and we now have a precious family record to be passed down to future generations.

I hope you noticed that the wonderful basket of lilies from the Texocon employees was placed right next to the casket, where it was seen and admired by everyone. And I must thank you again for the loan of your superb secretary the first two days to handle the telephones for us. That allowed Fred's secretary to join us as a member of the family, sharing our grief. You made everything so much easier for us. Our gratitude can never be properly expressed.

I'm sure you know how much Fred loved this company, and he would have been very proud that Texocon in a moment of crisis took such wonderful care of his family.

This kind of letter from the wife of the late CEO should be published, with her permission, in the company newsletter for the sake of the employees.

15

A Company Celebrates Its Anniversary

Acompany of any size should give top priority to the celebration of an important anniversary, because it's a perfect opportunity with which to remind the public, press, and employees of its accomplishments and future aspirations. The benefits of an effectively handled anniversary include these:

- Better employee morale
- Increased employee motivation
- A more highly polished company image within the community
- Great visibility of the company's products or services
- *Increased sales*

The really important anniversaries are the tenth, twenty-fifth, fiftieth, seventy-fifth, hundredth, and every quarter thereafter. If a company has a good reason for celebrating an in-between anniversary (such as a need for public visibility or a stimulus to employee morale), it should certainly proceed. The first through fourth anniversaries do not require any attention by the public, but they should be noted in-house, if for no other reason than it celebrates the fact the company has survived and is still in business. (The CEO might place a large bouquet of flowers in the reception area and circulate a memo to the employees, reminding them of the anniversary date and thanking them "for their large share in the progress of this company.") The fifth anniversary, while not major in terms of public visibility, is well worth celebrating by the company and its clients.

The employees' role in the celebration of an anniversary is paramount. Most senior managers do not have the noblesse oblige of the CEO of Gubelin, the Swiss watchmaker and jeweler, who, on the company's 125th anniversary, flew all of the American employees, from messenger to general manager, to Switzerland for a week-long celebration. (Some of them previously had not been outside the five boroughs of New York!)

It is important in an anniversary year to look ahead to what the company will be doing between now and its next anniversary. In this era of mergers and acquisitions, that can be difficult. Many of America's oldest companies have been merged into new identities. If a company is going through a merger, ideally someone within the new corporate entity will have enough sense of history to record carefully the history of the disappearing company so as to enable the new corporation to celebrate its roots dating back to the proud beginning of all of its divisions.

Planning a Celebration

A successful celebration of a company anniversary requires careful planning. A small company should begin planning a year in advance; a large corporation should begin at least three years in advance. (The total costs of a large anniversary celebration will not hurt quite so much if amortized over four years—from three years before the anniversary and including the anniversary year itself.)

One person within the company should be placed in charge of coordination of plans. A large corporation may need to retain an outside communications firm to handle the project. The first course of action after naming the in-house executive coordinator of the anniversary (and possibly retaining an outside agency for creative support) is to involve the employees. Three years before the anniversary date, they should be asked to volunteer written suggestions on how best to celebrate. It should be a competition, with prizes awarded for the best ideas.

Keep the employees abreast of planning activities through the employee newsletter or company magazine.

Play Up Company Nostalgia

It is impossible to overdo the nostalgic, historic aspects of your company while planning the anniversary celebration. Something from the past, whether it relates to people or their environment, has inevitable human interest impact. An accent on "yesteryear" is a great way to make people feel good about the company. Some of America's largest corporations have treasure troves of photographs and memorabilia of their past. When Ford, for example, celebrates its anniversaries, the old photographs in the archives are republished: Henry Ford and his original investors standing in front of the coal yard in Detroit in 1903, looking like tough guys on a Western movie set; photographs of the great old cars, showing the men drivers with caps, handlebar mustaches, and stiff tall white collars and the women passengers with dusters and large filmy hats anchored by chiffon scarves tied under their chins. Proctor & Gamble can reissue its nineteenth-century posters used for selling soap. A poster worth a million words shows James Gamble in his laboratory in 1878 working on the magic formula for a floating Ivory soap, of which millions of cakes would be sold in the next hundred years.

Most American companies do not have such rich archives from which to draw material. Most are not that old. However, there is historical interest in any company's first location, in how much its products cost twenty-five years ago, how its services were priced ten years ago, or how the company executives and employees looked and dressed ten years ago. You can make your company's past, short though it may be, the focus of photographs and anecdotes in the press kits, as well as the basis of decorations for your anniversary party. The more you can compare, item by item, your business of ten years ago with your business of today, the more interesting you are to a newspaper journalist.

The right touch of nostalgia is a key to success in any anniversary celebration, but don't forget the present and future. A newly formed company with any foresight immediately begins keeping archives (from which to cull pieces of the past when it's time to celebrate an important anniversary).

Duration of an Anniversary Celebration

A small company's anniversary may be celebrated in one day; a mid-sized company's anniversary might take place over two or three days of single events; a major corporation's anniversary might be scheduled throughout the year, with events in each city or town where the company has offices, branches, or plants.

Instead of a boring, repetitious overkill celebration, the planning should concentrate hard on events over a short period of time, then the company should move on to other projects.

A company with an important anniversary like the "50th Golden Anniversary" should incorporate the event into the company's graphics for that year: its stationery, all company ads, even supplementing the company logo for just that year on the side of the company trucks, the front doors of its major offices, etc. This kind of visual repeat reminder is very effective; what is *not* effective is to label every party or special event staged during the entire year a "Golden Anniversary" event. Enough is enough.

The Extent of Celebration
According to a Company's Age

Fifth Anniversary

- Makes a widespread mailing of a special press release to customers, friends, colleagues, and local press
- Holds cocktail party on office premises for staff, customers, vendors, and friends

Tenth Anniversary

- Makes a widespread mailing of an entire press kit to local and state media
- Holds cocktail party at hotel for enlarged list, adding VIPs and press
- Takes a quarter-page ad in the local newspaper, congratulating itself on its age and accomplishments

Twenty-fifth Anniversary

- Makes a widespread mailing of a press kit to include national media, TV, and radio, with full-scale publicity launch and media treatment
- Holds large reception in hotel for greatly increased list, including securities analysts
- Takes a full-page ad in the city newspapers of all its plants and offices on the subject of its anniversary
- Holds a party for employees (such as a family picnic in summer)
- Commissions an anniversary poster from a graphic designer as a gift for customers, employees, VIPs, etc.
- Has inexpensive souvenirs made for executives and employees to give away
- Makes a modest gift in the name of the employees to a local nonprofit institution chosen by the employees

A Large Company Celebrates a Major Anniversary

Some major companies share major birthdays with the world when they sponsor network television shows to mark their anniversaries. Other companies concentrate on the employees. R. J. Reynolds, for example, one year rounded up all their employees in the entire state of North Carolina and gave them (50,000 people) an all-day family picnic complete with bands, carnival rides, seven tons of barbecued pork, and 13,000 pounds of fried chicken!

Some companies rent an entire symphony concert hall for a concert performance; others invite customers and their families to the circus or even a rodeo. One CEO assembled all the employees in the parking lot and told the cheering throng that everyone was to receive an unexpected bonus in honor of the occasion.

Two of the most ambitious projects that may be undertaken to record the company history are:

· Writing a book
· Making a videotape cassette

Publishing a Company Book

The public relations power of a well-done book on the history of the company outlasts almost any other affirmative result of celebrating an important anniversary.

A company should be at least fifty before its history is written in book form (the brochure form will do until then). The text should be written with style and with wit; it should be handsomely illustrated. It should not be a saccharine puff-piece but "tell it like it was"—an honest, historically accurate book, even though written with affection, pride, and humor. It's a fine idea to have a photograph of the management team and board of directors (as well as a collage of photos of the employees) at the back of the book, but any overt accolades to present management will turn the book from a company history into a management-serving propaganda piece. If the company wants everyone to read the entire book and thus learn about the company, the company history should be written as just that, negatives included (and the CEO should restrain his own ego!).

This kind of book requires careful planning, research, and a healthy budget. The giving away of many copies should be budgeted into the total anniversary plan, and a prestigious press party launch should be organized.

The company should first find a book producer to help put together the book. Book producers serve as editorial and manufacturing services. They will help your company find a writer and researcher, then work with the writer through the completion of the manuscript and then on to bound copies of the book. Book producers are listed in the book industry publishing directory, *Literary Market Place,* available at your public library, or through R. R. Bowker Company, 1180 Avenue of the Americas, New York, NY 10036. If the book is interesting and well-written, without being a flagrant commercial, the book may merit publication by a regular publishing house (which would then distribute it to bookstores, assuring a much wider distribution).

A hypothetical time-table for such a book to appear on a company anniversary in the year 1989 might look like this:

July 1986:　　Researcher is retained to gather material relating to the company's history: photographs, anecdotes, interviews with old-timers, clippings from old newspapers, and memorabilia in general.

January 1987:　　Researcher supplies author with finished work.

December 1987: Author completes book and gives approved manuscript to publisher.

December 1988: Publisher delivers bound copies to company for distribution as Christmas gifts and for use during the anniversary year, beginning January 1, 1989. (Remember to allow at least six months between date final manuscript is submitted and date of finished books.)

The cost of privately producing a company history in book form could be anywhere from $25,000 to $100,000, according to the amount of photography and number of volumes printed.

A Videotaped Cassette of the Company's History

This project involves videotaping a history of the company in conjunction with a book or in place of it. The tape should be made available in both half-inch (for use with VCRs) and three-quarter-inch (industrial use) formats. The cassette should be no longer than ten minutes. The book illustrations could be part of it, but there would be a need for additional shots of executives and employees at work.

This cassette would be useful for:

· An executive to excerpt when making a television appearance
· Management to give (or sell at low cost) to employees
· Management to screen for employees, customers, friends, etc. (and to send customers who cannot attend a screening)
· Management to show at shareholders' meetings
· Management to show to securities analysts

From the minute the company gives the budget approval—through the script writing, production, editing, and processing—two months of a company executive's time would be required for supervising the project. The cost for using a first class production company would range between $100,000 and $200,000, depending upon the travel required and number of locations used.

Groups That Deserve Special Attention

The Employees

· The employees should be represented on the planning committee when it begins to function. Their input is invaluable on everything from the type of employee party to be held to the naming of the nonprofit institution that will receive a donation from the company in honor of the anniversary.

- The company book should be made available to them at a low price.
- The videocassette of the company history should be made available to them at a low price.
- A pep rally should kick off the anniversary celebrations.
- Raffles should be held, with prizes given to the lucky winners (a family weekend at a lake resort, two season tickets to the baseball game, membership to a health club, etc.).
- They should each be given an "anniversary souvenir" (key ring, pen, retractable metal tape-measure, etc.) stamped with the corporate logo.

The Shareholders

In the quarterly dividend mailing, send the stockholders a detailed announcement of the anniversary and the company plans.

- They should be able to order the hardcover or softcover version of the company book at a healthy discount.
- There should be a special anniversary program at the annual stockholders' meeting.
- Attendees at the stockholders' meeting should receive the anniversary souvenir.

The Top Customers, Vendors, VIPs, etc.

- They should receive the hardcover version of the company book, nicely wrapped as a gift. Very important customers would receive the book with a handsome Florentine leather bookmark, gold-embossed with the company name and anniversary years (in small letters) on the back.
- They should be invited to the anniversary reception held in their particular city.

The Press

- An impressive no-nonsense press kit should be compiled and a full-scale media plan should be implemented. Journalists should receive a careful selection of press releases (*not* an exaggerated number) at the beginning of the anniversary year and then again only when there are special events.
- Exclusive stories and interviews should be developed, using the anniversary as the springboard.
- Special company history visuals should be created for the executive to use on camera (if he does not have a cassette tape history) when making a television appearance.

- Important media figures should be given copies of the softcover version of the company book.
- They should receive invitations to the company reception and to any special events in their city.
- The company anniversary souvenir should be part of the press kit.

The Community

In all cities and towns where major company facilities are located:

- The company should stage a *celebration for the people of the community* or town, which might consist of:
  An *open house*
  An *evening fireworks display*
  An *outdoor band concert* (in summer)
- The company should *make a major gift to the nonprofit sector,* either nationally or locally—for example:
  A *beautification project* (planting trees, rehabilitation of an area, donation of small public park, donation of children's park playground equipment, giving the city new trash containers or bike racks, etc.)
  The *purchase of needed equipment for a local hospital*
  A *gift to a local museum,* such as a grant for the docent program, a gift to the junior museum education department, etc.
  A *research grant to a major institution*
  A *gift to local colleges or universities* for faculty enrichment or for a company-named scholarship (in perpetuity)
  A *work of art commissioned for the anniversary*
  A *sponsored concert, opera, play, or ballet*
- Consideration should be given to the placing of a large *institutional ad* in the local press on the exact date of the company anniversary (plus paid public service announcements on local television) in which the company announces its age with pride, gives salient points of its history, and thanks the community and its citizens for "being so supportive of us through all these years."

A Major Company's Traveling Road Show

It is wise, from the points of view of design, impact, and cost, to have a standard format for each branch office or plant to use in celebrating the company's anniversary. Within this format the following would be standardized:

- Anniversary graphics (for company stationery, labels, etc.)
- Order blanks for each office to write in their order for the number needed

of anniversary souvenirs, hardcover and softcover copies of the company book, copies of the tape cassette, etc.

- Ad campaigns, touting the anniversary but tied into each local office
- A "party planner" for the company reception and for the employee party in each community. These party planners would include suggested menus, type of entertainment, anniversary backdrops and decorating ideas, instructions on how to compile a guest list for the company reception, a dummy invitation to be printed (or engraved) locally, etc.
- Press kits
- Instructions on how to book interviews for the senior managers (who come to town to host the anniversary reception and employee party) in the local media
- An order blank for photographic blow-ups of the company's history, to use for the office reception area or for decoration for the parties, etc.
- Instructions on how to proceed with a gift for the local nonprofit institution
- A sample thank-you letter to acknowledge any congratulatory letters or flowers sent to the local company by people from the outside
- Instructions on how to stage a fireworks display for the community

16

The Art of
Business Gift Giving

Gift-giving, particularly in business, is an art. When done with sensitivity and imagination, it pleases the recipient, helps cement a new business relationship or regenerates an old relationship, and creates considerable goodwill. When done improperly or in a pedestrian manner, it may annoy the recipient or even create a major problem for that person.

Many people in business today have become paranoid about accepting gifts, quite understandably when one reflects on the bad publicity surrounding the offering of bribes in both the public and private sectors. *The donor should be aware of this problem and take every precaution to avoid any possible suggestion of bribery or impropriety in his gift.*

Good Timing and a Good Reason

If there is a good reason to send a gift, do it at that moment, not later. The impact is usually lost when the emotion of the moment is gone. Don't wait six months before sending your gift to a retired person. Send your sample of a new product *before* its launch, if possible, not when it's old news; send your client's wedding present within two months of his wedding, not a year later.

There should be a natural, proper reason for sending any gift, otherwise the act looks contrived and suspicious. No one is obliged to send a business associate a birthday present, but if you see a person constantly in your business dealings and he has become a good friend in this process, there is a reason for you to send him a modest gift on an important birthday.

You should never send a substantial gift to a business person with whom you are trying to negotiate a deal. It might be regarded as a material attempt to influence the outcome.

Most people would agree that *the very nicest gift is the one for which there is no special reason*—it's simply an act of friendship. I have my own store of thoughtful gifts that I will never forget—such as when another outside bank director showed up at our monthly meeting on an extremely cold, snowy February day with a bunch of fresh violets for everyone around the table, and when I received a large packet of the best kind of wild rice from a client who remembered a conversation in which I said I loved it, and when President Kennedy's father sent a ten-gallon carton of Louis Sherry's special ice cream to me and my staff in the White House because he had heard me say that we were all working so hard we couldn't even get out for an ice cream cone, and the day a fellow executive sent me a beautiful small leather address book for my handbag, with a card that said, "I realized how much you needed this when I saw you take out your address book one day and it looked like an Egyptian relic of crumbling papyrus!"

Some of the reasons for sending a small gift, flowers, or a letter to a business colleague are these:

To say thank you to	*To encourage someone who*	*To apologize for having*	*To wish good luck for*	*To congratu-late for*
Your host at the lunch or dinner in your honor	Is starting a new job or career	Put someone to a great deal of trouble	A birthday	Earning a promotion
Your host when you travel to another city	Is suffering from or recovering from an accident or serious illness	Offended someone	An anniversary	Winning an award
		Forgotten a promise or an engagement	A move to another city	Having a baby
The person who did you a great favor, whether personal or work-related	Has had a death in the family		A marriage	An act of courage
	Is in serious financial difficulties		The sale of the company	Performing well in public
			A retirement	Finishing further education
			A new financial venture	Giving a good speech

Choice of Item

Think before you act is the best advice I can give. Don't send bottles of liquor to every single person on your Christmas business list; not everyone drinks. Don't give someone a new piece of sports equipment you think is tremendous unless you know for a fact that the recipient is as enthusiastic about that sport as you are. Don't give someone (whose home you've never seen) a framed lithograph you have fallen in love with, because the recipient's taste may be the exact opposite of yours. Don't try to be funny at someone else's expense, such as giving a diet book to an overweight colleague. If you are a newly arrived executive, don't give your boss a present; it looks like apple-polishing, regardless of your motives. Never give anyone something in sized apparel, unless you are 100 percent positive of the recipient's size (and few people ever are). A gift of cash to a business colleague is something to avoid, unless it involves a very good friend and an unusual situation (such as financial distress following the death of a family member).

It's important to do your homework if you plan to give a substantive gift to a male or female executive. First of all, be aware of the person's hobbies, sports, and special interests. The two best confidential sources of research are the gift recipient's secretary or spouse, if you know them. If the recipient has just moved offices, for example, he might be able to use something for his office. If he is going abroad on business in the near future, a gift for the traveler would be appropriate. If he uses his car a great deal on business, an accessory for this kind of travel would be useful. Take into consideration the lifestyle and needs of the person who will receive your present.

Shopping for the Present

There are many ways in which to find the perfect gift:

- Appoint someone *whose taste you know is impeccable* to scout the gift for you.
- Visit your favorite bookstore.
- Peruse the leading mail order catalogs.
- Watch the newspaper and magazine ads.
- Poke around in antique shops.
- Attend weekend auctions at reputable auction galleries.
- Use personal shoppers at the department stores.
- Look around your local museum gift shops or check their catalogs.
- Watch for the new specials in your gourmet food shop.

Paying for It

Many companies have a standard gift for employees at Christmas, a standard gift for customers or clients, and inexpensive promotional items used mostly as giveaways. Obviously all of these are paid for by the company.

Beyond this kind of gift giving, there is great diversity in company policies about gifts. Some companies pay for all of the gifts given individually by all members of top management to the business community. Others pay for special gifts given by all executives, provided justification has been furnished and written approval has been received in advance. Most executives, however, frequently face a decision on whether giving a gift to someone connected in business is worth the outlay of personal funds. It is much like giving a gift to a personal friend. (The government allows a tax deduction on a business gift only up to $25 in cost as of this writing, which helps curb excessive gift giving practices.)

Most senior executives will agree that it is on occasion worthwhile for an executive to pay for a small gift to a business associate from his own pocket, provided the timing is right, the reason is justified, and the choice of gift is propitious.

What Should It Cost?

Gifts presented by junior executives and mid-managers to their clients should cost between $10 and $25 on the average.

Gifts presented by mid to upper managers might cost between $25 to $50. Senior executives might spend between $50 to $100 for top customers and close friends in the business world.

Gifts costing more than $100 are only for very important and rare occasions.

Manner of Presenting the Gift

The manner in which a gift is made is extremely important. It should be presented to show that the donor has high esteem for the recipient *and* for the gift.

- *A gift should be presented in person,* if possible. When you hand a present to the recipient, it assumes added importance and meaning because of the impact of your voice, expression, and perhaps even your handshake or mini-embrace as you present it.
- *It should be beautifully wrapped.* Nothing is more of a downer than receiving a gift that is sloppily presented. I remember seeing the fallen expression on an executive's face when he was handed an expensive

crystal bowl that had been beautifully wrapped but had been tucked inside a food chain's plastic shopping bag. The entire effect was ruined.

Many United States presidents have used as their gift wrapping a wonderfully handsome white paper, blind embossed in a repeat pattern with the President's official seal. Gold and white ribbons are used with the paper, and the effect is stunning. Any business could have its own paper made and blind embossed with its logo or symbol, a handsome way to display the company's imprimatur.

• *One should take pains with the enclosure card.* Enclosing your business card without a signature and a personal message is a cold and impersonal way to send a gift. It conveys the feeling the donor never saw the present or had anything to do with its dispatch. If you use your business card as an enclosure, put a slash through your name and write your given name in ink. Add a sentence on the front or back of the card, such as "Hope you can use this." Or, if you're sending a wedding present to colleagues, write something like "With best wishes to Susan and Jerry for a wonderful life ahead."

Always use a piece of good note paper or one of your correspondence cards, if you have this kind of stationery, for your enclosure card message. It's much nicer than your business card.

Be thoughtful about what you write on your card. A card enclosed with a dozen grapefruit that says, "Thanks for giving me the business, and I look forward to more," certainly does not have the impact of a card that says, "We've been having a long tough winter, you've been working too hard, so you deserve a little extra Vitamin C!"

If you're sending a gift to a married couple and you have forgotten the first name of the spouse, just write on your card, "To the Bradfords, with best wishes for . . ."

Enclose your gift card in an envelope, whether matching or not.

A gift worth giving is a gift worth presenting well. As the French say, in respect to a gift or a dinner: *"Il faut bien présenter les choses . . ."*

The Sending of Flowers

Flowers are an easy-to-send, quick-to-arrive gift. They may be ordered by telephone; you can either send your card to the florist, or you can dictate your message by telephone to the florist. Flowers are telegraphed throughout the world. They are an international symbol of greeting, celebration, and gratitude. An executive who goes abroad to any country should remember that he should send flowers before or after any meal at which he is an honored guest *in someone's home.*

In this country, flowers were traditionally sent by couples, by a woman to another woman, or by a man to a woman, but never by a woman to a man. In this new era of equality, that qualification has disappeared. Women should send flowers to men for the very same reasons they receive them themselves. Generally, if a woman is sending flowers to thank a male executive for a favor or to congratulate him, she would send them to his office. If she has been a dinner guest in his home, she would send them to his home.

It is always better to send flowers either on the morning of the party or the day after. If you arrive at the door with flowers in hand, your host will have to stop his or her activities in order to find the proper vase, to arrange them and to put them in the proper spot—an unwelcome interruption for the host.

If you are wondering whether to send an arrangement or cut flowers to someone, here is a good rule: *Send an arrangement to a person's office but cut flowers to his or her home.*

To an executive who is ill in the hospital, send a plant that requires little care. Flowers that need maintenance are neglected in busy hospitals. Send flowers when the patient is back home, recuperating from the hospital.

Flowers for Funerals
(*See* Chapter 14, When an Executive Dies)

Holiday Greeting Cards:
An Annual Communication of Friendship

When a corporation sends out its greeting cards, it has a choice:

· To send a Christian greeting card that might have a religious theme
· To send a Jewish greeting card, which might have the words "Happy Hanukkah and best wishes for 1987"
· To send a card devoid of Christmas trees, Santa Clauses, or any religious connotations, with this kind of greeting: "Seasons Greetings" or "Our best wishes for this joyous season"

If your company sends out cards with a religious scene because most of your customers are Christian, you can personalize the cards for your Jewish friends by writing "Happy Hanukkah to you and yours." If your customers are predominantly Jewish, send them Hanukkah cards. If you want to avoid the problem of separate cards, send the "Seasons Greetings" kind of card. Those to Jewish friends may be personalized by writing "Happy Hanukkah!" and those to Christian friends by writing "Have a Holy, Happy Christmas," or whatever you wish to say. The most important thing to remember is to personalize every Christmas card you send, whether it is personal or corporate.

When a company sends cards announcing that a "donation has been made on your behalf to . . ." the need for a personal note is even more urgent. I am all for donations to the needy, particularly during the holidays, but to make the donation announcement the primary message on the card is, to me, too much back patting. In the true spirit of Christmas and Hanukkah, the company should make a generous donation and mention it *very subtly* somewhere on the card. Then the recipient won't consider the greeting card as just another request for his donation in turn.

Getting Holiday Gift Lists in Order

If possible, one should computerize both Christmas card and holiday gift lists. These lists should be kept up to date with great care, with all changes in a person's company name, title, address, telephone number, and marital status carefully noted each time a change occurs. Keeping good records will keep you from making errors of omission or from giving someone the same thing you gave him last year! For example, you might keep a gift list like the following:

CODE: OS —office staff members
　　　　FE —fellow company executives
　　　　CU —customers
　　　　VE —vendors
　　　　VIP—goodwill gifts for VIPs
　　　　BD —board of directors
　　　　SA —service agency executives

HOLIDAY GIFT RECORD

Year_____Name of Executive_____

Name, title of recipient, address, company	Description of gift	Code	Value	How gift sent and date shipped or messengered

When to Tip versus When to Give a Present

Knowing when to tip is a tricky subject. Some people might be offended by tipping. You don't tip an airline attendant who serves you a meal on the plane, for example, but you do tip a restaurant waitress. In many beauty salons, you do not tip the owner who does your hair, but you do tip the other operators. You would give a tip to your gym instructor, but you would give a gift, not a tip, to your French language instructor.

The basic premise is that one gives a present to a fellow professional and a tip to someone in the basic service industry. In fact, you might make a combination of a small cash gift and a modest present to a person in a service job, such as a hairdresser or barber you see every week.

It is sometimes difficult to separate business from personal tips, because the two often intermesh, but it helps to computerize your holiday tipping so that you will not forget who should receive that important envelope. The office tipping list of a successful executive might look something like this:

Cash Holiday Gifts for 1985

Hairdresser or barber: from $10 to $50, depending on how often you go

Shampoo person: $15 (if you are her steady customer)

Manicurist: $25 (if you are her steady customer)

Gym instructor: $20 (if you do not belong to a club and if you go often)

Maîtres d'hôtel at restaurants you use often: normally $10 each, but should be $20 each for first class big city restaurants

Employees' Christmas fund at club: $100

Office garage employees' fund: $50

Presents Exchanged Between Employer and Employee

Company Policy at Holiday Time

Bonuses are given for performance and are earned, even if they are distributed during the holiday season, so they are not considered gifts. Companies differ quite dramatically in the way they approach holiday gift giving, depending on how good their business is, the practices in the various regions where the company has offices or plants, and the type of industry.

Here are the options in Christmas gift giving:

- To have no company policy whatsoever
- To prohibit any gift giving
- To give employees a food package, a transistor radio, a Christmas turkey, or something of this nature
- To give employees a gift catalog from which they order an item of their choice or receive the equivalent (such as $25) in cash
- To consider the company Christmas party as the gift

- To consider the company Christmas card, signed by the CEO, as the gift
- To distribute gifts to the needy instead of giving employee gifts

The decision management makes on this subject is an important one, in that it is related to employee morale and to how well the company is doing. Certainly it is an individual decision. What is good for one company may not be good for another.

The Employer Remembers "the People Backstage"

An executive may certainly supplement the standard company gift with a small personal one of his own, paid for out of his own pocket, for the people who serve him and make his life more efficient and comfortable. This is a very personal act, for which there are no rule books. How it is handled depends upon the executive's own degree of thoughtfulness and sensitivity to other people. There are those who manage to carve immensely successful business careers for themselves without ever giving a thought to office gifts, other than a token present to a secretary at Christmas. Many people feel that if company employees receive their salary checks and their benefits, that is sufficient, and if the employees also receive the standard company gift, then that is more than sufficient.

From the viewpoint of the human side of business, however, that may not be sufficient. A thoughtful executive is aware of those who serve him, including some who are not even on the payroll but work under service contracts. His gift—even a small one like a basket of fruit, a cake, candy, or cheese—is shown to the recipient's family and friends with great pride, particularly because the executive donor "certainly didn't have to do this." The people who receive these small gifts from him might be the switchboard operators, for example, hidden away from sight but carrying an enormously important responsibility for the company's public relations; the elevator starters who smile at him warmly each day and call him by name; the cleaning person who cleans his office every night and with whom he sometimes chats when he's working late.

It's nice when an executive acknowledges with a small gift the existence of the employees who are involved with him on a constant basis—and adds a note that says, "Thanks for your help this past year."

The Employee's Gift to the Boss

Employees should *not* give presents to their employers except in the case of an employee who has been very close to his employer for a long time and views him as almost family. The average employer is embarrassed by having to accept gifts from someone who works for him. There are, of course, exceptions to this rule, such as those infrequent spur-of-the-moment occasions when an employee will bring to the office some freshly cut flowers from his garden or something delicious made in his kitchen. (This kind of simple gift is an act of thoughtfulness, not one of apple-polishing, particularly if the supply of lilacs from the garden or the brownies from the kitchen are shared with others in the office as well.)

An employee should refrain from giving the boss an expensive gift (over $25). If he or she does, the boss should diplomatically but firmly return it, so that the employee will not attempt it again. ("Look, I can't accept this. You were so nice to give it to me, but it is much too important a gift. I'm returning it, even though I am very grateful for your thought.")

Presents Exchanged Between a Secretary and Boss

A secretary is not obligated to give her boss a present. However, a devoted professional secretary who has been with her boss for a long time is in a class by herself. If she is close to her boss and his family, she might give him a modest, impersonal gift for the holidays and for his birthday, such as a bottle of fine wine (if she knows he loves wine) or a book relating to one of his interests, some good cigars if he has that unfortunate habit, or something resulting from her own talents and handiwork. I remember the pleasure a secretary gave her woman boss when she needlepointed a telephone book cover for her. Another made a drawing of her boss's beloved boat and had it framed; and another, an excellent amateur photographer, enlarged and framed an excellent photograph she had made of the boss and his family on the Fourth of July.

As for what the boss gives his secretary, a mid-manager who has had the same secretary for two years might spend $25 on her Christmas present, whereas a senior executive whose secretary has been with him for ten years might spend as much as $100 or more on her Christmas present. It all depends on how long the secretary has been in service, the responsibilities she shoulders, and the importance of her boss within the company.

An executive should remember that he or she is setting a precedent in raising the value of the gift, and that the secretary will expect something of equal value, not less value, when the next Christmas comes around.

If your secretary is in a difficult financial bind for the moment (paying exorbitant hospital or tuition bills), it is certainly appropriate for you to give her a check. Otherwise it is more personal to give her a gift or a gift certificate from a store you know she favors.

During my years in the working world, I have heard some wonderful stories of thoughtfulness and creativity in the gifts exchanged between boss and secretary, but I have also heard the opposite kind of story. There was the secretary in Atlanta, for example, who worked for a firm dealing in imported French merchandise. She had great difficulty with the French language, so her boss gave her as his Christmas present a book on the subject of *Improving Your French*—a mean gift. She remembered that all year; the next Christmas she gave him a book called *How to Improve Your Character,* as her present, with a card that read, "Touché."

If an executive's children make demands upon his executive secretary, ideally those children should remember the secretary at Christmas with some small gift, which might be a $2 gift from a high school child, or a hand-made Christmas card from a second-grader.

As with the giving of all gifts, it is the personal thought that matters.

When Several Share a Secretary

If two or more people share a secretary, they should each donate from $10 to $15 to buy her a gift certificate from a department store or mail order catalog. A Christmas card should accompany the gift certificate, signed by each of the bosses.

"Secretary's Day"

Some executive secretaries choose not to celebrate this day, which appears in the spring with the regularity of Mother's Day, since they consider it nothing more than a commercial ploy for stores and florists. Most secretaries, however, in spite of what they may say on the subject, really appreciate it when they find a small bouquet of flowers or a box of chocolates on their desks, left there by their bosses on Secretary's Day. I personally feel that taking one's secretary to lunch on Secretary's Day is ridiculous. (I'm for taking her to lunch on any other day.)

Office Collections for the Purchase of Employee Gifts

The practice of asking executives and employees to contribute to a gift for "Suzy's baby," for "George's wedding," or "for Angela in the hospital" has become a nuisance at best and a financial hardship at worst for some people.

The ideal situation is that which exists in a few companies where there is a fund at corporate level to pay for any gifts or flowers sent from the employees to an individual executive or employee on occasions like these:

- When there is a death in the person's family
- When the employee is ill or injured
- When the employee gets married
- When the employee has a baby
- When the employee retires

Unfortunately this system is very expensive for management and quite impossible for a large organization. Many companies cover the cost of flowers or a plant for each headquarters employee on his or her birthday but allow collections to be taken for the other occasions that call for condolences or celebrations.

Regardless of whether employee gift collections are permitted or not in your company, you should have no compunction about saying no *politely* when you are asked to contribute. "I'm very sorry. I can not make a contribution at this time. I prefer to write a note to Angela in the hospital."

Questions Concerning Wedding Presents from Executives to Employees

Some company chairmen and presidents receive wedding invitations from every person in their organization who gets married. If certain weddings are attended and others aren't, hurt feelings will result. It is very understandable, therefore, if members of senior management make a policy of regretting the wedding invitations of all employees except for those on their own personal staffs and for people serving in a senior management function.

Company executives do *not* have to send a present when they regret an employee wedding invitation, but they should send a nice note wishing the couple great happiness in their future.

When an executive gives a wedding present to someone on his or her own staff, it is very nice to have it monogrammed, engraved, etched, embossed, or incised with the couple's initials, the date of the wedding, and the executive donor's initials.

Employees should not give their bosses wedding presents. (An exception, of course, is when a secretary wishes to give her boss a *small* token gift or volunteers her free time to hand address all his invitations or announcements.)

The Company Gifts to Clients, Customers, and VIPs

The company's annual holiday gift for clients, customers, suppliers, VIPs, and possibly others like the company's lawyer, banker, and presidents of the advertising, public relations, and accounting firms should not be expensive. It should certainly be thoughtfully chosen and in good taste. It should also be:

- Attractively presented (gift-wrapped)
- Packaged, if at all possible, in a reusable, handsome container to further its impact
- Something relating in a logical fashion to the donor's products or services
- Of a quality equal to or better than last year's gift (or it is better not to send one)

The enclosure cards should be hand-written by the executive donors. (If one person must write hundreds of gift-enclosures, his greeting and signature on his card should be rendered as a facsimile.)

I admit that I eagerly await the arrival each year of certain gifts from companies that never disappoint. I know there will be a useful kitchen utensil tucked inside the American Home Products box full of the items they manufacture and that the box may be used again for shipping the most fragile of objects. I know that Hennegon Press in Cincinnati will send me the most beautiful Audubon wall calendar to hang in the same place each year. I know that a liquor company will be sending me half a dozen glasses in the same pattern they send each year (allowing me to break some of them without ever running out). I know that *Life* magazine will be sending me something useful like a superb desk calendar or something totally crazy like a can of red sequin confetti to throw about on New Year's Eve. I feel there is no hint of bribery in these gifts, only wafting breezes of goodwill.

Using the Corporate Logo on Company Gifts

A gift from a business person becomes more special if it contains his company's small printed, engraved, etched, or incised corporate logo or trademark. The smaller and more inconspicuous the symbol is, the more appreciated the gift becomes. The logo might be put on the underside of an object, or on the inside cover or the back cover of the gift.

For small "giveaways" and promotional items, the corporate symbol may be shown in a much bolder manner, as long as its design is tasteful.

Giveaways

The company's promotional items, used by salesmen to give to customers and potential customers, and used generally by everyone in the marketing and sales force as a public relations tool of goodwill, should never be shoddily designed or manufactured. Even if it is a $1 item, a giveaway should never be allowed to detract from the company's first class image.

Promotional items, ranging in cost from fifty cents each to $25 each can be tastefully manufactured in the following categories:

Brushes	Credit card cases	Sewing kits	His/her aprons
Bar glasses	Penknives	Measuring tapes	Frisbees
Highway emergency kits	First aid kits	Ponchos	Thermos bottles
	Puzzles	Shoeshine kits	Tie clips
Keychains	Legal pads in covers	Belt buckles	Zippered sports totes
Expense account kits	Tennis hats	Combs	Balloons
Radios	Manicure kits	Plastic rainhats	Boxes or baskets
		Picture frames	

Buttons	Pen and pencil sets	Neckties	Decorative file
Yardsticks	Cutting boards	Shower caps	folders
Map cases	Golf shirts	Posters	Paper napkins
Caps	Calendars	Calory counters	Diaries
Sweat bands	Tennis balls	Tee shirts	Garment bags
Golf balls	Beach towels	Calendars	Jewelry items for
Scarves	Bumper stickers	Playing cards	women
Baseball jackets	Game sets	Umbrellas	Sweatshirts
Small staplers	Cufflinks	Shoebags	Racquet covers
Combination locks	Memo pads	Carving knives	Pocket dictionaries
Scissors	Business card	Self-stick notepads	Flashlights
Paperweights	cases	Stick pins	Stop watches
Handkerchiefs	Tennis towels	Ski hats	Cosmetic cases
Mugs	Thermometers	Posters	

Business Gift Ideas

Food as a Business Gift

Food is a wonderful gift. Somehow it does not smack of bribery, even when it is expensive. It is a gift that is shared by the recipient with the others in his family or in his office, so it has a widespread influence. It is a gift that leaves a fleeting, pleasurable kind of memory behind it.

Gourmet food shops and mail order catalogs today make it possible for foods of all kinds to be shipped and handled properly, so that they arrive at their destination in good condition.

If the region in which you live is noted for a certain food (for example, peaches from Texas, grapefruit and oranges from Florida, pecans from Georgia, cheese from Wisconsin, etc.) your gift of that food to people in other regions is always a welcome one.

Popular Gifts of Food

Baked goods: cakes, cookies, breads
Jams and jellies
Fresh fruit
Candy
Nuts
Gourmet soups in tins
Pure maple syrup
Cheeses
Crackers
Frozen casseroles (for local use)

Expensive Gifts of Food

Beluga caviar
Smoked salmon from Scotland
Imported pâtés
Smoked delicacies
Frozen steaks flown in
Fresh lobsters flown in
Fresh-killed wild game and fowl
Gourmet food packages in reusable
containers
Special ice creams and sauces (for
local use)

Liquors and Wines as Gifts

A gift of liquor or wine requires reflection. It's very easy to call up a retailer and have him deliver "a case of good vodka" to someone as a gift. But if that person is a Scotch drinker, he is going to shrug his shoulders and say to himself, "Oh, well, some day I'll have a cocktail party and use it up," or "This will please my vodka-drinking friends when they come by." How much greater an effect this gift would have had if a case of Scotch had arrived! The recipient would have known that the donor had remembered or had researched what he liked to drink. And, of course, if the male recipient of the gift is a Scotch drinker and his wife drinks gin, what an impact a case of half Scotch, half gin would have! All that is required is a telephone call to the executive's secretary to learn the liquor preferences of the executive and his or her spouse.

Wine as a gift has a broad range of appeal, because if the recipient doesn't drink wine himself, he probably serves it at home to guests, whether during the cocktail hour or at the dinner table. You do not need to know the subtleties of your recipient's preferences—i.e., whether he prefers a Burgundy to a Bordeaux or vice versa—because wine is a gift meant to be shared, and a good bottle is appreciated by anyone who drinks wine, particularly in tandem with good food.

If you arrive at someone's home for dinner with a bottle or two of wine in hand, say immediately to your host, "Here's something to put away and enjoy on a *future* occasion." By party time, any good host has his wine selected and perhaps already opened and "breathing." Actually it's nicer if your gift of wine is delivered the day *after* the dinner, with your thank-you note attached.

Champagne is a luxurious symbol of celebration, rejoicing, and special occasions. Many people feel as do I, that if you can't afford a good bottle of champagne, don't buy it; buy a bottle of wine instead as your gift.

Good cognac (brandy) and after-dinner liqueurs are welcome presents. It's not necessary to know your recipient's taste in this respect, as your host can always use them when entertaining others. Don't send a gift of liqueurs, however, to someone who rarely entertains at home; they will sit on the shelf for years gathering dust.

Remember never to send a gift of alcohol to someone who is not of legal drinking age, and naturally never to someone who doesn't drink, even if you think he will use it for entertaining others. Never send alcohol to a person's office, always to his home address.

In deciding how much to send a business contact, here is a general guide:

- As a gift of friendship or to say thank you for a meal in someone's home or in a restaurant:
      One or two bottles of a modest wine or
      A bottle of liquor or

A bottle of sherry, aperitif, or liqueur
- A more significant gift for someone's birthday or anniversary
      A bottle of good champagne or
      Two bottles of good liquor
- An important gift (when you and your family have spent the weekend)
      A case of champagne or
      A case of good wine or
      A case of good liquor or
      A bottle of exceedingly rare wine or brandy

Bar Accessories

These make great presents. Look around your business friend's bar in his home or office to notice what he needs. The bottle opener may be old and tarnished; he may be missing a bar knife. If the glasses are of different patterns, it is a sign that a set of a dozen bar glasses would be useful.

Here are some gift ideas:

- Small serving tray (with a rim to keep glasses from sliding off)
- Bar pitcher (a small one, to hold water)
- Martini pitcher and stirrer
- Ice bucket (the gift recipient can usually use a new one!)
- Ice tongs
- Bar knife and cutting board (for slicing lemon peel, sectioning limes, etc.)
- Strainer for mixing cocktails
- Coasters (for drinkers' glasses)
- Cocktail napkins in paper or in fabric
- Wine cooler
- Wine bottle coasters (to put on the dining table for protection)
- Bar glasses and other glasses needed for a party:
      Martini "straight up" cocktail glasses
      Old-fashions
      Highball glasses
      All-purpose wineglasses
      Champagne flutes
      Sherry-liqueur glasses
      Brandy snifters

If you are buying glasses as a gift for a business friend, purchase a minimum of six or eight.

For Special People and Special Occasions

For the New Executive

Pocket calculator
Leather desk calendar
Pocket calendar
Pen and pencil set
Pen set for desk
Dictionary-thesaurus set
Desk caddy (for paper clips, rubber bands, tape, etc.)
Leather scrapbook
Card case

The ultimate gift: the briefcase
Latest book on management techniques
Subscription to an important financial newspaper or magazine
If executive begins career in another city, a year's subscription to his hometown newspaper
Membership in a health club

For the Traveler

A piece of needed luggage (to match or in keeping with his existing pieces)
Portable smoke detector (could save his life)
An expandable tote
Travel iron
Folding umbrella
Magnified folding cosmetic/shaving mirror

Toilet kit for man; cosmetics kit for woman
Shoe bags
First aid kit
Luggage tags with name and address
Sewing kit
Good face soap in plastic container

For the International Traveler

Foreign dictionary
Wallet-passport case
Battery-operated hairdryer
Battery-operated radio-alarm clock
Money exchange calculator
Rolls of film (to fit his camera)

Diary for trip notes
Address book for foreign addresses
List of world holidays (such as Guaranty Trust's "World Calendar of Holidays") so traveler can avoid the national holidays

Newly Decorated Office

Desk set with matching wastebasket (match the basic colors of the office)
Desk or wall clock
Ashtrays
Magazine rack

Thermos set with glasses and tray
Bar glass sets (if senior executive has bar)
Letter opener
Antique container for pens and pencils

Picture frame
Large standing plant in handsome container
Bookends
Crystal jar containing hard candies

Wall mirror (if secretary or executive's spouse says it would be useful)
Leather telephone directory cover

From a Houseguest to His Host

(*See also* Food as a Business Gift; Liquors and Wines as Gifts)

Books relating to host's hobbies
Subscription to an art, decorating, or food magazine you know host does not have but would enjoy
Box of cans of tennis balls or golf balls (according to what host plays most)
Records and tapes (find out from secretary what host's equipment is)

Kitchen accessories, cookbook, or cooking equipment for hosts you know like to cook
Pot pourri
Box of guest soaps
Set of towels or beach towels
Tray
Picnic basket or cooler
Barbecue set

Special Birthday Gifts

As previously mentioned, birthday gifts are not usually given in the business world, but an executive's special birthday (the thirtieth, fortieth, fiftieth, seventy-fifth) is often celebrated in some way by his or her close personal friends in the business world—with a birthday card, if nothing else.

The Birthday Card

One of the smartest public relations gestures in the business world is for the executive to make a note of all of his clients', customers', and friends' birthdays and send a card regularly each year to salute them. One of the most celebrated advocates of mailing birthday cards is Mr. Morita, the chairman of SONY in Japan. He keeps adding to his list the names of people he meets during the year. The list is monumental, and everyone whose name is included looks forward to receiving his card.

Wedding Gifts

(*See also* When a Colleague or Client Marries, in Chapter 2.)

The wedding gift to a customer or business associate is either a company expense (for a senior executive), or it may have to come out of the executive's pocket. Since it creates so much goodwill and is so important to an executive's personal friendship, it is usually worthwhile for the executive to pay for it himself if that is what it takes.

From an Executive to His Good Customers

Many young executives are ingenious at finding gifts that look expensive, even when they are not. One woman I know scouts antique shops in each city to which she travels on business. She buys small, low-priced items (under $20) that look unusual. The shop owner writes on a card the *provenance* of the object (where it came from, how old it is, etc.) and she places that card inside a gift box with the object. She has it beautifully wrapped, tagged, and put away in her closet until she needs a wedding or anniversary gift. Another executive I know attends the post-Christmas sales in the fine stores and buys greatly marked-down pieces of fine English bone china (small boxes, serving bowls, cachepots, creamer and sugar, etc.). He has each one wrapped as a gift, ready to go with his card, for special events like weddings.

A Company's Gift for VIPs and Their Senior Executives

Some companies have a standard wedding present for senior managers and VIPs, and a less expensive gift for mid and junior managers for their weddings. The following are examples of both:

Expensive ($150 or over)	*Less Expensive* (up to $50)
Steuben crystal bowl	Porcelain salad bowl
Small engraved Tiffany silver box	Large crystal pitcher, with etched monogram on the side
Boehm porcelain bird or flower sculpture	Serving tray
Mantlepiece clock	Dozen glasses (six wine, six water)

Company Service Anniversary Presents
(*See also* Chapter 15, A Company Celebrates Its Anniversary)

It's a tremendous morale booster to an employee to be able to look forward to a small gift marking his or her anniversary with the company, beginning in the fifth year and recurring every five or ten years thereafter. It's important for management to recognize loyalty.

An example of a fifth anniversary gift is a small leather address book marked with the employee's name, the name of the company, and the words *Fifth Anniversary* in gold lettering on the cover.

For the tenth anniversary, a gold tie tack for the men and small gold stickpin for the women, engraved with a tiny company logo, is an appropriate gift.

By the fifteenth anniversary, a tie for the men and a scarf for the women, with the company logo integrated into the design of the custom-designed pure silk fabric, is a handsome way to mark the employee's record of service.

The twentieth anniversary might be marked by a gold tie clip for the men and a small gold brooch for the women, both engraved with a tiny logo. For the twenty-fifth anniversary (silver) the employees might receive handsome silver boxes, suitably engraved.

For the Jade Anniversary (thirty-fifth), the employee might receive a piece of jewely with jade, or a clock with jade on the base. By the fiftieth anniversary, the company should have something like a very fine gold watch or bracelet to give its employees. If the employees make it to their sixtieth anniversary, they deserve something with diamonds!

For an Important Customer's Baby

(*See also* Congratulations for an Executive Mother, in Chapter 2)

If someone like the company's most important customer or client or an outside director of the company has a baby, it is good business to send the parents a gift to mark the occasion. In most cases, a gift for the new baby means much more to the parents than a gift sent to them.

When a very small company logo is engraved on the back or underside of a piece of silver, along with the baby's initials and birth date, the results are usually visually attractive. Objects in silver that lend themselves to this kind of engraving are:

· Baby Mug
· Baby spoon
· Small picture frame
· Rattle (barbell kind is the best)
· Small box

For Someone in the Hospital or Ill at Home

Here are some suggestions for those who are sick or injured:

· A flowering plant (that requires a minimum of watering)
· An amusing soft sculpture
· A tape recording of the person's colleagues all sending their good wishes and relating the office gossip

- A taped recording of a good book
- Music tapes of the convalescent's choice
- Good bath soap
- Cologne
- Room spray
- Bed jacket (for a woman)
- Bathrobe for either a man or woman
- An amusing book
- A book of magnificent photographs

Occasions on Which Fine Gifts Should Be Given

Gifts for the Retiree
(*See also* Chapter 13, When an Executive Retires)

The gift a company chooses for a retiring executive should logically depend upon his length of service and rank achieved. Some companies give standard items, such as clocks and gold watches (inscribed with the dates of the person's service to the company) for important anniversaries and retirements. Other companies become very creative for their distinguished retirees' gifts. A few ideas:

- Give something related to the person's activities in retirement, such as new fishing equipment for someone who says he'll now be "gone fishin'" or a gift of art supplies for someone who claims he will now be "painting in earnest."
- Have a photograph taken of him in the office, with all of his staff and colleagues clustered around him; have the photo enlarged and framed, with an incised brass plaque on the frame.
- Have a handsome leather scrapbook made of career-related photographs, news articles, and memorabilia (which could be a wonderful surprise if the retiree's spouse becomes actively involved in the project). The cover of the scrapbook should contain a gold embossed inscription.
- Present the retiree and spouse with round-trip air or steamship tickets to a very desirable place. (Expense money should be included in the envelope for any retiree who could not otherwise afford the trip.)
- Ask the retiree's colleagues to participate in a kind of *Festschrift* (German for a "festival of writings"). Colleagues would write about their illustrious colleague, his career, and his ideas; they would include some ideas and predictions of their own. The collection of essays and tributes would then be loosely bound into a handsome cover for the retiree to savor and enjoy in the coming years.

- Find an attractive antique—such as a pair of decanters in a mahogany carrier, with a brass plaque added to the base and engraved with his name and dates of service.
- Commission an artist to paint his portrait or a sculptor to do a bust of him.

Gifts Relating to Art

A company or an individual who relates gift giving to the local art community knows how to impress and please the gifts' recipients. A company that has sponsored an art exhibit in a local museum should continue to reinforce that relationship by sending gifts related to the museum. Here are some of the ways in which business and the arts interrelate in the field of gift giving:

- A company gives a gift to its employees of tickets of admission to important museum exhibitions.
- The company gifts feature items from the local museum's gift shop or from the museum's gift shop catalog.
- An executive gives another executive a gift certificate to a reputable store selling lithographs, framed posters, reproductions, and drawings.
- The company gifts center around art books of the local museum's treasures.
- The company gives a senior executive (for example, a retiring chairman of the board) a major gift: a commissioned portrait that can be placed:
  In the retired chairman's home
  In the board room
  In both board room *and* the chairman's home (a copy is made)

Commissioning a Portrait

The commissioning of an executive's portrait is a wonderful way to honor a retiree—or mark any important occasion in an executive's life. A good artist might do a pastel or water color portrait for approximately $1000. Artists who work under the aegis of a group like New York's Portraits Inc. charge between $5000 and $60,000 to do a portrait—the latter price includes a portrait and a copy made by a famous artist (like Aaron Schickler, Clyde Smith, William Draper), who must go through the same exercise twice.

A portrait usually takes from one to five sittings to complete. When the artist uses good photographs, it may greatly accelerate the process. A company involved in commissioning a portrait must remember to budget in the cost of the frame (from $300 to $1000). The metal plaque affixed to the bottom of the frame or to the pedestal of the sculptured bust should be engraved with the subject's name and either his dates of service to the company, his retirement date, or just the date of the presentation of the portrait.

A portrait need not show an executive seated stiffly in a pinstripe suit. The figure should be full of life, reflecting his spirit and charm. Today an executive's portrait may show him relaxing in his garden, sailing his boat, or riding his horse—however he best wishes to be remembered. A portrait is a gift that personifies its subject.

A sculptured portrait bust may cost anywhere from $5000 upward. Alexandra E. Whitney in New York, for example, who receives many corporate commissions, charges about $6500 for a bronze bust and $5000 for a copy.

The base for a bronze head should be chosen with care. It may be placed on a pedestal or on a table or in a bookcase. Great care should be taken with the lighting, so that the warmth of the bronze and the subtlety of the three dimensional planes can be appreciated.

The third kind of portrait to be commissioned by the company as a gift is the photographic one, made by a reputable firm like Bachrach or by famous photographers like Irving Penn, Francesco Scavullo, or Richard Avedon. The prices can range from $300 to $10,000.

One executive received the gift of four handsomely framed photographic portraits (13″ × 18″) of his most precious possession, his garden, shown in the four seasons of the year.

An Exchange of Gifts at Merger and Acquisition Time

By the time a merger or acquisition deal has been completed, a tremendous amount of blood, sweat, and tears will inevitably have been expended behind closed executive doors.

After the merger is concluded it is thoughtful for the head of the acquiring company to present the CEO of the other company a gift commemorating the new partnership.

One of the most striking merger gifts I ever saw was a dark blue Mark Cross leather desk set, consisting of a blotter holder, pen set, letter opener, scissors, clock, and letter box. The two former company logos were stamped in gold on the left side of the blotter holder, while the logo of the newly created company was stamped on the right side. The CEO presented this desk set to the former CEO of the acquired company, who had now become chief operating officer of the new corporation.

Another particularly thoughtful executive I knew made a list of the names of every person who had worked around the clock in the final two weeks of the merger, including his own executives, the outside financial consultants, lawyers and accountants, secretaries and typists. Two weeks later, after the regulatory agencies granted their permission for the merger, each person received a gift from him—a sterling silver letter opener, engraved simply with the words *Well Done* and the date of the signing of the agreement. (This same executive had also ordered gourmet dinners sent in from a leading New York restaurant for everyone who worked through dinner; late at night he would send everyone home in taxis, a particularly welcome luxury for those who would have had a long subway ride.)

Giving and Returning the Inappropriate Gift

The giving and acceptance of gifts is not an easy art. An inappropriate gift that is too expensive, too inexpensive, too personal, or just in bad taste may cause embarrassment, even distress to the recipient. But it may have even worse repercussions on the sender. Danger signals are in order

- When an executive gives a lavish gift such as jewelry or furs to his secretary
- When a gift is related to a smutty joke and is supposed to be amusing but falls flat when presented. (Such gifts are in particularly poor taste during the Christmas season.)
- When a gift has not been researched, with the result that an executive gives a car accessory to an executive who does not own a car, liquor is sent to someone who doesn't drink, clothing of the wrong size is sent as a gift, or a piece of sports equipment is sent to a nonplayer
- When a gift with obvious sexual overtones is presented

Any gift with sexual or with bribery connotations should be returned immediately to the sender because if the recipient keeps the gift for a few days, the donor will consider it accepted. I remember a pretty young secretary who received from her boss on her first Christmas an 18-carat gold ankle bracelet. The boss's card read: "I'd like to see this wrapped around that beautiful little ankle of yours." She rewrapped it and put it on his desk right away with her own note attached: "And I'd like to see this wrapped tight around that beautiful little neck of yours." (The good part of this story is that she kept her job and he never bothered her again.)

If you receive something you know you shouldn't keep, return it at once. Retain a copy of the note you send back with it, including the date and the manner in which it was sent back. (This is obviously for self-protection.) It is not necessary to explain *why* you are returning the gift. It is enough to write, "I do not find it appropriate to accept this gift, so I am returning it at once."

Company Policy Prohibiting the Acceptance of Gifts

Many CEOs do not permit executives and employees to accept any gifts from anyone associated with their business, for fear of making the recipient obligated to the donor. Management should remind employees annually of this fact by circulating a memorandum or making an announcement in the company newsletter.

Some companies run "ethics awareness" programs for employees where the subject of gifts is discussed in detail; others make new employees sign a conflict of interest agreement that spells out the gift policies. An employee who accepts a gift should also remember his personal liability in the eyes of the IRS—he may be taxed for the value of a gift as "ordinary income."

Some people are naturally generous by nature. They enjoy giving presents to people and do not have bribery in mind. An executive should be sensitive to the donor's real motives in such a situation and handle him with kindness and tact.

Accepting and Acknowledging a Gift

Part of good manners is knowing how to accept a gift "with grace." This means putting a big smile on your face even when you open the package and find a neon orange scarf that you would hesitate just to hang on a clothesline, for fear of ruining your image. It means saying "How *very* nice" with enthusiasm when someone has given you a leather desk calendar and you already own four of them. It means being warm and gracious about a gift of an office dictionary with the name of the company in large letters all over the leather binding. Little white lies are in order at this time, and kindness decrees that you say you like something even when you don't.

If you feel that company products you receive are inferior, do not praise them in your thank-you note. Instead, simply thank the donor "for being so nice to remember us this holiday season." But if you really liked the company products, let the donor know with as much enthusiasm as you can generate. It will please him immensely.

Epilogue

I hope that in reading these pages you have gained insight, received assistance, gleaned information and support—or even reaffirmed the appropriateness of your own behavior. If so, then all of my work will have been worth it.

We are all after profit in the business world. My thesis is that we can go after it with business toughness, but with consideration and good manners at one and the same time. Professionalism and polish oil the wheels of commerce; they support morale, productivity, and profitable relationships in the marketplace. Far from being polar opposites, good business and good manners become compatible—and even identical—when practiced with sincerity and care. The executive or professional who sustains that vision—who recognizes that people and profits are equally essential for success—has the edge on all of us.

Index

A

Abortion, diplomatically handling news
    of, 60
Acceptance and regret, letter of, 108
Accessories
    man's evening, 155
    woman's, 144
Acknowledgment and thanks, letters of,
    120–27
Address, proper forms of, 394–419
    in conversation and writing, 410–11
    foreign business people, 398–99
    letters and envelopes to nonofficial peo-
        ple, 397–98
    military rank, 399–401
    official business, 412–19
    religious officials, 402–4
    Royal Family (in Great Britain), 413–15
    "sir" or "ma'am," 396–97
    titles before names, 395–96
    U.S. officials, 404–10
    women, 411–12
Addressing female colleagues, 41–42
Administrative assistant, 422–29
Admission tickets, formal dinner event,
    314
Adopted child, 59
Air Force officers, according to rank, 399

Alcohol, serving or not serving, 353–54
American Association of Fund-Raising
    Counsel, 432
American Association of Retired Persons,
    445
American Speech, Language and Hearing
    Association, 68
American University (Washington, D.C.),
    160
*Amy Vanderbilt Complete Book of Eti-
    quette* (Baldrige), 278, 310, 394
Anniversaries. *See* Company anniversary
    celebration
Anniversary of service letter, 116
Announcement cards
    addition to medical practice, 253
    birth or adoption, 60
    business, 245–55
    retirement, 446
    "Save the Date," 360
Annual Report, noting death of an ex-
    ecutive, 459
Annual "review," 20–24
    being let go and finding new job, 23–24
    handling with sensitivity, 21
    letting someone go, 22–23
    receptive to criticism, 21–22